MULTICULTURAL AMERICA

A Resource Book for Teachers of Humanities and American Studies

Syllabi, Essays, Projects, Bibliography

Betty E. M. Ch'maj, *editor*
Professor of Humanities and American Studies
California State University, Sacramento

with Annette Hansen, M. Kathleen Hanson, and Jan Petrie

Foreword by Reginald Wilson
American Council of Education

UNIVERSITY
PRESS OF
AMERICA

Lanham • New York • London

Copyright © 1993 by
University Press of America®, Inc.
4720 Boston Way
Lanham, Maryland 20706

3 Henrietta Street
London WC2E 8LU England

Library of Congress Cataloging-in-Publication Data

Multicultural America ; a resource book for teachers of humanities
and American studies / edited by Betty E.M. Ch'maj.
      p.   cm.
Includes bibliographical references.
1. Intercultural education—United States—Curricula.
2. Intercultural education—United States—Bibliography.
3. Pluralism (Social sciences)—United States. 4. Education,
Higher—United States—Aims and objectives. I. Ch'maj, Betty E. M.
      LC1099.3.M8   1992
   370.19'341'0973—dc20   92–33140 CIP

ISBN 0–8191–8916–2 (cloth : alk. paper)
ISBN 0–8191–8917–0 (pbk. : alk. paper)

The paper used in this publication meets the minimum requirements of
American National Standard for Information Sciences—Permanence
of Paper for Printed Library Materials, ANSI Z39.48–1984.

ACKNOWLEDGEMENTS

This book began as a bibliographic project for which I was to supervise three student assistants paid with funds from a "mini-grant" from California State University in 1990-91. Kathleen Hansen began the work while I was recovering from surgery during the summer of 1990; she was joined by Jan Petrie and Annette Hansen in the fall. However, when, during California's teeth-clenching budget crisis, the funding for the project was cut in half and a second mini-grant the following year could not retrieve it, I undertook the editorship of a larger publication, soliciting materials from authors across the country as well as faculty from our campus. Reginald Wilson, an intellectual colleague who had been involved (as had I) in the educational controversies that had erupted in the city of Detroit during the 1960s, and who today as Senior Scholar for the American Council of Education in Washington, D.C. had been following the PC debate as assiduously as I, was persuaded to serve as consultant.

Despite the cuts to our budget, I appreciate the impetus given the project by the mini-grants and by my colleagues on our beleaguered California campuses. I appreciate as well the enthusiastic support from colleagues in the fields of American Studies and American music--their insistence on the urgency of getting such a resource book into print, even if parts would necessarily remain incomplete. To Lucy Lippard for permission to reproduce her bibliography, Macmillan Publishing Company for permission to reproduce the Table of Contents of one of its readers, and to those who furnished illustrations, my thanks. I am deeply and profoundly grateful to Reggie, Annette, Jan and Kathleen for their dedication to the project through its difficult stages; to Debi Holmes-Binney for her editorial expertise and wit; to computer wizards Vicki Pearson-Rounds, Terry Manns, Jim McCormick, Maria Chmaj, and especially Karin Kawelmacher for converting and formatting files; to Al Hansen and Arlene Altman for photography; and to Karl Hillstrom for his careful proof-reading of the final text. The eagerness of the staff at the University Press of America to get this volume into the hands of teachers as soon as possible lifted my spirits during the last frantic days of editing, just after I had returned from lecturing in China. Most of all, I am grateful to the contributors--each one, every one--for the time, intelligence, sensitivity and energy that have made this volume possible.--BC

August, 1992.

TABLE OF CONTENTS

PART I: SYLLABI

A. Courses with a Deliberate "American" Emphasis

B. Courses with a Deliberate "Ethnic" Emphasis

C. Transforming "Basic" or "Mainstream" Courses

PART II: ESSAYS

A. "Looking for Patterns": Analysis, Assignments, Resources

B. "From the Inside Out": Essays Using Personal Testimony

PART III: BIBLIOGRAPHY AND CHECKLISTS

FOREWORD

by Reginald Wilson

As a child in elementary school in Detroit during the Depression, I could rise with my classmates and recite the Pledge of Allegiance, saying "with liberty and justice for all" with no sense of the contradiction in the applicability of those words to me. However, as a young GI during World War II, as I watched German prisoners of war being marched to a U.S. Army dining hall where I could not eat, the contradiction became stunningly apparent. The captured defenders of fascism, the killers of Jews, could eat in that Army mess hall because they were white and I, an American citizen, allegedly fighting for democracy and freedom, could not eat there because I was black. The agony of confronting the contradictions imbedded in American society and encoded in American education is wholly encompassed in that moment, an epiphany of historical experience. Confronting those contradictions is the essential first step toward achieving what today we call the multicultural perspective, a perspective that is transforming the curricula of our universities as they move toward the twenty-first century.

Socialization into American society has in the past more or less required the acceptance of certain assumptions as part of an American mythology: that Western territorial seizure was progress; that Europe was the creator of most that was of value in human civilization; that women's subordinate place in society was determined by nature; that the lesser social status accorded to people of color was the result of their personal deficiencies, and so on. Not only did the dominant "WASP ascendancy" (to use Joseph Alsop's elegant phrase) accept that mythology; acceptance was required of all those, native born and immigrant, who would aspire to membership in the polity. Thus it was regarded as singularly unremarkable that I, a young black American, should volunteer to go to war to defend a country whose mythology and social practice not only viewed me as a lesser being but legally required that I be segregated from full social participation with my fellow citizens.

The challenge to that mythology burst full force in America with the explosion of the black civil rights movement in the 1950s and 1960s. When Rosa Parks in

1955 refused to move from her seat on a segregated bus in Montgomery, Alabama, and eight black college students in 1960 sat in at a segregated lunch counter in Greensboro, North Carolina, the contradictions had to be confronted. Suddenly America had a mirror held up to its ideals and was forced to read its own words: "We hold these Truths to to be self-evident: that all Men *[sic]* are created equal, that they are endowed by their Creator with certain inalienable rights, that among these are Life, Liberty and the Pursuit of Happiness." The contradictions were made manifest. Was it possible to claim these truths were universal without applying them to *all* people?

Following the lead and inspiration of the black movement, other marginalized groups began to press to be included into what was being called the "center" or "mainstream" of society: women, Latinos, American Indians, Asians, and gays. However, upon critically scrutinizing the center, these groups soon discovered that the "truths" which presumed to legitimize centrality were insufficient to explain either their own oppression and marginalization or the dominant majority's presumed entitlement to privileged status. In universities, that discovery led to what is today called "challenging the canon" and "reconstructing" the curriculum, a process that became especially subtle and especially contentious when applied to the arts and humanities.

Although many social activists, political reformers and academics throughout American history had challenged the legitimizing "truths"—that is, the traditional canon that had sustained the presumed superiority of Euro-American male society and its "natural" right to rule others—it has been primarily through the creation of ethnic studies and women's studies programs in colleges and universities, particularly those growing out of the social protests of the 1960s, that the current outburst of race- and gender-based scholarship has been developed. The establishment of these programs, often over the vociferous and organized protests of academic traditionalists, has generated an impressive body of original research and scholarship, which has significantly shifted perspectives in one discipline after another, at times virtually transforming the discipline to which their criticism has been directed.

Although attacks on race- and gender-based scholarship have not abated (as in the satirizing of "political correctness" and "thought police," addressed in this book's introduction), there has now developed such a significant body of critical scholarship and research that increasing numbers of faculty in colleges and universities are requesting textbooks, syllabi, reference and resource material to assist them in infusing multicultural content into their courses in a variety of liberal arts disciplines. The volume in hand, *Multicultural America*, is an especially outstanding response to these requests. As Senior Scholar at the American Council of Education (ACE), I have had the good fortune to witness first-hand the increasing enthusiasm behind these mounting requests over the past decades while visiting dozens of campuses each year to consult on the implementation of diversity programs (affirmative action, curricular infusion, etc). Moreover, as the leading higher education organization, ACE has published a number of books and monographs designed to give colleges and universities specific guidance in initiating these endeavors. *Multicultural America* is a particularly welcome and original addition to this body of literature.

The consequence of race and gender critiques in academic discourse has been not only to expand and enrich the often excluded experiences and perspectives of people of color and women; it has served as well to legitimate newer and more complex evaluations of the American experiences of European immigrants, of gays and lesbians, and of other marginalized groups. This expanded vision of ethnic diversity and multiculturalism is the controlling perspective behind *Multicultural America*. Its various chapters are replete with suggestions for introducing diverse perspectives into classrooms and research work. The accompanying bibliographies, videography, and musicography will be of immense value to pedagogy and research. But what makes this volume unique is Ch'maj's decision to focus on the arts--that is, to approach multicultural issues through the arts--literature, painting, music, film; popular arts as well as fine arts, oral as well as written traditions--and to demonstrate how to "read" from them cultural and social meanings. Ch'maj is uniquely qualified for this extraordinarily path-breaking task, since she brings to it thirty years of experience as the the only scholar in her field to have held the double title Professor of Humanities and American Studies, first at Wayne State University in Detroit and then at California State University, in Sacramento--which is to say, she has insisted for thirty years on making strong the connection between art and society, aesthetic values and social urgency, the humanities and the social sciences, culture and context.

What will be immediately apparent is that a multiplicity of voices speak though this volume--there is no "politically correct" line of thought. The richness and complexity of the discourse here emphasizes that the discovery of truth is an ongoing and never-ending search. Indeed the exciting search becomes itself not just a process but the goal. And that is as it should be as we expand our vision beyond rigid orthodoxies of both the past and the present, ever open to new perspectives and interpretations, in our long historical struggle to come to terms with each other as distinctive human beings on this small planet we must all share.

This is an excellent collection of syllabi and essays for use by faculty members and department chairs who are engaged in restructuring their curricula to include the latest of the new scholarship on multiculturalism and prepare their students for the twenty-first century.

REGINALD WILSON is Senior Scholar at the American Council of Education in Washington, D.C., having served for eight prior years as ACE's Director of Minority Concerns. He was president of Wayne County Community College, Detroit, for ten years before moving to ACE. He has published widely on issues of racial equity, desegregation in higher education, multiculturalism, and affirmative action, and regularly consults on these subjects at colleges and universities throughout the United States, Canada and the Caribbean.

INTRODUCTION:
MULTICULTURAL AMERICA AND THE PC DEBATE

by Betty Ch'maj

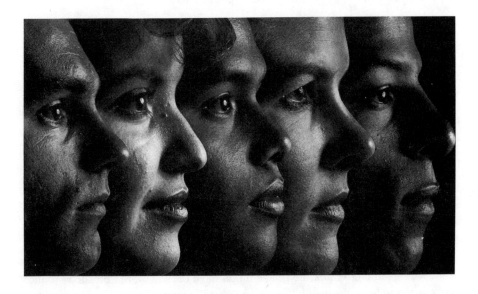

FIGURE 1.

When I first saw the image of five faces on the cover of the 1990 Spring class schedule at my university, I was mesmerized by it. What semiotic message was here? What was the university trying to say to students, to the community, to anyone and everyone who reads class schedules? Was the message intentional or unintentional? Five profiles, transfixed, facing the light—was it The Future they were staring at? Surely these were five students looking ahead to the twenty-first century and wondering, would they be ready for it? Would their education prepare them? But were they male or female, dark-skinned or light? The middle face— could it not be *either* male or female, black or white? Race and gender are the cultural categories of highest visibility, yet here the distinctions had been persuasively blurred. How serious they all looked! how *equal* in their seriousness!

Given the centrality of the debate over multiculturalism on college campuses at the time, it did not take long to guess that this was somebody's comment on the rise of multiculturalism in America and how it was transforming universities like ours.

I began to reflect on the politics of visual images. Could these clean-cut faces with their well-proportioned features, clear-eyed, light-skinned, clean-shaven, be five variations on a single all-American profile—an anglo-conformist standard of beauty acceptable to "middle" America?

I was musing over the image when a colleague walked into my office.

"What do you think?" I asked him. "E pluribus unum?"

"Come again?"

"This image on the catalog cover—it's stunning, it's powerful, but what is it supposed to be saying? Doesn't it emphasize sameness over difference? and wouldn't that mean it privileges unity over diversity? Isn't this an indirect way of asserting 'E pluribus unum'—out of many, one? Might it even betray a subtle bias toward uniformity, collapsing the many *into* the one? This is the way we're all supposed to look—like the faces in some TV commercial."

"Oh *that*," he countered, as if settling the matter. "I heard they discontinued using it. Too controversial. Some hotheads objected—faculty *and* students."

"But why?"

"It's not politically correct. You can't tell for sure if the women are women or if those are really people of color. How come all five have brown eyes? They purport to be different but they really look alike. Somebody goofed."

I hadn't noticed the eyes. (Here, in black and white, their color doesn't show.) But I was appalled to think the image might have been *censored* on such grounds and curious to learn the details. Tracking down the story a year later, I learned that Sam Parsons, our talented campus photographer, had composed an image from five separate plates. The original had been a four-color product designed to distinguish clearly among five images, underscoring difference at the same time that it affirmed similarity — a semiotic of American "twoness." The idea for the image originated in the College of Engineering and Computer Science in the mid-seventies, a time when its faculty was seeking ways to advertise its commitment to diversity in order to attract more candidates from underrepresented areas—specifically, women and ethnics. "It wasn't the image itself that made the difference, it was the policies we structured into our program after about 1976," explained the Dean of Engineering.

"The image simply helped us announce these policies on our brochures."[1] He added that he was of course speaking of the original four-color image used by the College, not the image on the 1990 class schedule. What? I had never seen the original? Oh, I really should. He brought it over so that I could judge for myself.

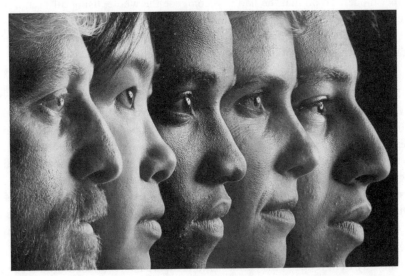

FIGURE 2.

I was shocked by the difference. Here the first man was blonde and hirsute, the woman next to him identifiably Asian, the middle figure darker-skinned, the end man profiling—in Sam Parson's words—"someone's idea of a Jewish—or was it Aztec?—nose." (The choice of profiles had been made by committee, he explained, from a range of possibilities.) It took careful scrutiny to discern that all five faces were different in the two versions, but an overall difference stood out at once. Gone was the intriguing ambiguity! Here the image plainly catalogued diversity, variety, pluralism. The *many* in the one. This was indeed a clearer translation of Engineering's aims, but as the image gained in clarity, it lost in complexity—that is, its power to convey the complex relationship between the "unum" and the "pluribus" in American culture—and I regretted that loss.

---

[1]Telephone conversation with Don Gillott, Dean of Engineering and Computer Science, CSUS, June 19, 1991. In 1971, Gillott said, only 0.8% of its enrollment was female, about 5% ethnic minorities; in 1991, it was 15% female and 20% ethnic--a dramatic change. He was clearly proud of what had been accomplished in so short a time. I am grateful to Gillott, Parsons, and Geri Welch for going out of their way to get me the story and for permission to use both photographs.

Setting out to find out what had happened, I learned that university administrators had received permission from Engineering to use their image on the 1990 schedule, but on learning that a four-color image costs four times more than a one-color image, asked Parsons if he could eliminate three colors to produce a cheaper model. To do that, he had to recompose the whole, using different faces, different lighting, "browning" the composition down—which explains how all the eyes ended up brown, the faces clean-shaven, and the skin shades more uniform. Budgetary necessity, not political correctness, had dictated the decision.

This tale of two images can be read as a paradigm to illuminate the simultaneous development of the enthusiasms, the confusions, and the suspicions which have accompanied the debate over American multiculturalism as it has evolved during recent years. To be sure, there are cultural categories a visual image alone can *not* tell us about: it is not capable of coding identity related to class, nationality, religion, region, or sexuality as readily as it can tell us about race, gender, age, and lifestyle. But if we imagine our paradigm as one extending to *all* elements of cultural difference, we can use it as a model for introducing the variety of issues and emphases to be found in this book—issues and emphases related to what in the early nineties came to be called the debate over "political correctness" (PC).

One way to introduce these issues is to compare and contrast attitudes toward race and gender in terms of change over time. The differences in our responses toward the two images can be explained not only as changes in the image itself or the political leanings of viewers but also as differences created by historical perspective. Belief influences what we see and what we know, and viewers of the nineties found their beliefs about ethnicity and gender changing rapidly as they were exposed to the events and experiences of the era.[2]. Figure 2 may have looked "safe" in 1976 to many well-intentioned viewers—a familiar and easily legible

---

[2]Reactions to the movie *Dances with Wolves* can illustrate the speed at which such changes can occur. When the film first appeared, my students and most of my colleagues liked it, as did most students of other colleagues who assigned it. When it won the Oscar, they joined in debating whether it had portrayed *white* men fairly, but less than a year later--say, by the time our neighboring city of Berkeley announced that it was changing October 12 from Columbus Day to Indigenous Peoples Day--students were seeing the movie differently, many arguing, as does Shoots the Ghost (in Essay #10, below), that its unfairness lay in making *the hero* white, the West pristine, empty and grand, while casting Indians into subsidiary roles. It had by then become politically correct to disdain the film. Six months later, it was being described as a perspective on Native Americans solely through a white man's eyes, a "first step" toward helping us all to see.

emblem of diversity, while Figure 1 looked suspect to some by 1990 because, within the course of a few years, they had learned to see differently.

That difference will emerge from a summary of recent history. Although the PC debate seemed to surface around 1990, the events leading up to its emergence had been underway for some decades. Breaking in on American history in the middle of the 1960s at about the time the "civil rights movement" was becoming the "black liberation struggle"—let us say, when Martin Luther King was joined by Malcolm X in national headlines and the national consciousness—we can trace, one by one, the parallel emergence of a number of other movements related to American identity: the women's movement (after Betty Freidan's *The Feminine Mystique* of 1963), the Indian Rights movement (after the founding of AIM in 1968), the Chicano movement (after the farm workers' boycotts led by César Chavez beginning in 1965), the gay rights movement (after Stonewall in 1971), and so on. We can track the interest in ethnicity—especially in exploring one's "roots"—as it spread outward from the black movement and Alex Haley's book to many other ethnic groups, including white ethnics. By the mid-seventies, all of these movements had been affected by another major development, the new immigration from Latino and Asian/Pacific nations. In short, by 1976, when the CSUS College of Engineering designed its brochure, coding multiple identities into the official language and images of college campuses and other institutions was so commonplace—at least in California—that it had become cliché. Such images were merely reporting on a new reality of American life.

The rise of neo-conservatism throughout the seventies and eighties coincided with the extension and legitimation of this emphasis on diversity—that is, on the rights of individuals to be different and the importance of affirming difference.[3] The decade of the eighties saw the consolidation of conservatism in America as a whole—in national politics, in a backlash against feminism and civil rights, in the empowerment of the evangelical Right—but at the same time, it witnessed the emergence of a "me generation" with an interest in careerism (the Yuppie phenomenon) and a "new narcissism" (as expressed not only in self-awareness movements but also in those same ethnic celebrations that followed after, and were first inspired by, the 1977 TV adaptation of *Roots*).[4] Both developments had an

---

[3]See Peter Clecak, *America's Quest for the Ideal Self* (Oxford University Press, 1983), a book which, growing out of a disagreement between us on the relation of the 1970s to the 1960s, makes an excellent case for continuity rather than disjunction between the two decades.

[4]Steven Watts has used the phrase "the Age of Self-Fulfillment" to describe this eighties-into-nineties phenomenon, a term which might substitute for "me generation" (first used by Tom Wolfe) and "narcissism" (as in Christopher Lasch's *The Culture of Narcissism*) which have so far

impact felt on college campuses. Those involved in the process of legitimation ranged from older campus liberals who had moved into power positions to younger radicals just moving up to a generation of postmodernist scholars newly arrived on the scene. It is striking today to look back and note how little coalition work there was among different ethnic groups, between feminists and ethnics, or between older liberals and new postmodernists during this period of retrenchment. By the end of the eighties, the insistence on the right of individuals to be different had led to what was called "identity politics"—the assumption that one's politics are (and should be) shaped by one's identity as determined by race, ethnicity, gender, and/or sexuality. The emphasis in many disciplines had shifted from stressing *equality* to stressing *difference*—indeed, *insistence* upon a recognition of difference. Thus, by the time Sam Parson's second image surfaced on the CSUS class schedule, the entire emotional burden of history had shifted. Rather than merely applauding evidence of diversity, the newly-sensitized were inclined to suspect images of not being different *enough*. The stage was set for the PC phenomenon.[5]

THE EMERGENCE OF THE PC DEBATE

Like many American academics, I first became interested in the PC debate in 1991, when a rash of attacks on multiculturalism began to appear in the journals. At the time, Dinesh D'Sousa's *Illiberal Education* was climbing the best seller list, and, quite suddenly, *Newsweek*, the *Atlantic Monthly*, *The New Republic*, the New York *Times*, the *Nation*, and *Time* were all viewing life in our universities with alarm. In June of that year, President George Bush chose the graduation

---

been popular in descriptions of attitudes of the 1970s, as contrasted to the 1960s. Of the role of Leftist scholars on campuses, Watts writes: "By the 1980s, what had once been a disgruntled political retrenchment gradually evolved into a sophisticated political disengagement. . . . By the 1980s, aging radicals from an earlier era in search of regeneration increasingly crossed paths with a younger breed of Leftist scholar, for whom the 1960s are irrelevant as much as inspirational." Steven Watts, "The Idiocy of American Studies," *American Quarterly* 43, 4 (December 1991).

[5] By then, a conservative backlash had also been generated by the perception that the radicalisms of the 1960s had "gone too far." That resistance found expression first in two hugely influential books which focussed national attention on campuses by Allan Bloom and E.D. Hirsch who, along with William Bennett, Secretary of Education under Ronald Reagan, became its most articulate, popular, and maligned spokesmen; they were followed in 1990 by Dinesh D'Sousa's *Illiberal Education*. See Bloom, *The Closing of the American Mind* (Simon and Schuster, 1987), E.D. Hirsch, Jr., *Cultural Literacy: What Every American Needs to Know* (Houghton Mifflin, 1987), and Bennett, "'To Reclaim a Legacy': Text of Report on Humanities in Higher Education," *Chronicle of Higher Education*, November 28, 1984, 16-21.

ceremony at the University of Michigan as occasion to denounce what he called "assaults on freedom of speech" taking place on American campuses. Acrimony seemed to erupt all over Academe. What might have been the subject of interesting *discussion* seemed to be transformed overnight into an increasingly political, increasingly shrill *debate*. On one side of the debate were scholars challenging the canons of courses in literature, art, history and the humanities; some feminists; advocates for black, Latino, Native American, gay and lesbian and other groups; affirmative action supporters; and student groups seeking to enforce speech codes in an effort to control a growing number of incidents of racism, sexism, and homophobia on campus. They were the new "thought police" (*Newsweek's* term) whose tactics were compared to McCarthyism—a "McCarthyism of the Left."[6] On the other side of the debate were new and old conservatives and traditionalists, a new organization calling itself the National Association of Scholars, and an odd assortment of alarmed liberal humanists.

At first I suspected that everyone was overreacting, that the speech codes campuses had adopted were getting attention because some universities *had* taken them to extremes, and that the right-wing was merely attacking liberals on a new front. In the media pieces, valid examples of overzealousness were mixed with superficial examples, and much of the evidence seemed so silly, the tones of voice so frenetic, that I was sure the debate would soon collapse of its own weight. But the anger boiling up behind the differences of opinion was more troubling, and so, having three times before in my career spent time looking for the motivating forces that kept improbable right-wing movements afloat,[7] I began to look for patterns.

First, I noticed that not everybody claiming to discuss PC was talking about the same things. For instance, some saw feminism as central to the debate while others seemed oblivious to gender, assuming multicultural meant multiethnic, identity determined by racial and ethnic groups.[8] By the end of 1991, however, PC had

---

[6]In its December 24, 1990 issue, *Newsweek* had "THOUGHT POLICE" in big block letters on its cover, followed by a subtitle, "Is This the New Enlightenment or the New McCarthyism?" Christopher Phelps refuted the analogy in "The Second Time as Farce: The Right's 'New McCarthyism,'" *Monthly Review*, October 1991, 39-48.

[7](1) Unpublished M.A. essay on Senator Joseph McCarthy, Wayne State University, 1956; (2) "Paranoid Patriotism: the Radical Right in the South," *Atlantic Monthly*, November 1962, and "Circuit Riders to the Right--Religion and the Patriots," *Universitas*, ed. Clifford Davidson, 1963; and (3) "The Agony and the Ecstasy: The Rise of the Christian Right," one of several titles for unpublished lectures on the evangelical Right delivered on twenty-some occasions, 1984-1987.

[8]Among groups, by 1990, the Big Four had long since emerged as the major categories of ethnic identity: African American, Native American, Hispanic American and Asian American,

expanded—especially in the popular press, including its comics pages—to include an even wider variety of issues, not only sexism and homophobia but ageism, ableism, animal rights, and environmentalism.[9] Secondly, I noticed that while some of the debaters focused on ideas, such as Afrocentrism as against Eurocentrism in discussing the fate of Western civilization, others concentrated on demographics, using the history of ideas merely as backdrop to concerns over admissions and hiring policies, revision of high school textbooks, speech codes, ethnic studies requirements, and school policy.

Thirdly, as the debate unfolded, I was often uncertain where the debaters stood on a given issue. One moment the position of the multiculturalist "thought police" would seem perfectly clear—as when Amoja Three Rivers in *MS.* Magazine refuted a whole body of history with the single line, "Columbus didn't discover diddly-squat."[10] The next moment their position would seem so fraught with partisanship—as with the relation of Afrocentrism to the disclosures in the volume *Black Athena,* or the debates in music over jazz and jazz criticism—that I despaired of ever finding time to track down the evidence and read it all so I could piece out the arguments for myself. How could I answer students' questions if I was unsure myself? Were the essentialist arguments about origins real discoveries or exercises in ego affirmation aimed at solving contemporary social problems by increasing self-esteem among excluded groups? Why were scholars I had once respected joining in the chorus defending the canon and attacking multiculturalism, among them Irving Howe, Eugene Genovese, Max Lerner, C. Vann Woodward, and especially Arthur Schlesinger in a strange little book called *The Disuniting of the United States?*[11] What role had been played by postmodernist theory (by which I

---

often cited in that order. In terms of right-wing history, however, the opposition to feminism and gay rights made more sense since they were seen as the newest threats to the American status quo.

[9]Thus in Sacramento during a single week in January, 1992, citizens were cooperating with a "politically-correct plan" for disposing of our Christmas trees, the city's art museum announced an exhibit of Alfred Jay Miller's paintings that exposed his "fraudulent" portrayals of Indians, and the local paper reported Hollywood's willingness to make films with "PC Ratings." See The Sacramento *Bee* for the week of Jan. 7, 1992; art review on Miller, "Artful Deceit: Paintings of the 'Wild West' reveal a fraudulent vision," Jan. 12, 1992, Encore, p.3.

[10] *MS Magazine: The World of Women,* II, 2 (1991).

[11]Schlesinger, *The Disuniting of the United States: Reflections on a Multicultural Society,* (W.W. Norton [Whittle Books],1991). The Whittle version of the book has ads for Federal Express interspersed throughout. What made Schlesinger's role painful for many was that he had been one of the best historians to explain the concepts of unity and diversity in American history.

mean to include poststructuralism, literary theory, feminist theory, and culture theory—all theory influenced by the new continental scholarship) in shaping the discourse over pluralism and cultural difference?[12]

I soon reached the conclusion that the PC debate was related to far more fundamental developments than those cited in the newsmagazines and TV talk shows. However problematic definitions were, the threat was real, and the danger was different from what I had originally supposed. Whether intentionally or inadvertently, the attack on PC was threatening to undo much of what had been taught in American universities during the previous forty years. It was affecting our personal and professional lives as teachers and scholars, and questioning the very existence of American Studies. Some scholars had sensed danger early on. In May of 1991, the Modern Language Association had felt the need, for the first time in its century-long history, to speak out against a perceived threat:

> [The Modern Language Association] has noted with dismay the recent appearance of a number of books and articles that decry 'political correctness' on American campuses. These texts charge that teachers of language and literature, with the support of the MLA, are eliminating the classics of Western civilization from the curriculum and making certain attitudes towards race, class, gender, sexual orientation, or political affiliation the sole measure of a text's value. Some teachers, it is said, intimidate colleagues who do not comply with their own political agendas, and they subvert reason, truth, and artistic standards in order to impose crude ideological dogmas on students.

That is the chief burden of this book, which thoughtfully reviews familiar concepts and milestones in ethnic history until, upon introducing the subject of Afrocentrism, the author turns coldly critical as he reviews the scholarship, lining up its advocates in order to refute them, calling on others (including D'Sousa) to back him up. Schlesinger does not similarly take up, much less try to refute, feminist advocacy; indeed he largely avoids the subject of women and feminism.

[12]I first became disaffected with theorists who presented themselves as opponents of the Right in June 1991, while attending a conference in Minneapolis on "Feminism and Music Theory," a stunning event jam-packed with formal papers on theory. (The planners had expected perhaps 30-40 women sitting cross-legged around a room *talking* ideas.) Since then, the writings I have found most helpful to explain both my sense of betrayal by the theorists and the dynamic that has led them to wield such authority are Paul Lauter's *Canons and Contexts* (Oxford, 1990); Paul Berman's "The Fog of Political Correctness," *Tikkun*, 7, 1 (January/February 1992), 53-58, 94; and especially the controversy over Steven Watts' compelling "The Idiocy of American Studies," *American Quarterly*, 43, 4 (December 1991); see *American Quarterly* 44, 3 (September 1992).

What is most disturbing . . . is the persistent resort to misrepresentation and false labeling. . . . Far from having discarded the established canon, most teachers of literature and language today continue to teach the traditional works of Western culture, even as a growing number introduce new or neglected works of Western and other cultures. . . . Contrary to the charge that such questions and perspectives debase standards, they have stimulated students to think more critically, rigorously, and creatively.[13]

While I know of no other professional association which has taken as strong a stand, new organizations soon sprang up to oppose the National Association of Scholars, and scholarly associations were pressed to state their views. More and more, their analyses have moved beyond the initial outrage that characterized reaction in 1990-91 toward a recognition that the debates over multiculturalism and political correctness are challenging us on a more fundamental level.

THREE CHALLENGES FROM MULTICULTURALISM

Among these challenges, three seem to me especially relevant to this book. I propose to set all three into context briefly before turning to the specific content of this book's chapters, to which all three are related.

1. Multiculturalism challenges us to rethink the meaning of the university. The cultural changes taking place have become so urgent that universities have found themselves being pressured simultaneously from within and without—and this at a time of severe budget crisis. From the outside, demographics are impacting on educational systems faster than they can respond; from K-12 through graduate schools, they are struggling to increase percentages of students and faculty to approximate those in the society, as well as prepare students through their course work for citizenship in their newly multicultural world. Meanwhile, from within the university, scholars have issued challenges to the canon of works we teach and the way we draw conclusions. The results of these challenges have become so sweeping as to be frightening, especially to older scholars who are not eager to revise their lecture notes or expand the scope of their research.[14] New and

---

[13]MLA statement quoted in *ASA Newsletter,* Vol. 14, No.2

[14]Two statements by two past presidents of the American Studies Association will illustrate the sweep and scope of change. In 1986, Sacvan Bercovitch spoke for the contributors to a collection called *Reconstructing American Literary History* (Oxford University Press) in writing:

> [We believe] that race, class, and gender are formal principles of art, and therefore integral to textual analysis; that language has the capacity to break free of social restrictions and through its own dynamics to undermine the power structures it seems to

old scholars alike are struggling to cope with the startling scope of change--for starters, with sheer information overload.[15]

That is to say, the PC debate is not really about being fashionably correct—knowing when to say Hispanic or Latino or Chicano, or realizing that the musical "mainstream" in America, as Albert Murray once put it, is not white but mulatto, or deciding whether it is inelegant to say herstory instead of history and spell womyn with a *y*. The challenge goes beyond race, class, and gender, beyond changing the canon; as Robert Berkhofer has rightly said, "These new perspectives challenge our very ways of understanding what we are about as scholars and persons and how

---

reflect; that political norms are inscribed in aesthetic judgment and therefore inherent in the process of interpretation; that aesthetic structures shape the way we understand history, so that tropes and narrative devices may be said to use historians to enforce certain views of the past; that the task of literary historians is not just to show how art transcends culture, but also to identify and explore the ideological limits of their time, and then to bring these to bear upon literary analysis in such a way as to make use of the categories of culture, rather than being used by them. (p. iii)

In 1989, Robert Berkhofer, addressing "the new scholarship" in American Studies, summarized what he saw happening in the field:.

New subject matter and new terminology would seem to indicate . . . a new approach to American Studies, if not a new American Studies. The concern with myths, symbols, and images, which marked the classical period of American Studies, has given way to an overwhelming interest in class, ethnicity, race, and gender. Such once popular terms as *paradox, ambiguity,* and *irony* have been replaced by *domination, hegemony,* and *empowerment.* The definition of culture has changed from one stressing eclecticism but unity to one emphasizing division and opposition. The exemplary works have moved from stressing the basic homogeneity of the American mind and uniformity of the American character to noting the diversity of the American population and the divisiveness of the American experience. As a result, the idea of society as a system of structured inequality receives priority over the concept of culture as the basis for understanding American life. ("A New Context for a New American Studies?" *American Quarterly,* 41, 4 [December 1989]).

[15]"Traced to their source, many of the complaints about multiculturalism stem from the fundamental fact that there is too much to read," writes Patricia Nelson Limerick, asking that we "recognize that much of the grumpiness currently aimed at studies of gender, race, class, and ethnicity is, in fact, a response to a vast, worldwide rush to publish information," and concluding: "A multicultural approach is, simply, a more accurate way of telling and interpreting the planet's complicated stories. In the intertwined stories of people of diverse origins and perspectives lies the basis of our true national and global identity." See Limerick, "Information Overload Is a Prime Factor in Our Cultural Wars," *The Chronicle of Higher Education,* July 29, 1992, p. A32.

we represent our understandings."[16] The PC debate is about *what a university is and should be*, and what we as scholars are supposed to be doing in it.

To come to terms with such sweeping changes, teachers feel they need not only new textbooks, not only add-and-stir recipes for changing their syllabi (add ethnics and stir, add women and stir); they need new anthologies, new *ways* of teaching, new ways of conceiving their roles as scholars, and quite possibly wholesale curricular revision. It will take some time before a response adequate to the challenge emerges. This volume is intended to serve in the interim as an aid to those who wish to hasten the day, and who need suggestions on how to begin making changes.

2. Multiculturalism challenges us to a dialogue that will bridge across borders and span the chasm of theory.[17] Here I am speaking of a more subtle expression of the PC debate, one that is unfolding within the scholarly community, with implications for all who teach. "As everyone in the profession well understands, 'theory' of any kind is at present a code word for the politicalization of literature," wrote a critic of multiculturalism in *The Chronicle of Higher Education* in 1991, urging that theory be banned from the literature classroom.[18] In some circles, theory is equated with a leftist political agenda. In others, theorists are characterized as "formalists"[19]—detached intellectuals who

---

[16]Berkhofer, "A New Context for a New Americans Studies?" *American Quarterly,* p.3.

[17]I use the words "bridge" and "border" deliberately, conscious of the ways multicultural artists and American Studies scholars alike are exploring *borders* both as *barricades* and *bridges* See the chapter called "Mixing" in Lucy Lippard's *Mixed Blessngs: New Art In a Multicultural America* (Pantheon Books, 1990), and Gloria Anzaldua's *Borderlands/La Frontera: The New Mestiza* (Spinsters/Aunt Lute Book Co., 1987). See also the session titled "Theorizing Border Culture," with [as yet unpublished] papers on "Changing Border Theory" and "Borders/Diasporas," for the meeting of the American Studies Association, Costa Mesa, CA, Nov. 5-8, 1992, as well as the chapter called "Border Pedagogy in the Age of Postmodernism" in Stanley Aronowitz and Henry A. Giroux, *Postmodern Education: Politics, Culture and Social Criticism* (University of Minnesota, 1991), which has subsections called "Border Pedagogy as a Counter-text," "Border Pedagogy as Counter-Memory" and "Border Pedagogy and the Politics of Difference."

[18]Peter Shaw, in the *Chronicle of Higher Education,* November 27,1991. Shaw did not believe "the new, more politically oriented theories belonged in the classroom in the first place." His article inspired a great many responses, most of them hostile, several quoting the sentence above as proof of Shaw's "shallow" outlook.

[19]Paul Lauter uses the word "formalist" to describe literary theorists but adds in a footnote: "'Formalism' may no longer be the most appropriate label for all that is now being put into the bottles of criticism. Certainly, poststructuralist, hermeneutic, speculative, philosophical, or theoretical modes of criticism are different from those of the New Criticism and its various

may abstractly support diversity but, having discovered during the eighties how well theoretical writing is rewarded, became so enamored of their own agility with language and concepts that they lost connection with (some say betrayed) their original mission. In still other circles, theorists are credited with discovering, in the nick of time, that theoretical discourse could be a subversive strategy for keeping alive a radical intellectual critique through a period when the conservatives seemed to have taken over everything else in American intellectual life.[20] We are led to ask: how can bridging be done when we cannot even see the shore, when we do not know where the border is?

Two contrasting attitudes toward theory, in two books published in 1991, will illustrate the dilemma. In the name of democracy and diversity, and in the interest of educational reform, Aronowitz and Giroux in *Postmodern Education* argued on behalf of adopting a "critical postmodernism," "a postmodernism of resistance":

> At its best, a critical postmodernism signals the possibility for not only rethinking the issue of educational reform but also creating a pedagogical discourse that deepens the most radical impulses and social practices of democracy itself. . . . At its best, a postmodernism of resistance wants to

---

successors. . . . I prefer 'formalism' since it accepts the formalist stance by analyzing texts, including its own, primarily as autonomous objects isolated from their social origins and functions." (p.20) He also suggests such theory might be called *ludic* because it spends much time in play. Lauter, *Canons and Contexts* (Oxford University Press, 1991). I find "formalism" persuasive, and I am more impressed by the similarities to New Criticism than by the differences.

[20] See, for example, Robert Scholes, "Deconstruction and Communication," *Critical Inquiry*, 14 (1988), 284-85, for the view that deconstruction appealed to those influenced by the politics of the 1960's because it "allows a displacement of political activism into a textual world where anarchy can *become* the establishment without threatening the actual seats of political and economic power. Political radicalism may be thus drained off or sublimated into a textual radicalism that can happily theorize its own disconnection from unpleasant realities." I am grateful to Clifford Davidson for calling my attention to this remarkable passage, in his *On Tradition: Essays on the Use and Valuation of the Past* [in manuscript, 1992], p. 178, n.17. Condemnation of postmodernist theory has also come from feminists. For example, Jill Dolan, speaking of postmodernism's influence on feminism and performance, in 1987 found it "debonair and complacent, wallowing in empty formalism" and accused feminists of "abdicating their responsibility for creating social and political meaning." ("Is the Postmodern Aesthetic Feminist?" *Art and Cinema*, New Series, 1, 3 [Fall 1987]) Camille Paglia, always flambuoyant, has characterized postmodernism as a "70s French fad [that was] a flight from 60s truths, a reactionary escape into false abstraction." (Quoted in *Image*, July 7, 1991, and September 27, 1992. See also Paglia, *Sexual Personae* [Yale University Press, 1990]).

redraw the map of modernism so as to effect a shift in power from the privileged and the powerful to those groups struggling to gain a measure of control over their lives . . . . a postmodernism of resistance challenges the liberal humanist notion of the unified, rational subject as the bearer of history. . . . Postmodernism views the subject as contradictory and multilayered, and rejects the notion that individual consciousness and reason are the most important determinants in shaping human history.

Clearly these authors see postmodernism advancing the cause of multiculturalism and helping us all rethink the purposes of education. Equally committed to democracy and diversity, equally concerned about educational reform, Paul Lauter—as if in answer—in the same year wrote:

It is my view that, especially at this historic moment of reform in American higher education, the power exercised by formalist, ludic modes of criticism in American academic circles is peculiarly pernicious and needs consciously to be contested. . . . We need . . . to understand why speculative criticism developed such an enormous vogue in the late 1960s and 1970s, why its practitioners have come to be dominant figures in the American literary establishment, why its terminology slips so trippingly from the tongues of serious graduate students, why job lists multiply calling for practitioners of "theory," and, finally, why so much of it has spun increasingly into irrelevance to the concerns we face every day as teachers and as intellectuals. [21]

The dialogue I envision will be one that accomodates both statements, more than one school of thought. While it is beyond the scope of the present discussion to compare "postmodernism" *as against* "poststructuralism," "culture theory" *as against* "literary theory" or unravel the debate over what is sometimes simply called "criticism,"[22] it is important for readers of the volume to question the easy assumption that all theorists are on the same side. On the contrary. Not only do they

---

[21]Stanley Aronowitz and Henry A. Giroux, *Postmodern Education: Politics, Culture and Social Criticism* (University of Minnesota, 1991), pp. 187, 115, 116. Lauter, *Canons and Contexts* (Oxford University Press, 1991), pp. 135, 138. I have reordered their sentences out of context for the sake of coherence and brevity.

[22]As in Giles Gunn's *The Culture of Criticism and the Criticism of Culture*-- my favorite example of a postmodernist title--(Oxford University Press, 1987) and Terry Eagleton's *The Function of Criticism* (1984). Eagleton, whose books defining the history and forms of literary theory have been highly influential, has called postmodernism "a form of discourse that is almost entirely self-validating and self-perpetuating," and concludes that it had by 1984 become as bloodless, cloistered, and hermetic as the forms of New Criticism it displaced.

differ in political alliances, their own perception of what they do is quite different from the way they appear to others.[23]

To some extent, the schism over theory is generational. Speaking for an older generation, I find in the schism a gigantic irony: a younger generation that had begun by embracing my generation's "radical" concerns, in the course of *expanding* on the cultural critique we had championed, managed to *reverse* the direction in which we had sought to guide scholarship by focusing single-mindedly on method, theory, and forms. The new scholars became conspicuous not for dogmatism as such, but for a particular combination of dogmatisms (a pattern I recall witnessing among my graduate students of the early 1960s)—a combination of great naiveté in politics and great sophistication in scholarship. It is a scholarship whose forms appeared so opaque, so obtuse, so private, that even early on I feared only an elite could understand them. An elite has since emerged. Articles, books, whole new journals devoted to theory have emerged.[24] By the end of the eighties, younger scholars had learned to speak the language as if it had always been there, and they responded to complaints over jargon and obfuscation by saying it was not their problem but everyone else's if not even the people they were studying could make sense of what they were saying. As one pair of critics put it, they spoke as if those who do theory must know more than those being theorized.[25]

To be multicultural in our teaching will require breaking the silence that surrounds the schism over theory. "Speaking up presents far too high a risk," writes Lauter, in an observation about the silences at academic conferences after papers addressing theory. "To ask a question might imply the inadmissible: that you

---

[23] Gregory Jay, for example, speaking as a theorist, claims that "the production of new knowledge" by theorists was not by tenured radicals, as the Right had claimed, but by "the have-nots of academe" who had turned to French poststructuralism and British Cultural Studies in reaction against New Criticism, in order to "stress how works of culture belong to the larger struggles of their societies." Jay called on theorists to "go public" to "explain aspects of the new scholarship and show how valuable it can be in practice." *The Chronicle of Higher Education*, February 26, 1992, p. B2. Jay's critics took him on in subsequent issues of the *Chronicle*, where the debate over political correctness was in full swing in letters to the editor during this entire era.

[24] Among the new journals devoted to theory are *Critical Inquiry, Diacritics, New Literary History, Cultural Critique, Representations* and *differences: A Journal of Feminist Theory* [sic]. Interestingly, a collection from *Representations* was published in 1991 under the title *The New American Studies* (University of California Press, 1991). Also symptomatic are the expanding sections on "Critical Theory" in the catalogs of university presses.

[25] Lucy Lippard attributed this phrase to two black feminists during her lecture, "Towards a Post-Columbian World," at California State University, Sacramento, October 8, 1991.

do not understand part, or even all, of a paper. . . . Better silence, gravity, and pretense."[26] The challenge to cope with theory will mean looking at book lists and assignments not with an eye to determining whose "bias" prevails, which form of "discourse" is being used, but for ways to open up dialogue and increase possibilities for bridging across the borders. The contributors to this volume, many of whom cope with diversity and democracy on the front lines—in the classrooms, often with students from disempowered and dissident groups, often suffering burnout from their daily efforts—convey a partiality for the sheer exuberance of doing multicultural work and for the openness it brings that leaps across that chasm of silence, risking error, defying formalism, welcoming controversy, with an ease the cloistered theorists would do well to emulate.

3. Multiculturalism challenges us to rethink the single most basic question in American Studies: What does it mean to be American? By and large, debates over the answer to that question have revolved around a polarity between, on the one hand, unity, consensus, sameness, and on the other hand, diversity, pluralism, difference—the unum and the pluribus in our national motto, "E pluribus unum." The PC Debate pits the "insurgents" and "innovators" who emphasize difference—primarily differences based on race, ethnicity, gender, class, and sexuality—against those "traditionalists" or "humanists" who give primacy to unity—to an ideology of synthesis, commonality, devotion to Western values, to holism and togetherness, to the idea of a mainstream, to cooperative models that assume, even without saying so, a smiling acceptance of an American common ground.[27]

As sides have become polarized in the PC debate, a battle line has been drawn down the middle of the term Multicultural America, in effect creating an oxymoron, the word "multicultural" pointing to diversity, "America" assuming there is one—a a single ideology, an agreed-upon definition of what America is. Among many teachers, it has become PC to ignore "America" in American Studies, deflecting

---

[26]Lauter, *Canons and Contexts,* p. 13.

[27] The Federal Express advertisements that interlard Schlesinger's unnerving little book, *The Disuniting of the United States* [in the original edition, published by Whittle] illustrate at a glance how, in everyday images, multicultural unity is commodified. Out of twelve ads, eight are of men, five of them white, only one a woman (black), and one—the culminating ad at the end—a collective portrait in which we see the "pluribus" in a mass of smiling workers' faces while the "unum" to which they all give allegiance is a monolithic red, white, and blue airplane looming over them. These are emblems of the happy acceptance of commonality under the umbrella of American capitalistic enterprise; admirers of Schlesinger are bound to wonder what he had in mind when he agreed to have them in his book.

attention to *eras* (modern, postmodern), to *groups* (racial groups, gender groups, subcultures) and *regions* (Southern Culture, California Studies, West Texas folk music), partly out of an unspoken fear that studying "America," meaning the United States, implies giving assent to Western values, to dead white Eurocentric males (nicknamed DWEMs), to "exceptionalism," to hegemonic patriarchal WASP culture—a whole cartoon image of what America is presumed to be. That fear of being criticized has already left in its wake a trail of timidity and a habit of self-censorship among younger scholars caught up in the stormy PC atmosphere.

At the same time, another and contrary fear has emerged with the PC debate—the fear that emphasizing diversity will lead to balkanization, fragmentation, and self-segregation, and that this new "separatism" could tear us apart as a people. Parallels to the current divisions in Eastern Europe are used as warnings against what could happen in America if our fragmentation continues. Such fears reveal a loss of faith in America's basic cultural cohesion, the faith that there will always be a unum to bring us together, that the unum will triumph—"E pluribus unum," out of many will come the one. It is here, I believe, at this point in the analysis, that we arrive at the central issue in the PC debate, the one that underlies most of the material in this book. It is the crucial realization that PC may be new, but the debate between the unum and the pluribus is not. Over the course of American history, there have been not one but several theories put forth that have attempted to reconcile the many with the one, primarily in relation to ethnicity, theories which can now serve as models for other categories of difference.[28] Implicitly, such "reconciliation theories" underlie most of the chapters in this book.

The question, What does it mean to be American? has always been asked with special urgency during times of crisis. Often it has been the dispossessed and oppressed who have cared the most about the answers. The proof is in the frequency with which "protest" works appear on the syllabi and in the essays— protest in music, the visual arts, and literature, especially conspicuous in works created during the eras of the 1930s and after the 1960s. Protest and celebration are twin themes that have simultaneously characterized the art of ethnic artists in the several fields of art, and they are now the themes appearing in the work of the newer groups factored into the equation called multiculturalism—women, gay men and lesbians, and "new immigrant" groups. Although there has been a temptation to use the same protest themes and appropriate the same protest language in teaching about all groups, a more conspicuous emphasis today is on factors of difference in responding to American experience. Some teachers, for example, are asking if

---

[28]See "Theories and Stages of Ethnicity," in the appendix to Syllabus #2, in Part I, above.

"America" has been a more empowering idea for women than for men, more empowering for minorities than for the majority. Peter Frederick makes a point of structuring his syllabus (#1 in Part I) to force students to realize that the black response to American experience has been quite the reverse of the Indian response, the former seeking to be counted in, the latter asking to be allowed out.

Similarly, although the experience W. E. B. DuBois long ago described as "twoness" remains very real in the readings and syllabi, having been extended to cover gender and sexuality as well as race and ethnicity, the twoness has often been redefined so as to acknowledge a continuing tension between equality and difference, unity and diversity, in the struggle to define who the American has become.[29] Also characteristic of the new directions in scholarship is a new "essentialism" in the definition of the American, based on the claim that certain groups have a unique experience of twoness—that is, an insider's knowledge in coping with double consciousness which has earned them a right to greater attention. The claim is frequently made for women, sometimes for homosexuals, but most often, I think, for Chicanos. A good illustration appears in a conclusion offered by Marcos Sanchez-Tranquilino to a 1989 essay on Chicano mural art: "the Chicano experience represents a model for all Americans to acknowledge their current identity as an outcome of two (or more) living histories coming together . . . the word 'Chicano' is an American word (not only an English, or only a Spanish word) because it signifies the unique amalgamation of the old and new identities without the denials of one in favor of the other. *That is Chicano; that is American.*"[30]

In one way or another, all of the entries in this book, ranging from those which acknowledge obvious forms of twoness (as in the Table of Contents to

---

[29]Here is the famous passage from *The Souls of Black Folk* (1903): "It is a peculiar sensation, this double consciousness, this sense of always looking at one's self through the eyes of others . . . . One ever feels his twoness: an American, a Negro; two souls, two thoughts, two unreconciled strivings; two warring ideals in one dark body, whose dogged strength alone keeps it from being torn asunder. The history of the American Negro is the history of this strife,--this longing to attain self-conscious manhood, to merge his double self into a better and truer self. In this merging he wishes neither of the older selves to be lost." On DuBois' own later modifications of "twoness" as a self-defining strategy, see Thomas Holt,"The Political Uses of Alienation," *American Quarterly*, 42, 2 (June 1990), and the chapter by Keith E. Byerman in *Multicultural Autobiography: American Lives*, ed. James Robert Payne (University of Tennessee Press, 1992).

[30]"Murales del Movimiento: Chicano Murals and the Discourses of Art and Americanization," in *Signs from the Heart: California Chicano Murals* (Venice, CA: Social and Public Art Resource Center, 1990), p.85. (Emphasis added.) See also Gloria Anzaldua's *Borderlands/La Frontera*.

In one way or another, all of the entries in this book, ranging from those which acknowledge obvious forms of twoness (as in the Table of Contents to *Crossing Cultures*) to those with more complex self-contradictions (as in Langston Hughes' "Let America be America Again," or the lyrics to "America" from *West Side Story*, both in Essay #2) to those describing modern "mosaics" (Part I, Syllabus #7), are connected by a common theme: they all confront the challenge to define—to redefine; indeed, at times, to recreate—what it means to be an American.

WHAT THIS BOOK IS ABOUT

> *In the clash of cultures, artists have always had a special capacity to illuminate the differences among peoples and expose the reasons for conflict. They may not provide solutions, but their insights can be crucial in helping us understand and accommodate diversity and change.*
>
> — from a pamphlet, *The Arts and Government: Questions for the Nineties, 1990.*

This book is grounded in the conviction that artists not only have a special capacity to "illuminate differences" when cultures clash but also, in their own way, to provide solutions—once we learn to interpret what their art forms can tell us. At least one art form is included in each syllabus or essay in this volume, but since there is so much material available elsewhere on *literature*, musical and visual materials have been given preference, albeit their relationship to literature may be emphasized. Many syllabi cross over borders with ease, not only borders between art forms and ethnic groups but between highbrow and lowbrow, cultivated and vernacular forms of art. I have rigorously excluded syllabi and essays that focus only on a single group (using as my guideline the "multi" in multicultural), but I have included examples of courses that lean on team-teaching, guest lectures, and video materials, and I have been partial to projects that encourage border-crossing by students. It is the creativity of the teacher in using art forms in multicultural teaching that explains most of the choices made for the book.

The volume is divided into three parts— Part I. *SYLLABI,* Part II. *ESSAYS,* and Part III. *BIBLIOGRAPHY AND CHECKLISTS.*

Part I grew out of my interest in course syllabi as documents to measure change—footprints in the sands of our multicultural times. Some of the syllabi are enhanced with comments and appendices; others are not. The dates of the syllabi range from 1976 to 1992. Those who composed them are aware that their assignments and structures reflect the views of the times. The rapidity with which we are transforming "survey" courses, as the comments by teachers attest, is an index to the speed with which new perspectives are having an impact upon universities and their humanities programs.[31] I have divided the syllabi into three groups—those with an *"American"* emphasis, those with an *"ethnic"* emphasis, and *"basic"* or *"mainstream"* courses—but these divisions themselves become partly arbitrary. No two of the syllabi are alike; each has something unique to offer. Collectively they will provide teachers with a wealth of ideas for creating and amending courses, but more than that, a comparison of their different approaches to similar subjects will reveal different responses to the challenges from multiculturalism and the PC debate I have outlined above.

It will be noted that several of the syllabi in Part I can be cross-referenced with essays by the same authors in Part II and in one case (Atwater) a checklist in Part III. In five cases, pairs of syllabi appear together—for different reasons, explained by editorial notes. Several authors provided me with commentaries specifically for the benefit of this book. Otherwise the syllabi are addressed to students in the language and format the teachers actually used, at times with handouts and/or reading lists appended. (I have omitted office hours, telephone numbers and other data if they seemed really extraneous to this book's purposes.)

Part II of the volume, "Essays," is divided into two sections. The essays in the first section, "Looking for Patterns," range from general analyses to specific projects. The two lead essays, the first by Pamela Fox and the second by Annette Hansen and me, might well be paired as explorations of the unum and the pluribus in scholarship, Fox's exploring efforts toward synthesizing (unity), ours offering examples of cataloguing (pluralism). Even their comparative length is instructive: Fox's charts concentrate huge ideas and amounts of material onto a single page; Hansen's and my examples spread outward from Whitman to Kingman, page after page, in order to provide examples of diversity, this multivocal chapter becoming the longest single essay in the book. While California teachers will have an advantage in using the third essay, on California Post Office murals, since their students can visit the post offices John Carlisle describes, there are similar murals in every other state in the union (he cites in a footnote his own work on murals in Texas and Indiana murals); thus the essay has broad value.

---

[31] I learned to appreciate the value of syllabi to reveal new perspectives and locate the frontiers of thinking in our universities, first, from the Women's Studies series published by Know, Inc., Pittsburgh (which also published my two volumes, *American Women and American Studies* (1971, 1974), both including syllabi), and more recently, from Paul Lauter's *Reconstructing American Literature,* published by The Feminist Press (1986), a forerunner to the multicultural movement which boldly announced on its cover its aim to see that "the work of Frederick Douglass, Mary Wilkins Freeman, Agnes Smedley, Zora Neale Hurston and others is read with the work of Nathaniel Hawthorne, Henry James, William Faulkner, Ernest Hemingway and others."

The next six essays offer practical suggestions for assignments, projects, and stages to consider in transforming courses. In the course of doing so, they describe the arc of change underway in our universities in response to the challenges of multiculturalism. Peter Frederick's appeal for using emotion in the classroom (Essay #4) is followed by my outline of two ways to introduce courses on multiculturalism (Essay #5), both of us recommending the use of media. Sherry Sullivan's account of the stages she experienced in transforming her American literature survey course (Essay #6) may be read along with her "Before" and "After" syllabi in Part I (15A & B). Similarly, Susan Willoughby's report (Essay #7) to a college ad hoc committee—called, intriguingly, the "Beyond the Canon" Committee—may be read in relation to her syllabus (17B) for an American music survey course and the "Trialogue" in Essay #6, while Scot Guenter's essay on team-teaching a basic American Civ course (Essay #9) refers to the two-semester survey course described in Syllabi 18A & B. In their different ways, these essays all track out patterns-—steps, stages, or interdisciplinary presentations to show how a changing mindset is emerging in the humanities and the arts.

The second section of essays, "From the Inside Out," targets a particular emphasis brought into the classroom by multiculturalism—namely, perspectives based on personal experience or reported from an inside point of view. A Lakota-Sioux student calling himself "Shoots the Ghosts" gives a searing review of the movie *Dances with Wolves*, the most controversial film of 1991; a minister gives a sermon reporting his experience growing up gay in America; a Bay Area Career Woman tells of becoming an aspiring lesbian; and a working-class student reports on her experience going to graduate school at UC-Santa Cruz. I have had one reader react to these four essays by asking what they are doing in this volume; I have had two others call them, hands down, the best things in the book. The last two essays in this section are also informed by the emphasis on inside points of view. For the essay on "The Roots Project," I have composed a kind of scrapbook of responses from my own students (1989-1992), using their evaluations, outlines, personal experiences, and—in Kathleen Hanson's case—a retrospective account of the whole "Roots" experience. The last essay contains the Table of Contents for *Crossing Cultures*, reprinted by permission from Macmillan, a composition reader in which an array of witnesses report on their experiences from the inside out.

Part III, which will probably be the most immediately useful to most readers, contains bibliographies and checklists on literary, musical, and visual materials for use in humanities classes. Section A, "The Visual Arts and Multicultural America," is an annotated bibliography by Jackie Donath, and is indeed mostly (but not exclusively) on the visual arts. It is a treasure-house of materials, with subdivisions on architecture, research guides, exhibition catalogues (an impressive collection on major ethnic groups), photography, fine arts and folk arts. I am enormously grateful to Jackie for this contribution, as I am for Keith Atwater's "Resource Guide" in Section B, which is organized around the four major ethnic groups, with examples of each group's forms of expression—literature, art, music, films—listed under each category, plus a list for comparing Japanese American internment camps with Native American reservations. Section C is a "videography" of videotapes, 16mm films, and movies available on video teachers might consider using. Section D is a "musicography" that includes four categories of materials—musicals, videos on music, discography, and books about music. Kathleen Hanson's highly personal bibliography of Fictional Favorites follows in Section E, with Lucy Lippard's bibliography from her path-breaking volume *Mixed Blessings* concluding in Section F. There are also bibliographies appended to several syllabi which are distinctive for different reasons—Victor Greene's for his categories related to attitudes on race, Jeff Lustig's for his listings on California themes, my own for its comments addressed to students, Peter Frederick's "Wonderful Teachable Autobiographies," and Olivia Castellano's lists on Chicano resources. Since each of the lists represents the personal choices of its author, I have made no effort to edit out duplications—indeed, the duplications are themselves of interest. I have also left intact the idiosyncracies of format and style in the syllabi and bibliographies.

Finally, how does one offer up a book whose listings one knows are inevitably incomplete? Does one apologize for leaving out data that came to our attention too late, or that we smply did not know? Or does one gloat that such lacunae, revealing how much still needs to be done, are proof of contemporary relevance? Early in 1992, a colleague had persuaded me, in the name of Relevance, to abandon my ridiculously cumbersome subtitle, "A Resource Book for Teachers of Humanities and American Studies," in favor of a jazzier subtitle, "New Perspectives for the 21st Century." During the final editing, as the oratory of the national presidential conventions sounded on television while I typed, that dashing new subtitle began to sound more and more like hype. I returned to my clumsier original, confident that America was entering a period when lumpy language was becoming more trustworthy than slick sloganeering as a route to accuracy, and that in this small way—as in its very appearance at this juncture in our history—this book reflects the spirit of America in our time.

August 1992

Part I: Syllabi

==

AMERICAN AUTOBIOGRAPHY:
THE EURO-AMERICAN, AFRICAN-AMERICAN, AND INDIAN TRADITIONS

Peter Frederick, Wabash College
History 25A, Fall 1990

SOME REFLECTIONS ON THE COURSE

I have taught variations of an American Autobiography course for some 15 years, sometimes taking a more American Studies approach and sometimes focusing on literary genres, but always featuring the multi-cultural American experience. My African-American culture and history course, taught since 1968, is organized around reading classic black autobiographical documents. The syllabus included here, representing the latest version of my interest in life-writing, reflects a year's work at The Newberry Library in Chicago studying American Indian autobiographies and ethnographies.

The statement of goals on the syllabus, which is for me much more than a rhetorical exercise, reflects my increasingly experimental approach to the course, especially as I explore ways of helping students connect *their* lives and issues (intellectual, emotional, physical, spiritual) to the various ways these issues play out in other Americans from diverse cultures. In both the journals and the various paper assignments these connections were made; students were able to see both universal themes of the human condition *and* cultural differences.

The divided structure of the course reflects an organizational idea borrowed from H. David Brumble ("Black autobiographies, it seems, characteristically imagine themselves *into* white society, while Indian autobiographies imagine themselves *out*") that placed the black autobiographical style in the Euro-American tradition: individual self-development stressing the rise from rags to riches or "up from slavery" and the discovery of identity and a "name." American Indians, although sharing issues of bicultural identity with African-Americans, were far more focused on "place" than on "name" because a specific spiritually-charged geographical location, unlike for the displaced African, conveyed origins, continuity, survival, land, purpose and group identity. "Place" distinguished Native Americans from all those immigrant Europeans and even Africans.

Other than some splendid papers, three of which won major student awards at the end of the year (one for creativity in writing on "the margins of knowledge"), the highlights of the course occurred as students gradually discovered in both the texts and themselves similarities as "Americans" and distinctive cultural differences (in the class of 15 were two Blacks, one Asian Indian, and a range of socio-political attitudes among the whites). The most illuminating discussions were over the identity choices made by Washington, Malcolm X, Rodriguez, Eastman and Black Elk. It was fascinating to see many white students, who resisted and resented black student choices to be more "African" than "American," reverse themselves in the case of Indians, preferring that Black Elk or Eastman, for example, reject the Catholic or American parts of their identity and remain Lakota. The stormiest discussions of these questions of biculturality came with Rodriguez' *Hunger of Memory.*

--Peter Frederick

Syllabus: History 25A

AMERICAN AUTOBIOGRAPHY: The Euro-American, African-American and Indian Traditions

> *"'The most democratic province in the republic of letter . . is open to all. . . .. The range of personality, experience, and profession reflected in the forms of American auto-biography is as varied as American life itself."* —
> William Dean Howells and Albert Stone

My Goals and Dreams for this Course (for me and for you)

1.   to understand and find value in the purposes, patterns, forms and issues of life-writing,

2.   to understand the Euro-American, Black and Indian traditions of auto-biographical writing, including similarities and differences,

3.   to learn some [more?] American history through the study of American lives,

4. to experience and appreciate the exterior and interior complexity of human lives,

5. to achieve deeper insights into one's own life,

6. to improve one's powers of expression, oral and written, about matters of both the heart and the head,

7. to appreciate learning in collaboration with others,

8. to learn how to think analytically by ferreting out themes, patterns, and interpretive viewpoints in books and lives,

9. to learn how to think synthetically by making connections among diverse lives, cultures, disciplines, and ways of thinking,

10. to continue to push my boundaries as a teacher in new directions by exploring how the teaching/learning dynamic is affected by such issues as emotions, myth, metaphor and images, drama, spirituality, contact, and ritual space.

[These things, by the way, are present in some form in all teaching/learning situations all the time; I just want to be more reflectively aware of them; that is my concern primarily, not yours, except as you may find these issues interesting and helpful to your own learning.]

> *"Autobiography is an unparalleled insight into the mode of consciousness of other men [and women]."* —Roy Pascal

> *"My whole life has been a chronology of—changes."* —Malcolm X

Some (further) Reflections on Dynamics of Teaching and Learning

I have thought a good deal about these goals and dreams and take them very seriously. The whole list, not just #10, suggests new directions in my thinking (and feeling) as a teacher. The course topic itself—the process of expressing the Self—is central to my evolving reflective-ness as a teacher and person.

You should also know that I believe strongly in a classroom climate that is highly interactive, participatory and cooperative, one in which all of us assume responsibility for our own—and others'—learning, where we pursue (or wait for) insights and truths actively and together.

This means keeping up regularly with the readings and assignments and coming to class ready to be involved both intellectually and emotionally with questions and responses to the texts. That's the way I'll come to class; plus I have the additional responsibility (at least at the beginning) for planning how best to facilitate our mutual explorations of American autobiography. I am aware that some of this may be a bit scary to some of you —it is to me as well— so let's talk about our anxieties as well as our exciting dreams early in the course.

Course Assignments and Basis of Grade

As long as the Goals and the Teaching/Learning dynamics seem to be working for us, evidenced by widespread and shared engagement in the readings on and issues about American autobiography, I see no reason why this course need any formal testing. Instead, I foresee *several* writing assignments of varying lengths (from a paragraph to perhaps 8-9 pages), done both as individuals and perhaps in pairs or small groups (because I believe in the importance of learning how to learn collaboratively). The writing will constitute 50% of your grade. The other 50% will be based on class participation, which includes keeping an autobiographical journal of your developing thoughts and feelings about the life-writing and life-living issues raised in the course in terms of both the people we read and yourself.

> "*In most books, the* I, *or first person, is omitted; in this it will be retaine. . . . I should not talk so much about myself if there were anybody else whom I knew as well.*" —Henry David Thoreau

> "*That is my home...in that place of ruins is the evidence of my beginning. My roots are there. A part of me is there still . . . in the very dust that whispers in the streets where I played so long ago. Is that where I belong now?*" —Polingaysi Qoyawayma

> "*Although no man knoweth the things of a man but the spirit of a man which is in him, yet there is something of a man which neither the spirit or man that is within him knoweth.*" —St. Augustine

> "*An autobiographic instinct may be as old as Man Writing; but only since 1800 has Western Man placed a premium on autobiography.*" —Karl Weintraub

Required Reading:

First Half of Semester: The Euro-American and Black Traditions

Articles on autobiography by James Olney, Robert Sayre, Albert Stone, Shirley K. Rose, & others. Jonathan Edwards' Personal Narrative (handout)

The Autobiography of Benjamin Franklin (Bookstore)

Short selections from H. D. Thoreau, Walden, Walt Whitman, "Song of Myself," and *The Education of Henry Adams* (handouts)

Frederick Douglass, *My Bondage and My Freedom* (Bookstore)

Booker T. Washington, *Up From Slavery*

Maya Angelou, *I Know Why the Caged Bird Sings*

either Maxine Hong Kingston, *Woman Warrior* or Richard Rodriguez, *Hunger of Memory*

Second Half of Semester: Indian Autobiography

Everyone: Charles Eastman, *From Deep Woods to Civilization*, John Neihardt, *Black Elk Speaks*

Peter Nabokov, *Two Leggings: The Making of a Crow Warrior*, Ruth Underhill, *The Autobiography of a Papago Woman*

Choose two or three from among a list, including:

Polingaysi Qoyawayma, *No Turning Back, Mountain Wolf Woman, Sun Chief, Lame Deer: Seeker of Visions*, Standing Bear, *My People the Sioux*, Crashing Thunder, Wooden Leg, Pretty-Shield, Plenty-Coups, Black Hawk, Maria Campbell, *Halfbreed*, Zitkala-Sa, *American Indian Stories*, N. Scott Momaday, *The Way to Rainy Mountain* and *Names*

==========================

I. The Euro-American and Black Autobiographical Traditions

> *"The very idea of autobiography has grown out of the political necessities and discoveries of the American and French revolutions."* —James M. Cox

Aug. 28/30-- Introductions: of Ourselves and of the Themes, Patterns, Issues, and History of Autobiographical Life-writing. Reading: articles by Olney, Sayre, and Stone

Sept. 4/6-- Edwards' *Narrative* and Franklin's *Autobiography*

Sept. 11/13-- Thoreau, Whitman and Henry Adams

Sept. 18/20-- Douglass, *My Bondage and My Freedom*

Sept. 25/27-- Douglass, DuBois, and Washington, *Up From Slavery*

Oct. 2/4-- article by Rose; Angelou, *Caged Bird Sings*; & review *Autobiography of Malcolm X*

Oct. 9/11-- Kingston, *Woman Warrior*, and Rodriguez, *Hunger of Memory*

II. Indian Autobiography and Life-Writing/Telling

> *"Hear me, not for myself, but for my people."* —Black Elk

Oct. 18-- Review and Preview of Indian themes, patterns, forms...

Oct. 23/25-- Nabokov, *Two Leggings—Making of a Crow Warrior*

Oct. 31/Nov 1-- Neihardt, *Black Elk Speaks*

Nov. 6/8-- Eastman, *From Deep Woods to Civilization* and Zitkala-Sa

Nov. 13/15-- Underhill, *Papago Woman*

Nov. 20/27/29--Working (individually or in groups) on additional Indian autobiographies; reports and discussions of emerging patterns, themes, issues, etc., both unique to Indian life-writing and common to the Euro-American and Black traditions

Dec.4/6-- Turning autobiographical traditions & themes back into ourselves & our own life stories.

I haven't worked out the details, but it is likely that in addition to the writing of several paragraphs and 1-3 page "papers" throughout the semester, reflecting all aspects of the Medicine Wheel (mental, emotional, physical, spiritual), there will be a 4-5 page paper due in October and a longer (8-10?) paper due in November. This last paper will be wide open for a creative presentation of Indian autobiographical themes in whatever form you think appropriate.

APPENDIX A: Handouts for "American Autobiography"

ED. NOTE: The two "handouts" I have included in Appendix A illustrate themes that inform both Fredericks' syllabus above and his essay in Part II, "Using Emotion in the Classroom." Appendix B is a bibliography.—BC

Handout #1 on Journal Writing

In a course which explores writing about the self, we can hardly avoid thinking about and writing about our own self. We, too, are historical figures, and our life and writing becomes another "text" in the course. Therefore, throughout the course I would like each of you to keep a journal of your developing thoughts and feelings about (1) the themes, issues and patterns of autobiographical writing; (2) the people and life-writing texts we encounter; and (3) your own life-history. The Journal will be a series of autobiographical fragments and reflections, the basis, if we wish, for our own autobiography, "complete" at least up to the present. You might think of the Journal as a fragmentary autobiography of your head and heart from August to December, which includes telling some stories from your past.

In addition to your own story, as you feel free or wish to write it, and reflections on the issues and themes of the course, the Journal should include reactions to the various texts and people we read and talk about, the dynamics and content of our class discussions, and any favorite poetry, art work, quotations or whatever you wish to add. The emphasis is on introspection and spontaneity. Use a pen, not word-processing. Do not worry about such things as spelling, syntax, use of evidence, etc., in the Journal. Just write freely, and be aware of possible insights about both course issues and yourself.

Date each entry (your biographers will need that) and write in your Journal *at least* twice a week. Journal writing goes best when you make it a regular part of your day, or week. Find a time when you make it a habit to write in the Journal. There will be times when the writing seems forced and unnatural; deal with this by writing about the impasse you are feeling. Often, one can write through a block by confronting it directly.

From time to time I will ask to see the journals and will return them as soon as I possibly can with some marginal responses (in pencil so you can erase them if you wish, or, if you'd rather I not write in them at all, tell me, please). Even though I have your Journal, do not stop writing entries, which can be stapled in when you get it back. All Journals, of course, will be treated with confidence and respect. No one else will see them but me, though as I said in class, there may be times when you will want to share a particular entry or story or thought with others in the class. Please do not let the fact that you are putting thoughts and feelings into the Journal prevent you from bringing them into our class discussions. Finally, the "grade" on your Journal (what an absurd thought; one's life is not graded!!) will be a holistic part of your general participation and discussion in the class.

Handout #2: "On Reading Well to Discuss Well"

Fundamental to the process of reading and discussing well is our *active interaction* with a "text" (a reading, poem, painting, document, or artifact). Effective reading is not just going quickly through a text, but rather is a process of questioning it actively, looking for key issues, themes, events, characters, forms and images. Underlining and even writing marginal comments in a "text" highlights these key points and makes them accessible during class discussions and in reviewing for exams. Some people find it helpful, while still fresh in their mind, to summarize at the end of a chapter/scene/section the main ideas and issues *in their own words.* This serves not only to aid the memory but also to make sure they understand what they've read.

In reading these classic, timeless texts, look for the main message the author intends to convey. What are the key themes? Depending on the length and complexity of the document, there may be several sub-themes as well. Note also how the structure, or form of the text, as well as how its language (imagery and symbolism) supports and reinforces the ideas. *Underline and circle words and phrases that have power for you.* Note also how the text reveals the historical traditions and cultural way of life of the time and place about which the document is written. Finally, think about how the themes and issues of the text still have applications in the modern world, contemporary culture, and in your own life.

In summary, then, in reading, look for and makes notes on:

1. The author's point of view, main message, themes.

2. The structure/form/plot of the text. Important characters.

3. How language, words, images, metaphors, create an emotional tone which supports the message and form of the text.

4. Cultural and historical context and information.

5. Contemporary connections to our lives.

When we come to class having not only read but thought about a text in these five ways, with underlining and marginal comments that reflect our thinking and feeling as we read, we are well-prepared to discuss thoughtfully, listening well to the observations and ideas of others and trying out our own developing thoughts. Focused, even personalized, underlining of texts prepares us in particular for discussions that begin with such questions as:

"What are the major points or themes that X is trying to make in this text?"

Or, "what did you particularly like or dislike about the text?"

Or, "what quotations seemed particularly important to you?"

Or, "what do you learn about how people lived and thought?"

Or, "what words, phrases, or images had emotional or intellectual power for you?"

Or, "what's this reading say about what's going on in our world today, or in my own life?"

Happy reading! — PETER FREDERICK

APPENDIX B:

Wonderfully Readable/Teachable American Autobiographies

Adams, Henry. *The Education of Henry Adams*. (Houghton-Mifflin, 1918)

Addams, Jane. *Twenty Years at Hull House*. (New Amer. Lib.,1964)

Angelou, Maya. *I Know Why the Caged Bird Sings*. (Bantam, 1971)

Black Elk Speaks, the Life Story of a Holy Man of the Ogala Sioux, with John Neihardt. (Univ. of Nebraska, 1979)[1931]

Campbell, Maria. *Halfbreed*. (Univ. Nebraska, 1973)

Crashing Thunder. *Autobiography of an American Indian*, ed. Paul Radin. (Nebraska, 1983) [1926]

Du Bois, W. E. B. *Dusk of Dawn: The Autobiography of a Race Concept*. (1940)

Du Bois, W. E. B. *Souls of Black Folk*. (Signet Classic, 1969)[1903]

Kingston, Maxine Hong. *The Woman Warrior*. (Vintage, 1975)

Lame Deer, John (Fire) and R. Erdoes. *Lame Deer: Seeker of Visions*. (Pocket Books, 1972)

McCarthy, Mary. *Memories of a Catholic Girlhood*. (1957)

Momaday, N. Scott. *Names: A Memoir*. (Harper & Row, 1976)

Moody, Anne. *Coming of Age in Mississippi*. (1964)

Mountain Wolf Woman: Autobiography of a Winnebago Woman, ed. Nancy Lurie. (Univ. of Michigan Press, 1961)

Mourning Dove: A Salishan Autobiography, ed. Jay Miller. (Univ. of Nebraska, 1990)

Narrative of the Life of Frederick Douglass. (Anchor, 1973)[1845]

Peter Nabokov. *Two-Leggings: The Making of a Crow Warrior*. (Univ. of Nebraska, 1967)

Pretty-Shield: Medicine Woman of the Crows. edited by Frank Linderman(Univ. of Nebraska, 1974) [1932]

Qoyawayma, Polingaysi [Elizabeth White]. *No Turning Back: A Hopi Woman's Struggle to Live in Two Worlds*. (New Mexico, 1964)

Rodriguez, Richard. *Hunger of Memory: An Autobiography: The Education of Richard Rodriguez.* (Bantam, 1982)

Shaw, Anna Moore. *A Pima Past.* (University of Arizona, 1974)

Standing Bear, Luther. *My People the Sioux.* (Nebraska, 1975)[1928

Stein, Gertrude. *The Autobiography of Alice B. Toklas.* (Random House, 1933)

Talayesva, Don. *Sun Chief: Autobiography of a Hopi Indian,* ed. Leo Simmons. (Yale Univ. Press, 1942)

The Autobiography of Benjamin Franklin. (Signet, 1961)

The Autobiography of Malcolm X, with Alex Haley. (Grove, 1964)

Thoreau, Henry David. *Walden.* [1854]

Underhill, Ruth. *The Autobiography of a Papago Woman* [Maria Chona]. (Holt, Rinehart, 1979) [1936]

Washington, Booker T. *Up From Slavery.* (Bantam, 1956) [1900]

Whitman, Walt. *Leaves of Grass* ("Song of Myself"). [1855]

Wooden Leg: A Warrior Who Fought Custer, interp. by Thomas Marquis. (Nebraska, 1962) [1931]

Wright, Richard. *Black Boy.* (Harper Perennial, 1966) [1937]

Zitkala-Sa [Gertrude Bonin]. *American Indian Stories.* (Nebraska, 1979) [1900-01]

MULTICULTURAL AMERICA

Betty E. M. Ch'maj, California State University, Sacramento
Humanities 101, Spring 1992

CATALOG DESCRIPTION

This is an introductory course in the humanities that explores the meaning of America as a multicultural nation. By integrating video, audio, and literary materials, the course links expressions in the arts (fine arts and popular arts) with their social and historical contexts in order to investigate cultural issues relating to race, ethnicity, gender, class, sexuality, region, and religion. Students report on their own multicultural heritage (oral or written reports) in relation to the central themes of the course. These themes include the experiences of migration and immigration, gender identity, racial or ethnic identity, marginality, and the core themes of unity vs. diversity and equality vs. difference. *Fulfills the G.E. Requirements for a Course in Ethnic Studies.*

COMMENT: The course is designed around four general characteristics:

(1) Rather than being structured around ethnic or cultural *groups*, this course will be structured around *ideas* and ways to "read" cultural and social ideas in the arts. It is organized around nine topics or themes, but it also uses the students' own experiences and histories to illuminate the themes, along with lecture, discussion, slides, video material, music, and readings. That necessarily means interrupting the development of the themes in order to accommodate the rhythm of students' lives as they prepare for their assignments and complete their readings. This is especially true for the "Roots Project."

(2) Multi*cultural* in this class does not just mean multi*ethnic*. We will consider images and issues relating to gender, class, region, religion, sexuality, and generation as well as--and in relation to--race and ethnicity as we seek to understand what makes America a multicultural society.

(3) A natural organizing principle for the course is the polarity between unity and diversity, center and margin, individualism and community--the classic "*E Pluribus Unum*" of American history. It should be understood from the outset, however, that the course will not favor a single interpretation of the motto, "out of many, one." It does not assume that diversity will disappear into a melting pot, that individual identity will fade into some form of national unity. The course validates as well the motto's reverse, "*E Unum Pluribus*,"

"out of one, many," meaning that out of one original (Jeffersonian) idea has come a great deal of cultural diversity, interaction and pluralism, as experienced among different peoples over the course of American history.

(4) The implications of that diversity will be *illuminated* as well as *illustrated* through the study of the arts in relation to American culture. We will be experimenting with combinations of video, audio, and literary material and trying out patterns that are subject to change. Music, music videos, and musicals will demonstrate different cultural voices and styles of cultural interaction and conflict. You should also be aware of videos, old movies, and TV programs available at local video stores, programs on PBS and other networks, and popular music related to our inquiry. Throughout the semester, suggestions from you on all of these materials is welcome!

REQUIRED READINGS

Thornton Wilder's *Our Town*, Ralph Ellison's *Invisible Man*, assigned chapters from Dorothy Allison's *Trash* and two works from Reading List A are required; one of these works should be *similar* to your own cultural identity, the other *different* in some way. Also required is the video version of *West Side Story*, for sale at the Bookstore, for rent at video stores, and on reserve at the Media Center.

POLICIES

GRADING: "Roots" Project=25% of grade. Term paper=30%. Three quizzes=30%. Class participation, including in-class evaluations & a written report on one "outside event"=15%.

ATTENDANCE: Regular attendance is expected. The Humanities Department policy is that for each absence over two (excused or unexcused), a student's grade must be lowered half a step (from A-to B+, then B+ to B, etc.), so if you must be absent more than twice, see me about make-up assignments.

EXTRA CREDIT: You may turn in up to 5 written reports on additional outside events relevant to the class, approved films or videos, or books from Reading List B. These may help make up excess absences or compensate for unsatisfactory grades. For extra credit, you may also volunteer for oral book reports or student panels in relation to relevant units of the class.

SYLLABUS: Hum. 101: MULTICULTURAL AMERICA

Note to my Students on the First Day of Class: This outline may seem hard to read until you get used to the system It is organized around nine main themes and their subsections, but I interrupt this system to alert you when assignments are due and your tests will be given.--BC

I. Introduction—Basic Concepts and Overview

Week 1 TuTh: INTRODUCTION TO THE COURSE. (1) First-day "quiz" followed by answers by "experts" on "Portrait of the American" tapes. (2) SURVEY OF KEY ISSUES: Unity vs. diversity. "E Pluribus Unum" as a theme in American history. Ethnicity and "twoness." Mainstream vs. margin, hegemonic vs. counter-hegemonic. Equality vs. difference.

> *ASSIGNMENT 1*: For next week, read *Our Town* and view *West Side Story*, taking notes on plots, character, music lyrics, and the dances. Be prepared to compare the two works.

> *ASSIGNMENT 2*: Immediately when the course begins, students should begin thinking about, and gathering material for, the "Roots Project," due to begin the 6th week of class. We will make up a calendar for oral reports by the 4th week. Make an appointment to see me if you are uncertain how to begin research

II. "Hegemonic" Small Town vs. "Tragic" Urban Conflict

Week 2 Tu: Discuss "hegemony" as a concept. Discuss *Our Town*, with scenes from video. Compare to video of 1950s middle-class suburban culture.

Week 2 Th: "Counter-hegemonic" American cultures. Discuss *West Side Story*, especially its songs. Compare to *Our Town*, several interpretations.

III. Stereotypes of Race and Gender

Week 3 Tu: Overview of stereotypes--a slide lecture. Why and how stereotypes emerge, how they function. "Difference versus equality" in stereotyping.

Week 3 Th: VIDEOTAPES: Parts of "Ethnic Notions" or "Color Adjustments" & "Seeing Women and Seeing Anew" on stereotypes of race and gender.

IV. The Drama of Migration in American History

Week 4 Tu: The "classic" version of the immigrant story. Discuss scenes from the video, "Ellis Island." Begin comparing to scenes from "El Norte." COMPLETE CALENDAR FOR ORAL REPORTS.

Week 4 Th: Complete viewing and discussing "El Norte."

Week 5 Tu: QUIZ #1 on readings and lectures to date.

Week 5 Th: MIGRATION, cont.--A QUICK AND DIRTY OVERVIEW of: the Puritan migration. The migration across the continent; the "winning of the West." Recent challenges to such interpretations. South-to-north migration. Rural-to-urban patterns. Horizontal-to-vertical patterns. Other patterns.

Weeks 6-8: ORAL REPORTS plus parts of the following videotapes to illustrate migration, generational conflict, and interactions among ethnic & cultural groups: *These may be shown along with student reports or afterward.*

(a) James Baldwin's account of his father's life, PBS--entire.

(b) Bill Moyers' PBS program, "One River, One Country"--selected scenes.

(c) "Where the Spirit Lives," along with scenes from documentaries on Indian schools. (Entire film can be seen in the library media center.)

(d) Scenes from Spike Lee's "Do the Right Thing" and John Singleton's "Boyz 'n the Hood."

FIRST MAJOR CLASS ASSIGNMENT: "THE 'ROOTS' PROJECT."

(Oral reports 6th through 8th weeks. Written reports due first day of 6th week):

Each student gives an oral (8-10 min.) or written (6-7 pp.) report tracing his or her own roots, *not by recounting genealogy as such* (that kind of report may mean a lot to the reporter and his/her family but it's often a bore to listen to), but by putting together a story to illustrate significant migrations, issues involving identity (racial, regional, gender and/or generational identity), stereotypes, conflicts, interactions, and, where possible, the expression of these in the arts. As guidelines for what to include, begin with the themes introduced in the class lectures so far. If you are not scheduled for the first day, it's a smart move to incorporate ideas from the autobiographies you are reading (see top of next page) into your oral report--that's a great way of impressing classmates and giving them an insight into your books.

V. *Multiculturalism and Autobiography*

In relation to the "Roots" project, as soon as you have completed the "Roots" report, you should begin reading the two autobiographical works from Reading List A. See handout on multiculturalism and autobiography.

ASSIGNMENT: BEGIN READING TWO WORKS FROM LIST A

VI. Theories and Stages Ethnicity

Week 9 TuTh: LECTURE on theories of ethnicity & stages in American ethnic history. These are summarized on a handout and illustrated with readings from literature coupled to scenes from documentaries--(1) Noriko Bridges' "Sometime in My Past" plus documentary on Japan-bashing; (2) passages from Rodriguez' *Hunger of Memory* and Gloria Anzaldua, *Borderlands/La Frontera* to pair with Moyer's "One River, One Country"; (3) passages from *The Woman Warrior* and *The Joy Luck Club*. (The lecture's themes will overlap what we have covered so far, so this is also a review and summary.)

Week 10 Tu: Continue "Theories and Stages," with readings and videos.

Week 10 Th: FORMAL LECTURE: "Multicultural America and the PC Debate"-- my super-duper controversial prize-winning formal lecture on the emergence of the PC Debate during the 1990s (with handout). This will be a public lecture.

VII. Protest in the Arts --*from Ellison to Allison*

Week 11 TuTh Discuss Ellison's *Invisible Man*. Have it read by now and bring your copy with you to class, along with the Study Guide on Ellison.

ASSIGNMENT: TERM PAPER: 8-10 pages. A comparative paper using the two books you have read plus any two or more other works we have covered in the course; not merely a book report but a paper centering on some central theme that has come up in the course so far. Due right after Spring break.

Week 12 TuTh: MULTI-MEDIA LECTURES ON PROTEST IN THE ARTS. Includes (1) protest based on race, class, gender, ethnicity, and sexuality, (2) protest in visual, musical, and multi-media forms.

Week 13 Tu: MULTI-MEDIA ON PROTEST ART, completed. Discuss assigned stories in Allison's *Trash* as protest, as a portrait of extreme marginality.

VIII. California as a Study in Regional Multiculturalism

Week 13 Th: STUDENT PANEL on the writings of Kevin Starr, Mike Davis, and J. S. Holliday in conjunction with segments of a taped performance of Dan Kingman's "The Golden Gyre" (based on Holliday's *The World Rushed In)*, a "revisionist" 100-minute epic cantata that tells the story of the Gold Rush.

Week 14 Tu: QUIZ #2, on all material since the last quiz.

IX. Perspectives from the Border and the Margin

Week 14 Th: GUEST LECTURE by Keith Atwater: "The Aztlan Connection"--A multi-media presentation on art, music, and literature on Aztlan Cultures (Chicano, TexMex, Southwestern, Native American interactions). This will be a case study in the kind of perspective from the margin that is now redefining America.

Week 15 Tu: STUDENT PANELS ON MARGINALITY AND OTHER ISSUES-- panelists & themes to be selected by 14th week.

Week 15 Th: Complete panel(s). Review for the final.

Week 16: FINAL EXAM WEEK

==

READING LISTS FOR HUM 101

List A: Fiction, Autobiography, Oral History, Journalism

(You are required to read two works from this list, one similar to your own roots or identity in some way, one on the roots and background of a culture very different from your own. Your choice of works to pair for comparison is important, so take your time in selecting. Note that there are many ways to interpret "similar" and "different.")

Abbott, Shirley. *GROWING UP DOWN SOUTH* (1991). "Vibrant family memoir as a meditation on myth & tradition; honest look at Southern women & families, servants, religion, relationships." Compare to *I'll Fly Away* on TV.

Adams, Henry. *THE EDUCATION OF HENRY ADAMS.* Major work by a mainstream writer, an Adams of Boston, how his opinions were shaped by his heritage and his age.

Allen, Paula Gunn. THE WOMAN WHO OWNED THE SHADOWS and other works. Native American feminist author who writes in a way to capture authenticity of experience.

Anaya, Rudolfo. *BLESS ME, ULTIMA.* See essays in Paul Vassalo, ed. *The Magic of Words: Rudolfo Anaya and his Writings.* Leading Chicano novelist.

Anderson, Sherwood. *WINESBURG, OHIO.* Classic of traditional white small town America. A collection of stories to produce overall impression.

Angelou, Maya. *I KNOW WHY THE CAGED BIRD SINGS* & later works in her autobiography. Black woman, contemporary, tells story of her life movingly in a series of works.

Antin, Mary. *THE PROMISED LAND.* A classic version of the immigrant story.

Anzaldua, Gloria. *BORDERLANDS/LA FRONTERA.* Wonderful novel of "twoness" from a new perspective, new definition of identity. Cf. Moyers' "One River, One Country."

Baldwin, James. *GO TELL IT ON THE MOUNTAIN.* Major black author's first novel; role of father, family, church in life of young man growing up in New York after the family migrates north from the rural South.

BLACK ELK SPEAKS, the Life Story of a Holy Man of the Ogala Sioux, with John Neihardt. (1979)[1931] The title says it all.

Bulosan, Carlos. *AMERICA IS IN THE HEART (1946).* By a Filipino immigrant who comes to California, works in the fields & gambles in the back rooms.

Cahan, Abraham. *YEKL, THE IMPORTED BRIDEGROOM, & OTHER STORIES.* The urban immigrant experience, Jewish Americans. The film "Hester Street" is based on *Yekl.*

Campbell, Maria. *HALFBREED.* (Univ. of Nebraska, 1973)

Cather, Willa. *O PIONEERS! or DEATH COMES FOR THE ARCHBISHOP* or *MY ANTONIA .* Works by Cather will give you a good perspectives on the "classic" American frontier & immigrant stories. If you have never read Cather, here is your chance.

Chin, Frank et.al. *AIIIEEEE! ANTHOLOGY OF ASIAN-AMERICAN WRITERS (1975).* Representative cross-section of Chinese-American, Japanese-American, Filipino-American literature.

Crashing Thunder. *THE AUTOBIOGRAPHY OF AN AMERICAN INDIAN,* ed. Paul Radin. (Nebraska, 1983 [1926])

Douglass, Frederick. *NARRATIVE OF THE LIFE OF FREDERICK DOUGLASS.* The best-known of all slave narratives. As an autobiography, this can be paired with Benjamin Franklin's.

Dreiser, Theodore. *AN AMERICAN TRAGEDY.* How striving for the American Dream by moving up in class led to tragedy for a young man imbued with "desire" yet limited by conflicts in values.

Faulkner, William. *LIGHT IN AUGUST, THE SOUND AND THE FURY or AS I LAY DYING or ABSALOM! ABSALOM!* These are too difficult for some students, but Faulkner's great novels tell the story of the struggle with identity in the South as no others do, so take advantage of this opportunity to read one.

Franklin, Benjamin. *AUTOBIOGRAPHY OF BENJAMIN FRANKLIN.* Used to be required reading in America, it is so "classic" in its outline of "mainstream" American ideals! Try using it to compare to your other work.

Galarza, Ernesto. *BARRIO BOY* (1971). Mexican-American novel about a boy growing up in an American city. Good for California Studies also.

Gold, Michael. *JEWS WITHOUT MONEY.* Not as good as Howe's *World of Our Fathers* but a good book to pair with it & highly readable.

Haley, Alex. *ROOTS* plus the TV series on video. This would be a different sort of reading experience--tracing the impact of TV and comparing book to the series. Good choice for Comm Studies majors.

Hansberry, Lorraine. *RAISIN IN THE SUN and "RAISIN" Reader.* Hansberry was *Young, Gifted and Black* and this one play is still the leading classic of black American life. It's nteresting to trace the changing views about it.

Houston, Jeanne Walatsuki & James D. Houston. *FAREWELL TO MANZANAR:* . Easy-to-read story of the Japanese internment & its implications for identity.

Howe, Irving. *THE WORLD OF OUR FATHERS.* Not fiction but a wonderful book about East European Jews who came to America. Gets my vote as best book on ethnicity in America.

Jackson, Helen Hunt. *RAMONA.*There is new interest in this influential 19th-century story of Indians in the Southwest. She tried to do for Indians what *Uncle Tom's Cabin* did for blacks. There is even a yearly outdoor Ramona pageant in Hemet, California. Compare to video, *Where the Spirit Lives.*

Jacobs, Harriet. *INCIDENTS IN THE LIFE OF A SLAVE GIRL,* ed. Jean Pace Yellin. It's Yellin's introduction that makes this such a fascinating study!

Kingston, Maxine Hong. *THE WOMAN WARRIOR & CHINA MEN.* These are classics by now for the story of Chinese Americans during the 20th century.

Kotlowitz, Alex. *THERE ARE NO CHILDREN HERE (1991).* Easy read (some say oversimplified), but strong stuff on life for the young in American cities.

Lame Deer, John (Fire) and R. Erdoes. *LAME DEER: SEEKER OF VISIONS* (1972). Good example of counter-hegemonic view from the Indian perspective--a long way from *Dances with Wolves!*

Lewis, Sinclair. *BABBITT,* 1922. A comic version of what has been seen as the "typical American" (white, middle-class, upward-striving) and Lewis offers an array of caricatures we can all recognize!

Lewis, Sinclair. *MAIN STREET,* 1920. Like *BABBITT*, this is classic Lewis--supposedly the "typical" American story built around a "typical" Main Street in America--but with a woman at the center. This is the story of her struggle with the town's & her husband's biases.

M. BUTTERFLY & MISS SAIGON. These two modern plays (very different from each other) may substitute for one novel. Both take on stereotypes and biases about Asians and Americans.

MALCOLM X, THE AUTOBIOGRAPHY OF. A classic by now. The story of striving to succeed inside & then outside white society. Black protest.

McCarthy, Mary. *MEMORIES OF A CATHOLIC GIRLHOOD.* Another classic.

McCullers, Carson. *THE HEART IS A LONELY HUNTER.* White Southern woman author with strong views reflecting her region.

Momaday, N. Scott. *THE WAY TO RAINY DAY MOUNTAIN & HOUSE MADE OF DAWN.* Best-known Native American author until recently.

Morrison, Toni. *BELOVED, or SONG OF SOLOMON.* Modern classic black author. Here's your chance to read *Beloved*--not easy but very moving. *Solomon* is an easier read & some say her best.

Qoyawayma, Polingaysi [Elizabeth White]. *NO TURNING BACK: A HOPI WOMAN'S STRUGGLE TO LIVE IN TWO WORLDS.* (New Mexico, 1964)

Rodriguez, Richard. *HUNGER OF MEMORY.* Hispanic American tells his story (I'll talk about this book in class)..Also read my collection of reviews on it.

Rolvaag, Ole. *GIANTS IN THE EARTH.* Powerful "classic" story of Norwegian immigrants who come to America, settle in the midwest.

Santiago, Danny. *FAMOUS ALL OVER TOWN.* Classic Mexican-American story

Silko, Leslie. *CEREMONY.* Highly acclaimed Native American novel, about Vietnam soldier who comes home and struggles to rediscover identity.

Smith, Betty. *A TREE GROWS IN BROOKLYN.* A favorite of mine when I was growing up--about a young girl coming of age in Brooklyn. Irish Americans coping with poverty, politics, & ethnicity.

Tan, Amy. *THE JOY LUCK CLUB.* A terrific book that explores third-generation Asian experience; strong attention to mother-daughter tension in the transition.

Thoreau, Henry David. *WALDEN.* [1854], if you have never read it. Much depends of which book you compare it with.

Underhill, Ruth. *THE AUTOBIOGRAPHY OF A PAPAGO WOMAN* [Maria Chona]. (1979) [1936].

Washington, Booker T. *UP FROM SLAVERY* [1900]. Another classic in the history of black American experience. Use edition with introductory essay.

Wright, Richard. *NATIVE SON or BLACK BOY*. The first great black novelist in
20th century American fiction; his novel is gripping (and good to compare and
contrast to Ellison); his autobiography is too.

Yezierska, Anzio. *BREAD LOVERS*. My students have *loved* this story of a
Russian Jewish immigrant woman & her struggle against her father as she
seeks to assert autonomy.

Zangwill, Israel. *THE MELTING POT*, 1908, plus "afterword" added in 1915 &
my collection of essays on the play.

List B: History, Theory, Social Analysis--General Checklist

*(These are among works mentioned in lectures or on the tapes
Use books like these to help you on your paper, as necessary.)*

Bellah, Robert et. al. *HABITS OF THE HEART: INDIVIDUALISM &
COMMITMENT IN AMERICAN LIFE*.

Berkhofer, Robert. *THE WHITE MAN'S INDIAN: IMAGES OF THE
AMERICAN INDIAN FROM COLUMBUS TO THE PRESENT*, 1978.

Mike Davis, CITY OF QUARTZ: EXCAVATING THE FUTURE OF LOS
ANGELES, 1992.

Dearborn, Mary. *POCAHANTAS' DAUGHTERS: ETHNICITY & GENDER IN
AMERICAN LITERATURE*.

Dinnerstein, Leonard, Roger L. Nichols and David M. Reimers. *NATIVES AND
STRANGERS; BLACKS, INDIANS, AND IMMIGRANTS IN AMERICA.
2nd edition, 1990*.

Douglas, Ann. *THE FEMINIZATION OF AMERICAN CULTURE*.

DuBois, W. E. B. *THE SOULS OF BLACK FOLK*.

Feldman, Saul D. and G. W. Thielbar. *LIFESTYLES: DIVERSITY IN
AMERICAN SOCIETY*.

Freidan, Betty. *THE FEMININE MYSTIQUE*, 1963.

Giddings, Paula. *WHEN AND WHERE I ENTER: BLACK WOMEN AND
FEMINISM*.

Glazer, Nathan and Daniel Patrick Moynihan. *BEYOND THE MELTING POT:
THE NEGROES, PUERTO RICANS, JEWS, ITALIANS AND IRISH OF
NEW YORK CITY*, 1963.

Gordon, Milton. *ASSIMILATION IN AMERICAN LIFE: THE ROLE OF RACE,
RELIGION, AND NATIONAL ORIGINS*, 1964.

Handlin, Oscar.*THE UPROOTED: THE EPIC STORY OF THE GREAT MIGRATIONS THAT MADE THE AMERICAN PEOPLE*, 1951. "Once I thought to write the history of the immigrants in America. Then I discovered the immigrants *were* American history."--Handlin.

HARVARD ENCYCLOPEDIA OF AMERICAN ETHNIC GROUPS, 1980.

Higham, John. *SEND THESE TO ME: JEWS AND OTHER IMMIGRANTS IN URBAN AMERICA*, 1975. "Pluralistic integration" introduced in this volume.

Higham, John. *STRANGERS IN THE LAND* (this book discussed on tape).

Holliday, J. S. *THE WORLD RUSHED IN* (on the California Gold Rush).

Hsu, Francis. *AMERICANS AND CHINESE: TWO WAYS OF LIFE..*

Hunter, James Davison. *CULTURE WARS: THE STRUGGLE TO DEFINE AMERICA, 1991.*

Ibson, John Duffy. *WILL THE WORLD BREAK YOUR HEART? DIMENSIONS AND CONSEQUENCES OF IRISH-AMERICAN ASSIMILATION*, 1990. An exception to my rule not to focus on a single white ethnic group.

Joseph, Gloria I. and Jill Lewis, editors. *COMMON DIFFERENCES: CONFLICTS IN BLACK AND WHITE FEMINIST PERSPECTIVES.*

Kallen, Horace. *CULTURAL PLURALISM AND THE AMERICAN IDEA*, 1956.

Kolodny, Annette. *THE LAND BEFORE HER* (2 vols).

Lucas, J. Anthony. *ON COMMON GROUND.*

Mann, Arthur. *THE ONE AND THE MANY*, 1979.

Novak, Michael. *THE RISE OF THE UNMELTABLE ETHNICS.*

Sollors, Werner. *BEYOND ETHNICITY: CONSENT & DESCENT IN AMERICAN CULTURE.*

Starr, Kevin. *AMERICANS AND THE CALIFORNIA DREAM and INVENTING THE DREAM* and *MATERIAL DREAMS* (all on California).

Stern, Stephen and John Allan Cicala, eds. *CREATIVE ETHNICITY* (new idea).

Terkel, Studs. *AMERICAN DREAMS, LOST AND FOUND, WORKING*, other.

William Whyte, Jr. *THE ORGANIZATION MAN*, 1955 (book discussed on tape).

Yans-McLaughlin, Virginia. Editor, *IMMIGRATION RECONSIDERED*, 1990.

==

APPENDIX: THEORIES AND STAGES OF ETHNICITY

NOTE: In teaching about theories and stages of ethnicity to beginning students in Humanities 101, I begin by giving the "Quixotic Quiz"--up to the point when students protest (they always do) against the generalizations. Then I spend three class periods explaining the theories and stages outlined below, illustrating them, after which we return to the "quiz" and discuss the answers at greater length. In the course of the lectures, I cite relevant bibliography on ethnicity (which they have on handouts) as well.--BC

A Quixotic Quiz (tongue-in-cheek type)

1. Stereotypes of Ethnicity. Answer true or false.

T F   The darker your skin, the more ethnic you tend to be.

T F   The closer your ties with the old country, the more ethnic you probably are.

T F   The higher you move up the economic ladder, the less ethnic you tend to be.

T F   The more education you get, the less ethnic you tend to become.

T F   The further you move from an ethnic neighborhood, the less ethnic you tend to become.

T F   The further west you travel (to California, say), the less ethnic you become.

T.F   Ethnicity in America is slowly but surely withering away.

T F   Protestants tend to be less ethnic than Catholics and Jews.

T F   In America, we are all ethnics.

On Group Stereotypes:

T F The trouble with Hispanic Americans is that they can't speak English.

T F By and large, history has shown that Native Americans can't handle alcohol.

T F It's been proven that African Americans have more natural rhythm than whites.

T F Generally speaking, Japanese Americans can't be trusted.

T F The reason people don't like the Indochinese is because they eat dogs.

2. Which word best describes your own conviction about ethnicity?

a.___sentimental: It's a nostalgic yearning by old-timers for a simpler ethnic past.

b.___fashionable: It's a fad for Yuppies & boomers eager to prove they are PC.

c.___sinister: The Nazis in Germany showed us where ethnic thinking can lead.

d.___conservative: Ethnicity embraces traditional values and the good old days.

e.___radical: Basically, ethnicity is concerned with oppressed ethnic underclasses.

f.___ reactionary: The bottom line for those who preach ethnic pride is really to oppose intermarriage.

g.___unfair: Ethnicity really works to take jobs away from Americans

3. *So is Ethnicity Good or Bad? Select the best answer.*

a.___ *good*, because we need to learn about our roots; we need to cherish and respect group differences. (Who wants to be melted in a melting pot?)

b.___ *bad*, because ethnicity disguises our more important identities. (We are all Americans. Why exaggerate cultural differences?)

c.___ *good*, because it preserves our heritage--and ethnic festivals are fun!

d.___ *bad*, because inevitably groups end up thinking they are better than others.

e.___ *good and bad:* "Ethnic consciousness is good. Ethnic confrontation is bad."

f. ___ *neither:* "Ethnicity is a fact. It is neither good nor bad. We are all ethnics. American history *is* ethnic history."

American Ethnicity:
SUMMARY CHART OF THEORIES AND STAGES

I. Four Theories of American Ethnicity;[1]

1. the melting pot theory (assimilation, integration, "Americanization")

   formula: $A + B + C = D$

   meaning: "Here [in America] individuals of all races are melted into a new race of men, whose labours and posterity will one day cause great changes in the world." --*Crevecoeur, Letters of an American Farmer, 1782.*

---

[1]For some of the ideas in this section, I am grateful to Werner Sollors, "Theory of American Ethnicity," and John Ibson, "Studying the Ethnicity of White Americans, " both in *American Quarterly*, 33, 3 (Bibliography Issue 1981), 257-308. These two essays, taken together, are a good place to begin exploring theories of ethnicity.

2. Anglo-conformity (assimilation by conforming to WASP hegemonic standards)

   formula: $A + B + C = A$

   meaning: all ethnic groups acquire the identity of the original or
     dominant group

3. cultural pluralism {Kallen} [stresses cultural diversity, "democracy," belief in
   persistence of ethnic identity into later generations)

   formula: $A + B + C = (A + B + C)$

   meaning: all ethnic groups retain and cherish their separate identity
     within the national whole--collectively, they are the national
     whole; tendency here toward identity politics

4. pluralistic integration {Higham} [stresses complex, ambiguous, identities)

   formula: $A + B + C = (\{[\,A + B + C\,]\}) = (D)$

   meaning: groups retain & affirm identity yet act as part of--indeed,
     help create--the larger national whole through interactions of
     ethnicity with class, gender, religion, occupation, generation;
     assumption that identity shifts--and can be "constructed"
     differently--for political, economic, social, or cultural activity

II. Five Stages in the History of American Ethnicity

1st stage, up to ca. 1930: melting-pot theory comes to dominate; assimilation
    assumed to be good--the expectation that all will be Americanized "eventually";
    hysteria for Ango-conformity leading up to 1924 immigration restriction.

2nd stage, 30s to WWar II: "old ethnicity"=conscious efforts to challenge
    assimilation in the name of cultural pluralism; ethnic identity linked to class
    identity--"common man" of the 30s; cultural diversity celebrated.

3rd stage, WWII to 1960s: One World era--stress on Americanization and
    universality; colorblind, raceblind liberalism; modernism; international
    unionism; cold war mentality; "holism" affirmed.

4th stage, 1960s to 1980s: "new ethnicity"=fierce attack on holism and Anglo-
    conformity; new interest in "roots," diversity, pluralism; the "new social
    history"; concern with "new immigration" (Asian, Latino).

5th stage, 1980s to 1990s: 80s reaction against excesses of "ethnic celebration";
    rise of postmodernism and "theory"; 90s debate over political correctness;
    various proposals to combine ethnicity with other identities; 90s return of
    feminism; rise of interest in multiculturalism and comparative world cultures.

MULTICULTURAL AMERICA

Keith Atwater, Whitworth College
EL 228: 1990
A three unit, one-semester, lower division course.

   This course explores the rich and varied artistic contributions of African-Americans, Asian-Americans, Mexican-Americans, and Native-Americans. Rather than teaching each ethnic group separately, which may tend to compartmentalize or polarize these groups as outside the plurality which is America, the course stresses unity within diversity of these uniquely American arts by studying the painting, literature, music, drama, and dance of all these groups as they respond to four broad and significant themes or concerns: 1) identity, 2) community, 3) spirituality, and 4) struggle. Responses to these often overlapping areas produce a vibrant, living art that is often in "creative tension," as Dr. King would say, to the forces of the dominant Eurocentric Judeo-Christian cultural, academic, and art worlds. But this creative tension can help Americans see their world anew as they look through the eyes of artists of color to a different vision of America. The course cannot hope to cover the history of the arts of these four cultural groups, so--with the exception of the Harlem Renaissance and Mexican muralists of the 1930s and the Nisei internment--the course studies arts and artists from 1960-1990. Important contributions of often overlooked women artists will be featured.

GOALS. Five goals direct and focus our activities:

1) Discover and understand the many artistic contributions of women & men of Asian-, African-, Mexican-, & Native-American ancestry, primarily through examinations of literature, painting, & music.

2) Use the study of these arts as one approach or tool for a deeper understanding of the religion, ritual, sociology, politics, culture, lifeways, and "soul" of American people of color.

3) Become aware of different perspectives, tensions, racism, ethnocentrism, and sexism in American society; also find ways to build bridges of respect and understanding through arts appreciation.

4) Learn the techniques of literary, artistic, and aesthetic appreciation, interpretation, and criticism that will lead to deeper understanding of many art forms encountered outside the classroom.

5) Sharpen college level skills of analytical thinking; clear, concise writing; thoughtful questioning; and stimulating discussion through classroom activities designed to open our eyes and ears to these arts.

STUDENT INFORMATION

Required Readings: The following serve as an introduction to multicultural literature and as a springboard for exploration of themes and ideas in other genres such as music and painting.

Anaya, Rudolfo: *Heart of Aztlan*. Univ. of New Mexico Press, 1976.

Baldwin, James: *Go Tell It On the Mountain*. Doubleday & Co., 1952.

Okada, John: *No No Boy*. Univ. of Washington Press, 1957.

Rosen, Ken, ed: *The Man to Send Rainclouds*. Random House, 1974.

Requirements: The following written work is required for course credit. Papers should be typed or word-processed, double-spaced, one side, standard paper

Four unit short answer tests (25 points each) 100 points

Arts analysis paper (3 pages) 40 points

One book/movie/VCR/music review (2 pages) 30 points

One off campus arts field trip and report (1 page) 30 points

Grading: Letter grade is based on points accumulated from 200 points offered (unless pass/no credit is chosen). A = 90-100 percent of points earned; B = 80-89 percent; C = 70-79 percent; D = 60-69 percent; F = 0-59 percent. Excessive absences result in point deductions. Improvement over time (especially in writing) and active discussion will help your grade. Students are *strongly encouraged* to see the instructor with topics and rough drafts of written work.

Format: The course uses a variety of approaches--slides, music, VCR tape viewing, oral poetry reading, lecture, discussion, field trip, small group work, lots of discussion. The format includes detailed discussion of how to look at/ listen to appreciate works of art in a variety of media, from sculpture to photography to dance. You need not be an arts major to succeed in the class.

Suggestions: Keep up with the reading, take many notes (including in margins of books), study visual arts closely and jot down what you see; avoid plagiarism in your writing; be open to several possibilities or meanings and responses to the arts studied --their complexities and sometimes disturbing messages--as you let these arts touch you in meaningful ways.

WRITTEN ASSIGNMENTS

Arts and Analysis Paper

Typed, 3-page. Designed to help investigate specific course ideas in depth.

Using your own analysis, class materials, and some outside investigation, compare and analyze the connections between *two* art forms in *one* multicultural group. Show how these arts reflect key concerns and ideas of the artists. As examples: You might look at connections between land and people (farms, crops, geographical home) of the Chicano tradition. Or compare expressions of God(s), Sacred Mystery, Great Spirit in painting/sculpture and the literature of Scott Momaday or Leslie Silko. Or look at jazz to find connections between this music and poems of selected black poets. Or look at conflicts of generations as seen in the Chinese-American movie, "Eat a Bowl of Tea," and the Japanese-American novel, *No No Boy*. Or choose any two favorite art forms within one cultural group and investigate. Instructor will O.K. your topic as "doable" before you begin.

Book/ Movie/ VCR/ Music Review. *Typed, 2-pages, in the style of book and movie reviews found in better magazines and newspapers.* Describe themes and images found in outside viewing/ listening/ reading experience as they connect with the goals of the course. Include title, author or director, year produced, and your candid opinion of its merits; mention some particularly memorable scenes.

POSSIBILITIES FOR YOUR REVIEW:

African-American: "Mo Better Blues," "Do the Right Thing," "Bird."* Current TV shows, such as "Creativity with Bill Moyers--Maya Angelou" (PBS). A jazz, reggae, or soul concert or album.

Asian-American: "Eat a Bowl of Tea," "Come See the Paradise."* Current TV shows, such as "American Playhouse--Hot Summer Winds" (PBS). A play by Frank Chin.

Mexican-American: "La Bamba," "The Milagro Beanfield War,"* "The Ballad of Gregorio Cortez,"* "Stand and Deliver."* Current TV shows such as "Mi Otro Yo" (PBS)." A Los Lobos or Linda Ronstadt ("Canciones de mi Padres") concert video.

Native-American: "Dances With Wolves,"* "Little Big Man."* Current TV shows such as "The Trial of Standing Bear" or "In the Spirit of Crazy Horse" (PBS). A flute recording by Carlos Nakai.

---

* Not made by a minority film maker; see instructor before watching.

SYLLABUS/ SCHEDULE:

WEEK/DAY, THEME   ASSIGNMENT

1. **Introduction:** Why study multicultural arts?   read syllabus
   Student ethnicity responses.
   How to analyze arts: 3 models.
   Seven characteristic patterns in arts as seen in literature.

2. **Identity:** Problems with identity, stereotypes.   read handout A
   Forbes, Silko short stories.   Rosen 149-154
   Images of the Native-American.
   Slides of Catlin, Curtis, Scholder--
   Analysis and discussion of slides

3. **Identity:** Social activism & stereotypes in
              Chicano theater; Valdez "Acto"   read handout F
   The soul search for roots: Hughes, Angelou,
              music: blues.   read handout D
   Dilemma of split identity:
   Ichiro's pain in Okada's novel   read Okada 111-49

4. **Identiy:** Surviving in America: analysis of characters, incidents
   Artists' expressions of the Indian:"   Okada 50-171

   Video, "Fritz Scholder"
   Analysis, discussion of video

5. **Identity:** Psychological, physical, social pain.   Okada 172-251
   Analysis of Ichiro, Kenji.
   Slides.
   No No, Yes Yes: conclusions and themes in Okada's *No No Boy*.
   Short answer test: Unit 1, Identity.

6. **Community:** Introduction to expressions of community
              family, clan, roots   read handout E
   Stories and generations and ghosts:
   Video, "Talking Story" with M.H. Kingston--
   analysis, discussion of video

7. **Community:** Field to barrio: arts and literature of the Chicano
   community.   read handout B
   Uptown, Downtown: arts and literature of Harlem, New York.
   Analysis, discussion of the Harlem Renaissance--.
   Cullen, Hughes, et al, & for *music*, jazz.   read handout G

8. **Community:** Tensions, coping in the community:
   stories & poems of Walters, Silko, Ortiz.
   Analysis of stories and poems.
   The Sacred hoop, circle of life: music, dance of Native Americans
   read Rosen 3-8, 9-13,
15-26, 82-92, 93-99.

9. **Community:** Black community in drama, music, and videos:
   "The Colored Museum," "Goin' Home to Gospel."
   Analysis, discussion of videos
   Short answer test: Unit 2, Community

10. **Spirituality:** The East-West connection:
    poetry and stories of Asian-Americans   read handout C
    Spirituality in arts and lifeways;
    video "Hopi: Songs of the Fourth World"
    Catholicism and folk religion in Chicano and Native American culture.

11. **Spirituality:** Images of the feminine: Earth Mother,
    Corn Woman, Virgin.
    Spirituality in arts and lifeways.
    Video "Hopi: Songs of the Fourth World."
    Catholicism and folk religion in Chicano and Native American culture.
    read handout H
read Rosen 33-45

12. **Spirituality:** Baldwin and the Black Church experience.
    Music of African Americans: gospel, soul, spirituals.
    Discussion, analysis of Baldwin & music.
    read Baldwin 11-90

13. **Spirituality:** Analysis of John, Gabriel, Florence and theology in
    Baldwin.
    Short answer test: Unit 3: Spirituality.
    read Baldwin 91-221

14. **Struggle:** Struggle, resistance, assimilation, and survival: the
    internment. Slide presentation.
    Social and political protest in Chicano arts.
    Video, "Mi Otro Yo."
    Analysis, discussion of videos, slides.

15. **Struggle:** La Raza: The People on the March--
    murals of Diego Rivera and Jose Orozco.
    Out of the barrio: the power of Aztlan in works of Rudolfo Anaya.
    Analysis of Anaya's novel.

    DUE: book/movie review.
    read Anaya 1-118

16. **Struggle:** Corridos, protest songs,
    folk music of Los Lobos & others.
    Themes and images in Anaya.
    Power to the People—Black, Red, Brown:
    resistance & rage in arts of the 60s.

    DUE: analysis paper.
    read Anaya 119-200.

17. **Conclusion:** Putting it all together: what did we learn?
    Short answer test: Unit 4, Struggle.
    Share field trip experiences orally.

    DUE: field trip report.

==

ED. NOTE: For more on Atwater's resources, see his Resource Guide in Part III.

THE IMMIGRANT EXPERIENCE:
ALIENS AND ANGLO-SAXONS IN AMERICAN SOCIETY, 1830-1930

Lois Rudnick, University of Massachusetts at Boston
Spring 1991

Because this is a research seminar in which you are expected to be a full participant, discussion is the primary way that we will conduct class. One-third of your final grade for the course will be based on your oral work, which includes the following three reports: a brief commentary on some aspect of your family or community's ethnic history as it relates to the issues raised by Handlin in *The Uprooted*; a brief summary of one chapter in Higham's *Strangers in the Land* (5 to 10 minutes); an analysis of an outside reading related to one of the issues we are studying at the time or discussion leader for one of the texts we are studying in the second half of the course (10 to 15 minutes). The second and third reports can be done in teams.

The written work for the course is as follows: a 1-page summary of the chapter report in Higham; 2 short papers (5 pages) in which you will apply theoretical readings on prejudice and assimilation to primary source readings; a research paper of 12 to 15 pages that can take a variety of forms, depending on your interests. Suggested topics will be handed out after mid-semester and I will meet with each of you individually to discuss your topics. There will be no extensions for papers unless you have a medical emergency. Readings for the course include part or all of the following texts and assignments in the reading packets (noted on syllabus as RP). Most of the texts (*) are on reserve in the library. There will be a $6.00 charge for the reading packets.

Oscar Handlin, *The Uprooted*, 2nd edition*

John Higham, *Strangers in the Land**

Jane Addams, *Twenty Years at Hull-House*

Hamilton Holt, ed. *The Life Stories of Undistinguished Americans**

James Riordan, ed. *Plunkitt of Tammany Hall*

Ole Rolvaag, *Giants in the Earth**

Abraham Cahan, Yekl, *The Imported Bridegroom, and Other Stories**

List of articles and book chapters on reserve in the library for oral reports:

1. J. Smith, "Our Own Kind: Family and Community Networks in Providence"

2. T. Smith, "Immigrant Social Aspiration and American Education"

3. G. Rosenblum, Ch. 6, Immigrant Workers, "The Immigrant and Business Unionism"

4. S. Thernstrom, Ch. 6, The Other Bostonians, "Yankees and Immigrants"

5. W. Shannon, Ch. 1, The American Irish, "The Irish Inheritance"

6. E. Levine, Ch. 5, The Irish and the Irish Politician, "The Politicization of the Irish"

7. D. Hoerder, "Introduction," 'Struggle a Hard Battle': Essays on Working-Class Immigrants

8. Ewa Morawska, Ch.7, Immigration Reconsidered, "The Sociology and Historiography of Immigration"

Syllabus

February

5   Introduction

7   **Course Overview:** RP: "Some Questions," "Family History," "Pros and Cons of Ethnic Identity," "Welcome to Ethnicity," "Groups to Examine Ethnic Differences," "Chronology"

12   **Immigration:** Handlin, THE UPROOTED, Chs. 1 and 2 and RP: IMMIGRATION AS A FACTOR IN AMERICAN HISTORY (IFAH), pp. 10-28; IMMIGRANT WOMEN (IW), pp. 15-22; 34-36; "The Isle of Tears"

14   Handlin, Chs. 3-5

19   Handlin, Chs. 6-10, 14

21   RP: Karen Larson, "Review of THE UPROOTED"; John Buenker, "Mainstream America and the Immigrant Experience"

26   **What is an American?** RP: Potter, "The Quest for National Character." *First paper assignment handed out*

28   RP: Allport, "The Scientific Study of Group Differences" and "Theories of Prejudice"

March

5 Higham, STRANGERS IN THE LAND, Ch. 1, RP: Appel, "Notes on Stereotyping"; in-class slide show, "The Distorted Image" (media images of ethnic stereotypes)

7 Higham, Chs. 2-5 student reports

12 Higham, Chs. 6-8 student reports

14 **FIRST PAPER DUE** (based on Allport and RP readings on prejudice against Chinese, Jews, and Italians)

16 - 24 SPRING VACATION

26 **Becoming an American:** RP: Gordon, "Assimilation in America"; Addams, TWENTY YEARS AT HULL-HOUSE, Chs. 1-4. *Second paper assignment handed out*

28 Addams, Chs. 5-8. In-class film, "The Fights of Nations"

April

2 Addams, Chs. 11, 13. Student reports on Seller, pp. 185-195, Higham, Ch. 9

4 **Immigrants Respond to Americanization:** Community Life and Education RP: IFAH, pp. 76-93; IW, pp. 157-65; 174-79; 197-205; 215-221. Student reports on immigrants and education; women, family, and community

9 *SECOND PAPER DUE* (based on Gordon and *The Life Stories of Undistinguished Americans*)

11 **Immigrants and Work:** RP: IFAH, pp. 53-59; 64-71; Seller, pp.81-89; 99-110; 264-68; "Some facts about American industry." *In-class discussion of research paper*

16 Immigrants and Work (continued); Immigrants and Politics RP: IFAH, pp. 94-100; "The Greening of the Police." Student reports on immigration and labor unionism, ethnic mobility, the American Irish, the Irish and politics

18 Riordan, PLUNKITT OF TAMMANY HALL: student-led discussion

23 **The Pioneer Immigrant Experience:** in-class slide show, "Pioneers on the Frontier." Rolvaag, GIANTS IN THE EARTH, pp. 3-106

25 Rolvaag, pp. 107-90

30 Rolvaag, pp. 191-344

May

2 Rolvaag, pp. 345-end. Student report on letters of Scandinavian immigrants

7   **The Urban Immigrant Experience:** Cahan, "YEKL"—student-led discussion

9   **World War I and the Closing of the Gates:** Student reports on Higham, Chs. 10 and ll; the sociology and historiography of immigration *1-page prospectus and bibliography due for research paper*

14 RP: Susan Izzicuppo, "Graduation Poem," UMB, 1975   in-class movie, "The Inheritance"   RESEARCH PAPER DUE Thursday, May 23

===

CLASS TRIP TO ELLIS ISLAND AND
    THE STATUE OF LIBERTY--May 25-26

Movie Schedule: the full-length feature films will be shown at 2:30:
week of April 30: Max Von Sydow, Liv Ullman "The New Land" (Norwegian immigrants on the Minnesota frontier)
week of May 7: "Hester Street" (based on Cahan's "Yekl")

===

Syllabus #5

AMERICA AND AMERICANS[1]

Marilyn Patton, University of California, Santa Cruz
American Studies 1, 1990

This is an introductory course, usually enrolling between 100 and 180 students, which fulfills both the Introduction to Humanities and the Ethnic Studies requirements, so it is popular with students from a wide variety of disciplines and from diverse backgrounds. It is also required of American Studies majors.

I designed this course to concentrate on three very specific historical periods. The first is the year 1882 as the year of the Chinese Exclusion Act, an approximate divide within European immigration between northern European immigrants and southern/eastern European immigration and, serendipitously, the year in Cather's *My Antonia* when Jim and Antonia arrive in Nebraska. Jim is a migrant and Antonia is an immigrant, so this conjunction allows me to discuss and distinguish the two movements. The second period is World War II, covered primarily from the point of view of American Indians. The third period is the Civil Rights Movement from 1955 to 1965, which I place into its context as a progenitor of the Women's Movement, Gay and Lesbian Liberation, and the Third World Liberation movement, which involved ethnic consciousness for Chicanos/Latinos and Asian Americans.

The primary themes developed during the course, which cut across the historic dividing lines, are: cultural pluralism and its alternatives, the relationship of American people with the American land, the role of religion in American life, the place of media in American politics, the requisite conditions for social change, and the social construction of race, class and gender. Students primarily read fiction, autobiography and selections from historical texts, while my lectures combine history, politics, sociology, anthropology and "popular culture." Because I am a non-"ethnic" person teaching an "E" course, I invite several guest speakers each quarter, and use films to broaden the perspective of the class.

Each week, students are required to attend a 70-minute discussion section as well as three 70-minute lectures. One lecture period per week is set aside for films,

---

[1]This course was developed originally by Professor Ann Lane, UC Santa Cruz, to whom I owe a tremendous debt for her second ideas, her encouragement, and her constant support.

which are then discussed and critiqued along with the readings. The lectures include some time for discussion, but we all enjoy the small group (15-20 student) discussion sections, in which a real sense of mutuality develops. Leaders are graduate students, advanced undergraduates and myself. The undergraduate leaders get course credit for an independent study because they meet weekly with me for a thorough discussion of the larger issues involved, as well as specific techniques for that week's material.

TEXTS

(1) **Class Reader***:* selections from histories such as Ronald Takaki's *Strangers From a Distant Shore*, Rudolfo Acuna's *Occupied America* & John Dower's *War Without Mercy*.

(2) **Novels***:* Willa Cather, *My Antonia*, Leslie Marmon Silko, *Ceremony*, Houston and Houston, *Farewell to Manzanar*, Alice Walker, Meridian (We may change to King's *Why We Can't Wait*), Gloria Anzaldua, *Borderlands/La Frontera*.

CALENDAR

Week I: 1882—America as a Nation of Immigrants —Introduction —Robert Frost's "Gift Outright" and Chief Seattle's Speech —Four directions of U.S. Immigration: South (Native American), North (Latin American), West (African, European and Mid-Eastern), East (Asian and Pacific Islander) — America as both a Utopia and a Dystopia —Reading: Begin *My Antonia.*

Week II: 1882—Migration and Immigration, Horrors and Joys —History of United States Immigration/Citizenship Policy —Judy Yung: Angel Island and Chinese immigration —Letters, poems, art of immigrants —*My Antonia*, the "dark side" of immigration, attitudes of "natives" toward immigrants, two kinds of history (linear and circular), and consideration of a "lesbian" reading of the novel —Reading: Finish *My Antonia* —Film: *The Chosen*, first half.

Week III: World War II and the American Land —Nuclear Testing at White Sands, Hiroshima, Nagasaki —Native American theories of history and myth — Internalization of oppression, assimilation, cultural pluralism —*Ceremony*: American Indian participation in World War II. "Enemy Way" ceremonies, relationship between the fly/hummingbird story and the Tayo plot —Reading: Begin *Ceremony* —Film: *The Chosen*, second half.

Week IV: World War II and Cultural Pluralism —The Holocaust, Internment Camps, and Reservations —Laguna myth and the chants in *Ceremony* —Epic structures and *Ceremony* —Political Cartoons and racism in World War II —

History of Native American resistance –Religious components of Native American resistance —Reading: Finish *Ceremony.*

Week V: World War II and the Japanese American Experience. —Visit to class by Jeanne Wakatsuki Houston. —History and politics of the internment camps. —Poetry and photos from the internment experience. —Reverberations through other Asian American groups. —Reading: *Farewell to Manzanar* plus reader. —Film: PBS *A Family Gathering,* by Lise Yasui.

Week VI: 1955-64–the Civil Rights Movement. —Class watches "Eyes on the Prize" I, parts 1-5 —Reading: Begin *Meridian.*

Week VII: 1955-65–the Civil Rights Movement. —Nonviolent tactics of achieving social change —*Meridian*: a feminist view of Civil Rights, the place of caucasians, the Church in the movement, music —Black Power —Women's Movement —Reading: Finish *Meridian* —Film: *El Norte,* first half.

Week VIII: Chicano response to Civil Rights —Chicano Theater and the Delano Grape Strike —Educational issues in Chicano communities —Panel of Student Activists —Reading: *Occupied America* and pieces by Gomez, Rodriguez — Film: *El Norte,* second half, to end.

Week IX: America as a Borderland/Frontera —Guest lecture by Alfred Arteaga on Columbus, Cowboys, Cars and Chicano culture —Multicultural art — Borderlands/Frontera, beyond cultural pluralism —Reading: *Borderlands/La Frontera.*

Week X: Coalition Politics–Coalition Building across lines of class, race, gender and sexual preference. —America as a coalition or mosaic rather than melting pot –Talk by a gay activist, summing up and evaluation —Film: *The Times of Harvey Milk.*

WRITTEN WORK

Students hand in a 1-2 page typewritten essay every week. The essay must respond to that week's reading, but may also touch upon ideas raised by the film or by the lectures. I suggest topics and questions each week. These essays are called "talking papers" because the discussion sections usually begin with people dividing into pairs and reading their papers to each other; the ideas shared often ignite a lively discussion.

The students also write one longer essay as a conclusion to their quarter's work. A variety of options is available, but all require that students make use of several of the class texts. One popular option is an oral history of a person who was involved in World War II or in the Civil Rights Movement; another is a study of the student's family's immigration or migration experience, again often using oral histories.

Syllabus #6

RELIGIOUS DIVERSITY IN THE UNITED STATES

Jeanne Halgren Kilde, Cleveland State University
Department of History, 1991

COURSE SUMMARY AND GOALS

This course examines the worship practices, beliefs and concerns of several groups of Americans with respect not only to each group's cultural identity but also each group's situation within the national American society. The religious beliefs of a people naturally define the "religious world" of that community, and they also affect the way that community participates in the national context. Our study will examine both historical and contemporary issues and practices, leading to an understanding of the ways in which religion functions as a social strategy with national and local contexts as well as personal ones.

REQUIRED TEXTS

Momaday, N. Scott. *House Made of Dawn.*

Moore, R. Laurence. *Religious Outsiders and the Making of Americans.* New York: Oxford Universdity Press, 1986.

McLoughlin, Wm. G. *Revivals, Awakenings, and Reform: An Essay on Religion and Social Change in America, 1607-1977.* University of Chicago Press, 1978.

Rudolph Anaya. *Bless Me Ultima.*

REQUIREMENTS AND GRADING

Class Participation (see below)–20%. Midterm Exam –20%. Final Exam–30%. Project (see below)–30%.

All students must come to class prepared to discuss both the major themes of the works assigned for the day and their relationship to previous readings. Students are expected to contribute to class discussions.

All students must complete an independent research project on some topic relevant to me study of American religious diversity. Topics for the study may deal with any group discussed in class or a religious group not specifically examined. Specific subjects may focus on such things as worship practice, political ramifications of religious thought, relations between a religious group and broader society, internal issues of theology or organization, position of women within a religious group. Each project must be the equivalent in research and analysis of a 10-page term paper. You may write a paper or choose an alternative format with the consent of the instructor. Possible approaches: an ethnography of an unfamiliar worship service, a slide presentation on the material culture of a religious group, a group project, a video or cassette tape with narration and analysis, a historical docudrama--be imaginative! All projects will be presented in class—sign up for a time-slot early!

READINGS AND LECTURES –

Week 1: **Approaches to the Study of Religious Diversity.** "Religion as a Subject Matter" and "Worlds" from William E. Paden's *Religious Worlds: The Comparative Study of Religion* (Boston: Beacon Press, 1988). PACKET.

"Zones of Conflict: Encounters with Otherness in America" from David Chidester's *Patterns of Power: Religion and Politics in American Culture*, (Englewood Cliffs: Prentice Hall, 1988.) PACKET

"'An Infinite Variety of Religions': The Meaning and Measurement of Religious Diversity" and "'A Motley of Peoples and Cultures': Urban Populations and Religious Diversity" from Kevin J. Christiano's *Religious Diversity and Social Change: American Cities, 1890-1906* (Cambridge University Press, 1987). PACKET

Religious Outsiders. "Introduction: Protestant Unity and the American Mission– The Historiography of a Desire."

Weeks 2 and 3: **Protestantism in the U.S.** Themes: Evangelicalism, individualism, negotiating for position within national and local cultures.

Revivals, Awakenings and Reform: An Essay on Religions and Social Change in America, 1607-1977. ALL

Religious Outsiders. CHAPTERS 4-6

Film: *The Holy Ghost People*

Music: "Nearer My God to Thee" &"Amazing Grace" (Joni Mitchell)

Weeks 4 and 5: **African-American Religious Experience.** Themes: Evangelical Protestantism, religious foundations of the Civil Rights Movement, worship styles.

"Slavery and the African Spiritual Holocaust" from Jon Butler's *Awash in a Sea of Faith: Christenizing the American People.* (Cambridge: Harvard University Press, 1990). PACKET

Sisters of the Spirit: Three Black Women's Autobiographies of the Nineteenth Century. Wm L. Andrews, ed. (Bloomington: Indiana University Press, 1986). Excerpts. PACKET

King, Martin Luther, Jr. "Letter form Birmingham Jail—April 16, 1963." PACKET

Cone, James H. "Black Theology and the Black Church: Where Do We Go from Here?" *Cross Currents* 27 (Summer 1977),147-56. PACKET

Religious Outsiders. "Black Culture and Black Churches--The Quest for an Autonomous Identity."

Murphy, Larry B. "A Balm in Gilead: Black Churches and the Thrust for Civil Rights in California, 1850-1880." PACKET

Jackson, Mahalia. "Singing of Good Tidings and Freedom" from *Movin' On Up* (New York: Hawthorn Books, 1966) PACKET

Gospel Music: Rev. C. J. Johnson—"You Better Run (to the City of Refuge)" (1982); Aretha Franklin—"Amazing Grace" (1972); Mitchell's Christian Singers– "I'm Praying Humble" (1937); Mahalia Jackson—"Nobody Knows the Trouble I've Seen"; Abyssinian Baptist Choir; The Jubilee Singers; Dixie Hummingbirds (Many of these selections are available on the two volume set, "The Gospel Sound").

Review and Midterm Exam

Weeks 6 and 7: **Immigrant Churches—Judaism and Catholicism.** Themes: Assimilation, doctrinal integrity, maintaining cultural traditions within the American context, religious discrimination.

Dolan, Jay P. "The Immigrants and Their Gods: A New Perspective in American Religious History" *Church History* 57 (March 1988) 61-72. PACKET

Gaustad, Edwin Scott. "Faithful Immigrants and the Varieties of Religious Experience" from *A Religious History of America: New Revised Edition* (San Francisco: Harper & Row, Publishers, 1990). PACKET

Higham, John. "The Rise of Social Discrimination," from *Send These to Me: Immigrants in Urban America.* rev. ed. (Baltimore: Johns Hopkins University Press, 1984). PACKET

Religious Outsiders, "American Jews as an Ordinary Minority."

Film: *Hester Street* (1974)-- Jewish immigrant life in New York City ca. 1906.

Music: Polka Masses.

Week 8: **Latino Catholicism.** Theme: Similarities and differences in cultural situations and strategies between the immigrant church and the Hispanic church.

Campbell, Francis M. "Missionology in New Mexico, 1850-1900: The Success and Failure of Catholic Education," from *Religion and Society in the American West: Historical Essays,* Carl Guarneri, ed. (Lanham, MD: University Press of America, 1987). PACKET

Burns, Jeffrey M. "The Mexican-American Catholic Community in California, 1850-1980" from *Religion and Society in the American West.* PACKET

Bless Me Ultima.

Film: *The Shrine* (1990) El Santuaro church in New Mexico.

Week 9: **Native American Religious Experience.**

Gill, Sam D. "Native American Religions" in *Encyclopedia of the American Religious Experience.* PACKET

Readings from Christopher Vecsey's *Imagine Ourselves Richly: Mythic Narrative of North American Indians* (1988). PACKET

Readings from Sam Gill's edited work, *Native American Religious Action: A Performance Approach to Religion* (1987). PACKET

Bowden, Henry Warner. "North American Indian Missions" in *Encyclopedia of the American Religious Experience.* PACKET

Momaday, N. Scott. *House Made of Dawn.*

Week 10: Finish Presentations. *Final Exam*

SUPPLEMENTAL READINGS

Ahlstrom, Sydney E. *A Religious History of the American People* (New Haven, 1972).

Marty, Martin E. *Pilgrims in the Own Land: 500 Years of Religion in America* (Little, Brown & Co., 1984).

Sernett, Milton C. *Afro-American Religious History: A Documentary Witness* (Durham: Duke University Press, 1985).

Vecsey, Christopher. *Religions in Native North America* (1990).

CALIFORNIA MOSAIC:
LITERATURES OF A MULTICULTURAL SOCIETY

R. Jeffrey Lustig, Director, Center for California Studies
Proposed Syllabus for a Summer Institute, 1992

> *California has often been regarded as "America, only*
> *more so," and it is through California that the nation has*
> *often glimpsed its future, for good or ill.*

California has never been an easy place to understand. Its apparent openness, the motley richness of its subregions, explosive pace of its development and image-making capacities of its films have all worked against a clear and accurate image of the state, its master trends and implications. "Maybe I did have all the aces," remarks a character from a Joan Didion novel. "But what was the game?" Over the past decade, a growing number of Californians have turned their attention to the task of achieving that understanding and developing a socio-cultural map of their region. People from many walks of life have revealed an interest in identifying the real character of California culture, the real burden of its past, the precise meaning of "California" as ideal and reality. A burgeoning array of journal articles, books and conferences addressed to a "sense of place" attest to the heightened curiosity on the part of scholars, writers, and community leaders about the dense and richly-textured culture which has emerged beyond the cinematic stereotypes, a culture flowing from discrete eras and regional experiences, productive of recognizable identities, and evocative of new impulses and tensions. Many Californians now seek to answer Didion's question and identify the game, its rules, players and stakes.

Coincident with this effort has been the profound recognition of California as a genuine, tangible and deeply-rooted multicultural society, and the scholarly and aesthetic commitment following from this recognition to understand the ways ethnicity, racism, and cultural differentiation have affected, indeed constituted, the regional consciousness. California has always been a multiethnic society and always possessed an extraordinarily rich ethnic and social tapestry. The struggles of Hispanic, Asian, and Indian cultures for expression in the face of dominant Anglo-European culture—indeed, the struggle of lone Anglo champions of cultural synthesis, like Charles Fletcher Lummis—are key parts of the history of the state, little known though they may be by most westerners.

Recent immigration and changing social circumstances have forced a new recognition of this multicultural condition and lent new urgency to the task of its comprehension. California, of course, is not the first of the world's global cross-roads. Rome, the Austro-Hungarian Empire, India, and Beirut of mid-century also made claims to this status. The very mention of these precedents, however, suggests the character of the deeper questions facing us. To what extent do multicultural relations define a caste society, a balkanized array of warring nationalities, or a two-tier society, instead of a democracy? What is the precise character of the experience of those relations as revealed in the outlook and insight of a region's literature? . . .

Complementing the new interest in a regional culture is a growing recognition of the part of writers, educators and philosophers of the critical importance of locale to culture and understanding. Whether we look to anthropologists following Clifford Geertz's lead in *Local Knowledge,* post-modernists overturning the significance of the nation-state as locus of citizen identity, teachers discovering the importance of grounding lessons in lived experience, or social theorists reminding us that while we may think in universals, we live in particulars, pedagogical and epistemological emphases of the significance of "regional 1 knowledge" now abound.[1] Further encouraging this new focus is the fact that the literature of the United States has always been largely a regional literature, expressing a national voice through the dictions and rhythms of its major sections. The California poet, Gary Snyder, strait-forwardly declares, "The nation is a fiction. The region alone is real." (Kevin Starr notes less severely—on the cover of the Wyatt volume cited below—that California "as a landscape of fact and symbolic encounter . . . is becoming increasingly recognized as a significant variant, in life and art, of the American national experience.")

The Summer Institute will focus attention on those literary works which best give expression to California society as constituted by different ethnic voices and visions, which best offer opportunities for understanding the commonalities and conflicts between those cultures as they have confronted core experiences, and which best equip institute members for comprehending the larger historical, ethical and aesthetic aspects of relations between the cultures of this Pacific commonwealth. What will be sought through a study of these literatures of the

---

[1] "Of course regionalism has had a bad press since the advent of the Modernist movement . . . . Over against this perspective I believe that the impress of place on man's artifacts is something not only authentic but absolutely ineradicable, and in affirming it I have sought to isolate the energy shaping the specific Western experience." Everson, Archetype West, The Pacific Coast as a Literary Region, 1976, p. xiv.

barrios, ghettos, chinatowns and other ethnic communities are the differing visions which may have been fulfilled, defeated, preempted or transformed, but which together have defined California as a cultural "place," as opposed to a bare geological location.

These are concerns of clearly more than regional significance. California has often been regarded as "America, only more so," and it is through California that the nation has often glimpsed its future, for good or ill. America too was settled by immigrants from many nations. It too offers the example of peoples residing in the same location and yet entertaining different concepts of place. It too is being compelled by a changing world position to rethink the meaning of multicultural pluralism. The first "boat people," we realize, arrived on the *Mayflower*. What has extended over three centuries for the nation at large, however, and has often been hidden by the hegemony of a dominant culture, has been compressed into half that time in California and broken through efforts at evasions with the efflorescence of a most diverse and multi-voiced regional literature. Questions of cultural interpretation which will be taken up by humanities scholars over the next few decades in the nation at large are forced upon California scholars and students in a sharply focussed manner now. In looking at California, then, we will be looking at questions of national significance.

The disciplines of the humanities are uniquely suited to address these questions for a number of reasons. The first is that California since discovery has been associated with a state of mind, and not simply a physical domain. Particular attitudes have always been associated with the state, particular ways of seeing the world, and particular expectations *from* the world . . . .

The insight underlying this seminar is that these "states of mind" have in fact been multiple and diverse. "California" has been constituted by different peoples. To confront this multiculturality it is necessary to understand various world-views, various ways of apprehending realities, various ways of living a life. Different people are doing different things in California; indeed, they possess and endure different "Californias." We shall therefore also seek to push beyond surface stories and immediate concerns in the works we study, as William Everson did in *Archetype West, the Pacific Coast as Literary Region*, and to discover the archetypes, basic motifs, and repository images of the different cultures' narratives.

As truly as Anglos see California as the culmination of the move West, Hispanics see it as El Norte, and Southeast Asians as the first step East to America. Contemporary California turns out in fact to also be compounded of other places. Part of California is *Mexico afuera* ("Mexico outside"); part of Santa Ana is little Phnom Penh; part of Fresno is Laos. Implicit in these divergent perspectives are divergent senses of time, of relations to history, of community, and of the scope of human effort.

Central to institute inquiry, then, will be matters of ethics and values, and the comparison of ethics and values. These topics, like those of world-view and archetype, are accessible only through an interdisciplinary approach combining literature, philosophy, history, and political theory—i.e., only through the outlook of the humanities. . . . To summarize: "The California Mosaic" proposes a study of the multicultural literatures of California to extend an appreciation of those literatures, of world-views and contributions of the groups whose experiences they express and of the real character and legacies of California's multiethnic culture.

COURSE MECHANICS

Course meetings are planned for four days a week (except for the last week which will include a fifth, summation discussion). They will be scheduled to run from 8:30 a.m. to 12:00 p.m. with a break from 9:45-10:00. Lecture topics are assigned among the four instructors and one guest lecturer each week; the lectures will conclude before the break. Discussions will follow the break. The number of Institute Faculty makes it possible to break down into separate discussion groups on the days when guest lecturers are not attending. . . .

Site visits to locations of value to students of literature and society are planned for weeks 1, 3 and 4, and films for Week 2 [and] as time permits to the California State Archives, the State Library (possessing significant literary collections), or the State Railroad Museum. Students will be invited to form separate study groups on specific topics pertinent to the coursework, and to convene these groups on occasional afternoons. They will also be assigned a fifteen-page paper to write on a seminar topic. These will be distributed to all participants and a few of the papers, selected by the students, will be presented on the afternoon of July 18 and during class July 19, at the conclusion of the course.

Institute participants will be sent the following selected works

before the course begins:

Patricia Nelson Limerick, *Legacy of Conquest, the Unbroken Past of the American West* (major reinterpretive work on historiography of the West, will provide historical and cultural context for discussions)

Gerald Haslam, "California Writing and the West," *Western American Literature*, Nov., 1983, (pp. 209-222)

Institute attendees will also be asked to read the following:

Kevin Starr, *Americans and the California Dream, 1850-1915* (1973)

David Wyatt, *The Fall into Eden: Landscape and Imagination in California* (1986)

The Haslam article will be reprinted in a specially-prepared course reader which will also include the following:

Elliott, George P., "Why are they Driving Me Crazy?" *Contact*, (III, 6), April, 1963.

Haslam, G., "Western Writers and the National Fantasy," from *Western Writing*, Univ. of New Mexico Press, 1974 (pp. 1-8)

Dobie, J. Frank, "The Writer and His Region," ibid. (pp. 16-25)

Stewart, George R., "The Regional Approach to Literature," ibid. (pp. 40-49)

===================================

SYLLABUS

NOTE: Reading assignments below are indicated for lectures and discussion the next day. Institute participants are expected to participate in the seminars in the morning, small groups in the afternoon, and field trips and special events on evenings and weekends, as indicated. Small-group discussions of syllabus components will be critiqued on successive Fridays, July 17 and 24. Papers from the course are expected by the last day; comments and evaluation of effectiveness of syllabus and course materials will take place in February, 1993.

Presentation of First Theme: Land--Week 1

Tuesday: **Introduction:** Themes and Scope of the Course. Introductions.

Requirements of Course, Including Small-Group Assignments

The first day of the institute will introduce attendees to selected themes, texts, and approaches. After Institute participants introduce themselves, and staff are introduced, Haslam and Moore will make brief presentations. Expectations and requirements of the course will be clarified. Possibilities for small-group workshops will be listed and volunteers solicited. Goals and criteria for evaluation of the Institute and effectiveness of syllabus will be discussed.

Haslam and Moore will introduce the topic of the next Institute day: **Indigenous Californians: Relationship to Land.**

Required reading for next session: LaPena, Frank, *The World as Gift* (brief book of poetry)

Wednesday:. Institute Lecturer Frank LaPena will present a slide-illustrated lecture on the significance of Mount Shasta to Native Californians. Reprints of Darryl Wilson's "Gedin Ch-Lum- Nu: Let It Be This Way" will be distributed.

Required reading for next session:

Arthur Quinn's *Broken Shore: The Marin Peninsula in California History* (Chs.1-3, 68 pp. a poetic reflection on European ambition and conquest)

LaPerouse, "Monterey in 1786" (60 pp. in recent Margolin reprint of original)

Haslam, G., and J. Houston, *California Heartland, Writing from the Great Central Valley*, Part I (California Indian myths, 15 pp.), Captain Pedro Fages "Valley Indians" (2 pp), F. Garces, "Encountering the Yokuts" (2pp.)

(See additional suggested texts in selected bibliography at end of syllabus))

Thursday: **Indigenous Californians**: The Encounter With Diversity

Darryl Wilson will read from his story, a tribal account of early Hawaiians in a place now called California, as well as other works demonstrating the diversity of Native Californians and the significance of place to indigenous peoples.

News from Native California: Contemporary Tribal Relationships to Sacred and Other Natural Places

Malcolm Margolin will speak on the diversity of Native California life and contemporary expressions of traditional relationships to land.

Presentation of Second Theme: **PEOPLE**

Land and People: Early Spanish Presence

Friday and Saturday: Site visit to Mission San Juan Bautista, and lecture by Luis Valdez, founder and director of El Teatro Campesino. (Valdez was the keynote speaker, highly acclaimed, at the second California Studies Conference.)

Evening of July 10: theatrical performance by El Teatro Campesino.

Return home by way of the University of California, Berkeley, with stop at The Bancroft Library, nationally-known repository of major collections of California letters and historical documents.

Assigned reading for next session: Kevin Starr, *America and the California Dream* (Ch.1, Ch. 13, i-ii; 50 pp.)

(see additional suggested texts in selected bibliography, end of syllabus)

Supplementary activities:

Visit to California State Indian Museum in Sacramento, and Trading Post in Folsom, CA

Film Screening, "Ishi." Discussion with filmmaker N.Jed Riffe and key consulting archaeologist, Jerald Jay Johnson.

*Week 2--***Spanish Presence,** *continued*

Monday: Spanish Land Grants & Early Relations with Indigenous Peoples. Lecture by Ed Castillo, Professor of Ethnic Studies, Sonoma State University

Assigned reading for next session:

Walt Whitman, "Looking West from California Shores" (poem)

Allen Ginsberg, "A Supermarket in California" (poem)

Henry George, *Progress and Poverty* (first 10 pp of selections)

J. S. Holliday, *The World Rushed In, An Eyewitness Account of a Nation Heading West* (Chs. 3, 6; 49 pp.) (diary literature of the goldseekers)

Haslam, Gerald, *Okies* (two of its stories)

Tuesday: **Search for the Promised Land:** The European and Asian Presence. "Westward Ho!" Pioneer Ideals and Okie Realities. Lecture by Co-Leader, Gerald Haslam

Assigned Reading for next session:

Maxine Hong Kingston, *Woman Warrior, China Men* (novels of legend, mythology, migration)

(see additional texts in selected bibliography, following)

Wednesday and Thursday: **The Sojourn in Gold Mountain.** Maxine Hong Kingston, reading from and discussing her work

Friday: First Report from Small-Group. Draft of Annotated Bibliography

Supplemental activities (Friday of 2nd week, cont.)

Field trip to Pena Adobe, site of early Spanish presence in near Vacaville in Solano County.

Site visit to General Vallejo's home, where Bear Flag Republic took command of the Mexican Governor.

Field trip to Sutter's Fort, Sacramento, early haven for European immigrants coming from the East

Film screening, "Grapes of Wrath," based on novel by John Steinbeck, directed by John Ford

Guest lecture by Charles Wollenberg, editor of "Harvest Gypsies on the Road to the Grapes of Wrath," notebooks from migrant labor camps kept by Steinbeck on which novel was later based

Presentation of Third Theme: **Community**

Land, People, and Community. *Week 3*

Monday: Site Visit to Mother Lode country, the gold country in foothill of Sierra which were home to Twain and Bret Harte, inspiration to John Muir

> *Required reading for next session:*
>
> McWilliams, C., *North from Mexico* (Chs. 9-12, 82 pp.) (1949 classic still-cited work on Mexican migration)
>
> Bezzerides, A. I., *Only When You're Sleepy* (farm work novel of 1938, basis of Hollywood film, "They Drive By Night")
>
> Bulosan, Carlos, *America is in the Heart* (20 pp. selection)
>
> Fante, John, "Helen, Thy Beauty is to Me" (1941) (re: Filipinos and Italians in pre-war California as depicted by premier mid-century California author)
>
> Saroyan, William, "Our Little Brown Brothers the Filipinos" (1936), "The Cornet Players" (1950) (Sikhs, Turks, & Assyrians in the 30's Central Valley)
> All assignments but Bulosan under ten pages. (See also suggested readings in selected bibliography, following)

Tuesday: **Strangers in a Strange Land.** Chicanos and Blacks as Migrants and Workers, Lecture by Co-Leader Shirley Moore.

Evening activity: Film Screening, "The Trail North," by Paul Espinosa (award-winning film, funded partially by California Council for the Humanities, 1988)

Wednesday and Thursday: **The Central Valley:** A Fresno Childhood and the Multi-Cultural Experience.

Readings, lecture and discussions with Gary Soto, Chicano poet

Friday: Small Group Reports. Filmography.

Classroom Assignments: Paper Topics, Suggested Themes, Activities

Review of Annotated Bibliography

Required reading for following session: Young, Al, Things Ain't What They Used To Be

Supplemental Activities:

Site Visit to original Chinese-American settlement of Locke, on the Delta

Film Screening of "Locke," funded by the California Council for the Humanities

Film Screening, "Rock and Hawk"; discussion with filmmaker Alan Soldofsky, former Executive Director, Poetry Center, San Jose State University

The Meaning of Community. *Week 4*

Monday: The Contemporary African-American Experience. Reading, lecture, and discussion with Al Young.

Required reading for the next session:

Jeffers, Robinson, "Continent's End"; "Roan Stallion" (from Roan Stallion), "The Purse-Seine" (from *Tamar and Other Poems*) "Natural Music" (ibid.), "Hurt Hawks" (from *Cawdor and Other Poems*), "Fire in the Hills" (from Thurso's *Landing and Other Poems*), "Oh, Lovely Rock" (from *Such Counsels You Gave Me*) (about 75 pp.)

Everson, Wm. *Archetype West: The Pacific Coast as Literary Region* (150 pp.)

Tuesday: Readings, Lecture, and Discussion. James D. Houston on Jeffers and West Coast Literature. Jeanne Wakatsuki Houston on Problems in Community: the Japanese Internment.

Evening Activity: "Farewell to Manzanar," film screening and discussion with screenwriters Wakatsuki and Houston

Required readings for next sessions:

Royce, Josiah, *The Problem of Christianity* (Chs. 2-4, 9-10; 125 pp., his most focussed discussion of the theory of community)

Hine, Robert, *California's Utopian Colonies* (Chs. 1, 5, 7, 9; 69 pp.)

McWilliams, Carey, *Southern California Country* (Ch. 9, "I'm a Stranger Here Myself" re: the absence of community in California, and Ch. 14 on "The Politics of Utopia," early political communes; 52 pp.)

Haslam, Gerald, "Diversity and Identity: Perils at the 'Edge of Mexico'"

Rodriguez, Richard, *Hunger of Memory*

(see also additional texts in selected bibliography)

Wednesday: **The Search for Community.** Project Director Jeff Lustig presents remarks on "Royce's Theory, California, and Classical Political Theories of Community"

Thursday: The Search for Community, cont. Jim Heffernan, Professor of Philosophy, University of the Pacific, Stockton, California, presents lecture, "Scepticism and Moral Insight: Josiah Royce on Community"

Co-Leaders Moore and Haslam lead discussion on a pluralistic society and the moral ideal of a harmonious whole

Friday: CONCLUDING SESSION: Farewells, oral evaluations of Institute by faculty participants

ADDITIONAL SELECTED BIBLIOGRAPHY

Week 1:

Ordonez de Montalvo, Garcia, *Las Sergas de Esplandian, 1510* (original myth of "an island called California")

Forbes, Jack, *Native Americans of California and Nevada*

Kroeber, Theodora, *The Inland Whale* (collection of California Indian stories)

Kroeber, Theodora, *Ishi in Two Worlds, A Biography of the Last Wild Indian in North America*

Margolin, Malcolm, *The Ohlone Way*

Muller, Tom & Tom Espanshade, *The Fourth Wave, California's Newest Immigrants*

Royce, Josiah, *California* (1886)

Starr, Kevin, *America and the California Dream*

Starr, Kevin *Inventing the Dream, California Through the Prog-ressive Era*

Takaki, Ronald, *Iron Cages, Race and Culture in Nineteenth Century America*

Week 2:

Daniel, Cletus, *Bitter Harvest, A History of California Farmworkers, 1870-1949*

Eisen, Jon and David Fine, *The Unknown California*

Galarza, Ernesto, *Barrio Boy*

Gregory, James, *American Exodus: The Dust-Bowl Migration and Okie Culture in California*

Ichioka, Yuji, Issei, *The World of the First Generation Japanese Immigrants, 1885-1924*

Kingston, Maxine Hong, *Woman Warrior*

Saroyan, William, *My Name is Aram*

Schwendiger, Robert, *Ocean of Bitter Dreams, Maritime Relations Between China and the U.S., 1850-1915*

Stein, Walter, *California and the Dustbowl Migration*

Steinbeck, John, *Grapes of Wrath*

Tan, Amy, *The Joy Luck Club*

Uchida, Yoshiko, *Picture Bride*

Week 3:

Austin, Mary, *The Land of Little Rain* (pp. 3-38 of Pearce reprint of 1903 volume)

Brautigan, Richard, *The Confederate General from Big Sur*

Didion, Joan, *Run River* (re: Sacramento compared with Galarza or Gardner)

Everson, William, *San Joaquin*

Everson, William & Robinson Jeffers, *Fragments of an Older Fury*

Galarza, Ernesto, *Barrio Boy*

Galarza, Ernesto, *Merchants of Labor*

Gardner, Leonard, *Fat City*

Haslam and Houston, *California Heartland* (any of selections from Parts 3 - 4 , "Awakening" and "Exploring")

Jeffers, Robinson, *The Women at Point Sur*

King, Clarence, *Mountaineering in the Sierra Nevada*

Kushner, Sam, *The Long Road to Delano*

London, Jack, *Martin Eden*

Muir, John, *The Mountains of California* (1-173)

Norris, Frank, *The Octopus*

Smith, Michael L, *Pacific Visions* (Chs. 1, 2) (re: Muir as scientist)

Snyder, Gary, *Rip Rap*

Soto, Gary, *California Childhood* (recollections of California childhoods of major California writers)

Soto, Gary, *Elements of San Joaquin*

Starr, Kevin, *Americans and the California Dream* (Chs. 6, 7, 13)

Stegner, Wallace, *Angle of Repose* (pp. 215-235 to contrast Clarence King's rapacious view of the Sierras with Muir's)

Stewart, George, *Fire*

Wyatt, David, *The Fall into Eden: Landscape and Imagination in California*

Week 4:

Chan, Sucheng, *This Bittersweet Soil, The Chinese in California Agriculture,* (Ch. 11, "Survival and Commuity")

Didion, Joan, *Play it as it Lays*

George, Henry, "The Chinese on the Pacific Coast" (1868)

Gregory, James, *American Exodus: The Dust Bowl Migration and Okie Culture in California*

Haslam, Gerald, *Okies*

Hine, Robert, *California's Utopian Colonies* (remaining chapters.)

Houston, James, *Californians, Searching for the Golden State*

Houston, James *Continental Drift*

Irons, Peter. *Justice at War* (Japanese internment)

McWilliams, Carey, *Brothers Under the Skin* (also chapters. on Indians & Mexican-Americans in Southern California Country)

Royce, Josiah, *The Philosophy of Loyalty*

Saxton, Alexander, *The Indispensable Enemy, California Labor and Anti-Asian Prejudice, 1865-1910*

Shinn, Howard, Mining Camps: *A Study in American Frontier Government* (1885, a classic document linking western community with racism)

Soto, Gary, *California Childhood, Living Up the Street; or The Elements of San Joaquin*

Tan, Amy, *The Joy Luck Club*

Uchida, Yoshiko, *Desert Exile*

Valdez, Luis, *Zootsuit* (the play; film if available)

Wakatsuki, Jeanne with J. Houston, *Farewell to Manzanar*

Young, Al, *Sitting Pretty* (re: Black community in Bay Area)

====================

Syllabus #8

INTRODUCTION TO ETHNIC STUDIES

Victor Greene, University of Wisconsin-Milwaukee
for National Humanities Institute, 1976
A design for a three unit, seminar-type entry course in ethnic studies.

This is a design for a course required in the B.A. undergraduate major in Ethnic Studies at the University of Wisconsin-Milwaukee. Most students will have declared their major and therefore will be at the start of their junior year. Students will come from Black, Latino, and Native American organized elements since interest for ethnic studies has come from them, although there will also be some white students who are sympathetic to social change and movement, chiefly of Roman Catholic, Orthodox, and Jewish background. The university and community it serves are good resources for a program in ethnic studies. For example, the university, with a mission statement as its founding objective to educate the population of the state's largest city and a wide array of off campus courses in its urban outreach division, will encourage the ethnic studies course's field work. In addition, the city, itself an ethnically diverse laboratory where ethnic consciousness is the norm, has an annual international folk festival in which the city's ethnic organizations participate, sponsored by the International Institute of Milwaukee County. As ethnic groups emerge, persist, and decline, they provide a vital cultural and social framework by which people identify themselves and acquire values. Recognizing this source of self identity without shame for minority status is particularly valuable to adolescent students going through the difficult process of identity-consciousness (re Erik Erikson and Kurt Lewin on this subject). Students will have a good opportunity to view preparations and involvement in the folk festival and in the community at large.--Victor Greene

COURSE RATIONALE

This Ethnic Studies course consists of a broad theoretical introduction to ethnicity. Structurally it will serve as an initial step for the student to explore a particular topic or group in future course work. People have both public and private lives, performing in their vocational/professional spheres as well as in their more intimate, leisure, and casual moments; however, it is in the latter sphere that ethnic attachments are most visible.

GOAL OF THE COURSE AND PROGRAM

To illuminate the nature, parameters, and dynamic quality of ethnic feeling from the
individual in her/his American context. An assumption is that this exploration
will not be an exercise of discovery, but a revision/refinement of pre-conceived
notions of ethnicity. The ethnic bond, for example, can exist within an
individual without being a part of the existing ethnic community--much
ethnicity, then, is repressed, as well as expressed. The presumption is that
neither outsiders nor group members fully realize the sociological as well as
psychological dimensions of ethnic feeling. Ethnicity is a far more complex
and elusive phenomenon, often with more influence on individual behavior
than we heretofore assumed. Since ethnic feeling exists at both the group and
individual levels, the objective is to have the student recognize both and
explore their interrelationship. This will be done through class work--reading,
discussion, writing--as well as through newer forms of learning, field
observations, and interviewing.

COURSE OBJECTIVES

To explore the extent and impact of, as well as intellectual attitudes toward, ethnic
feeling in America at both the social and individual levels. The assumption is
that we have yet to understand just how pervasive such feelings are in our
society, particularly in the way in which they affect and condition the
individual. Emphasis is placed on beneficial creative resources that such
feelings offer in our culture. In introducing the field of ethnic studies, the
student will be encouraged to consider a particular subject concerning one or
several groups for exploration in the ethnic studies program.

COURSE METHOD

To determine and assess parameters of ethnic feeling, several complementary
learning approaches will be employed, to bring together a more sophisticated
understanding of the ethnicity-individual relationship by the conclusion of the
seminar. Most important is the field work, conducted after some classroom
reading, guidance, and discussion. After necessary administrative contact with
the organized ethnic group(s), the student will observe groups to determine the
role that such associations have for their members. In addition to the field
work, readings and classroom discussion will illuminate and interrelate
independent student observations. The innovative and interdisciplinary
character of the program requires close teacher-student contact, aided by the
seminar form.

COURSE DESCRIPTION

First, introductory meetings will explain the independent, out-of-class field activity. The student will prepare for this activity by selecting a group for study, acquiring certain basic techniques of field work, then proceeding to observe the group in its meeting places--church, meeting hall, home, etc. The instructor will have assisted in negotiating with the group's officers to ease the transition. If possible, the student will interview a member of the group in an attempt to determine how and why that individual commits to the group. Results will be presented at one of the last meetings of the course. While the student is involved in the field, class work is all related to determining the relationship of the individual to her/his group.

There are three major sections:

1. First, broad sociological theories of assimilation and cultural pluralism in America. This part will cover the ethnicization process, how ethnic groups were organized and developed in America, with some finally dispersed. Some attention will be to compare and relate American diversity to that of other nations.

2. Second, proceeding directly to the individual level, how and why do some people need group identification. A related inquiry is to learn what ethnic affiliation provides for a person in self-perception and values. Readings will stress adolescent psychology and the power of ethnic stereotypes, that is, the potency of ethnic images and their effect on group members.

3. The third module considers ethnic tradition as a positive, creative force within the individual--how group membership consciously and unconsciously aids and conditions individuals in making and refining their culture. (For example, writers and artists frequently draw upon group traditions in their art). While Black and Native American folk cultures have been studied for their richness, those of other ethnic groups with their dress, dances, crafts, foods, and folk tales still remain obscure to scholars and students and largely uncollected and unpreserved; students should find considerable evidence of ethnic folk culture among all ethnic groups.

4. Finally, the last section of the course will be synthetic. Students present their findings from field work to each other in written and oral presentations, to be discussed in consideration of previous readings and assignments, as well as of the findings of the other students.

Student Assignments: 1. Reading assignments. 2. Individual research project. 3. Final report. 4. Oral presentation on individual project during final two weeks of course. 5. Final exam.

Suggested Syllabus for "The Introduction to Ethnic Studies":

Week 1. *Introduction to the course.* Explain in detail course objectives and requirements. Offer initial guidance to field work (bibliography to be supplied).

Weeks 2 and 3. *Further instruction* & discussion in field work, preparing students for observation.

Weeks 4 and 5. *The Issue of Ethnicity in America's Melting Pot* Racist and Cultural Pluralist Views. Assimilation and persistence viewed broadly.

Weeks 6, 7, and 8. *Discussions of Ethnicity and Psychology.* Readings on identity, self perception, the nature of prejudice, and the potency of stereotypes.

Weeks 9, 10, 11, and 12. *Discussions of Ethnicity and Creativity.* Class reading and discussion on how one's group affiliation stimulates and provides a resource for creativity and the aesthetic. Traditional fine arts media covered, as literature, painting, sculpture, and folk art --needlework, dress, foods, etc.

Weeks 13, 14, and 15. Student papers presented in which field work and class work are compared.

BIBLIOGRAPHICAL LIST (Student level works are asterisked)

Assimilationists

*Hector St. John Crevecoeur, *Letters from an American Farmer* (London, 1782), especially Letter III, "What is an American." A classic statement of the early American assimilative power.

Daedalus issue of 1961 on American Ethnic Groups. A much neglected early anthology of views by scholars on transformation of white ethnic groups; the essay of Oscar Handlin on permeable boundaries is the best.

Nathan Glazer, "Ethnic Groups in America: From National Culture to Idealogy" in Morroe Berger, et al., *Freedom and Control in Modern Society* (New York, 1954). How the nature of ethnic groups changes over time from spontaneous social enclaves to self-conscious bodies.

*Milton Gordon, *Assimilation in American Life* (New York, 1964). A sociological view of acculturation without assimilation, i.e., ethnic groups can have commonly held values yet remain apart structurally.

*Oscar Handlin, *The Uprooted* (New York, 1959). Beautiful lament on the tragic disorientation of America's immigrant minorities.

*Will Herberg, *Protestant-Catholic-Jew* (New York, 1955). A dated theory by a theologian that religious diversity has supplanted ethnic diversity in a continuum of group evolution.

H. L. Mencken, *The American Language* (New York, 1919). A classic study of our language indicating its malleability as it accepts and adopts ethnic terminology.

*C. Wright Mills, *The Power Elite* (New York, 1956). A sociological view of American society that shows how homogenous our society is becoming through oligarchic control.

*Gunnar Myrdal, *An American Dilemma* (2 vols., New York, 1944). Classic study of America's treatment of its Blacks; a work that looks forward to the inclusion of this racial minority in the American Dream.

Robert E. Park, *Old World Traits Transplanted* (New York, 1922). Traces the difficult though inevitable course of immigrant assimilation. Compassionate, but expects an early end to cultural diversity.

*Michael P. Rogin, *The Intellectuals and McCarthy* (Cambridge, 1967). Case study that rejects the value of ethnic politics practiced by politicians, which, Rogin advises, uphold special interests atthe expense of the public good.

William Smith, *Americans in the Making* (New York, 1939). Like Park, Smith concentrates on marginality and sees ethnic persistence as a very transitory, though painful, phenomenon.

William I. Thomas and Florian Znaniecki, *The Polish Peasant in Europe and America* (5 vols., Boston, 1918-20). Sociological classic on the destructive social impact of the New World modern civilization upon a peasant people.

Warner and Leo Srole, *The Social Systems of American Ethnic Groups* (New Haven, 1945).

*Max Weber, "Ethnic Groups," in T. Parsons, ed., *Theories of Society* (2 vols. in one, New York 1969), pp 305-309.

*William White, *The Organization Man* (New York, 1956). Sociological work depicting American life in homogenous terms in a post-industrial context, implying that suburbanization has made for social (and ethnic) conformity.

*Israel Zangwill, *The Melting Pot* (New York, 1908). Famous play expressing the assimilationist ideal. Far from a masterpiece, but the enthusiasm of the hero for America & his distaste for the Old World are clear.

Cultural Pluralists

Peter and Brigitte Berger and Hansfried Kellner, *The Homeless Mind* (New York, 1973). While not deliberately advocating cultural pluralism, the authors imply the satisfactions that ethnicity offers people in modern society, including a greater sense of self and meaning.

*Randolph Bourne, "Trans-National America" in Van Wyck Brooks, *A History of A Literary Radical and Other Essays* (New York, 1956). A 1916 attack on conforming pressures in America and an endorsement of preserving ethnic diversity.

*Stokely Carmichael and Charles V. Hamilton, *Black Power: The Politics of Liberation in America* (New York, 1967). Fervent appeal to Blacks to use the political system to achieve ethnic autonomy.

John Collier, *Indians of the Americas* (New York, 1947). Liberal statement urging abandonment of the policy of trying to assimilate Native Americans but rather allowing them to maintain their tribal culture.

*Harold Cruse, *The Crisis of the Negro Intellectual* (Ann Arbor,1967). Penetrating study with the goal of allowing Blacks to handle their own affairs.

*Vine de Loria, *We Talk, You Listen: New Tribes, New Turf* (New York, 1970). Rallying cry for a new Indian militancy.

Horace Kallen, *Culture and Democracy in the United States* (New York, 1924). Defense of ethnic diversity using the term cultural pluralism. The author foresees no acculturation, rejecting all attempts of Americanization.

Harold Isaacs, *Idols of the Tribe* (New York, 1975). Most recent recognition of the value of ethnic persistence, in America as well as elsewhere. Focus is on the individual.

John Higham, *Send These to Me* (New York 1975). Collection of essays by a leading American historian; the most original section is an appeal for "pluralist integration" where group nuclei are strengthened rather than group boundaries.

*Michael Kammen, *People of Paradox* (New York, 1972). Stresses decentralized, fluid nature of our formative era, described by the term "unstable pluralism."

*James Madison, Federalist Essay No. 10 in *The Federalist Papers*. Not a specific support of cultural pluralism, yet Madison knew the tendency to form into factions to achieve political ends. The Constitution was to permit that development, but through compromise to achieve essentially democratic goals.

*Melville Herskovits, *Myth of the Negro Past* (New York, 1941). Indicates the vital importance of African survivals in American Black life.

*Patrick Moynihan and Nathan Glazer, *Beyond the Melting Pot* (New York, 1963). First major work to question a universally held notion among sociologists that ethnic feeling was vestigial among whites.

Richard Niehbur, *Social Sources of Denominationalism* (New York,1929). Classic investigation of American religion; shows cultural and social bases of our various religious groups.

*Robert Nisbet, *Twilight of Authority* (New York, 1974). Conservative's attack on nationalization of social and economic life, stresses value of local communities.

*Michael Novak, *The Rise of the Unmeltable Ethnics* (New York, 1971). Personal attack of a Slovak American on oppressive WASP establishments and a rallying cry for Southern and Eastern European Americans to mobilize politically in the 1970's.

*Joan Micklin Silver, *The Immigrant Experience* (FILM). Film study of a young Polish immigrant wanting to "succeed" as an American; a subtle satire on the American achievement myth.

*Alexis de Tocqueville, *Democracy in America*, section on "Voluntary Association." Tells of the need for voluntary associations to blunt the potentially anarchic and tyrannical tendencies of American individualism, as these bodies can defend the common good from unrestrained egotism.

Ethnicity and Psychology

*T. Adorno et al., *The Authoritarian Personality* (New York, 1950). Classic psychological exploration of the sources of prejudice. A major finding is that fears of other groups rest on insecurities about one's self.

*Erik Erikson, *Youth: Identity and Crisis* (New York, 1968). Well known psychological inquiry into youth, particularly the period of identity consciousness. Suggests that being aware of one's group tradition leads to the holistic personality.

*Suzanne Gordon, *Lonely in America* (New York, 1976). Recent, popular work reiterating Berger's theme of "homelessness" in the post-industrial age. For Gordon, a recent glorification of "singleness" is forced, masking an uncomfortable loneliness.

*Kurt Lewin, *Resolving Social Conflicts* (New York, 1948). Regrettably, a little known collection of essays by a perceptive psychologist concerned with intolerance and group identity. Best essay is on self-hatred felt by the Jewish minority and other white ethnics in America.

Morris Rosenberg and Roberta Simmons, *Black and White Self-Esteem: The Urban School Child* (Washington, D.C., 1971).

Ethnic Stereotypes (Use with Psychology and Ethnicity)

*John and Selma Appel, *The Distorted Image* (Anti-Defamation League, New York). 60 slides of cartoons about various ethnic groups published in journals between 1815-1922; a graphic survey of public opinion in visual form.

*Gordon Allport, *The Nature of Prejudice* (New York, 1954). Ch 12. Excellent introduction on origins and impact of stereotypes, by an important sociologist.

*Ray A. Billington, *The Protestant Crusade* (New York, 1938). Concentration (perhaps too heavy) on anti-Catholic hysteria of 1825-1855 in America. Valuable, but more descriptive than analytical.

George Frederickson, *The Black Image in the White Mind: The Debate on Afro-American Character and Destiny* (New York, 1971).

L. Perry Curtis, Jr., *Apes and Angels* (Washington, D.C., 1971). Valuable (and partially entertaining) review of the Irish in Victorian caricature.

*Oliver La Farge, "Myths that Hide the American Indian" in Roger L. Nichols and George R. Adams, eds., *The American Indian* (Waltham, 1971), pp. 1-15. Straightforward assault on the popular myth of the "typical Indian," stressing the very wide cultural differences between Native Americans.

*Winthrop Jordan, *White Over Black* (Chapel Hill, N.C., 1968). Outstanding investigation of sources of Anglo-American attitudes toward the Black African.

*Roy Harvey Pearce, *The Savage in America* (Baltimore, 1953). Similar to Jordan's work on Blacks, this superb study reviews early reactions of Englishmen to American natives during the 17th through early 19th centuries.

Robin Williams, *Strangers Next Door* (Englewood Cliffs, N.J., 1964). Author is interested in reducing intergroup (especially interracial) tensions, like Adorno's Authoritarian Personality. Surveys the images individuals of one group have about others in a particular American community. Survey somewhat dated.

Racist Theorizers

*George Fitzhugh, *Cannibals All* (Richmond, 1857). A justification of Black slavery by a Southerner.

*Madison Grant, *The Passing of the Great Race* (New York, 1916). Very popular work distinguishing ethnic rankings genetically, with Nordics being superior and darker skinned people most inferior.

William Ripley, *Races of Europe* (New York, 1899). Early attempt to formulate a genetic theory based upon geographical location.

*Edward A. Ross, *Old World in the New* (New York, 1914). A sociologist's fear that continued inundation of south and east Europeans will prove the death of American civilization.

*A. R. Jensen, "How Much Can We Boost I.Q. and Scholastic Achievement?" *Harvard Educational Review* 39 (1969), pp. 1-123. A much-discussed, recent suggestion that Blacks have genetically inferior achievement potential in education. (See also "Ethnic Stereotypes.")

Creativity and Ethnic Culture

*Daniel Aaron, "The Hyphenate Writer and American Letters," *Smith College Alumnae Quarterly* (July 1964), pp. 213-217. Brief but interesting typology on the evolving character of ethnic writing, emphasizing Blacks and Jews.

Jonas Balys, "Lithuanian Folk Music in the United States," *Folkways Records*. Faithful collection of group songs sung by the people themselves in their most intimate settings; includes explanatory text.

*H. D. Bossert, *Peasant Art in Europe* (New York, 1925). More visual than verbal, on the richness of folk art in dress and crafts.

Allan Eaton, *Immigrant Gifts to American Life* (New York, 1931). Early recognition of the artistry, both folk and fine, in various media.

Allan Guttman, *The Jewish Writer in America: Assimilation and the Crisis of Identity* (New York, 1971). Broader than the title suggests, explores the reciprocal relationship between pluralism and assimilation in American writing.

*Irving Howe, *World of Our Fathers* (New York, 1975). Popular and affectionate --and badly needed--analytical work on Yiddish culture of the Lower East Side; especially good on literature, with superb analysis of Jewish American humor.

Jean Lipman, *American Primitive Painting* (New York, 1942). Probably the first work focusing on excellence in plastic painting by untrained artists. Emphasis is on individual creativity rather than the artists' subcultures.

Bruno Nettl, *North American Indian Styles* (Austin, 1954). Concentrates on the quality of Native American music.

*James A. Porter, *Modern Negro Art* (New York, 1943). Valuable survey of both trained and amateur Black American artists, including Horace Pippin.

Christine Wilson, "Food Habits," *Journal of Nutritional Education.* Vol. 5 (January-March 1973). Excellent, recent bibliography on food and ethnic cuisine as part of culture.

=======================================

Syllabus #9

ETHNIC AMERICA

Otis P. Scott, California State University, Sacramento
Ethnic Studies 100, 1991

COMMENTARY

"Ethnic America" is designed to be an interdisciplinary excursion into the heart, soul and spirit of the ethnic group experience in the United States. And while I introduce students to several institutional, historical and other key factors shaping the experiences of selected European ethnic groups, the focus of course content is on the experiences of people of color—indigenous people and subsequent arrivals. My intent in this course is to bring students inside the social-historical and cultural experiences of people of color. The pedagogical approaches I use to accomplish this "drawing in" are several. In the main, I require students to read the words and thoughts of people of color. Most reading assignments are authored *by* people of color; students are seldom assigned works *about* people of color. I also use videos/films similarly. I want my students to experience the experience as related by ethnic group members themselves.

At the conclusion of this class, I want my students—all of them—to be different from the individuals who entered the class. I want students to confront themselves with the information provided. I want students to be dissatisfied, puzzled, and most of all, involved.--Otis Scott

---

COURSE DESCRIPTION: Through an interdisciplinary approach, this course will introduce students to the experiences of four American ethnic groups-- African American, Native American, Chicano (Mexican-American) and Asian American. The course will focus on themes common and distinct to all four groups and to American social, cultural, political and economic life. 3 units.

COURSE OBJECTIVES:

1. To develop a sophisticated understanding of American society and the roles non-European groups have played and play in shaping this society.

2. To develop an appreciation for interdisciplinary pursuits of knowledge.

3. To develop an understanding of the concept of ethnicity.

4. To develop a sophisticated understanding of the several factors, e.g., historical, institutional, cultural, economic, etc., which shape the social realities of major non-European groups in the United States.

5. To encourage you to become intellectually involved in problem solving.

6. To develop writing skills to a level where you can express your comprehension of the subject matter in a clear, intelligent and coherent fashion.

COURSE METHODOLOGY: I will use the lecture/discussion approach in this course. You will be expected to keep current with the reading assignments in order to participate in class discussions.

ATTENDANCE: I will take roll the first couple of weeks. After this I will know who is in class and who is absent. More than three unexcused absences may result in a one letter grade reduction at semester's end.

WRITING ASSIGNMENTS: This is an advanced study course. My expectation is that you demonstrate your mastery of course subject matter through writing. This is not a "how to write" course, but I will provide information as to strengthening your writing skills; I will make note of writing errors and consult with you concerning these.

You can expect five writing assignments. At least two of these will be in-class blue book essays. You can expect a minmum of two "take home" assignments. Normally, at the class meeting prior to the writing assignment, I will provide a list of study questions which should prepare you for the in-class assignment.

You can expect to participate in in-class writing exercises. Periodically I will ask you to write your reactions to, thoughts about, and understanding of, a topic, subject, or concept pertaining to the course subject matter. This writing will be collected, commented on and returned.

REQUIRED TEXTS:

Ethnic America: Reading and Sources (Scott)

From Different Shores (Takaki)

Bless Me Ultima (Anaya)

Ceremony (Silko)

America is in the Heart (Bulosan)

If He Hollers Let Him Go (Himes)

Course Syllabus

Sept. 4—Explanation of course. Distribution of syllabus.

> Begin reading Chapter II in *From Different Shores;* begin "Strangers in the Lands" (Takaki)

Sept. 6—Theoretical considerations. Concepts and models shaping the social reality of ethnic groups. The immigrant experience—strangers and others.

> Begin "Colonized and Immigrant Minorities" (Takaki). "Beyond the Stereotype: A New Look at the Immigrant Woman"

Sept. 11—Continue lecture/ discussion. *Begin Himes novel, complete by Sept. 27.*

Sept 13—WRITING ASSIGNMENT #1, BLUE BOOK.

Sept. 18—The African American Experience: An Overview.

> Read "First Impressions: Libidinous Blacks," "White Women, Black Woman," and "The Black Community in the 1980s" (Takaki), and Article #3 (Scott)

Sept 20/25—Factors and Issues shaping the social realities of African Americans.

Sept. 27—Contemporary Issues/Trends/Status.

Oct. 2—Discussion of *If He Hollers Let Him Go.*

Oct. 4—WRITING ASSIGNMENT #2, BLUE BOOK.

Oct. 9—The Chicano/Latino Experience. Factors and Issues Shaping the Chicano/ Latino Social Reality.

> Begin *Bless Me Ultima*, complete by Oct. 18. Read Article #4 (Scott) and "Americanization and the Mexican Immigrant," "Chicano Class Structure," and "Puertoriquenas in the U.S." (all three in Takaki)

Oct. 11 con't—Key Policy issues—immigration, bilingualism

Oct 16—Contemporary Issues/ Trends. WRITING ASSIGNMENT #3 TAKE HOME.

Oct. 18—Synthesis. Discussion of *Bless Me Ultima.*

Oct. 23—The Native American Experience.

> Begin *Ceremony*, complete by Nov. 8. Read Article #5 (Scott) and "Metaphysics of Civilization," "Identity and Culture," and "Wampum to Pictures" (Takaki)

Oct. 25—An Overview of "The First People."

Oct. 30—cont'd: Key Public Policy Issues.

Nov. 6—Sovereignty Issues.

Nov. 8—Contemporary Issues/ Trends. Discussion of *Ceremony.*
    WRITING ASSIGNMENT #4, TAKE HOME.

Nov. 13—The Experiences of Asian Americans.

    Begin *America is in the Heart,* complete by Nov 29. Read Articles 6-8 (Scott)
        and "Ethnic Enterprise" and "Slaying Dragons" (Takaki).

Nov. 15—Factors and Issues Shaping the Social Realities of Asian Americans.

Nov. 20—Key Public Policy/ Immigration Issues.

Nov. 22—THANKSGIVING BREAK.

Nov. 27—Contemporary Issues/Trends/Status

Nov. 29—Synthesis; Discussion of *America is in the Heart.*

Dec. 4—WRITING ASSIGNMENT #5, BLUE BOOK.

Dec. 6—"Ethnic America": Trends/ Directions. *Read Chapter VI in Takaki*

Dec. 11—Pluralism, Diversity, Multiculturalism: Whither the USA?

Dec. 13—Course Summary.

FINAL PAPER WILL BE ASSIGNED NOV. 6; DUE IN BY DEC. 2

=======================================

ETHNIC AND IMMIGRANT EXPERIENCE

Joanna S. Zangrando, Skidmore College
American Studies

The New Colossus

Here at our sea-washed, sunset gates shall stand

A mighty woman with a torch, whose flame

Is the imprisoned lightning and her name

Mother of Exiles. From her beacon-hand

Glows world-wide welcome;.cries she

With silent lips, "Give me your tired, your poor,

Your huddled masses yearning to breathe free,

The wretched refuse of your teeming shore.

Send these, the homeless, tempest-tost to me,

I lift my lamp beside the golden door."
　　　　　　　　　　　　—Emma Lazarus, 1883

The Unguarded Gates

Wide open and unguarded stand our gates,

And through them presses a wild, motley throng--

Men from the Volga and the Tartar steppes,

Featureless faces from the Hoang-Ho,

Malayan, Scythian, Teuton, Kelt and Slave,

Flying the Old World's poverty and scorn;

These, bringing with them unknown gods and rites,

Those, tiger passions, here to stretch their claws.

In Street and alley what strange tongues and these,

Accents of menace alien to our air,

Voices that once the Tower of Babel knew!

O Liberty, white Goddess! Is it well to leave the gates unguarded?
　　　　　　　　　　　　—Thomas Bailey Aldrich, 1892

This course focuses on the general immigration policy of the United States, as well as the experiences of specific immigrant, ethnic, and racial groups: Afro-American, German, Irish, Norwegian, Jewish and Italian.

We will examine the immigrant and ethnic experiences of several groups from a general background perspective and primarily from the mid-nineteenth through twentieth centuries. We will explore acculturation, assimilation, ethnic conflict and cultural survival by means of a variety of sources, including fiction, historical monographs, oral histories. Two threads of our exploration are immigration and responses to it by ethnic groups and by "native" Americans, and ethnicity as a manifestation of specific cultural survival and identity. Topics for readings and discussion include: who came to the United States, why and when; responses to immigrants over time; ethnic group creation of cultural survival mechanisms; ethnic group use of the institutions they found in the United States and institutions they crated for their communities; life within ethnic communities; tensions that have existed among ethnic groups and larger society, and within ethnic groups; and ways that tensions have heightened and diminished. Our concern, then, is with the larger society's reception to immigrants over time, and with specific ethnic groups' reception of the larger society—and attempts to maintain distinct cultural traditions and identity. There are many different segments and variations within individual groups; our collective examination is merely an introduction to the immigrant and ethnic experience in the United States.

COURSE REQUIREMENTS

Attendance at all class meetings, and completion of readings. Active participation in class discussions and projects. Library projects (magazine and journal research, census reports). Examinations: mid-semester and final (essay format) Response Papers: 3 typed papers.

REQUIRED READINGS: BOOKS

Diner, *Erin's Daughters in America*

Kessner, *The Golden Door: Italian and Jewish Immigrant Mobility in New York City 1880-1915*

Kingston, *The Woman Warrior*

Luebke, *Bonds of Loyalty: German Americans and WW I*

Rolvaag, *Giants in the Earth*

Steinberg, *The Ethnic Myth*

REQUIRED READINGS: ARTICLES

Namias, Selections from *First Generation* (Preface, pp. 68-78; 117-133; 139-153, 205-216).

King, "Letter from a Birmingham Jail."

Sample Syllabus:

Jan 20   Introduction: Ethnicity and Immigration.

Jan 22   *Eyes on the Prize* (film). Read: King, "Letter From a Birmingham Jail."

Jan 27   Myths and Realities. Read: Steinberg, *The Ethnic Myth*, chapter 8, pp. 201-221.

Jan 29   Library Assignment (hand in one page): Each of you select a journal of a professional nature (such as *American Historical Review, American Anthropologists, American Journal of Sociology*) or a magazine of popular nature (*North American Review, Harpers, Scientific American, Atlantic Monthly*).

Select one year's run in the a) 1880, b) 1890's and c) 1890-1910 periods and note for each of the three years selected the following: a) name of the journal, b) date c) author and full title of the article(s) in the year's issues you have selected that pertain to immigration, ethnic groups, questions concerning race. We will discuss your findings in class.

Discussion of findings in class: Contemporary immigration (newspaper handout.)

Feb 3   Beginnings: Opening the "Golden Door." Read: Steinberg, Ch. 1

Feb 5   Library Visit Census Reports, 1790—present; Immigration legislation.

Feb 10   An Assault on the "Brahmins": The Irish Influx.
Read: Diner, *Erin's Daughters*, pp. 1-80.

Feb 12   Irish Mobility? Read: Diner, pp. 80-119; 139-153

Feb 17   Jews and Italians in the City: Mobility Behind the Door?
Read: Kessner, The Golden Door, Fwd pp. 3-70
Storm of Strangers: Jewish-Americans (film)

Feb 19   Read: Kessner, pp. 71-103; 127-156
Storm of Strangers: Italian-Americans (film)

Feb 24   Education: The Road to Mobility? Read: Steinberg, chap. 3 and chap. 5

Feb 26 Unionization: the Road to Mobility? "The Inheritance" (Film)

Mar 3 Closing the Door: Immigration Restriction Begins
Read: Steinberg, Ch. 2

Mar 5 Survival Beyond the Golden Door: Midwestern Toilers
Read: Rolvaag, *Giants in the Earth*, Introduction and pp 3-224

Mar 10 Read Rolvaag, pp. 225-453

Mar 12 EXAMINATION

Mar 24 Immigrants & the Question of Loyalty: German-Americans and World
War I
Read: Luebke, *Bonds of Loyalty*, preface, pp 3-111; 115-151

Mar 26 Read: Luebke, pp. 199-331. RESPONSE PAPER IN CLASS

Mar 31 Reactions to Restriction
Read: Namias, *The First Generation*, Preface, pp. 68-78, 117-133, 139-153, 205-215

Apr 7 Immigrants and the Questions of Loyalty: "Japanese-Americans and WWII
Japanese Relocation" (brief film)
"Unfinished Business" (film)

Apr 9 Immigrant Survival in the West: The Chinese Experience
"Storm of Strangers: Chinese-Americans" (film)

Apr 14 A Chinese-American Woman's Account
Read: Kingston, *The Woman Warrior*, pp. 3-127

Apr 16 Read: Kingston, pp. 131-243. RESPONSE PAPER DUE

Apr 21 Contemporary Issues of Race, Ethnicity, Immigration in the United
States.

In Class Team Reports based on library research: newspapers, journals, census materials, legislation. This is an opportunity to select an issue or an ethnic group that we have not read about or discussed as a class. I will give some basic "guidelines" for this assignment. Reports continue until the end of the term.

===

IMMIGRATION AND ETHNICITY
IN AMERICAN LIFE

Betty Ann Burch, Ph.D., Metropolitan State University
St. Paul, Minnesota
Faculty-designed Independent Study

Metropolitan State University (MSU) in St. Paul, Minnesota, where this course was offered from 1977 to 1982, is a competence-based university for upper division and Master's degree students. Student average age is 34, and most students work and have families. MSU has a small full-time faculty and a much larger part-time Community Faculty, of whom I was one.

I originally designed the course for a class which would go on field trips together and then discuss the books and trips. When only 3 people enrolled the first year, I reorganized it as a Faculty-designed Independent Study which gave options so that students could fit it to their schedules and interests. I always had two or three students at any given time. They usually liked the course very much, and it had a completion rate of about 65 percent, a high rate for an independent study.

In the beginning, I specified all five books, but as book prices increased, I specified only three and let students choose the other two, which they could usually borrow from a library. In this way, they could read more about one ethnic group or whatever they were interested in.

It has always been a tenet of my teaching that education and life should not be compartmentalized. Immigration history is an ideal subject for integrating school and life. The students themselves initiated taking wives or husbands, mothers, children, sisters, in-laws, and friends with them on their field trips. As that helped integrate the course into the students' lives, I incorporated that into the syllabus. My study questions were designed to integrate the history of the students' families into the history of America. Thomas Bell's novel provided an excellent device for such integration. One of his characters, the daughter of immigrants, works as a "hired girl" in a middle class home. By asking the students if anyone in their family had been a hired girl, I connected them with the novel and with a phenomenon of immigrant life. Every student found a hired girl in his or her family background, even the Vietnamese student, an immigrant himself, whose mother had worked in a wealthy home in Saigon.

The flexibility of this independent study led students to new experiences, such as their first visit to an art museum, an interview of a Vietnamese restaurant manager about the philosophy of Vietnamese cooking, and revelations of family history they had never heard before. The course was rewarding for me, too. I enjoyed learning about what they were learning, their ingenuity in choosing field trips, and their enthusiasm about the books they read and the new experiences they had.— Betty Ann Burch, 11/91

IMMIGRATION AND ETHNICITY IN AMERICAN LIFE (as independent study)

Competence Statement

Student will know the general history of immigration to the U.S., theories of assimilation and acculturation, and the place of ethnicity in American life from historical and sociological perspectives well enough to use as background in observing contemporary political and societal events. (The "well enough to" section can be modified to reflect the student's needs in taking the course.)

Learning Strategies

Reading 5 books, making 5 field trips, keeping a journal.

Measurement Techniques

Evaluation of journal, one-hour final oral exam. The student will be able to define terms used in immigration history: Melting Pot, Anglo-conformism, structural pluralism, nativism, cultural pluralism, new ethnicity, "old immigrants," "new immigrants," push factor, pull factor, and to list the major waves of immigration in the Colonial period and the 18th, 19th, and 20th centuries.

Required Reading

Maxine Seller, *To Seek America: A History of Ethnic Life in the U.S.* Jerome S. Ozer, Publisher, paperback, 1977. History.

Edith Blicksilver, *The Ethnic American Woman: Problems, Protests, Lifestyle,* Kendall/Hunt Publ., paper, 1978. Biographical essays, short stories, poems.

Thomas Bell, *Out of This Furnace,* University of Pittsburgh Press paperback, 1976 (originally published by Little-Brown , 1941). Fiction.

One (more or less) classic book in the field of immigration history and one other suitable book. See reading list.

REQUIRED JOURNAL

A written record of reactions to readings, field trips, current events pertaining to immigration and ethnicity, and thoughtful responses to suggestions and questions below. Date each entry and keep the journal current. State clearly what you read or did and then give your reactions, thoughts, conclusions. Write in your best style in complete sentences. Be clear, be thoughtful.

On the first page of your journal, record the dates of the major waves of immigration as you read Seller. This list will serve as a framework for your understanding of the history of immigration. Who came when? Why? Who are called "old immigrants"? Who are called "new immigrants?"

In your journal, narrate your family's immigration history and point out if it does or does not fit in with the general pattern of their ethnic group's immigration history. For example, did your Irish ancestors come in 1847 when the great wave of Irish immigration occurred — or in 1927 or 1977? You might include what you feel has been important in your family's life in America. Discuss why and how they came, what problems they faced here, how your family feels about the Melting Pot idea and about the new ethnicity, what they have accomplished here, what disappointments they may have had.

You may write about either side of your family or both sides but only as much as you can readily find out. Perhaps you can interview your parents, grandparents, or aunts and uncles. The purpose here is not to produce a full - blown genealogy; it is to take the study of immigration history out of the realm of the textbook into your life. If you know an immigrant, interview that person about the immigration experience. Why did she leave home, what drew her to America (rather than some other county), what drew her to Minnesota, to her present neighborhood? What were the push and pull factors working on that person? That is, what conditions or events in the home country pushed that person out? What conditions, events, or people pulled that person to America? Minnesota? her present neighborhood?

In 1964, sociologist Milton M. Gordon proposed his theory of structural pluralism, arguing that each ethnic and racial group in the.U.S. has its own social structures or institutions (churches, schools, banks, bars, bakeries, funeral homes, insurance companies, etc.) often clustered in one neighborhood or section of a city and its own class structure (upper--middle--lower class). Examine your own neighborhood or neighborhood where you work with Gordon's theory in mind. (This can be one of your field trips--see below.)

Before starting Blicksilver's book, look at Appendices A and B, which give
alternate ways of reading the works. Look over topics on pages 360-67 for
possible journal entries. Did Blicksilver's book provide information or insights
that Seller's did not?

What were the generational differences among the characters in Bell's novel? You
can comment on the first, second, and third generations' attitudes toward
America, work, labor unions, sex, or any other attitude that strikes you. What
was the effect of Mary's working as a "hired girl" in a middle class home? Do
you know any women who were hired girls or who took in roomers or
boarders? Ask around among your women relatives; you may be surprised.
Do you know any women like Dorta? What does Bell have to say about
Anglo-conformism?

Record in your journal news stories you see in papers or magazines about
immigration or ethnicity or an individual ethnic group, neighborhood, person,
or event. If the stories are long, you need not summarize them. Instead, attach
them to your journal. Analyze these news stories or articles for push and pull
factors and underline what you find. Analyze them also for what they say
about the Melting Pot and underline this term. Respond to these articles in
your journal. Putting in a clipping lets me know you're alert, but I want
analysis and commentary!

THINK ABOUT THESE QUESTIONS AS YOU OBSERVE AND READ:

Record your thoughts and conclusions in your journal. What is the Melting Pot
theory? Has the Melting Pot worked? What is Anglo-conformism? What is
nativism? (See Seller, Chapter 5) What is cultural pluralism or new ethnicity?
(See Seller, Chapter 13) What is an ethnic group? Try defining the term
before you read the books and then define it again after you read them. What
are the components of an ethnic viewpoint?

How has religious ethnicity shaped American cities physically? Observe our city
skylines — spires, steeples, domes, single-bar and double-bar crosses.

What part do ethnic groups play in city and state politics? Should they play more?
less? What parts do ethnic groups play in American foreign policy? Could
they play more? For example, the federal Commission on Foreign Language
and International Studies reported in 1979 that the pool of bilingual persons in
the U.S. is a valuable resource and should be encouraged by funding of ethnic
language schools & teaching of many more languages in schools & colleges.

How is ethnicity and the recent influx of new ethnic groups shaping American life?
attitudes? public and private relationships?

Field Trips

Visit any five of the following and write about them in your journal. Family members of friends may accompany you, and you may include their reactions and comments in your journal.

Immigration History Research Center, University of Minnesota, 826 Berry St., St. Paul (near Highway 280 and University Ave.S.E. Phone the Curator at 627-4208 to arrange a tour of the Center and its archives of materials on 24 Eastern and Southern European and Middle Eastern ethnic groups.

American Swedish Institute, 2600 Park Ave.S., Minneapolis, 871-4907. Open to the public some days and Sunday afternoons. Check the Arts & Entertainment sections of Sunday papers, The Twin Cities Reader, and other sources for exhibits, films, classes, and other events.

Ethnic neighborhood — Examine your own neighborhood. Observe the names of stores, bars, bakeries, churches, pastors (in the phone book), restaurants, funeral homes, owners of banks and savings & loans, clubs, meeting places. See what ethnic groups are represented and which, if any, group predominates. I f you live in a fairly new suburb, you may not find one predominant ethnic group. If not, make a trip to an older, ethnic neighborhood in Minneapolis, St. Paul, or wherever convenient.

Ethnic restaurant — Eat an ethnic meal; observe the decor, the waiters, cooks, or other staff; listen to the music. Notice if this restaurant is part of an ethnic neighborhood. (For example, Emily's Lebanese Deli on University Ave. N.E. in Minneapolis is within a block of St. Maron's Lebanese Catholic church.) Observe the clientele of the restaurant. What is ethnic about this restaurant? What atmosphere or ambiance did you feel? What did you learn about the people who prepare and eat this food?

Ethnic church — Attend a service at an ethnic church, especially one different from your own. Observe the decoration and style of architecture inside and out. Ascertain when the congregation was founded. Was it during the time when that ethnic group was arriving in the U.S. in great numbers? shortly after? or a generation after? See if there are foreign language materials in use or for sale — newspapers, hymnals, bulletins, pamphlets, prayer books. If there is a parish cemetery, see what names predominate. How many ethnic groups are represented? Which came first?

Or visit several ethnic churches and study the styles of architecture and decor.

Dance troupes — local or visiting. What kinds of dances did they do? What was the music like? What did you learn about that ethnic group's attitudes towards courtship, marriage, old age, war, or other life events from their dances or music? (For example, a courtship dance in one Eastern European country is very fast and very long. At one time, it served to eliminate from consideration those who dropped out quickly due to tuberculosis, which was prevalent in that area then.)

Art and craft exhibits — look in the Sunday papers or other sources for listings of exhibits of foreign paintings, sculptures, or decorative objects, the work of one foreign artist or foreign art movement, or for ethnic and folk art exhibits at the Minneapolis Institute of Arts, Walker Art Center, Minnesota Museum of Art, Minnesota Historical Society, or other public or private museum/gallery. What do these works of arts or crafts say about the people who made them? What materials did they use? What events or people were portrayed? What feelings were projected to you? (The exhibit "Where Two Worlds Meet; the Great Lakes Fur Trade" at the Historical Society is excellent. It shows how European and Native American cultures shaped each other in the settlement era.)

Films and television—check listings of foreign films; attend films about your own ethnic groups or others. The U Film Society shows films from many countries. Check listings of KTCA-TV for programs on public issues, etc.

Other at your choice or opportunity: Ask your friends to tell you of events — an independence day celebration, a dance, a banquet, bazaar, wedding, religious service of particular interest, whatever — that will help you know that friend's ethnic background better. Most people are pleased at someone's interest.

SEND ME YOUR JOURNAL WHEN YOU ARE HALFWAY THROUGH THE COURSE — that is, when you have read THREE books and made TWO field trips or read FOUR books and made ONE field trip. I will read and comment on your journal and return it to you. When you have completed all of the work, send me the rest of the journal. I will read it and arrange the final oral examination.

RE-READ THIS COURSE OUTLINE AS YOU GO THROUGH THE COURSE. EVERYTHING IN IT IS HERE FOR A REASON

Syllabi #12A & B:

THE WHITE ETHNIC IN AMERICA and

AMERICAN ETHNIC CULTURES

John Ibson, California State University, Fullerton

>   *ED. NOTE: To John Ibson, ethnicity does not mean people of color. Below are two syllabi for two courses he has taught in a Department of American Studies. Both courses use the history and experience of "micks, kikes, wops" and others to explore the "framework of beliefs, expressive symbols, and values in terms of which individuals define their world." — BC.*

=============================

SYLLABUS 12A: THE WHITE ETHNIC IN AMERICA

American Studies 411
Spring 1989

>   *"Are we living the dream our grandparents dreamed when on creaking decks they stood silent, afraid, hopeful at the sight of the Statue of Liberty? Will we ever find that secret relief, that door, that hidden entrance? Did our grandparents choose for us, and our posterity, what they should have chosen?"* —Michael Novak, *The Rise of the*
>   *Unmeltable Ethnics,* 1972

>   *"It wasn't what my parents or relatives said so much as the way they said it that I seemed to remember. Not so much what they did but how they did it. I guess I know believe that the Irish — if I can generalize from those I knew — eat, drink, love, fear, sing, and get angry in a very special way. I suppose people of other backgrounds do to. But what I know, what is part of me, inescapable, is this that I call the Irish way. It feeds my vision and conjures for me dreams I would not have had without this Irish heritage. I feel it in my bones and know very little about it in my head."* —Irish-American writer Philip F. O'Connor, 1975

Required Reading: Books:

>   John Bodnar, *The Transplanted: A History of Immigrants in Urban America.*
>   Eugene O'Neill, *Long Day's Journey into Night.*
>   Mary Gordon, *Final Payments.*

Alfred Kazin. *A Walker in the City.*

Philip Roth, *Goodbye, Columbus.*

Helen Barolini, editor, *The Dream Book: An Anthology of Writings by Italian-American Women.*

Required Reading: Articles

John Ibson, "Virgin Land or Virgin Mary: Studying the Ethnicity of White Americans"

Irving Howe, "The Limits of Ethnicity"

Mary Gordon, "'I Can't Stand Your Books': A Writer Goes Home"

Course Requirements:

This course will examine the past and present experience of American white ethnic groups. It's commonly assumed that ethnic differences among white Americans are rapidly disappearing and may, in fact, already be largely gone. We will consider the degree to which that's true looking at the nature and extent of "Americanization" among whites. While the white ethnic experience in general will be covered the Irish and the Jews will receive special attention as examples for close analysis.

As befits a course in American Studies, this is at the heart an examination of culture: in Clifford Geertz's words, "the framework of beliefs, expressive symbols, and values in terms of which individuals define their world, express their feelings, and make their judgments." We will, of course, observe what groups have *done*, but we will be most interested in getting at what it has *meant* and means today to be, for example, Danish or Polish, Irish or Italian. After studying the amount of ethnic distinctiveness among whites that American society has experienced in the past and exhibits today, we'll consider how much distinctiveness is likely to exist — and how much ought to be encouraged — in the future.

Although I'll lecture from time to time, I expect you to be active participants in the class. All of the reading assigned in the course will be discussed in the classroom, and our discussions will form a very important portion of the course. It's essential that you attend regularly and do the reading as it's assigned on the Course Outline. As you'll note on the Outline, we will devote more than one meeting to certain pieces of reading; I'll keep you posted well in advance regarding how much of a book should be read for a particular session.

There will be two essay midterms at the times indicated on the Outline. They will both be take-home exams, due back within one week after they are assigned.

There will be a comprehensive take-home final, also essay, to be passed out during the last week of classes and due back during Final Exam Week.

The final will consitute 40% of your course grade, the other two exams 30% each. If you choose, the second midterm may be an optional exam. If you do not take it, the final will count 60% and the one midterm 40%. I will pay close attention to the quality and extent of your participation in our discussions; excellent participation may raise your course grade as much as one full letter.

Course Outline

M 1/30 Introduction to the Course: Review of Basic Concepts in American Studies

I. The White Experience: A Dream Come Too True?

A. Understanding White Ethnicity: Theory, History, and Current Meaning

M 2/6 1. Theoretical Approaches and Issues (lecture)

W 2/8 2. Historical Review of the White Ethnic Experience (lecture)

M 2/13 READ: Ibson, "Virgin Land or Virgin Mary?"

W 2/15 3. The Meaning of White Ethnicity in Contemporary America: The Problem of Holding on or Breaking Away.

    READ: Howe, "The Limits of Ethnicity"

B. Becoming American: The Complex Legacy of the Americanization Process

W 2/22 1. *Kikes, Micks, and Wops*: Slide Presentation and Discussion of Ethnic Stereotypes

W 3/1 2. *Beneath the Melting Pot*: The Cultural Ordeal of Americanization — Discussion of

M 3/6 3. John Bodnar's *The Transplanted*

W 3/8 READ: Bodnar, *The Transplanted*. First Essay Assigned, due in one week

II. Divided Loyalties, Divided People: Catholic Irish in Protestant America

M 3/13 A. *Will the World Break your Heart?* Dimensions and Consequences of Irish-American Assimilation (lecture)

M 3/27 B. *Irish-America's Most Distinguished Cultural Document*: A Discussion of Eugene O'Neill's *Long Day's Journey into Night*

W 3/29 READ: O'Neill, *Long Day's Journey into Night*

M 4/3 C. *Accommodating: The American Irish Today*

W 4/5   READ: Gordon, *Final Payments* and "'I Can't Stand Your Books'"
Second essay (Optional) Assigned, due in one week

III. American Jews: Exiles Still?

M 4/10 A. *Outsiders*: The Jew in Western Society and Culture (lecture)

W 4/12 B. *Another Promised Land?* The Cultural Situation of American Jews
(lecture)

M 4/1   C. *Growing Up . . . and Out*: The Ghetto and Beyond

W 4/19 READ: Kazin, *A Walker in the City*

M 4/24 D. *The Suburbanization of Ethnicity*: American Jews Away from the
Ethnic Neighborhood

W 4/26 READ: Roth, *Goodbye, Columbus*

M 5/1   E. *Is Nothing Sacred, Is Nothing Left?* The Present and Future State of
Jewishness in America

READ: Roth, "Defender of the Faith," in th same volume with *Goodbye,
Columbus*, pp. 115-143 and Roth, "Eli, the Fanatic," pp. 179-216

IV. Is the Story Drawing to a Close? The Future of White Ethnicity

M 5/8   *Assimilation, Pluralism, or Pluralistic Integration?* The Distinctive
Awakening of Italian-American Women

M 5/15 READ: Barolini, *The Dream Book*

FINAL EXAMS DUE ON FRIDAY, MAY 26

SYLLABUS #12B: AMERICAN ETHNIC CULTURES

American Studies 502 :Graduate Colloquium, 1982

> *"I want to tell you something about myself that will help to explain a lot of things about me. You might as well hear it now. First of all, I am a Mick." — James Malloy in John O'Hara's* Butterfield 8

REQUIRED READING: BOOKS

Maxine H. Kingston, *Woman Warrior: Memoirs of a Girlhood Among Ghosts*

Tom McHale, *Farragan's Retreat*

Barbara Myerhoff, *Number Days: A Triumph of Continuity and Culture among Jewish Old People in An Urban Ghetto*

Michael Novak, *The Rise of Unmeltable Ethnics*

Stephen Steinberg, *The Ethnic Myth: Race, Ethnicity and Class in America*

Virgina Yans-McLaughlin, *Family & Community: Italian Immigrants in Buffalo, 1880-1930*

REQUIRED READING: ARTICLES

John Ibson, "Virgin Land or Virgin Mary? Studying the Ethnicity of White Americans"

Stephen Whitfield, "Laughter in the Dark: Notes on American-Jewish Humor"

Mark Zborowski, "Cultural Components in Response to Pain"

COURSE REQUIREMENTS

Class sessions will be devoted to our intensive discussions of the assigned readings and your research projects. As befits a seminar, there will be no lectures or instructor's monologues. Needless to say, it is essential that you attend regularly, do the reading as assigned, and ponder it carefully before coming to class. The reading assignments are all specified on the Course Outline.

One half of your grade in this course will be based on your participation in our discussions of the readings. If you do not want to be evaluated on oral participation, please see me to arrange additional writing assignments.

The remainder of your grade will be based on a research paper of at least 20 pages which is in some fashion related to the seminar's general topic. Your paper may be the result of your own work in primary sources or it may be an interpretive essay which surveys and analyzes the work of other scholars.

No later than the fourth week of class, you must give me a brief written description of your project, accompanied by an annotated bibliography of the sources you plan to employ. The final three class meetings will be devoted to presentation and discussions of your work; if necessary, we'll meet for an additional two hours during the Final Examination Week to discuss these projects.

Before and after you give me the description of your project, please see me outside of class as frequently as necessary to discuss your research. It is most important that you select a topic which not only intrigues you but is limited enough in scope that you're able to retain a semblance of sanity this semester and to learn and say some significant things. If you are currently working on an M.A. thesis, you should select a project which complements this work in some way, if only by using sources akin to the ones used in your thesis.

COURSE OUTLINE

Week One: Introduction to the Course

Week Two: Cultural Dimensions of Ethnicity
    READ: Ibson, "Virgin Land or Virgin Mary?"; Whitfield, "Laughter in the Dark"; Zborowski, "Cultural Components..."

Week Three: Ethnicity as a Souvenir: The Assimilation Argument
    READ: Steinberg, *The Ethnic Myth* ·

Week Four: New Bottles, but the Same Old Wine? The Notion of Cultural Persistence
    READ: Novak, *The Rise of the Unmeltable Ethnics*

Week Five: Ethnicity from a Developmental Perspective: Using the Historical Record
    READ: Yans-McLaughlin, *Family and Community*

Week Six: Capturing Ethnicity: Ethnography and Ethnic Studies
    READ: Myerhoff, *Number our Days*

Week Seven: Individual as Cultural Representative: Using the Ethnic Autobiography as a Cultural Document
    READ: Kingston, *Woman Warrior*

Week Eight: Fiction as a Window on Fact: Using the Ethnic Novel as a Cultural Document

Week Nine: Presentation and Discussion of Research Projects.
This schedule continues until end of semester.

Syllabus #13

THE AESTHETICS OF MINORITY LITERATURES

Team-taught by Olivia Castellano and Chauncey Ridley,
California State University, Sacramento, 1990.

A three-unit graduate course in the Department of English.

BASIS AND OVERVIEW

Although works by minority writers are being included in traditional American literature courses, the essential explanation of culture which forms the bases for understanding are often not covered. Many English department graduates will be teaching a multi-ethnic student population and most likely multicultural literature. Student responses often convey a sense of awe after exposure to this kind of literature when given a way to understand its larger socio-political context. The politics of minority literature is integral to the course, as everything that is presented came about as a result of political awareness. For instance, Afro-centric literature must be understood by its roots and cannot be judged by the same standards one would use for Euro-centric based works. In the first section, Henry Louis Gates's *Signifying Monkey*, which presents literary theory based on an Afro-centric foundation rather than a Euro-centric one, is used as a beginning to understanding the different critical approaches in the black tradition, each black writer signifying or reacting to previous black writers in his or her writing. Embracing Gates's view means a radical move for the instructor; the great challenge is to teach the Afro-centric view of criticism side by side with the Euro-centric.

The next area of study begins with the critical theories of Juan Bruce-Novoa, Chicano writer and critic who writes of the chaos that results when a people's culture is not recognized by the larger society — a way of saying Chicano culture has no validity and no importance, threatening cultural extinction. Premises are that the human spirit can only live in space which is secure, safe and self-affirming, and that it is through the arts that the roots of a culture are reaffirmed and rediscovered and a space for that culture is made in society through new literature and the creation of new myths. Novoa's essays then deal with the need to create sacred space that is one's own, a necessity in order to make sense of the chaos of living in two worlds, one of which is hostile. Team teaching was chosen as a means to bring together separate experiences of teaching Chicano and Afro-American fiction and poetry.

Required Reading Summarized:

THE SIGNIFYING MONKEY: A THEORY OF AFRO-AMERICAN LITERARY
CRITICISM, by Henry Louis Gates, Jr. 1988.

NATIVE SON, a novel by Richard Wright. 1940.

THEIR EYES WERE WATCHING GOD, a novel by Zora Neale Hurston. 1937.

THE COLOR PURPLE, a novel by Alice Walker. 1982.

THE MAN WHO CRIED I AM, a novel by John A. Williams. 1967.

THE IDENTIFICATION AND ANALYSIS OF CHICANO LITERATURE, ed. Francisco
Jiminez. Bilingual Press. 1972.

BLESS ME ULTIMA, a novel by Rudolfo A. Anaya. First published by Tonatiuh
International, U.C. Berkeley. 1972.

POCHO, a novel by Jose Antonio Villarreal. First publ. by Doubleday in 1959.

TRINI, a novel by Estela Portillo Trambley. Bilingual Press. 1986.

THE ROAD TO TAMAZUNCHALE, a novel in magical realism by Ron Arias. West
Coast Poetry Review. 1975.

COURSE SYLLABUS:

*NOTE: The three major sections of the course are: Afro-American literature
and literary criticism: weeks 1-7; Chicano literature and literary criticism:
weeks 8-13; student presentations: weeks 14-15; final exam. Presentations are
based on research on a topic selected from the reading lists. Students interested
in Asian American or Native American literatures are encouraged to pursue
research in these areas. Issues related to the "politics of minority literatures" are
also examined such as (1) the dynamics by which a minority literature emerges
and seeks validation in a dominant culture; (2) the need to create a space for
minority literatures in the accepted canon; (3) the historical circumstances that
have led to belated recognition of Chicano and Black writers and their
exclusion from the canon; and, in effect, (4) how a canon evolves.*

I. Afro-American Literature and Literary Criticism

Examination of Afro-American literary criticism includes the critical debate over
the polarity of the Eurocentric tradition of expression and Afrocentric oral
traditions, focusing on the question of literary privileging in these two radically
different traditions. Focus is on the vernacular research and critical insights which
Henry Louis Gates offers in *The Signifying Monkey*, guiding students through the
book and discussing the novels. The evident relationships between Wright's

Native Son, Williams' *The Man Who Cried I Am,* and Walker's *The Color Purple* illustrate the "signifying" relationships argued by Gates's criticism (discussion of the novels is therefore important, but less detailed than discussion of Gates).

Week 1: Introductions and assignments. Introduction to the class.
Background on Chicano and Afro-American literature and literary criticism.
Information on projects and suggested reading lists.
Student introductions--background, goals, reasons for taking class, etc.
Assignments: READ: (1) to p. 88 of *The Signifying Monkey* and (2) handouts by James Weldon Johnson and Richard Wright.

Week 2: Class discussion. Explain assigned reading.
Assignment: Gates pp. 89-127; Wright's *Native Son*; students prepare for detailed discussion of the Introduction ("How Bigger Was Born").

Week 3: Class discussion: Gates chap. 3 and Wright's "hidden signifying"; complete novel. *Assignment:* Gates pp 128-169; begin Hurston's *Their Eyes Were Watching God,* to be completed by week 5.

Week 4: Class discussion: Gates chap. 4; continue with Wright. Brief update on research projects. *Assignment:* Gates pp. 170-216; complete Hurston.

Week 5: Class discussion: Gates chapter 5; Hurston's "speakerly text."
Assignment: Gates chapter 7; Walker's *The Color Purple.*

Week 6: Class discussion: Walker's revision of Hurston.
Assignment: Williams, "The Man Who Cried I Am."

Week 7: Class discussion: Williams' revision of Wright. Update on research projects. *Assignment:* readings for next section.

II. Chicano Literature and Literary Criticism

This is a comprehensive overview of current trends in Chicano literary criticism. Emphasis is on four works: two novels, *Bless Me Ultima* and *Pocho;* a newer Chicana voice; and the best example of South American magical realism. The underlying theme proposed for all four is what Yale critic Juan Bruce-Novoa has called the "Chicanos' response to chaos"; for Novoa, to be Chicano is to live in that space between "Mexican" and "American," refusing to be swallowed up by either, standing in the center of chaotic space and creating order despite threat of perpetual disintegration. As Novoa said (in his masterful study, "Chicano Poetry: A Response to Chaos," 1982), "Chicano literature has been reacting to a threat of Chaos, of the culture disappearing into something other than itself." With faith the culture can survive, Chicano writers also recognize the threats. How their protagonists respond are lessons in heroics the class will learn as they gather in the ritual of reading to celebrate these "ordered existences." (How does one find salvation and self worth, or order one's space and life, when forced to act according to rules that do not arise from one's own form of life? How does Antonio Marez synthesize experience so chaos makes sense? How does Richard Rubio reject aspects of his father's Mexican culture while refusing to become "assimilated" like his friends? How does Trini adapt U.S. life to her memories of and allegiances to her beloved Mexico?)

Week 8: Discussion of reading: (1) Novoa's "Introduction" essays from "Chicano Poetry: A Response to Chaos" and "Chicano Authors: Inquiry by Interview." (2) Articles from *Identification and Analysis:* Leal, "The Problem of Identifying Chicano Literature," Parr, "Current Trends in Chicano Literary Criticism," Sommers, "Critical Approaches to Chicano Lit." (3) *Bless Me Ultima.*

Week 9: Discussion of *Ultima.* Begin reading *Pocho* and articles on Villareal and Anaya. *Assignment:* Read Tatum, "Contemporary Chicano Prose Fiction: Its Ties to Mexican Literature" and "Chronicle of Misery" from *Identification and Analysis.* Read Grajeda, "The Novelist Against Himself."

Week 10: Discussion of *Pocho.* Begin *Trini. Assignment:* Read articles on Chicanas in Chicano literature, and Salinas, "The Role of Women in Chicano Literature" from *Identification and Analysis.* UPDATE on research projects.

Week 11: Discussion of *Trini. Assignment:* Begin to read *Road to Tamazunchale.* Read Dwyer's analysis of Arias's novel in *Identification and Analysis.*

Week 12: Finish discussion of *Road to Tamazunchale.* Close discussions of African American and Chicano texts. Begin student presentations.

Weeks 13, 14 and 15: Student presentations and class discussions. Final exam.

===================================

APPENDIX: *Suggested Readings on Chicano Literature and Criticism*

DARKNESS UNDER THE TREES, poetry by Omar Salinas. Published by Chicano Studies Library/ UC Berkeley, CA.

EMPLUMADA, poetry by Lorna Dee Cervantes. Published by University of Pittsburgh Press; also available through Bilingual Review Press.

TORTUGA, novel by Rudolfo Anaya. Published by Editorial Justa/ Berkeley, CA.

SILENCE OF THE LLANO, stories by Rudolfo Anaya. Tonatiuh International, Inc.

RAIN OF SCORPIONS, short stories by Estela Portillo Trambley. Tonatiuh International, Inc.

NAMBE YEAR ONE by Orlando Romero. Tonatiuh International, Inc.

DAY OF THE SWALLOWS, play by Estela Portillo Trambley. Included in the anthology, CONTEMPORARY CHICANO THEATRE, ed. Roberto Garza.

CLEMENTE CHACON, novel by Jose A. Villarreal.

THE MOTHS AND OTHER STORIES, short stories by Maria Helena Viramontes.

RAINBOW'S END, novel by Genario Gonzales.

DELIA'S SONG, novel by Lucha Corpi.

II. Recommended Bibliographies

CHICANO LITERATURE: A REFERENCE GUIDE, annotated bibliography with essays ed. by Julio A. Martinez & Francisco A. Lomeli, 1985. Published by Greenwood Press/ 88 Post Rd West/ Westport, CN, 06881. Note: Contains an excellent analysis of BLESS ME ULTIMA.

BIBLIOGRAPHY OF CRITICISM OF CONTEMPORARY CHICANO LITERATURE, 1980, 1982. Compiled by Ernestina N. Eger. Published by Chicano Studies Library, UC Berkeley, CA. (Publication Series No. 5).

LITERATURA CHICANA: CREATIVE AND CRITICAL WRITINGS THROUGH 1984. Compiled by Robert G. Trumillo and Andress Rodriguez., 1985. Order from: Floricanto Press/ 604 William Street/ Oakland, CA.94612.

CHICANO PERSPECTIVES IN LITERATURE: A CRITICAL AND ANNOTATED BIBLIOGRAPHY. Compiled by Francisco A. Lomeli & Donaldo W. Urioste, 1976. Pajarito Publications, 2633 Granite NW, Albuquerque, NM, 97104.

Note: Books can be purchased & catalogs requested from these most active Chicano publishers:

Arte Publica Press University Park, Univ. of Houston, TX 77004. Phone orders: (713) 749-4768

Bilingual Review Press publishers: Gary D. Kerrer and Karen Van Hooft. Hispanic Research Center, Arizona State University, Tempe, Arizona, 85287.

III. Recommended anthologies

THE GRITO DEL SOL COLLECTION: AN ANTHOLOGY. Ed. Octavio Romano, 1984. Tonatiuh International.

EL ESPEJO (THE MIRROR): AN ANTHOLOGY OF CHICANO LITERATURE. Edited by Octavio Romano, 1969. Eds. Romano and Herminio Rios, 1972. May be out of print; check with Tonatiuh International.

IV. Recommended anthologies of Chicano literary criticism

MODERN CHICANO WRITERS: A COLLECTION OF CRITICAL ESSAYS. Eds. Joseph Sommers and Tomas Ubarra-Frausto, 1979. Prentice-Hall.

CONTEMPORARY CHICANO FICTION: A CRITICAL SURVEY. Ed. Vernon E. Lattin, 1986. Published by Bilingual Review Press.

THE IDENTIFICATION AND ANALYSIS OF CHICANO LITERATURE. Ed. Francisco Jimenez, 1979. Published by Bilingual Review Press.

BEYOND STEREOTYPES: THE CRITICAL ANALYSIS OF CHICANO LITERATURE. Ed. Maria Herrera-Sobeck, 1985. Published by Bilingual Review Press.

LATIN AMERICAN LITERARY REVIEW: SPECIAL ISSUE OF CHICANO LITERATURE, Vol. V, Spring-Summer 1977, #10. LALR, Carnegie-Mellon University, Pittsburgh,. PA.

V. Literary Studies by Individual Critics

CHICANO POETRY: A RESPONSE TO CHAOS by Juan Bruce-Novoa, 1982. Published by Ustin: University of Texas Press.

CONTEMPORARY CHICANA POETRY: A CRITICAL APPROACH TO AN EMERGING LITERATURE by Marta Ester Sanchez, 1985. Berkeley: University of California Press.

VI. Recommended Journals and Periodicals

THIRD WOMAN. Ed. Norma Alarcon. Published by Third Woman Press,Chicano-Riqueno Studies, Indiana University, Bloomington, IN 47405.

IMAGINE: INTERNATIONAL CHICANO POETRY JOURNAL. Ed. Tino Villanueva. Published by Imagine Publishers, 645 Beacon Street, Suite 7, Boston, MA 02215.

THE AMERICAS REVIEW. Ed. Julian Olivares. Published by Nicolas Kanellos. Arte Publico Press, University of Houston, Houston, Texas.

VII. Other recommended works

THREE AMERICAN LITERATURES: ESSAYS IN CHICANO, NATIVE AMERICAN, AND ASIAN-AMERICAN LITERATURE FOR TEACHERS OF AMERICAN LITERATURE. Ed. Houston A. Baker, 1982. N.Y. MLA.

SPEAKING FOR OURSELVES: AMERICAN ETHNIC WRITING by Lillian Faderman and Barbara Bradshaw, 1969. Published by Scott Foresman.

THREE PERSPECTIVES ON ETHNICITY: BLACKS, CHICANOS, AND NATIVE AMERICANS by Carlos E. Cortes, 1976. Published by Putnam.

THE THIRD WOMAN: MINORITY WOMEN WRITERS OF THE UNITED STATES by Dexter Fisher, 1980. Published by Houghton Mifflin.

CHICANO CINEMA, RESEARCH, REVIEWS, AND RESOURCES. Ed. Gary D.Keller, 1985. Published by Bilingual Review Press.

THE CHICANO: FROM CARICATURE TO SELF-PORTRAIT by Edward Simmen.

===

Syllabus #14

ETHNIC ORIGINS OF FANTASY
AN EXPERIMENTAL GRADUATE SEMINAR

Jesper Rosenmeier and Andrew Gouse
Tufts University, 1988
American Studies 101/ Cross-listed as English 192H

CATALOG DESCRIPTION

Explores the questions raised by the immigration to America of so many ethnic and culturally diverse groups. Conducted in a small group format. Students are expected to actively participate in the lively discussion. Readings and films highlight the issues around immigration and assimilation into American culture. *Prerequisite:* Students must be interviewed by both Professor Rosenmeier and Dr. Gouse prior to acceptance. Enrollment is strictly limited to ten participants.

HISTORY OF THE COURSE

Professor Rosenmeier: In 1975, in response to the growing interest in ethnicity (including my own exploration of my Danish roots), I began to teach a course in immigrant literature. It was a traditional literature course. Every year, we would come to a point where some emotionally charged issues would emerge, issues that had to deal with the students' racial, ethnic, religious and gender differences. The issues were emotionally charged precisely because issues of race, ethnicity, and gender are at the very heart of our American identities. Feeling unable to deal with the issues, and not knowing what to do, I backed off. But I did so with a sense of frustration, for these "hot" feelings were clearly an important part of what the students brought to the readings and class discussions. So I decided to seek consultants who could help create a safe environment. The first consultant did not work out well. I next asked Andrew Gouse to participate in the course.

By creating an open-minded and accepting context, we found that understanding and acceptance of differences — racial, ethnic, gender, class — and the promotion of closeness could be achieved, a closeness not usually seen in academic classrooms, even though the University subscribes to ideals of ethnic and racial harmony. So when the first course was over in 1980, we decided to co-teach it again, and to make the format the center of the educational experience. Making the format central empowers students to appropriate — internalize and reformulate — the readings, films, and class encounters in personal ways that lead to a kind of learning that is very alive and — to us, the teachers — deeply moving.

PHILOSOPHY OF THE COURSE

Professor Rosenmeier [continued]: I need to preface my remarks on the philosophy of the course by saying that the course has always been advertised as experimental in nature, which is to say that we have constantly been open to suggestions and revision. . . . Through the past seven years, the following philosophical approach has emerged: Into new interpersonal contacts we bring with us certain cultural attitudes, biases, even prejudices that are based, to some extent, upon our experiences within the framework of our ethnic identity. One of the most powerful ways to learn about the impact of our ethnic heritage on how we related to others is to do the relating in the "here and now" — the spontaneous face-to-face sharing of experiences and the immediate expression of feelings and reactions to each other.

To learn about the process of immigration — the process of transformation of an ethnic heritage in a new land — what better way to learn than to experience it firsthand? And so, our course seeks to imitate the immigration experience by inviting into the "new land" of our group ten very different people, each from her/his own special "old land," who wish to accept the challenge of trying to immigrate into our "new neighborhood" — our classroom.

Milan Kundera in his novel *The Unbearable Lightness of Being* says about moving to another country: "Being in a foreign country means walking a tightrope high above the ground without the net afforded a person by the country where he has his family, colleagues, and friends, and where he can easily say what he has to say in a language he has known from childhood." We seek to replicate this precarious feeling of being suspended high above ground as it serves as the motivating force to find a *new* common language. We hope that the temporarily unsettling situation will stimulate the evolution of a group process. The group process has as its goals to answer certain key questions: How are we going to live in this neighborhood? Are we going to share of ourselves? Are we going to construct the walls of our own personal ghettoes? Will we chance self-revelation in order to establish new relationships? How do we find a common language to answer these questions?

Yet another risk becomes how to understand the choices we make. Why share or open up? Why not choose the perceived security of a silent retreat? How can our choices teach us about who we are? In this way we hope to reflect on our choices to better understand from where our response and choices spring. What emerges in the process of addressing these tasks is a greater understanding of how ethnic, familial, and cultural ideas, values, and myths influence and shape Human Nature.

And so the word "Fantasy" in our course title has a more encompassing meaning than implied in, say, a fairy tale. We mean it to take on the sense of how our individual heritage shapes how we perceive and react to our environment; and it highlights how we all bring our own personal fantasies from our former neighborhoods into our present experiences of art, of learning, and of relationships. "Fantasy," then, refers to the way we fantasize about other people and about their ethnic identities.

The decision to use a small group format originally rose, quite logically, because of the opportunity it afforded all the students to express openly their reactions to the ethnic and emotional issues raised in their readings and in the interactions among group members. Also we the group co-leaders feel that ten is a manageable number from the point of view of being able to keep track of each student's intellectual and emotional state during our meeting. Although there may be similarities with the general structure and operation of a psychotherapy group, this course by no means pretend to be group psychotherapy, nor is it advertised as such. Students who enroll are not doing so because of emotional problems. The fact that the course may have a therapeutic or healing effect comes more generally from its source of education and enlightenment, much in the way that any educational experience can be therapeutic.

The Role of the Teachers

As co-leaders we have debated about our definition and our roles — whether to be distant, aloof authorities who comment and observe or to be self-divulging participants who share our own personal fantasies and experiences. We have settled on a compromise.

We definitely see ourselves in the role of authorities who have designed, planned, and shaped this course. We choose the students; we assign the texts; and we grade the work. We also want to facilitate the discussion and remind students of the goals. In this context we assume more of a role of observing the interactions among class members and trying to tune in to the underlying "feeling states" of the session. The co-leaders sit across from each other to be able to view the facial and postural expressions of all the students while keeping in touch with each other's reaction to the class. We introduce ourselves as Dr. Gouse and Professor Rosenmeier and thereby establish ourselves as apart from the student-participants. We accept the fact that this may engender the usual range of emotions about authorities — which we welcome as part of the process of immigration and self-discovery.

On the other hand, we are not averse to discussing briefly our own ethnic identities and to frankly mentioning our reactions or feelings to the general atmosphere of a class session if we feel it would aid in furthering the process of the group. For example, if the class has come upon an obvious disagreement about an approach to a racial question and then suddenly grows silent, one or both of the co-leaders might share that he feels some tension in the air and that it's awfully uncomfortable. We might then ask if other people are feeling that way. We wish to emphasize that we see as our role to foster discussion of personal experiences and feelings in the service of promoting greater mutual acceptance and understanding.

With this in mind, the co-leaders feel it is our responsibility to meet frequently to discuss our reactions to the sessions and our interaction as co-leaders. In this way we hope to identify what the main theme of a given class was and to anticipate what to expect in coming sessions. We also try to be aware of problematic issues such as the tendency for the class to scapegoat one class member or an individual's inclination to monopolize class discussions. Upon returning to class, we will have formulated a plan to approach these issues, with the central aim of trying to understand what is transpiring. Although a tentative formulation may be in place, we still allow for an open-ended process.

FORMAT OF THE COURSE

Typically there is a great demand for the course. . . . Students interested in enrolling must arrange for a thirty-minute interview with each of the co-leaders. We select students based on the following criteria:

1. The student's interest in the topic of ethnicity and in his personal ethnic identity as demonstrated by work in the field and/or by enthusiasm for the course.

2. The student's ability to understand the need for commitment to the course.

3. The student's willingness to participate actively in a discussion group.

4. Lastly, we are interested in having an ethnically diverse group and we make an effort to compose the class accordingly, but we are most interested in students who demonstrate interest, commitment, and interpersonal relatedness.

The class meets twice a week for 75 minutes each time. We sit in a circle. Although there are assigned readings or films, there is no specific agenda for discussion. The discussion is open-ended — a source of some anxiety, like being precariously perched on the tightrope. But this is also a source of motivation for opening up.

THE SYLLABUS: WORKS AND ASSIGNMENTS

The syllabus has evolved over the past eight years to include a combination of novels, short stories, plays, and films. One year we even assigned Dvorak's *Symphony from the New World.*

The books and films often have as the main theme the individual's growth and development in immigrant and ethnic environments. *Studs Lonigan, A Long Day's Journey into Night, The Assistant, The Taylor Shop, I Know Why the Caged Bird Sings,* and *The Chickencoop Chinaman* are among the literary works. This year we have several films, three of which are documentaries and two others popular movies, *My Life as a Dog* and *Bread and Chocolate.* The selection varies with the composition of the class. We try to choose something to represent every ethnic group represented in the class, even if an individual has only a fraction of a particular ethnic heritage.

The students are asked to keep a journal of their reactions to the experiences related to the course. The entries can be reactions to the readings, to the discussion in class, to another classmate, or to a personal event in their lives that is evoked by the course material. The journals are graded based on the student's involvement in her/his writing. . . . (We have struggled with the concept of journal keeping, much as we have struggled with the philosophical foundations of the course as a whole. . . .) The journals are periodically collected and read by the co-leaders, who frequently make written comments to help the students resolve questions with which they are struggling or make suggestions that they share their thoughts with the group.

We have also added a requirement of a one-page ungraded reaction paper following each book or film, to insure that works on the syllabus are read by all group members at the same time in the semester.

Finally, students are requested to do a final project. This can be anything the student wishes to try, but we do express a preference for something written as that is what we feel best qualified to evaluate with a grade. In addition to receiving some very creative short stories, poems, and personal ethnic histories, we have gone on an ethnic tour of Boston and have participated in a "non-verbal" happening. What has been striking is the abandonment of the customary research paper in preference for highly creative, spontaneous individual and group efforts. . . .

CLOSING COMMENTS BY THE CO-LEADERS

Dr. Gouse: In the first years of doing the course together, Jesper and I divided the work into literature interpretations and group process interpretations. Jesper would provide some of the background for the texts and would help the group appreciate the works from an artistic, more traditionally literary point of view. Meanwhile, I would make comments about the group's "feeling states" and group interactions.

Thankfully, we discontinued this division of labor. But what especially enabled us to put this division aside was our increasing abilities in both spheres. Jesper felt more adept and secure in mankind group process interpretations and I felt more at home with literary analysis. In this way the experience of doing the course has been a wonderful enlightenment for both of us. . . .

Please rest assured that there is a lot of uncertainly in this kind of work — and that Jesper and I often feel lost and uncertain of what to say, which is one of the reasons our frequent after-class discussions are so important to us.

Professor Rosenmeier: From what we have said about the relationship between the group process and the students' appreciation of the texts, it will be clear that this is a different kind of literature course. The syllabus mirrors not the historical development of ethnic literature, but the stages of the individual's emotional and intellectual growth. Consequently, our primary aim is not to engage the students in traditional close analysis, though we certainly do not exclude it, but to a different kind of close reading: to invite them to read their own lives as well as the lives of their classmates, of people in their familial present and ancestral past, and of the characters they encounter in texts — to read all these lives as closely and deeply as they can with their feelings and minds. The astonishing — and to us, unexpected — result is that when they engage in this endeavor, they become story tellers, sharing their lives in the here and now, and in the telling, they come to accept that each of us sees her/himself as the center of the world — that we all see ourselves as centers of worlds.

AMERICAN LITERATURE, 1865-PRESENT

Sherry Sullivan, University of Alabama at Birmingham
Department of English, Fall 1980

> *ED. NOTE: This is the "Before" syllabus for Sherry Sullivan's "Before-and-After" Comparison. It is reproduced exactly as it appeared in 1980. Compare to 15B, which follows, and see her essay, "Transforming the American Literature Survey Course," Essay #6 in Part II. —BC*

COURSE DESCRIPTION

In this course we will cover the broad expanse of American literature from, roughly, the last quarter of the 19th century to the present day. It is a survey course, meaning that we will examine the work of a fairly large number of writers to see the value of each on its own merits and its place in modern American literature as a whole. The course will require, therefore, a lot of reading outside of class. You are expected to read each assignment carefully and be prepared to discuss it in class. Classroom participation can make a difference in your grade. Likewise, regular class attendance is strongly recommended, since exams and even paper topics will emerge directly or indirectly from what is covered in class.

EXAMS

There will be three examinations, each a combination of identification and short essay questions. I will give make-ups only in cases when there are compelling reasons for an absence and I have been notified by the student before the exam.

ESSAYS

Two essays are required: each must have an introduction with a clearly stated thesis, a body of paragraphs containing well developed ideas and evidence supporting the thesis, and a conclusion. I will discuss essay writing skills in class. Suggestions for topics will be made well in advance of the essay due date; late papers will be penalized. (Remember that submitting as your own any portion of another's work, without giving proper credit, constitutes plagiarism. Plagiarism not only results in an "F" for the essays, but can also lead to an "F" for the course.)

TEXT

The Norton Anthology of American Literature, vol. 2, 1st ed.

SYLLABUS

Tu 9/17: Introduction

Late Nineteenth Century: The Rise of Realism

Th 9/19: Harte, "The Outcasts of Poker Flat"; and Bierce, "Occurrence at Owl Creek Bridge"

Tu /24: Mark Twain, "The Literary Crimes of Fenimore Cooper"; and W. D. Howells, "Novel Writing and Novel Reading"

Th /26: Twain, *The Adventures of Huckleberry Finn*

Tu /01: *Huck Finn*, cont.

Th /03: *Huck Finn*, cont. Guide to Writing Essays

Tu /08: Edith Wharton, "The Bunner Sisters." First Essay Due

Th /10: Henry James, "The Beast in the Jungle"

Tu /15: First Exam

Between the Wars

Th /17: Ernest Hemingway, "The Big Two-Hearted River"

Tu /22: T. S. Eliot, "Love Song of J. Alfred Prufrock"; and F. Scott Fitzgerald, "Rich Boy"

Th /24: e. e. cummings, selected poems; and Hart Crane, "To Brooklyn Bridge"

Tu /29: Robert Frost, selected poems

Th /31: William Faulkner, "The Old Man"

Tu 11/05: Second Exam

Contemporary Period: New American Voices

Th /07: Ralph Ellison, from *The Invisible Man*

Tu /12: Saul Bellow, *Seize the Day*

Th /14: Flannery O'Conner, "A Good Man Is Hard to Find" and "Good Country People"

Tu /19: Michael Harper, Sherley Williams, Philip Levine (departmental visitors), poems

Th /21: Harper, Williams selected poems, cont.

Tu /26: Second Essay Due; Review Session

======================

SYLLABUS #15B: GENDER, RACE, AND CLASS IN AMERICAN LITERATURE

Sherry Sullivan, University of Alabama at Birmingham
EH 224-24, Spring, 1990

> *ED. NOTE; Below is the "After" syllabus for Sullivan's "Before-and-After" Comparison as it appeared in 1990, ten years later, under a new name, with a list of her "Ground Rules for Discussion" and a commentary appended. — BC*

COURSE DESCRIPTION

This course will focus on the many and varied voices in American literature, spoken and written and sung. In order to accommodate as many voices as possible in a coherent way, we will emphasize in the early half of the course those from the last third of the 19th century through the first third of the 20th, with forays into contemporary times in the final class periods. You will be encouraged to relate readings from this class to your own ethnic background and cultural heritage and gender experience. You are also encouraged to share your personal experience with the class, to actively pursue information from the experience of others, and when others share, to listen (see "Ground Rules for Discussion").

ESSAYS

The first essay, a genealogical history/ personal narrative of you or a member of your family, is optional. The second essay, a more formal literary analysis, is required. The first should be two-three pages; the second, three to four. Each must be typed, double-spaced, with proper margins. Neither essay is a research paper. The second, formal essay should have an introduction, which includes a thesis, and be well developed with supporting ideas and evidence. I will discuss writing skills in class and you are encouraged to consult me or work with a tutor in the Writing Skills Center if you need help.

EXAMS

There will be two examinations, a midterm and a final. I will give make-ups only in cases where there are compelling reasons for the absence and I have been notified in advance. In fairness to others, the make-up will be more difficult than the original exam.

GRADES

Optional first essay=10%, second essay 30% (20% if first essay is included), midterm exam 25%, final exam 35%, and class participation 10%.

TEXTS

The Heath Anthology of American Literature, vol. 2

Zora Neale Hurston, *Their Eyes Were Watching God*

SYLLABUS *(Based on 2-hour class meetings)*

Th 3/22: Introduction

Tu /27: Rebecca Harding Davis, *Life in the Iron-Mills*

Th /29: Louisa May Alcott, from *Work*; Elizabeth Stuart Phelps, from *The Story of Avis*; Julia A.J. Foote, from *A Brand Plucked from the Fire*; and Pauline Elizabeth Hopkins, from *Contending Forces*

Tu 4/03: Sarah Orne Jewett, "A White Heron" and "The Foreigner"; Mary E. Wilkens Freeman, "The Revolt of Mother"

Th /05: African-American Folktales (all)

Tu /10: Hamlin Garland, "Up the Coulee"; and Mary Austin, from *Earth Horizon*

First Essay: Geneological Narrative

Th /12: Theodore Dreiser, "Typhoon"; Corridos

Tu /17: Henry James, "The Beast in the Jungle." Exam Questions

Th /19: Exam Brainstorm Session

Tu /24: Midterm Examination

Th /26: W. E. B. Du Bois, from *The Souls of Black Folk*; Afro-American spirituals

Tu 5/01: Zora Neale Hurston, *Their Eyes Were Watching God*

Th /03: Richard Wright, "The Man Who Was Almost a Man" and video

Tu /08: Alexander Lawrence Posey (all); John Milton Okison, "The Problem of Old Harjo"; Standing Bear, "What I Am Going to Tell You Here"; Ghost Dance Songs; Charles Alexander Eastman, from "From the Deep Woods to Civilization"; Gertrude Bonnin, from *The School Days of an Indian Girl*; Leslie Silko, "Lullabye" (selections to be announced)

Tu /15: Edith Maud Eaton (Sui-Sin Far), "Leaves" and from *Mrs. Spring Fragrance* and Maxine Hong Kingston, from *The Woman Warrior*. Outline due

Th /17: John Okada, from *No-No Boy*; Grace Paley, "The Loudest Voice"; Martin Luther King, "I Have a Dream"

Tu /22: Saul Bellow, "Looking for Mr. Green." Second Essay Due. Exam Questions

Th /24: Exam Brainstorming Session.   Th /31: Final Exam, 2-5

GROUND RULES FOR DISCUSSION

1. Acknowledge that oppression (i.e. racism, classism, sexism, heterosexism, etc.) exists.

2. Acknowledge that one of the mechanisms of oppression is that we are all systematically taught misinformation about our own groups and about those we view as "others."

3. Agree not to blame ourselves or others for the misinformation we have learned in the past, but accept responsibility for not repeating misinformation after we have learned otherwise.

4. Agree not to blame victims for their oppression.

5. Assume that people (both the groups we study and the members of the class) always do the best they can.

6. Actively pursue information about our own groups and those of others.

7. Share information about our groups with other members of the class and never demean, devalue, or in any way "put down" people for their experiences.

8. Agree to actively combat the myths and stereotypes about our own groups and other groups so that we can break down the walls which prohibit group cooperation and group gain.

9. Create a safe atmosphere for open discussion. If members of the class wish to make comments that they do not want repeated outside the classroom, they can so request and the class will agree not to repeat the remarks.

10. When others talk, listen.

   (Adapted from "All Our Ways of Being: Taking on the Challenge of Diversity in the College Classroom," by Lynn Weber Canon, Director, Center for Women and Research, Memphis State University)

COMMENTARY: First Day Assignment--Telling Our Own Stories

In setting up a multicultural course in a tradition-minded University, the first class meeting is critical. This is especially the case when the course appears from without to be conventional, or when most students are taking the course in order to satisfy an undergraduate degree requirement. When I teach "Gender, Race, and Class in American Literature," which is listed in the University Class Schedule as a survey of "American Literature, 1865-Present," I am anxious to have students not only see but experience at the outset what the course is all about. Then they can decide, as I explain in class, whether they wish to fully commit to or drop the course (making this choice explicit, I think, significantly contributes to the success of the class). In addition to the kinds of works listed in the syllabus, the kinds of demands made of students in this course are non-traditional. Students are expected to draw upon and openly share their own class, race, and gender identities and cultures. They are expected to engage emotionally as well as intellectually with course materials and with one another in class discussions and activities.

In introducing the course, I first go over the syllabus, pointing out the diverse groups there represented, my own expertise (and limitations) in the material, and the course emphasis on issues of gender, race, and class. I note that each of us has a cultural heritage, particular ethnic, gender, and class identities, and personal experiences which will at one point or another bear on the material we read. We must be willing to share these in class and listen to others whose views and experiences are different from our own. I go over the "Ground Rules for Discussion." I then give students 5-10 minutes to prepare an informal oral statement on their class, race, or ethnic identity and what about it they are most proud. I do this as well, and report first (the interracial nature of my own extended family helps introduce—and somewhat defuse, I think—themes of conflicting cultural identities and crossing boundaries that will emerge later.)

The statements students make often reflect these themes in wonderfully unpredictable ways: the young Korean woman, for example, whose marriage to an Anglo-American caused her mother to "cry for three years"; the student from Iceland whose parents debate which of their Icelandic ancestries (both extending to the middle ages) is older; the two women (one hispanic, one Irish-American) whose fathers completely reject their ethnic heritages; the black woman whose parents only recently revealed to her the intermarriage of a grandmother; the student who is adopted and wonders just what comprises his identity; the black and white southern students whose families are enormously proud of their "Indian blood."

This exercise has many benefits, not the least of which is doing away with the usual first-day-of-class ritual of the teacher holding forth to an audience of passive students. Students are involved emotionally, intellectually, and experientially (it's hard to be passive and detached about your own life). Some clearly feel empowered by the very act of identifying their personal experience as expertise. All are obliged to observe, listen to, and implicitly to respect the diversity among themselves. (This diversity is often a silent part of traditional classroom dynamics, and quite invisible where a class appears homogeneous and mainly "white," as in the case cited above.) At the same time, by sharing their personal backgrounds, students begin to respond to the class itself as a kind of community which successfully encompasses sameness and difference, dialogue and disagreements.

This exercise, then, functions to model classroom procedure for the course as a whole. In a modest way it begins the process of deconstructing traditional hierarchies among students and between students and teacher, and thus reinforces the egalitarian and democratic impulse which also shapes the content of the course.

--Sherry Sullivan.

EARLY AMERICAN LITERATURE and
AMERICAN WOMEN WRITERS

Linda Palmer, California State University, Sacramento
Department of English, Fall 1990

COMMENTARY:

Thoughts on Adding Multicultural Literature to American Lit Courses

The most effective method of introducing multicultural literature to students is to share with them our own enthusiasm; inevitably, it is catching, and students become engaged because they know we are interested in the materials and because they appreciate being included in the experiment of reading new literature with new eyes. The students are generally unfamiliar with multicultural literature, and they find it more difficult than literature from the dominant Anglo-American culture. Therefore, it is helpful to encourage the students to ask questions, to allow them to respond personally as well as intellectually to the literature, and to respect their attempts to move into unfamiliar territory.

Teaching multicultural literature, I find that having students keep a journal or reading log is very productive. In journal assignments, I ask students to respond to the writing personally, to think about whether or not cultural differences (between their experience and Native American traditions, for instance) are causing reading comprehension or appreciation problems, to think about how the multicultural literature carries on a dialogue with the more traditional and canonized literature, or to interpret imagery that I think will be unfamiliar and challenging. I keep them writing about this literature steadily, believing that they learn through informal writing. I also rely more heavily on small group discussion than I do in most literature classes, when dealing with specific aspects of multicultural literature.

In our discussions, we often focus on the interesting dialogue that emerges between the canonized and the non-traditional literature we read. When students read Frederick Douglass' slave narrative alongside Emerson's "Self Reliance," or Chief Seattle's reflections on the Native American's relation to the land alongside Thoreau's *Walden*, their comprehension of one piece of literature is inevitably and richly altered by their reading of the other works. Their study of *Huckleberry Finn* is enriched by reading the slave narratives, particularly in terms of their understanding of the runaway slave Jim's plight.

I ask students questions in class that encourage them to see these connections between the literatures. When Franklin and de Crevecoeur paint pictures of the ideal American, I want students to see Douglass' narrative as an answer to that ideal picture, or at least as something that causes us to rethink what the other writers said. For instance, I asked them to evaluate in writing the images of Native Americans in the film "Dances With Wolves" as compared to limages in iterature by early Anglo writers and in traditional Native American tales. The students rightly compared the film's images of Native Americans favorably to some they had read in early American Anglo literature, but they argued too that the film had not fully captured the complex people they had come to understand while reading Zuni oral poetry or Chippewa traditional tales.

When students see literature in dialogue, of course, they become to some extent "resisting readers," raising questions about traditional American literature and its cultural assumptions. As a result, helping students recognize that there is a political issue involved in introducing multicultural literature into the syllabus seems only fair. We talk about this in class, and the students write about it in their later journal entries. I don't believe art can be neatly separated from politics. Keeping the old canon unchanged is as political as changing it; change, however, is more visible than stasis, and that can be threatening to those resting comfortably in the traditional. After reading criticism published nationally of "politically correct" teaching, however, the students in my classes wrote unanimously in support of a curriculum that broadens their thinking and reading experience and that opens their minds to the rich varieties of American literature.   --Linda Palmer, 3/91.

=====

Syllabus 16B: EARLY AMERICAN LITERATURE

English 150A, Fall, 1990

COURSE DESCRIPTION

We will begin the course with a discussion of the ways in which our earliest literature reflected and contributed to the development of a sense of identity for a new country. We will then conduct a careful analysis of some of that literature, from the beginnings to 1840. In this study, we will include the Puritans and other early settlers, Native American tales, slave narratives, and literature that expressed the optimism and hope of a foundling nation. The course places a particular focus on close critical readings of the multicultural and multiethnic voices of early American literature as well as on the more traditionally canonized works.

Texts:
>   (1) Supplemental text (available at Kinkos, 4765 J Street)
>   (2) HEATH ANTHOLOGY OF AMERICAN LITERATURE, volume 1

Course Format: This is an upper division course fulfilling a requirement for English majors. Therefore, I will expect full discussion and participation from class members. This is not a lecture course; I expect you to explore your ideas, analyze the literature thoroughly, and ask pertinent questions.

Special Notes about this Class: I would not ordinarily select an anthology for an upper division course; this is not a survey course, and we will examine these writers in considerably more depth than we would in an introductory course. However, I had three reasons for selecting the HEATH ANTHOLOGY: Many of the writers we will study are not available except in anthologies; the nature of early American literature encourages an inclusive rather than an exclusive study, a point I will explain in class; and this new anthology complements my desire to encourage your study of some of the richly varied voices that contributed to the formation of our nation's literature.

REGARDING THE SELECTIONS

English 150A covers the early years of American literature, before the great Romantics and Transcendentalists (who are studied in 150B). The writers in this course, then, reflect that emphasis. I have, however, occasionally ventured outside that time-frame either to provide us with a clear literary and cultural context for the writers we are studying (thus Emerson's "Self-Reliance," for instance) or to provide us with a sense of the ways in which our earliest literature has influenced modern writers (a short story by contemporary Native American writer Louise Erdrich, for instance). Finally, the slave narratives were published just after the dates generally covered in 150A, but because they make an important contribution to early American literature and as they were written about experiences these writers had during the period, I have included them here.

COURSE REQUIREMENTS

I expect you to read all of the work critically, closely, and by the due date noted on your syllabus. I also expect you to take part regularly in class discussion. In addition, you will have the following course requirements: 1. A mid-term. 2. A formal paper, approximately 5-6 pp. 3. A final exam (may be a take-home exam). 4. Regular in-class writing. 5. Occasional workshop discussions. 6. Regular journal entries. 7. A brief, formal presentation in class, based on your paper topic.

JOURNAL: Because I am convinced that writing about the literature you study will help you understand it better, focus your thinking, and clarify your questions, I will ask you to keep a reader-response journal. I will assign specific study questions and questions for exploration, but you are also free to make additional entries. I will collect the journal every 2-3 weeks. I will not grade the journal, just as I will not grade your frequent in-class writing-- unless, of course, you don't do the assigned work.

THE PAPER: I will assign topics well in advance. In this upper division course, I encourage you to consider designing your own topic; should you want to do so, please see me for help and approval. The paper will be approximately 5-6 pages long, typed, double spaced, with ample margins for my comments. The paper should have a clear and challenging thesis, stay clearly focused on your thesis, be thorough in its analysis, and provocative in its thinking.

TENTATIVE SYLLABUS

Sept. 5: Introduction to course

Sept. 7: Introduction to early American literature

An Errand into the Wilderness: Literature of Promise and Promotion

Sept. 10, 12: The Literature of European Settlement: JOHN WINTHROP

Sept. 14: WILLIAM BRADFORD

Sept. 17: JOHN SMITH. DANIEL DENTON

My Heart Rose Up: Voices in Conflict

Sept. 19, 21, 24, 26: ANNE BRADSTREET, "The Prologue," "The Author to Her Book," "The Flesh and the Spirit," "Before the Birth of One of Her Children," "To My Dear and Loving Husband," "A Letter to Her Husband," "In Reference to Her Children," "In Memory of My Dear Grandchild," "Here Follows Some Verses," "In Honour of That High and Mighty Princess . . ."

Sept. 28, Oct. 1, Oct. 3: JONATHAN EDWARDS: "Resolutions," "A Faithful Narrative of the Surprising Works of God," "Personal Narrative," "Sinners in the Hands of an Angry God"

Oct. 5: Midterm

"A Lively Resemblance of Hell": Captivity and Westward Movement

Oct. 8: 10: MARY ROWLANDSON

Oct. 12, 15: Captivity Narratives

Oct. 17: Diaries of the Westward Movement

"What is an American?": Creating the Dream

Oct. 19, 22, 24: BENJAMIN FRANKLIN: "Poor Richard's Almanac, "The Way to Wealth," "Information to Those Who Would Remove to America," *Autobiography*

Oct. 26, 29: HECTOR ST. JOHN DE CREVECOEUR

Oct. 31, Nov 2: PHYLLIS WHEATLEY

Nov. 5: The Frontier Humorist -- Crockett, Longstreet, Harris

Nov. 7: RALPH WALDO EMERSON, Self-Reliance

"What is an American?": Native American Voices

Nov. 9: Native American Traditions--CHIEF SEATTLE

Nov. 12: Native American Tales: Winnebago and Pima

Nov. 14: Native American Oral Poetry: "Sayatasha's Night Chant"

Nov. 16: "Oshkikwe's Baby," Chippewa "American Horse," Louise Erdrich

"What is an American?": Literature of Protest

Nov. 19: SARAH GRIMKE. MARGARET FULLER--from "Women in the 19th Century." Anonymous poem, "Verses Written by a Young Lady..."

Nov. 21: THOMAS NELSON PAGE: "Marse Chan"; FREDERICK DOUGLASS "What to the Slave...?"

Nov. 26: *PAPER DUE.* BENJAMIN FRANKLIN, "On the Slave Trade"; ANGELINA GRIMKE, "Appeal to the Christian Women of the South"

"What to the Slave?": Slave Narratives

Nov. 28, 30, Dec 3: FREDERICK DOUGLASS: *Narrative of the Life of Frederick Douglass, American Slave*

Dec. 5, 7: HARIETT JACOBS: *Incidents in the Life of a Slave Girl*

Dec. 10: JACOBS cont., and ZORA NEALE HURSTON, "Sweat"

"I Have a Dream": Literature of the Persistent Dream

Dec. 12: THOMAS PAINE from *Common Sense.* THOMAS JEFFERSON, "Declaration of Independence." ABRAHAM LINCOLN, "Gettysburg Address." MARTIN LUTHER KING, JR. "I Have a Dream"

Dec. 14: Course conclusion.

SYLLABUS 16B: AMERICAN WOMEN WRITERS

Linda Palmer, Department of English
English 250, Fall 1990

COURSE DESCRIPTION

We will begin the course with a discussion of feminist criticism, emphasizing its assumptions, concerns, and contributions and determining how the feminist perspective influences our serious reading of literature. With the points we have made in mind, we will then give close scrutiny to several American women writers. Our study will include a variety of writers: We will study Native American tales and contemporary writers who have used them as a source of creative inspiration (Erdrich, Silko); diaries of the westward movement, allowing us to discuss women's response to the landscape and its symbolic use; major writers, many of whom you know (Dickinson, Welty); writers long ignored (Hurston); writers at the peak of their careers (Morrison); and writers just building their reputations (Tan).

Texts: Supplemental text (at Kinkos, 4765 J Street)
  May Sarton, HOUSE BY THE SEA
  Zora Neale Hurston, THEIR EYES WERE WATCHING GOD
  Toni Morrison, BELOVED
  Eudora Welty, DELTA WEDDING
  Amy Tan, THE JOY LUCK CLUB
  Marilynne Robinson, HOUSEKEEPING

Course Format: This is a discussion seminar. Your ideas and literary analysis will be center stage at all times, and I expect each of you to be consistently and diligently prepared for that role. You should each plan on making regular contributions to the class discussion, and on the writers about whom you are writing. All of the discussion and analysis should be addressed by your independent readings in criticism.

COURSE REQUIREMENTS

I have designed this course with stringent requirements. I will expect you to read closely and analytically, to do outside reading, to discuss your ideas clearly (and frequently), and to write well in clearly-focused, well-developed and thought-provoking prose.

Two Papers: These papers will be approximately seven pages long. Though I will give you general suggestions, you are to design your own topic and submit it to me in writing for approval. While the papers should be interpretive (i.e., your own thinking), they must include reference to at least one outside source. One paper will be on a writer or topic assigned the second week of the course or sooner. The other can be on any of the writers/topics we cover in class, as long as you do not write two papers on the same writer. Your assigned paper will have a specific due date; your free paper will have a due date determined by the topic you choose. *Note bene:* I will not accept late papers. Your failure to turn your paper in on time will seriously disrupt the progress of the entire class, not to mention your grade.

Presentation: For the writer on whom you are doing an "assigned paper" (as opposed to your "free choice paper"), you will be responsible for (a) summarizing your findings for the class and (b) asking the class to address two or three clearly focused and significant questions about the work under study. You will lead a 20-30 minute discussion in class. All students will have read a copy of your paper before your discussion. You should come to class with a carefully prepared list of discussion topics, clearly focused on major issues in the novel and clearly related to topics of importance to the class. Be prepared to make provocative suggestions about the work, ask significant questions, and draw the other class members into a vital discussion of the work.

Criticism: You must submit summaries of four pieces of criticism, covering the writers/topics not covered in your papers. *These summaries must be turned in on the first day we discuss a writer.* They may be no longer than one page. I will make copies of each piece of criticism for the class members, so your criticism summaries are public. While the main point here is to summarize concisely, I do want you to include, in your final paragraph, your evaluation of the piece of criticism you read.

Journal: You are each to keep a reading response journal. Many of you will be reading literature in a new way this semester. While the course will be intellectually rigorous, it should also be an important personal experience-- sometimes joyful, sometimes disturbing. I look forward to contributions that reflect your response to the criticism, the literature, our discussions, and your re-vision of literature. A journal should help you formulate and crystalize those responses. For the most part, I will give you specific journal assignments, but feel free to write more open-ended responses to the writing as well. I will collect the journals every two-three weeks.

TENTATIVE SYLLABUS: AMERICAN WOMEN WRITERS

Sept. 5: Introduction to course

Feminist Criticism

Sept. 10: Woolf, "If Shakespeare Had Had a Sister," Kinkos p. 1; Morris, "Dick, Jane, and American Literature," Kinkos p. 3.

Sept. 12: Kolodny, "Dancing Through the Minefield," Kinkos p. 11; Baym, "Melodramas of Beset Manhood," Kinkos p. 23.

In Search of Our Mothers

Sept. 17: Alice Walker, "In Search of Our Mothers Gardens," Kinkos p. 32; Maxine Hong Kingston, "No Name Woman," Kinkos p. 39; Charlotte Perkins Gilman, "The Yellow Wallpaper," Kinkos p. 48.

Sept. 19: Chippewa Tale ("Oshkikwe's Baby"), Kinkos p. 56, and Louise Erdrich, "American Horse," Kinkos p. 60.

Sept. 24: Oneida Traditional Tales, Kinkos p. 67 and Louise Erdrich, "Fleur," Kinkos p. 71; also read Yellow Woman Tales, Kinkos p. 79, and Leslie Marmon Silko, "Yellow Woman," Kinkos p. 83.

Sept. 26: Diaries of the westward movement, Kinkos p 89

A Room of One's Own

Oct. 1: Emily Dickinson: letters, Kinkos p. 112.

Oct. 3, 8, 10, 15: Emily Dickinson: selected poems, Kinkos p. 133.

Oct. 17, 22: May Sarton, *House by the Sea* (completed by today)

In Search of the Self

Oct. 24, 29, 31: Zora Neale Hurston, *Their Eyes Were Watching God*

Nov. 5, 7, 12: Toni Morrison, *Beloved*

Women in the Family

Nov. 14, 19, 21: Eudora Welty, *Delta Wedding*

Nov. 26, 28, Dec. 3: Amy Tan, *The Joy Luck Club*

Dec. 5, 10, 12: Marilynne Robinson, *Housekeeping*

AMERICAN SOCIETY AND ITS MUSIC

Editor's Introduction to Syllabi 17A&B and Essays 7 & 8:

Almost all music transplanted to the New World underwent
change on American soil, absorbing and reflecting aspects of
American life and culture.— Charles Hamm, *Music in the New World.*

*A telling symbol of the changes affecting American universities in
our time is the decision made at California State University,
Sacramento, to change the title of its basic American music survey
course from "American Music" to "American Society and Its Music."
The responsibility such a name change imposes upon teachers can be
enough to frighten some, especially those trained to focus on "great"
composers and works (as American literature teachers have been
trained to teach "great books"), but the opportunity to move beyond
traditional boundaries of music courses is very exciting to others.*

*Until 1991, Music 129, "American Music," was a three-unit,
upper-division course at CSU. Its high enrollment as a "GE course"
(i.e., a course to fulfill a General Education requirement) was
achieved when it was redesigned to fulfill the "Advanced Study"
requirement of the School of Arts and Sciences—that is, the
requirement that students take one "advanced" course that would help
to teach them how to write, how to do research, and how to think
critically at the same time that it covered the subject matter of the
course. The course had been created by Daniel Kingman, who
remembers years when there was difficulty filling even one section;
now it fills from four to six. After Kingman's retirement, without
enough scholars trained in American music history on its staff, the
Department of Music redesigned the course so that it could be taught
by any of its teachers by using Kingman's* American Music: A
Panorama *as the text for all sections along with a body of films
related to its chapters, made available through the media center.*

*During the academic year 1990-91, an interesting experiment
called the "Beyond the Canon Project" was initiated at CSUS, at the
very time universities were beginning to debate the content of
courses that could be included on approved lists to meet new ethnic
studies requirements. That experiment provides the basis for the two
syllabi that follow. One section of Music 129 was selected by the
department to be a "target" section for bringing multiculturalism into*

the classroom. This section was taught by Susan Willoughby. Another member of the music staff, Jim Chopyak, has a strong interest in multiculturalism in world musics. But it was through Jim McCormick, who was teaching Music 129 for the first time that term, that I learned of the interest of the new, young, energetic music faculty in supporting American multiculturalism.

What follows, here and in Part II, is a four-part illustration of how courses in American music can move "beyond the canon" to incorporate new perspectives. First, McCormick's syllabus for his section of 129 (Syllabus 17A) is followed here by Willoughby's syllabus for the "target" section (17B). The two teachers have different styles, but both syllabi have useful suggestions. Then in Part II will be found a "Trialogue" in which Professors McCormick, Willoughby, and Chopyak respond to questions we asked of them about ways of "doing multiculturalism" in American music, and another essay by Willoughby in the form of a memo explaining how she plans to further transform her course, with a sampling from her students' research papers appended. Teachers will find in this material not only suggestions for ways to incorporate American musics into their courses but also hints of what to expect from their students after courses have been "multiculturalized."--BC

Syllabus 17A
AMERICAN SOCIETY AND ITS MUSIC

James P. McCormick, California State University, Sacramento
Music 129, Section 6, Department of Music

American Society and Its Music provides an excellent vehicle for our students to learn about who they are as young Americans. Since the best education is that which is founded in self-knowledge, this course offers a strong and versatile framework within which we can discover more about the various cultures that make up contemporary North American society. By examining where we have been musically, where we are currently, and where we are possibly heading in the arts, *American Society and Its Music* provides us a rich canvas on which we can paint an evolving panorama of musical styles reflecting a changing people with changing values and beliefs.

The United States during the 19th century was known as a singing nation. To make this course a unique and *feeling* experience, extensive musical involvement by the class is imperative. Invited under the right circumstances, students are willing to sing and make music in class. In so doing, they experience, in a deeper, more meaningful fashion, the emotional impact of the lyrics, the urgency of the message in the folk protest movement, and the joy of the spiritual and jazz music making. Active, ongoing participation in the music-making part of the course is characteristic of my section throughout the semester.

The course offers an excellent outlet for students to read about music, listen to music, view music, discuss music and make music. The plethora of styles examined throughout the course afford the student ample opportunity to witness how our cultural baggage (yes, we are all immigrants) continues to evolve as we witness cultures in transition that are continually bombarded by important changes with new technology and emerging musical styles.

Incorporating in-class performances by local artists from the community and generous, sharing "music majors" is a real advantage in making this course come alive. Assigning outside events draws the university milieu closer to the local community. *American Society and Its Music* can provide the teacher and the student with a barometer to tell us who we are as Americans—North Americans— and can help enrich our knowledge of our own selves and deepen respect for our individual cultural heritage. --JM

SYLLABUS (class meets three times per week)

class meeting #   **topics for the day**   **assignments**

1. *Introduction and welcome.* Who's who in the class: ethnic background, major, professional goals etc. *Music 129 Supplement and Resource Guide* explained. Discussion of *culture* and *society* followed by an overview of American musical styles. Student questionnaire. *Assignment:* Purchase Kingman's *American Music: A Panorama.* Read & make notes on Table of Contents, Forward and Introductions to individual sections of the text.

2. *What is Music?* Debate: What is music? What is its origin? Music as a phenomenon of man. The 4 basic elements of music: Tempo, Rhythm, Intensity and Pitch. (TRIP) Class involvement to demonstrate these elements. *Assignment:* Read the Carl Belz article in the *Supplement: The Story of Rock* for a clearer understanding of popular, folk, fine art treatments of music.

3. *Viewing*: Video Excerpt: *A Prairie Home Companion* hosted by Garrison Keillor--excellent patchwork of American musical styles demonstrated. Discussion of styles, characteristics, geographical origins in U.S. Music Overview tape distributed to individual students, with annotated guide for at-

home listening. *Assignment:* Listen to Overview Tape, Side "A," with a view to discerning what different musical styles you hear.

4. **Film:** *American Music from Folk to Jazz and Pop* as a platform for "America's Musical Melting Pot" discussion in class. Interrelations between folk, country, rock and pop. *Assignment:* Listen to Overview Tape, Side B. Outline styles for in-class discussion.

5. *So You Want to Write a Research Pape.* Class visit to Main Library, Music Section, with Music Librarian. View video on the joys of music research; hands-on experience with *Music Index* and the expanded version of *Infotrak.* Initial discussion of potential research topics for major paper in Music 129.

   Assignment: Browse through the Music Section of the Library. Determine the difference in contents between books shelved in the M, ML and MT sections. Bring one article to class you found by using the *Music Index* and *Infotrak, MLA Made Easy.* Cheat sheets distributed by instructor, guidelines for first page and "Works Cited" format described.

   Assignment: Read Kingman, Chapter One, "Anglo-American Folk Tradition.

6. **Film:** *Discovering American Folk Music.* Excellent for tracing the evolution of the ballad on American soil, following its transformation with the settlement of the American west, etc. Cultures in transition evidenr here. *Assignment:* Write a 12 line ballad based on one of your favorite American folk melodies--or, better still, create a new melody. We will sing a cross-section of these in class.

7. *Modern Folk Music.* Kingman, Chapter 4, "Folk Music in America." In-class protest song written: subjects vary from fee increases, parking nightmares, economic woes, student workload, part-time job, etc. Students gather round the piano (our 129 "folk" instrument) for performance.

8. *Recap of Folk Music/Modern Folk Music:* Impact on American Music Protest in Music: Folk Music of the 60s. Woodstock. Who were the hippies? How have young people's view of the "establishment" changed since the late 1960s? What were the key messages in the top 10 folk tunes of the 60s and 70s? *Assignment:* Listen to tape 4 in the library (for Chapter 4's Folk content).

9. *The Blues:* Introduction and Overview of this classic style. Video: *Good Mornin' Blues* featuring B. B. King. Discussion of the south, black music traditions, geography, history of the south, civil war and the movement north. *Assignment:* Read and take notes on Chapter 8: "Blues from Country to City."

10. *The Art of Writing Blues Lyrics.* 12-blues in action. Class Blues Theme Song: *Graduatin' Blues* lined out and performed in class complete with percussion, boogie-woogie background. *Assignment:* Listen to tape for Chapter 8: "Blues from Country to City."

11. *Blues Women*: Ma Rainey, Bessie Smith, Billie Holiday: "Mean Mothers," "Big Mamas," "Super Sisters." Images of women as portrayed in blues tunes. *Assignment:* Scour the area of a blues bar—pay a visit, if possible.

12. *In-Class Blues Performances*. Visiting artists and 129 class performers. *Assignment:* Begin work on your essay outline, bibliography, etc.

13. *American Indian and Inuit Music, Spanish & French Folk Strains*: Introduction function of the music of North America's aboriginal peoples. Effect of their music on the American Musical Tradition. Film: *Discovering American Indian Music*. and excerpts from the *JVC Anthology of World Music and Dance, Pt. 27*. *Assignment:* Read Kingman, Chapter 3: "American Indian Music, Spanish and French Strains." Write a "Weather Chant" to help us pray for rain during the California drought.

14. *Music of Mexico*. Examining the impact of the music of Mexico on mainstream Musical America. In-class demonstrations of certain key rhythms—dances demonstrated. In-class visiting artists perform a *corrido*. Video excerpts from *JVC Anthology*. *Assignment*: Listen to tape 3: "Music on the Fringe."

15. *Religious Music of Early America*. Introduction and discussion of psalms, hymnody, Calvinists. Cultural baggage of the Puritans, impact of the Shakers. *Assignment*: Read Kingman, Chapter 5, "Religious Music of Early America."

16. *Special visit* by an 18th century *Singing Master* to a class (small village in Maine) for a singing lesson in our "congregation." Lining out, hymn singing. *Assignment:* Visit a church of your choice and participate in the musical part of the celebration as much as possible. What style(s) of religious music seems prevalent in this church?

17. *Native Religious Music* During and After the Time of Expansion. *Assignment:* Read Kingman, Chapter 6, "Native Religious Music/Expansion."

18. *In-Class Performance*: Guest artist, soprano Bonnie Boles. Contemporary Christian/Spirituals/Hymns. Class participation. *Assignment:* Research for your major paper.

19. *Country Music*—Soul of America's Music. History and overview of country styles. Changing image of country music; million dollar, sophisticated industry. *Assignment:* Read Kingman, Chapter 7, "Country Music."

20. *Music of the Rural South*. In-class creations of contemporary country tunes to capture the style. In-class performances. *Assignment:* Listen to tape 7, "Country" and tune in FM 105—Country Station.

21. *Rock Overview and History: Rock 'n Roll: The Early Years.* Setting the scene. Post-war feeling, new sociological group: Teenagers. *Assignment*: Read Chapter 9, "Rock."

22. *Rock and its Permutations:* Evolution from the 50s - 90s. Here to stay? Are country and rap overtaking Rock? Images of women in Rock. *Assignment:* Listen to tape, Chap. 9, "Rock."

23. *Motown, Soul and Gospel.* Film: *Black Music in America from Then Until Now.* Styles discussed, performed in class. *Assignment:* Research for paper.

24. **Film:** *Black Music in America: The Seventies (Motown, Disco). Assignment:* Listen to radio station featuring these styles. (Discussion with parents about their musical experiences during the 1970s.)

25. *Fine Art Music in America:* The Planting of the Seeds. What is Classical Music Good For? Attitudes towards "long hair" music. Characteristics. *Assignment:* Read "Modern American Music" in Music 129 Supplement for overview of fine art music in 18th and 19th c. America.

26. *Fine Art Music in America:* The Pioneers: Gottschalk: A 19th c. American Consul. *Assignment:* Read Kingman, Chapter 13, "Eight Pioneers."

27. *New American Music—Characteristics.* Performance of contemporary vocal work. Psychology of Music and the New Music. *Assignment:* Try to attend a concert featuring new American Music to appreciate a live performance.

28. *Music with Film, Dance, Drama & Poetry:* Kingman, Chapter 14. Video, *Aaron Copland: A Tribute.* Use of jazz in classical music. The many faces of Copland. *Assignment:* Rent any video that relates to any aspect of American classical music composition. In-class discussion to follow. OR: Listen to KXPR Radio, to contemporary music.

29. *Contemporary Classical Music—American Style.* Music of Charles Barber and John Cage. Modern Music Notation: Graphic Notation by R. Murray Schafer. Film: *Music for Wilderness Lake.* (musique concrete) *Assignment:* Read Kingman, Chapter 10, "Broadway, Hollywood, and Tin Pan Alley."

30. *In-class Broadway Spectacular:* History of Broadway in Song. Visiting artists: cross-section of Broadway favorites. Discussion of lyrics, famous melody makers. *Assignment:* Listen to tape, Chapter 10, "Broadway, Hollywood."

31. *By George! A visit with George and Ira Gershwin.* In-class performance of Gershwin Piano Prelude. Video excerpts of Gershwin's musical contributions. *Assignment:* Where possible, rent a video featuring Gershwin's works or listen to any Gershwin album of your choice (in the music library).

32. *The American Musical.* Brief video history of the Musical. Introduction to *Showboat* and its importance in our American cultural legacy. *Assignment:* Rent a video of your choice featuring American musical content prior to 1950.

33. *Bernstein's West Side Story.* Romeo and Juliet, American Style. Musical comparison to *The Sound of Music.* Specific musical techniques used by Bernstein. *Assignment:* View a video with post 1950 content—American.

34. *Cole Porter and Irving Berlin*—Deans of American Popular composition. Excerpts from videos—styles, lyrics examined. *Assignment:* Listen to any Porter or Berlin album of your choice. What strikes you as being particular about their style?

35. *Jazz: America's Baby.* Video History: *Billy Taylor's History of Jazz. Assignment:* Tune into FM 88.9, a new Jazz Radio Station. What cross section of jazz styles are evident?

36. *In-Class Jazz Performance*: Piano, Vocals, Percussion, String Bass. How do jazz musicians communicate their art as compared to classical musicians? *Assignment.* Write new jazz lyrics for one of your favorite jazz melodies.

37. *Rap Music. Here to stay?* Move over Rock 'n Roll? Format. Artists. Images of society—and women—through rap lyrics. *Assignment:* Write your own rap lyrics—parental discretion advised. Be ready to give an upbeat, snappy in-class performance of these lyrics.

38. *Review: Looking Back.* Where have we come from? What styles will continue unchanged in American Music? What messages does contemporary American Music send out about our culture?

===============================

Syllabus 17B

AMERICAN SOCIETY AND ITS MUSIC

Susan Willoughby, California State University, Sacramento
Music 129, Section 3 ("Target" Section), Spring 1991

Music 129, Section 3 has been designated a "target class" in a new Academic Program Improvement study on campus this year on issues of race, ethnicity and gender in the curriculum. This campus project, entitled *Beyond the Canon: New Strategies for Pedagogy and Curriculum* has the single objective of initiating change in existing humanities and social science courses by:

1. Increasing the multicultural content of the curriculum.

2. Fostering the development of pedagogical practices suitable for a student population marked by diversity in race, ethnicity and gender.

Section 3 of 129 will address the first of these objectives during Spring semester 1991, with increased class time scheduled for study of music of Native Americans and Hispanic music in the United States, and increased focus on historical background of folk and popular music of the Afro-American tradition. The first reading assignment, listed on the class schedule, is the new chapter in Kingman's second edition: *Part Seven: Regionalism and Diversity.*

The writing assignments for the course will strongly reflect participation in this project by including (1) a concert review of a program of music by an ethnic minority group in the U.S., (2) A journal of thoughts, perceptions, and concerns about ethnic diversity and our semester study, and (3) a research project on an aspect of music of a cultural minority in the U.S.

ASSIGNMENTS:

1. *Journal on Race, Ethnicity and Gender.* 1000 words 10% of final grade. The Journal will consist of a series of 10 to 15 minute at-home and in-class writings of your own thoughts, perceptions and reactions to class study and discussion of the issues of race, ethnicity and gender. Writing for this Journal will be "No Fault," meaning that you will not be graded for style, spelling, or grammar. Your writings will be examined from time to time by the professor and a number will be given to each assignment: 0 for a non-response or a totally off-base response; 1 for all acceptable responses, and 2 for very exceptional responses. Several zeroes will affect your final grade negatively and several 2's will help your final grade. Since 129 is an Advanced Studies course and correction of writing style is required for assignments, you will receive non-graded corrections and suggestions on your writing style. First Journal assignment: Write 15 minutes at home answering the question: "What is my own experience with music of ethnic minorities in the U.S.?" *Due in class February 4.*

2. *Your Musical Autobiography.* 800 Words. (3-4 pages) Due Feb. 4--15% of final grade. A short paper on the role of music in your life—-your preferences, your experiences, and musical influences during your childhood.

3. *A Journal of Listening Experiences in American Music: Part 1.* 500 Words. (2-3 pages) 10% of final grade. Part One of the Listening Journal is a review of a live performance of a program of music by an ethnic minority group. The professor and students will keep the class informed of performances in the area this semester.

4. *Topic Proposal for Research Project.* 200 Words. Due March 18. 5% of grade. One or two paragraphs stating your topic, subtopics, research methods, basic plan/format for your material, and a minimum three sources. Sources may include books, periodicals, newspaper articles, television or film specials, or personal interviews. A list of suggested topics will be provided during the semester.

5. *Research Project.* 1700 Words (6-8 pages) Due April 22. 25% of grade. The Research Project is to explore some aspect of music of an ethnic minority as it exists in the United States, or on the influence of other cultures on American folk, popular or classical music.

6. *Journal of Listening Experiences in American Music: Part 2.* 800 Words. (3-4 pages) Due May 3. 15% of final grade. Part Two of the Listening Journal is to include reviews of two live performances of American music, or one longer review of the Sacramento Symphony concert of works by Aaron Copland: Community Center on March 17 and 18.

7. *Quizzes.* 15% of final grade. Three short quizzes will be given on the assigned readings, lectures and recorded music played in class.

COURSE INFORMATION

Text: *American Music: A Panorama,* 2nd ed. Daniel Kingman. N.Y. Schirmer Books, 1990, and "129 Supplement" (Both available at Hornet Bookstore).

Additional Reading: A list of books on reserve in the main library for Music 129 and a listing of reference works on American Music can be found in the "129 Supplement." There are also ample suggestions in the text for supplemental reading.

Writing Assignments: This is designated an "Advanced Studies" course; writing will therefore be an integral part of the course. The 5000-word minimum will be met by seven writing assignments detailed on a separate sheet. Please note that out-of-class papers must be typewritten and that none will be accepted late. Exceptions can only be considered in the case of personal emergencies.

Audio Assignments: Tapes keyed to the Kingman chapters and used in class will be available for student listening at the library media center on the first floor. Ask for tapes by course number (Music 129) and Chapter number. Listening to the tapes will aid you greatly in understanding the text.

Class	Reading	Assignment Due
Jan.28	Introductory	
30	Film: American Music, Folk, Pop & Jazz.	
Feb.1	Ethnic Diversity Program	Preface XIII-XIX;
		Ch. 20: 592-611
4	Folk Art, Fine Art, Popular	C. Belz, Supplement
6, 8	Anglo-Folk (Film)	Ch. 1: ALL
11	Anglo-Folk, continued	
13	Afro-Folk	Ch. 2: ALL
15	Afro-Folk, continued	Autobiography due
18	Native American Music	Ch 3 to p. 65
20	Native American Music, cont.	
22	Native American Music, cont.	
25, 27	Hispanic Traditions	Ch. 3: 65-84
March 4, 6, 8	Religious Music	Ch. 5: ALL
March 8		Journal due
11	Quiz # 1: Folk & Religious Music	
13	Classical Music	Ch. 16: 454-471;
		491-496
15	Classical	
18	Classical	Ch. 17: 504-528;
		Research proposal due
20, 22	Classical Experiment	Ch. 17: 531-537;
		539-541
March 25-29	SPRING RECESS	
April 1, 3	Technology: Aesthetics	Ch. 18 (Skim)
5	Beyond Modernism	Ch. 19: ALL
8	Quiz #2: Classical Music	
10	Blues-Country Music	Ch 7 (Skim)
12, 15	Blues	Ch. 8: ALL
17, 19	Rock	Ch 9: ALL
22, 24	Rock	Research Project due

26	Quiz #3: Blues & Rock	
29	Jazz	Ch. 13&14: ALL
May 1	Jazz Film: Billy Taylor	
3	Jazz continued	Journal ll due
6	Jazz	
8	Musical Theatre	
10	Showboat	Ethnicity Journal due
13, 15, 17	Showboat (continued)	
20-24	Finals Week	
	Class is Complete. Enjoy your summer!	

HANDOUT:
JOURNAL OF LISTENING EXPERIENCES IN AMERICAN MUSIC

The journal is to include a minimum of three reviews of performances of American Music. Each journal entry should occupy approximately one and one half pages, typed and double-spaced, though some entries may require more commentary. The journal assignment will be completed in two parts: The first part, due early in the semester, is to be a review of a performance of music of an American cultural minority group: Latin-American music, Mexican American music, Cajun music, music of the Hmong culture, Reggae, etc. The second part of the assignment includes two reviews of live performances of any American music, or one longer review of the Copland concert to be given by the Sacramento Symphony. Class members and professor will keep one another posted on suitable Journal events—concerts, TV specials, etc.

Rules and Suggestions:

1. Entries must be on American music, or music of ethnic minorities in the U.S.; not on European classical music such as Beethoven or Mozart.

2. Entries are to be concerts which occur during the semester the student is enrolled in 129. Exceptions may be made for very special festivals or concerts which occurred during the recent past.

3. When writing about fine-art music, always give the composer's name on any particular piece. Both composers and performers of fine-art music are referred to by their last names, not by their first names.

4. When writing on a concert of fine-art music, try to focus specifically on a few sections and aspects. When you attend, keep these questions in mind:

(1) *The performers*. What instruments are they playing? How many performers? Is their dress in any way noteworthy? Do they seem to communicate well with the audience?

(2) *Atmosphere*. What is the predominant age group and mood of the audience? Are they excited? bored? restless? Do they seem to be enjoying the concert? Is the room or the stage setting in any way significant to the experience?

(3) *The music*. What type/ style of music is being performed? Is it older style or contemporary? Are there original compositions? Give titles when possible.

(4) *Your reactions*. Are there selections you especially enjoyed? Would you recommend this group/program to your friends? Did this concert clarify or confirm the knowledge of styles you are gaining in Music 129? Did you think the performers were good performers?

Most important, listen and enjoy yourself. Allow the experience of the concert to provide your commentary. Your listening journal may be more a "folk art" paper than any of the other assignments, so be spontaneous and enjoy yourself!

===

Syllabus 18A & B

AMERICAN CIVILIZATION 1A & 1B

*ED. NOTE: See the essay by Scot Guenter about this course in Part II,
Essay #9, "Team-teaching an American Civ Course."--BC*

San Jose State University, 1990-1991
American Studies 1A, Fall 1990

Billie Jensen	**Kichung Kim**	**Scot Guenter**
Seminar: BC 103	Seminar: BC 209	Seminar: SH 347
Section: 01352	Section: 01363	Section 01374

Lectures: MWF 10:30-11:30, BC 014

TEXTS

    Paul Lauter, et al., *Heath Anthology of American Literature*, Volume 1
(Lexington, Mass.: D.C. Heath & Co, 1990)

    Frederick M. Binder and David M. Reimers, *The Way We Lived: Essays and
Documents in America's Social History*, Volume 1, rev. ed. (Heath, 1992)
[="B&R"]

COURSE SYLLABUS

American Studies 1A and 1B provide a chronological look at the rich and
diverse culture that has developed from the early days of European colonization
down to the present, in the area we know as the United States. This semester we
will trace the story down to the Civil War and its aftermath. In exploring American
civilization, we will look not only to monumental historical events and the works of
great thinkers and creative geniuses, but also to the everyday lives of earlier
Americans in a variety of social situations.

This course is by definition interdisciplinary. It is not a history class, a
literature class, or a political science class, although it draws heavily from all these
fields. It is rather a class on and about culture. Art, music, architecture,
technology, philosophy, religion — all play a part in the molding of "culture" and
will thus also be within our scope of consideration. We will strive to develop
connecting minds, reaching across the disciplines to use the social sciences, arts,
and humanities in an integrated fashion, probing more deeply the complex and
multifaceted layers of our cultural inheritance.

For purposes of fulfilling your General Education requirements in Areas C and D this course will prove most effective. . . . [and] you will also be well on your way to completing a minor in American Studies once this sequence is completed.

This course uses as its format a lecture to the entire group the first hour followed by smaller group seminar discussion the second hour. Attendance at all class meetings — both lecture and seminars — is essential and required. You must also ALWAYS bring with you to both lecture and seminar the assigned reading for that day. A looseleaf journal in which you respond to the readings will be an important requirement in this course: bring to each seminar class a written response (roughly one page per meeting) to the ideas, values, themes, and conflicts discussed in the reading for that day. These will be turned in to your instructor, and should serve as a good basis to provoke, evoke, or incite class discussion of the materials. In addition, this assignment serves several useful purposes: it ensures that you keep up with the readings; it encourages you to develop your skills in critical thinking; it stimulates you to improve your skills in written communication; and it provides you with a useful review guide when you begin preparing for the examinations.

Your grade will reflect your achievement in seminar and on the three examinations, the paper, and the journal. Though obviously your instructor will take such matters as attendance and improvement over the semester into account, as a rule of thumb these will roughly be apportioned as follows: First Examination 20%, Second Examination 20%, Final Examination 20%, Paper 15%, Journal 10%, Seminar 15%. What follows is an assignment sheet of readings for the entire semester that includes the wide range of topics we will cover in lecture. Plan your time wisely so that readings and journal responses are completed by the designated dates. Although we reserve the right to modify this syllabus, any such changes will be duly announced well ahead of time. You are responsible for all material covered in class wether you are there or not. Cheating and plagiarism will not be tolerated. The paper assignment will call for a thoughtful, modern response to the politics and culture of the Founding Fathers; it will be approximately 1000 words in length.

From the first interactions between European explorers and Native peoples to the post-bellum Reconstruction in the South, American life went through important shifts, shifts that profoundly shaped and influenced the everyday realities we take for granted today. A fundamental concern of this course will be not only to understand the institutions, subcultures, beliefs, and practices of the past, but also to get us questioning the institutions, subcultures, beliefs, and practices of the America we are part of today, and even more personally, how our individual attitudes are culturally determined, challenged, or reinforced.

COURSE SCHEDULE

Date	*Topic*	*B&R:*	*Heath Anthology:*
27-Aug	**Introduction**		
29-Aug	**European Image of the New World**		pp. 3-11; 67-80; 149-159
31-Aug	**The Puritan Experience (2 parts)**		pp. 11-17; 188-199; 204-210; 210-228
3-Sep	NO CLASS--LABOR DAY		
5-Sep	**City Upon A Hill: Puritans Come to America**		pp. 274-281; 295-307; 366-367
7-Sep	**Clash of European and Native American Cultures**	Ch. 1	pp. 22-25; 52-59; 176-180; 317-24
10-Sep	**Lives of Women and Slaves in Colonial America**	Ch. 3	pp. 256-257; 272-273; 674-76; 685-687; 712-14
12-Sep	**Salem Witchcraft**	Ch. 4	pp. 385-406
14-Sep	**Franklin, Edwards, and Woolman**		pp. 512-516; 555-566; 590-783; 823-838
17-Sep	**The Enlightenment {?}**		pp. 455-460; 650-51
19-Sep	**Crevecoeur and Tom Paine**		pp. 890-907; 936-957
21-Sep	**Living through the American Revolution**	Chs. 6,7	
24-Sep	**Editorial Cartoons and the Revolution**		pp. 994-1006
26-Sep	**The Development of the Constitution**		pp. 960-964; 978-981
28-Sep	**Ratification of the Constitution**		pp. 1007-1021
1-Oct	**Religious Diversity in the New Nation**	Ch. 5	
3-Oct	**Adams-Jefferson Letters**		pp. 925-935; 987-994
5-Oct	FIRST EXAMINATION		
8-Oct	**American Industry and Industrious Americans**	Ch. 8	
10-Oct	**Frontier Ideology and Disadvantaged Americans**	Ch. 9	pp. 1760-1772
12-Oct	**Virgin Land**		pp. 1280-91

======================================

Syllabus 18B: AMERICAN CIVILIZATION 1B

Billie Jensen   **Kichung Kim**   **Scot Guenter**
Seminar Section 11   Seminar Section 12   Seminar Section 13
SH435   BC209   SH347

American Studies 1B, Section 10, Spring 1991
Lectures: MWF 10:30-11:30, BC 014
Seminars MWF 11:30-12:20

TEXTS
Paul Lauter, et al., *Heath Anthology of American Literature*, Volume 2 (Lexington, Mass.: D.C. Heath, 1990)

Frederick M. Binder and David M. Reimers, *The Way We Lived: Essays and Documents in America's Social History*, Volume 2, rev. ed. (Heath, 1992)

PURPOSE
American Studies 1B continues the journey of interdisciplinary inquiry begun last semester in American Studies 1A. Together we will draw on insights from history, literature, political science, the arts, humanities and social sciences as we explore a range of themes focusing on the transformation and development of American civilization from the days of Reconstruction to the current war situation in the Persian Gulf. It is hoped that in crossing the disciplines and coming to grips with pertinent aspects of our personal and communal heritages we might develop "connecting minds," learning more about who we are as we evaluate the rich complexity of the American cultural experience.

You might recall that the successful completion of AS 1A and AS 1B fulfills the following GE requirements: a course in Area D (Social, Political and Economic Institutions); your state requirements in American History, the U.S. Constitution, and California Government; in Area C (Arts, Literature, Philosophy and Foreign Language); six of the twelve unit requirement. Should you decide to minor or major in American Studies, you will be off to a very good start, also.

Last semester we paid careful attention to the dynamics and development of America as a multicultural society. This will continue as a major theme for us;

building on this idea, together we will explore the complex mixture of forces, influences, and individuals who have contributed to the multifaceted American experience. It is hoped that our examination demonstrates the many different types of voices that have joined in the chorus Walt Whitman envisioned when he wrote his poem, "I Hear America Singing." Cutting across boundaries of gender, ethnicity, race, and class, we will learn about groups from which we might have sprung, about individuals with whom we might or might not identify, and about social structures that developed to meet the society's changing needs.

There are five other themes that will appear and reappear throughout our studies this semester. You are encouraged to consider these themes both separately and as they interconnect with each other. Along with the idea of *a multicultural society*, use them as springboards to dive into an analytical evaluation of our culture in your journals and seminar discussions. These themes are:

American Political Movements and the Modern Constitution
Industry, Business, Technology and Labor
War and Peace
The Pull of the Urban/ The Pull of the Rural
Modern Society and Mass Media

GROUND RULES

Attendance at all class meetings—lectures and seminars—is essential and required. You must also *always* bring with you to both lecture and seminar the assigned readings for that day. This semester we will again require a loose-leaf journal, which will consist of your written responses to the assigned readings. Bring to each seminar class a written response (roughly one page per meeting) to the ideas, values, themes, and conflicts discussed in the reading for that day. These will be read by your instructor and should serve as a good basis to provoke, evoke, or incite class discussion of the materials. In addition, this assignment serves several purposes: it ensures that you keep up with readings; it encourages you to develop your skills in critical thinking; it stimulates you to improve your skills in written communication; and it provides you with a useful review guide when you begin preparing for the examinations.

We reserve the right to make minor changes in the syllabus as the semester progresses, to be duly announced ahead of time in class. Plagiarism or cheating will not be tolerated. Critical inquiry, diligence, and perseverance, however, will be rewarded. The paper will be assigned prior to Spring Vacation and is due the second week of April. The assignment will be approximately 5-7 pages in length and will involve library research.

Your grade will reflect your achievement in seminar and on the journal, the paper, the two midterms, and the final. Though obviously your instructor will take such matters as participation and improvement over the semester into account, as a rule of thumb grades will be apportioned as follows: First midterm 20%, Second midterm 20%, Paper 15%, Journal 10%, Class Participation 15%, Final 20%

SYLLABUS:

DATE	TOPIC	B & R	HEATH ANTHOLOGY
28-Jan	**Introduction**		
30-Jan	**The Death and Life of the Frontier**	Ch. 2	
1-Feb	**The Ghost Dance**	Ch. 3	pp. 742-54
4-Feb	**Mark Twain**		pp. 214-17; 227-30; 243-52; 265-72; 289-309; 337-41
6-Feb	**Realism and Naturalism**		pp. 510-15; 530-47; 689-91; 697-714; 722-25
8-Feb	**Horatio Alger**		pp. 1298-1304; 934-36
11-Feb	**The "New" Immigration**	Ch. 5	
13-Feb	**The Populists**		pp. 658-88
15-Feb	**Jacob Riis**	Ch. 6	pp. 1599-1609
18-Feb	**Women in Turn-of-the-Century America**	Ch. 4	pp. 148-59; 760-73
20-Feb	**Frederick Law Olmstead**		pp. 877-84; 923-31
22-Feb	**The White City**		pp. 813-28; 842-49
25-Feb	**New Manifest Destiny, Imperialism, War**		pp. 548-90
27-Feb	**Washington and DuBois**	Ch. 7	pp. 851-72; 782-97
1-Mar	**Wilsonism in Peace and War**	Ch. 8	
4-Mar	**Harlem Renaissance**		pp. 1456-68; 1487-1506; 1553-63; 1581-86
6-Mar	**EXAMINATION**		
8-Mar	**The Red Scare and Immigration Restriction**	Ch. 9	
11-Mar	**Sacco and Vanzetti**		pp. 1225-58
13-Mar	**Disillusionment of the Intellectuals**		pp. 1164-66; 1168; 1170-74; 1287-96
15-Mar	**Religion in the 1920s**	Ch.10	

18-Mar	Scopes Trial		pp. 1088-99
20-Mar	Prohibition		pp. 1333-49
22-Mar	Crash of '29 and the Great Depression	Ch.11	
	SPRING VACATION		
1-Apr	The Dust Bowl		pp. 1616-24
3-Apr	Union Maids		pp. 1118-27
5-Apr	Women and the Depression		pp. 1648-62
8-Apr	New Deal		pp.1629-48
10-Apr	World War II, The Home Front	Ch.12	
12-Apr	Relocation Camps	Ch.13	
15-Apr	World War II, Popular Culture		pp.1786-1812
17-Apr	EXAMINATION		
19-Apr	McCarthy		pp. 1624-29
22-Apr	The Suburban Myth	Ch.14	pp. 2332-36; 2376-78; 2384-87; 1935-47
24-Apr	New Civil Rights & Feminist Movements	Ch.15,16	pp. 1957-69
26-Apr	Vietnam		pp. 2086-94; 1888-1900
29-Apr	Watergate		Review U. S. Constitution
1-May	Our Latino Heritage		pp. 1948-57; 2562-67; 2572-85
3-May	Asian Immigration		pp. 884-85; 895-901; 1755-62
6-May	Asian Immigrants		pp. 1747-54
8-May	Post-Modernism: MTV		pp. 2065-72; 2115-2126
10-May	And the Wars Came		pp. 429-31; 652-58; 691-97; 722-23; 1589-92
13-May	Asian-American Literature		pp. 1841-43; 1871-82; 1902-12; 2501-09
15-May	Conclusion		
20-May	Final Examination: 9:45-12:00		

Syllabus #19

AESTHETIC INQUIRY AND HUMAN IMAGINATION

Keith Ward, Denison University
Granville, Ohio, 1992

EDITOR'S INTRODUCTION:

Incorporating multiculturalism into a basic Freshman course on the American arts is the theme of the final syllabus in this collection. Here Keith Ward offers an extended commentary on the role the arts can play in a university-wide, multiculturally-oriented Freshman Studies program. His commentary is followed by his own syllabus for a course in the program called "Aesthetic Inquiry and Human Imagination" (alternately titled "Aesthetic Inquiry and the Human Condition"). Denison was one of the first universities in the United States to institute a diversity requirement in its General Education program. Supported by a two-year grant co-sponsored by the Ford Foundation and the university, Ward and his colleagues planned week-long Diversity Workshops for the teachers of these courses during the summers of 1991 and 1992. The second year in the continuing program is important, for it allows a follow-up to evaluate existing courses at the same time that new courses are designed.

A unique feature of Denison's plan is to have all incoming freshmen read a common text as part of freshman orientation — during the summer months, where possible — and then have faculty adopt it as a common reader in their courses. The text chosen is Lorene Carey's Black Ice *(Knopf, 1991), the story of a black teenager who goes to a prep school in New Hampshire from an inner-area in Philadelphia — an experience of a student in transition who must adjust to change of place, not unlike the experience the freshmen themselves are undergoing.*

As part of Denison's effort to incorporate diversity into freshman curriculum, the course described here may well serve as a model to other universities seeking ways to make multiculturalism integral to the whole college experience. Among other things, the syllabus offers an outstanding example of using campus and community events as an integral part of the learning experience — even coordinating the transportation! — BC

Commentary, by Keith Ward

CATALOG DESCRIPTION: FRESHMAN STUDIES 102. AESTHETIC INQUIRY AND THE HUMAN CONDITION. Directed towards the student who has had little exposure to the fine arts, this course attempts to enhance students' critical appreciation as well as their enjoyment of the visual, performing, and environmental arts. Students in all sections will be required to attend a minimum of seven events in the fine arts at Denison and selected off-campus events, as well as the fine arts common hour at which special lectures, films, and media events will be presented. There will be appropriate writing assignments, a library research paper, and readings in common texts. Freshman Studies 102 fulfills Artistic Inquiry requirement. — Denison University Catalog 1991-92.

This course is part of Denison University's Freshman Studies Program. Taught by faculty from all departments in the arts, it is geared toward freshmen who have had little or virtually no exposure to the fine and performing arts. Interdisciplinary in nature, the course attempts to awaken aesthetic appreciation in students who, for whatever reason, have not become involved significantly in artistic endeavors, either as observers or participants. Students are challenged to become engaged in and develop appreciation for human creativity, both inside and outside the sacred walls of the concert hall and art museum.

With such a general charge, teaching this course could be a daunting task! The world of the arts is so vast, and there are so many issues one could raise, that such a course could lose focus easily. One must choose topics carefully in order to weave the fabric whole. To this end, my colleague Lee Bostian and I have decided to focus a significant part of the course upon certain veins of multiculturalism in the artistic spheres of America. Our efforts have been supported generously by a grant from Denison.

There may be similarities between our experiment in multiculturalism and that of the "Beyond the Canon Project" at California State University at Sacramento described by Susan Willoughby and Betty Ch'maj. At the core of our course lies a series of events which are attended by both sections of FS 102. These events, which are chosen by Lee Bostian and me, determine the content of the course. We prepare students through readings, lectures, films, groups activities, and guest lectures in the weekly common hour. We follow each event with discussions and written assignments (see syllabus, below).

If we so wished, Dr. Bostian and I could use the open-ended format of FS 102 to define and preserve the canon of Eurocentered Western art. Obversely, however, this same format becomes the ideal forum for exposing students to experiences that confirm instead of ignore the multicultural present. By downplaying a canon of clearly defined norms and prejudices, we encourage students from the very start of their college careers to examine the world of the arts through a multicultural lens.

Unlike such courses as first-semester chemistry, which by nature have clearly defined and fairly standard contents, Freshman Studies 102 offers an instructor great flexibility in course design and class format. In an attempt to shape our course around aspects of diversity, Lee Bostian and I have tentatively settled upon a series of events, films, guest lectures, and readings that we believe reflects aspects of the multiculturalism we want to encourage. Its range extends from works of a more Eurocentric orbit to those by American women and native American artists. The series includes the following units (special group events are in italics):

Music that Engages
    Saud/Live Jazz (Denison)
    Branford Marsalis (The Vail Series, Denison)
    Guest lecture by Jazz scholar Mark Gridley, Heidelberg College
    Film, *Amazing Grace with Bill Moyers* (PBS Video)
    Film, *That Rhythm, Those Blues*, The American Experience (PBS Video)
    Film, *Desire, Sex, Power in Rock Video* (Univ. of Massachusetts, Amherst)

Dance, Theatre, and Elevating Our Consciousness
    Urban Bush Women (Martin Luther King Center, Columbus, Ohio)
    Guest lecture by members of the Urban Bush Women
    Twyla Tharp Dance Company (Ohio State University)
    Guest lecture by member of Denison's Dance Faculty
    Film, *Twyla Tharp: The Catherine Wheel*
    Film, *Configurations American Ballet Theatre, music by Samuel Barber* (Video)

Visual Art as Narrative
    Faculty Art Show (Denison)
    Discussion by Denison's Art Faculty of their works
    Panel Discussion/Roleplay: "The Museum Board"
    Exhibit of artifacts from the Cuna Indians and Indians from North America
    Guest lecture by Michael Jung, Professor of Art and collector of Indian artifacts

The Art Music Tradition
    Muir String Quartet (Vail Artists in Residence Program, Denison)
    Videodisc on chamber music, University of Delaware Music Series
    Videodisc on compositional and interpretative choices, University of Delaware
        Music Series
    Videodisc featuring the orchestra, University of Delaware Music Series

Licking County Symphony Orchestra (Denison)
Guest lecture by Prof. Frank Bellino, Conductor of LCSO

Hard Choices: Women in the Arts
Film, *The Turning Point*
Film, *Say Amen, Somebody* (Pacific Arts/Faucett Video)
Gerald L. and Margaret L. Belcher, *Collecting Souls, Gathering Dust: The Struggles of Two American Artists, Alice Neel and Rhoda Medary* (New York: Paragon House, 1991)
Guest lecture by Dr. Camilla Cai, Kenyon College
Panel Discussion by three local women artists

This list of issues and events is, necessarily, incomplete. There are many kinds of multiculturalism we do not address, such as Asian-American art and Hispanic art. We are not comprehensive in our coverage for two reasons: first, the events we choose are limited by logistical arrangements and offerings on concert series in the greater Columbus area; and second, celebrating diversity is a pervasive *theme* rather than a core *goal* of FS 102. It is the lubricant used as we address the overriding objectives of the course, which are 1) to develop further students' aesthetic appreciation of the arts, 2) to strengthen students' writing skills through various assignments, and 3) to develop the technical vocabulary that will enable students to identify, describe, and critique more clearly an art work or experience.

In Freshman Studies 102 we confront students with questions about art, and their appreciation of it, that they have either overlooked or never posed. Throughout the semester we repeatedly ask broad questions, such as those posed by Dennis Sporre ("What is it [i.e., an artwork or experience]? How is it put together? How does it stimulate the senses?") in his book, *Perceiving the Arts: An Introduction to the Humanities* (3rd ed., Prentice Hall, 1989), and we examine such pervasive issues of image, rhythm and form in all arts that Judy Nagle pursues in her textbook, *The Responsive Arts* (Mayfield Publishing, 1982). By asking these questions, we hope students will recognize some commonalities of artistic expression that may lie below the surface of striking differences. These broad questions will still be broached this Fall, only this time they will be posed for artworks that reflect the varying cultures found in America.

A final goal of FS 102 is to provide a good foundation for a growing, connected education. As part of the General Education Requirement all Denison students must take at least two courses in the arts. After a semester of exposure to various art forms, our hope and expectation is that students will be better prepared to choose the second arts course they should take, whether it is Music Appreciation, Elementary Acting, Art of Japan, Jazz Dancing, or something else.

Types of Assignments

FS 102 is a writing-intensive course. Assignments range from in-class essays as short as two paragraphs to a formal term paper. (Students also take quizzes on their developing analytical vocabulary, among other things.) Interim rough drafts are usually required for all longer assignments.

Write a review of an event. Students must not just evaluate a performance, but also must describe general aspects of an art work (works performed in a concert, themes of an artwork or show, synopsis of a play, etc.), the mise-en-scene of the experience, and how the experience affected them. These papers are usually three to five typed pages. Sometimes students write these papers individually and other times the papers are the results of a group effort by as many as three students. They may be shaped as formal reviews to model a piece one would find in a newspaper or magazine, a dialogue, or a letter.

Journals. One cannot downplay the power and influence of autobiography in the arts. Indeed, its importance is the primary reason behind our inviting artists to come to our class to talk about *their* art. They have not created their art in a vacuum; their art says something about them, their lives, and how they perceive the world. Similarly, students do not appear on the first day of class tabula rasa: unwittingly or not, the arts have affected their lives in some way and have contributed to their opinions and beliefs of the nature and value of art, be it fine art, folk art, or popular art. Through autobiographical essays we ask students to examine these fundamental issues. In the very first class students write and share essays on a significant experience they have had in the arts, either as performer, creator, or observer. In the past some instructors have required students to keep journals in which they record reactions to events, keep running logs of their involvement --in whatever guise-- in the arts, and reflect upon how art (outside of advertisements) is used to engage, cajole, or persuade them.

The Minute Paper. This is an assessment tool cited by Patricia Cross in her article, "Teaching for Learning" (*AAHE Bulletin*, March 1987, 3-7; see also Richard Light, *The Harvard Assessment Seminars: Explorations with Students and Faculty about Teaching, Learning, and Student Life, First Report*, 1990, pp. 35-38). So teachers could get feedback, students in a physics class were asked to answer two questions: 1) What is the most significant thing you learned today? and 2) What question is uppermost in your mind at the end of this class session? This same device can be used to elicit reactions to a guest speaker, a film, or a discussion. These "papers" are not given letter grades, but are recorded as part of students' class participation.

Term paper. The body of this major written work must be 8-10 typed pages. Pedagogically, I approach the paper as an ongoing project. Six weeks before the paper is due, students are required to discuss with me the state of their projects (i.e., how their thesis is developing, what sources they have found, and what questions are foremost in their minds). Outlines and rough drafts are required before the final drafts are handed in, but I assign a grade only to the final draft. Here is a sampling of some of the term papers I received one year:

> "Keith Haring: Artist Caught between 'Tasteful Exposure' and
> 'Commercialism'"

> "The Beatles and Bob Dylan: 'With a Little Help from Their Friend'"
> "Musicals during the Depression"
> "Bluegrass Music: Like No Other"
> "Censorship in the Arts: Mapplethorpe and 2 Live Crew"
> "The Legacy of the Country Blues"
> "Misunderstood Genius: Charles Chaplin"
> "I Woke Up This Moawnin' — Evolution of Harmonica in Blues Music"
> "Literary Illustration: Part of Our Heritage"; "Spirituals"

Special Activities. Here is a list of some activities that have been used in FS 102 to engage students: —small groups of 3-5 students, either for in-class discussions or group assignments —panel discussions in which students role play certain points of view (see "Museum Board," above); these panels then serve as foundations for further writing assignments —brainstorming to begin discussions or to initiate writing assignments —taking a dance class, directing and acting a scene from a play we are going to see, or conducting a live or videotaped musical ensemble --guest lectures or presentations by artists (see above) --structured writing exercises: providing topic sentences for three paragraphs and having students finish the paragraphs.--KA

======================================

SYLLABUS, 1992: "Aesthetic Inquiry and the Human Condition"

COURSE AIMS

The objective of this course is two-fold. First, through attendance at concerts, plays, art shows, and dance productions, the course will present you with a broad variety of the fine, popular, and performing arts. To this end there will be preparatory lectures and readings, guest lectures during the weekly Common Hour, and follow-up sessions after each event. The second goal of the course is to strengthen your writing skills through various assignments, such as reaction papers, in-class essays, and a term paper.

Most important, this course attempts to develop further your aesthetic appreciation of the arts. By experiencing and reacting to the arts first hand, you will become more cognizant of the artistic experience, which includes not only the creator and the performer (or, in the case of the visual arts, the artist and his/her created object), but you as the listener/observer as well. Experiencing art is not a passive exercise; even a painting is far from silent. Involvement at any level in the arts is part of the process of becoming involved in and reacting to one's inner and outer worlds. You will be asked to describe how art affects you and how you respond to particular works of art taken from the endless variety of human creativity. We will explore the ways art reflects its time, environment, and creator, and we will try to discern how such art affects and influences us today. This course will challenge you to become engaged in something that is vital to the human condition: the aesthetic experience.

In addition to the goals stated above, there are some pervasive themes that will run throughout the term. First and foremost, the common events we will attend with the other section of FS 102 were chosen to celebrate the diversity of human creativity. Though we will be experiencing Eurocentric works, we also will be looking beyond the standard canon of Western art. Throughout the term we will be recognizing and celebrating the diversity of our multicultural present. Second, while taking in this diversity, we will be seeking commonalities of artistic expression that may lie below the surface of striking differences. We also will work on developing a technical vocabulary so that we may identify, describe, and evaluate more clearly an artwork or experience. Finally, we will visit important contemporary issues as they affect the arts, especially those dealing with gender and censorship.

Required Texts (available at the bookstore)

Belcher, Gerald L. and Margaret L. *Collecting Souls, Gathering Dust: The Struggles of Two American Artists.* New York: Paragon House, 1991.

Sayre, Henry M. *Writing About Art.* Englewood-Cliffs, NJ: Prentice Hall, 1989.

Other readings, music listening, & films will be on reserve in the main library & Learning Resource Center.

Group Events — Mark the dates in your calendar NOW!

Fri, Sept 13: Saud/Live Jazz, Bandersnatch, Denison University, 8:00 p.m. Admission free with ID.

Sun, Sept 22: Branford Marsalis, saxophone (Vail Series), Swasey Chapel, Denison University, 8:00 p.m. Admission free, but pick up a priority pass at Slayter Union the week before the concert.

Thurs, Sept 26: Urban Bush Women, Martin Luther King Center, Columbus. Vans leave from Swasey Chapel parking lot at 6:00. Admission charged.

Fri, Oct 5: Twyla Tharp Dance Company, Mershon Auditorium, Ohio State University, Columbus. Vans leave from Swasey Chapel parking lot at 6:30. Admission charged.

Oct 8-23: Faculty Show, Burke Museum, Denison. Museum hours posted at entrance. Admission free.

Fri, Oct 18: Columbus Museum of Art. Vans leave Swasey Chapel 1:30 p.m., return 5:00 p.m.. Admission free.

Wed, Oct 23: Muir String Quartet, Burke Recital Hall, Denison University. Admission free.

Wed, Oct 30 : Film, The Turning Point, Learning Resource Center, shown at 3:30 & 7:30.

Wed, Nov 6: Film, Say Amen, Somebody, Learning Resource Center, shown at 3:30 & 7:30.

Nov 15-16: Play, Dangerous Liaisons, Ace Morgan Theatre, 8:00 p.m. Admission on weekend; you must purchase tickets in advance.

Sat, Nov 23: Licking County Symphony Orchestra, Swasey Chapel, Denison University, 8:15 p.m. Admission free with student ID.

Dec 5-7: Faculty-Student Dance Concert, Doane Dance, 8 p.m. Admission — reserve tickets in advance.

Dec 6-13: Artifacts from the Cuna Indians and Indians from North America, Burke Museum, Denison University. Admission free.

CLASS SCHEDULE

> *Please note:* Classes on Tuesday last two hours, classes on Thursday one hour, with the Common Hour (CH) lasting one hour on Thursdays.

9/3   Introduction: The Power of Narrative: The Arts in Your Life.
Events I & II: Music that Engages

9/5   Discussion of articles by Pereles and Sangeles.
CH (Common Hour): Film, *Dream Worlds: Desire, Sex, Power in Rock Video*

9/10   Musical Elements.

9/12   References & sources in Denison's library.
CH: Dr. Lee Bostian, "Jazz Heritage"

9/13   *Event I: Saud/Live Jazz, Bandersnatch*

9/17   Follow-up of concert; The universal, ineffable qualities of music: *Amazing Grace with Bill Moyers* (film)

9/19   Film, *That Rhythm, Those Blues.*
CH: Guest Lecture by Mark Gridley, Heidelberg College, on Branford Marsalis.

9/22   *Event II: Branford Marsalis, saxophone, Swasey Chapel*

9/24   Follow-up of Marsalis concert.. Quiz.
Events III & IV: Dance that Elevates Our Consciousness

9/26   Image, Rhythm, Form in Dance.
CH: Guest lecturer on Urban Bush Women, TBA.

9/26   *Event III: Urban Bush Women, Martin Luther King Center (Columbus)*

10/1   Follow-up of concert. Discussion of Anderson, Langer articles.

10/3   Modern Dance class, Doane Dance.
CH: Guest lecture on Twyla Tharp by member of the Dance Faculty.

10/4   *Event IV: Twyla Tharp Dance Company, Ohio State (Columbus)*

10/8   Follow-up of Tharp performance. Film, *Configurations.* Quiz.
Event V & VI: Visual Art as Narrative (Faculty Show, Burke Museum, through October 23)

10/10 Discussion of Introduction and Chapter 1 of Sayre.
CH: Tour of the faculty show by Art Department faculty

10/15 Visual Elements (line, shape & space, light & value, color, etc.),
Principles of Design (rhythm & repetition, balance, proportion, scale, unity & variety): Chaps 2-3 of Sayre. Discussion of the term paper.

10/17 Discussion of Chap. 4 of Sayre. Final preparations for Museum Board roleplay
CH: "The Museum Board of Directors" — a roleplaying experience.

10/18 *Event VI: Columbus Museum of Art*
Event VII: The Art Music Tradition

10/22 Quiz on Visual Art; preview of concert by Muir Quartet.

10/23 *Event VII: Muir String Quartet, Burke Recital Hall*

10/24 Follow-up of concert. CH: Presentation by members of the Muir String Quartet.
Events VIII & IX: Hard Choices - Women in the Arts

10/29 Individual appointments on term papers.

10/30 *Event VIII: Film, The Turning Point.*

10/31   Discussion of chapters 1-8 of Belcher.
CH: Guest lecture by Camilla Cai, Kenyon College.

11/5   Discussion of chapters 9-17 of Belcher.

11/6   *Event IX: Film, Say Amen, Somebody.*

11/7   Presentations on women artists. CH: Panel Discussion by Local Women Artists.
Event X: Theatre

11/12   Theatre as Art; excerpts from film, *Dangerous Liaisons.*

11/14   Discussion of play. CH: Lecture by director of the play.

11/15 or 16: Play, *Dangerous Liaisons*, Ace Morgan Theatre.
Event XI: The Art Music Tradition

11/19   Quiz on theatre. Compositional questions, interpretative choices.

11/21   Introduction to the orchestra. CH: Guest lecture — Prof. Frank Bellino, conductor, Licking County Symphony Orchestra.

11/23   *Event XI: Licking County Symphony Orchestra, Swasey Chapel*

11/26   Follow-up of concert.

11/28   THANKSGIVING BREAK

Events XII & XIII: Faculty/Student Dance Concert, Doane Dance and Cuna & North American Indian exhibits, Burke Museum).

12/3   Art: Mind and Body.

12/5   Preview of dance concert. CH: Guest lecture Art Department faculty on American Indian exhibits.

At the Close

12/10   Review.

12/12   The Mapplethorpe Exhibit: pros and cons. CH: Panel Discussion on Censorship.

12/20   FINAL EXAM, 2:00-4:00.

===================================

Part II: Essays

==

Essay #1

E PLURIBUS UNUM?
APPROACHES TOWARD SYNTHESIZING MULTICULTURAL AMERICA-- CULTURAL COUNTERPOINT IN HISTORY, MUSIC, AND ART

by Pamela Fox
Associate Professor of Music
Miami University, Oxford, Ohio

Reconstruction authority Eric Foner opened the 1990 essay volume *The New American History* with the definitive statement: "in the course of the past twenty years American history has been remade."[1] The agent of this transformation is the New Social History which emerged in the 1960s as a response to the civil violence, the new wave of feminism, and antiwar turmoil that challenged the consensus concept of a single national character. Responding to the obvious manifestations of a divided society, this new social history set out to free ordinary people from the bottom up. Universal causes and patterns of behavior were rejected. Private rather than public life became the major focus for specialized explorations of occupations, gender, generation, ethnicity, and family analysis. Rigorous quantitative methods and a new flexible sense of class divisions merged with widely debated new methods of literary criticism. Deconstruction, post-structuralism, historicity, Marxism, and expanded concepts of ethnography split historians and the general

---

[1] Eric Foner, ed., *The New American History* (Philadelphia: Temple University Press, 1990), vii.

academic community into various neurotic factions.[2] Intense polemics ranging from William Bennett's pronouncements to the phenomenon of Allen Bloom's *The Closing of the American Mind* have commanded national attention.[3]

Debates raged on, subsequently fueled by Dinesh D'Souza's bestseller *Illiberal Education: The Politics of Race and Sex on Campus*[4] and Arthur M. Schlesinger Jr.'s *The Disuniting of America: Reflections on a Multicultural Society*.[5] The proverbial tension between educational tradition and innovation currently revolves around many issues: modern versus post-modern, western canonicity versus democratic pluralism, content versus process, quality versus totality of everyday experience, homogeneity versus heterogeneity, fixed historical meaning versus historicity, popular culture as trash or treasure, and other issues.[6]

While the spirit of Foner's declaration is accurate, it is more realistic to state that many fascinating pieces of a new American history have been generated in the past twenty years but that no one is yet sure what the completed picture should look like. For women's historian Linda Gordon, adding new portraits to the pictures constructed in the past is like painting additional figures into the spaces of an already completed canvas. Gordon speaks for many newly recovered voices in stating that we must repaint "the earlier pictures, because some of what was previously on the canvas was inaccurate and more of it misleading."[7] Moreover, the New Social History which generated innovative components of many sizes, shapes and colors is no longer new. How should we connect the various voices of the new multicultural American history into a general pattern? For many, the challenge of understanding previously marginalized cultures in relation to canonical culture and the ideal of a national culture has renewed the quest for a current interpretation of our national motto: *e pluribus unum*. What do the *unum* and the

---

[2] A useful summary of these trends may be found in Alice Kessler-Harris's essay "Social History" in *The New American History*, 163-84.

[3] William Bennett, "To Reclaim a Legacy," *Chronicle of Higher Education*, November 28, 1984, pp. 16-21; Allen Bloom, *The Closing of the American Mind* (New York: Simon & Schuster, 1987). A broad sampling of reactions to Bloom has been gathered together in *Essays on The Closing of the American Mind*, edited by Robert L. Stone (Chicago Review Press, 1989).

[4] New York: The Free Press, 1991.

[5] Schlesinger's monograph (91 pages) is published by Whittle Books, 1991.

[6] A comparative critique of these issues is offered by Stanley Aronowitz and Henry A. Giroux in *Postmodern Education: Politics, Culture, & Social Criticism* (Minneapolis: University of Minnesota Press, 1991).

[7] Linda Gordon, "U.S. Women's History," *The New American History*, 185-86.

pluribus owe each other? In this essay I will summarize general suggestions toward such a synthesis, and then specifically illustrate how such synthesis can be facilitated for multicultural American music.

The imperative of synthesis resounded clearly within the historical community in the early 1980s. Philip Gleason's essay "American Identity and Americanization," in the *Harvard Encyclopedia of American Ethnic Groups*, concluded that "we cannot even begin to do justice to the problem [of cultural pluralism] as it is posed in our own time unless we grant the same kind of recognition to the imperative of unity that we give to the reality of diversity."[8] R. Herbert Gutman's article "The Missing Synthesis: Whatever Happened to History?" in *Nation*, November 21, 1981, and Bernard Bailyn's 1981 presidential address to the American Historical Organization passionately voiced similar concerns.[9]

The most ambitious attempt to frame a synthesis to date is William Woodward's two-part article "America As A Culture: Some Emerging Lines of Analysis," published in the 1988 *Journal of American Culture*.[10] Woodward first incorporates a broad array of specialized studies into four interdisciplinary historiographical approaches: the Republican Synthesis, the Organizational Synthesis, the Ethno-Cultural Synthesis, and the World-Historical Synthesis. In the second of two parts, Woodward proposes "a synthesis of syntheses" relating the above approaches to broader ideological traditions of what he calls "the multiplex culture that is America." He arranges four main heritages in a matrix overview, utilizing axes of cultural energy (as reproduced on the facing page; details on pp. 145-146). One axis ranges from gyroscopic to catalytic, or from the preservation of cultural stability to the reorientation of culture through change. Another axis ranges from generic values (common to the Old and New Worlds) to specific values instinctive to America. These two axes define four quadrants: the Modern Heritage (based largely on the organizational synthesis), the Pluralist Heritage (stemming from the ethno-cultural synthesis), the Western Heritage (relating to the world-historical synthesis), and the New World heritage (informed by the republican synthesis).

---

[8] Ed. Stephan Thernstrom (Cambridge: Harvard University Press, 1980), 57.

[9] Published as "The Challenge of Modern Historiography," *American Historical Review*, 87 (Feb. 1982), 1-24.

[10] William Woodward, "America As A Culture (I): Some Emerging Lines of Analysis" and "America As A Culture (II): A Fourfold Heritage?" *Journal of American Culture*, 11 (Spring 1988), 1-32.

Woodward's Multiplex of American Culture

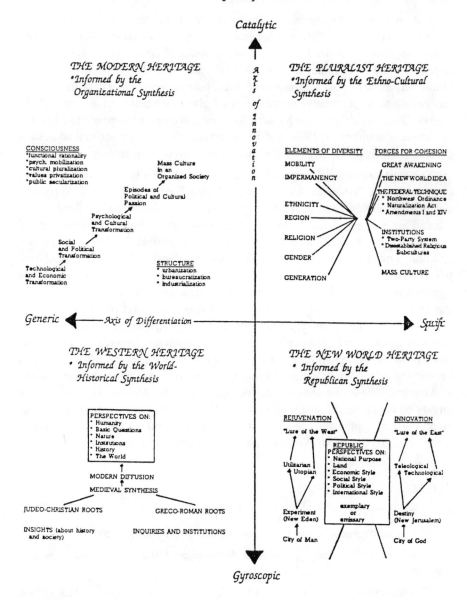

Woodward does not propose these quadrants as exclusionary, but rather as an "argument among competing visions."[11]

THE PLURALIST HERITAGE
Informed by the Ethno-Cultural Synthesis

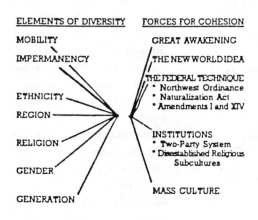

Detail #1 of Woodward's Matrix-- "the multiplex culture that is America"

Certainly we may contend that post-modernism and current global contexts are not represented fully, that class and socio-economic distinctions are not accounted for, that ethnicity is too isolated, and that region, gender and generation may cut through all four quadrants of Woodward's schematic diagram. Woodward does, however, effectively highlight the need to consider ideas and viewpoints as recurring encounters throughout American history. In considering the total cultural and ideological context of past and present events, Woodward proposes that a counterpoint of interpretations yields the fullest and fairest understanding.

---

[11] Woodward's article is rich in depth; a careful reading of the two parts is necessary to comprehend the significance of items contained within each quadrant. Woodward hopes to expose "identifiable patterns of inherent cultural tension [where] competing values begin to make sense." In a significant paragraph, he explains: . . . Imaging America in this way allows us to come to grips with the perplexing bipolarities in the American universe. We are a people who prize both liberty and order, both equality and success, both individualism and community, both unchanging principles and unending progress. We own a culture marked by homogeneity and heterogeneity, continuity and transformation, conflict and consensus. Ours is a culture that is both the sum and the cement of its constituent groupings, and both kin to and distinct from its parent Atlantic tradition." (p. 28)

The matrix was reproduced by kind permission of the author.

This concept of a deepened sense of textural depth, what I term *cultural counterpoint*, is emerging across disciplines as a central tool toward a synthesis of multicultural America.

Detail #2 of Woodward's Matrix:

THE NEW WORLD HERITAGE
* *Informed by the*
   Republican Synthesis

The concept of counterpoint, borrowed from musical language, offers a metaphor rich in interdisciplinary possibilities. As a property of polyphony, counterpoint combines several independent melodic lines. Instead of a single melodic line, "monophony," or a texture featuring one dominant line of melodic interest supported by other voices of lesser significance (homophony), counterpoint emphasizes a rich texture of interaction. Each contrapuntal line possesses coherence and individuality, yet the voices must be perceived simultaneously. As *The New Harvard Dictionary of Music* states, "perceptual balance is struck between the individualities of the lines and their combination; the ear's attention will ideally be focused now on one line, now on the other, and simultaneously on both."[12]

Counterpoint may involve a dialogue, as in a J. S. Bach *Two-Part Invention* or a complex conversation between six interwoven, overlapping lines of great individuality as in a second-generation Franco-Flemish Renaissance motet by Willaert or Gombert. As a flexible procedure, then, counterpoint offers an ideal metaphor for bringing contrasting ideas together. In order to accomplish a synthesis, we must blend and combine our perception of individual lines and relationships into a polyphonic whole. No one line need dominate. Voices may be consonant or dissonant with one another; they may proceed in contrary or opposite directions, in parallel motion, or obliquely while one part moves and the other

---

[12] *The New Harvard Dictionary of Music*, ed. Don Michael Randel (Cambridge, Mass.: The Balknap Press of Harvard University Press, 1986), 205.

remains fixed. Counterpoint does not imply a formal or structural rigidity, but allows an open-ended polyphonic unfolding. Woodward's matrix helps us visualize counterpoints of ideology and historiographical approaches as coexisting within the same space.

The cultural counterpoint of multicultural America is not necessarily a conversation of equality. African-American feminist writer bell hooks argues that we must make "space where critical dialogues can take place between individuals who have not traditionally been compelled by politicized intellectual practice to speak with one another." She continues: "Drawing from a new ethnography, we are challenged to celebrate the polyphonic nature of critical discourse, to--as it happens in traditional African-American religious experience--hear one another 'speak in tongues,' bear witness, and patiently wait for revelation."[13] She cautions against the mere appearance of difference, discouraging a "'celebration' that fails to ask who is sponsoring the party and who is extending the invitations."[14] As Hooks points out, we need to construct a cultural counterpoint which exposes the way history has been worked out through ideas, technology, language, power, gender, sexuality, regionalism, ethnicity, etc. Labor historian Alice Kessler-Harris offers an effective summary of needs and possibilities: the best social history attempts to integrate new research in institutional structures with consciousness and ideology in a way that creates understanding of broader political process and of the tensions that ultimately yield change. In so doing, it has already begun to develop a complex interpretation of American society that rests on neither conflict nor consensus but on a subtle and changing construction of relationships between groups of people, their orientations to social reality, and the actions they take to defend the world that is theirs.[15]

AMERICAN MUSIC AS CULTURAL COUNTERPOINT

The study of American music in cultural context has escalated since the 1950s, receiving a significant boost from the first edition of Gilbert Chase's *America's Music* in 1955.[16] In 1975, the Sonneck Society for American Music was founded

---

[13] Bell Hooks, *Yearning: Race, Gender, and Cultural Politics* (Boston: South End Press, 1990), 133.

[14] Ibid., 54.

[15] Alice Kessler-Harris, "Social History," *The New American History*, 180.

[16] Gilbert Chase, *America's Music: From the Pilgrims to the Present* (New York: McGraw Hill, 1955).

to foster the study of all aspects of American musical life. In 1987 the *New Grove Dictionary of American Music* was published.[17]

Several suggestions toward synthesis in American music have been offered. In 1985, Richard Crawford proposed a fivefold agenda for *Studying American Music.* His agenda centered around bibliography, biography, regionalism, economics, and canonicity; it did not establish a way of viewing relationships simultaneously, however.[18] Bruno Nettl's informal remarks delivered at the conference "American Music at Illinois," moved closer to synthesis.[19] Nettl implied the need for cultural counterpoint in perceiving simultaneously the interaction of musical and cultural lines. While not offering a refined agenda, Nettl listed eight significant aspects of American musical studies today. Among the eight were (1) the idea of viewing all of the music of a culture in its entire collection of strata [a contrapuntal or vertical vision], (2) the interest in "vernacular" music [a less oppositional term than than folk, popular, etc.], (3) the interest in music of ethnic [particularly immigrant] groups, and (4) the systematic examination of jazz and improvisatory practices.[20]

---

[17]*The New Grove Dictionary of American Music,* edited by H. Wiley Hitchcock and Stanley Sadie, with Susan Feder as editorial coordinator, 4 vols. (London and New York: Macmillan, 1986). Richard Crawford cleverly captured the significance of the four volume *"AmeriGrove" Dictionary* by heralding the B.A. or Before *Amerigrove* era, and the A{fter} A{merigrove} post-1987 era of our acceptance of American music's full pluralistic scope of activity. Despite the gathering of so much information together, Crawford also recognized that *Amerigrove* is a lexicographical monument, not a synthesis, and that our continuing challenge is to find a way to bring various constituents as diverse as Bing Crosby and Charles Ives together in meaningful conversation.

[18] Richard Crawford, *Studying American Music* (Brooklyn College: Institute for Studies in American Music Special Publications No. 3, 1985), 2. Utilizing a map-making landscape metaphor, Crawford suggested we explore the American terrain by asking:

1.What music have Americans made? [primarily bibliographical]

2.Who has made music in America? [primarily biographical]

3.Where and in what circumstances has music been made here? [regional studies]

4. How has the making of music been financially supported? [economic, professional]

5.What American music is the most important and why? [America's canon]

[19] Bruno Nettl, "An American Voice," printed in *The Sonneck Society Bulletin* 17/1 (Spring 1991), 6.

[20]Another approach has been advanced by Charles Hamm in "A Proposed Periodization of North American Music," a paper read at the American Musicological Society Meeting in Oakland California, 8 November 1990. (Despite the title, Hamm suggested unifying topics, not a

Viewing American music as cultural counterpoint involves, as Nettl points out, a vertical thinking of rich depth. All types of music stemming from written and oral traditions as produced by all socioeconomic levels and ethnic groups should be viewed in cultural context. Of the standard American music texts by Chase, Kingman, Hitchcock and Hamm, Gilbert Chase's *America's Music* deserves pride of place for continued efforts in this direction. The first edition of Chase broke profoundly with past Eurocentric presentations of the American musical past. Chase did not attempt to disguise his preference for and celebration of vernacular music. Now in a greatly revised third edition (1987),[21] Chase has continued to update, deepen, and expand the number of voices and issues and their interactions. In his introduction to the third edition, Crawford characterizes Chase's work as "a counterpoint of ideas, trends, voices, and sounds, issuing from many different layers of society, each distinct and eloquent in its own right, and each free to accept or resist outside influences."[22] Chase presents several viewpoints within individual chapters, and the dominant voices emphasized from chapter to chapter also counterpoint each other. Chase's prejudices have softened throughout each edition,[23] yet his opinions are ever-present. Even in the midst of an extensive quote, Chase does not hesitate to insert *his* voice through a bracketed comment.

---

chronological periodization.) His five topics, which reflect political and social history, can be applied to all musical genres, and move through time at varying rates:

1. Ritual and myth: music as an integral part of the ceremony and ritual of Native American peoples.

2. Colonization, immigration, and slavery: the importation into North America of complex musical styles and practices.

3. Emergence: syncreticized, distinctly North American styles and practices.

4. Commodification: music and genres as commercial products.

5. Amplification and reproduction: widespread application of electronic technologies.

[21] Revised second edition (New York: McGraw Hill, 1966); revised third edition, with a foreword by Richard Crawford and a Discographical Essay by William Brooks (Urbana: University of Illinois Press, 1987).

[22] Chase 1987, xvii.

[23] His prejudices against the cultivated Germanic dominance of the Second New England School composers run so deeply that in the first edition Chase asserted (325): "Most of the nineteenth century is merely an extended parenthesis in the history of American art music. Take it out and nothing vital is lost in the cultural continuity. (I am speaking, be it understood, of the cultivated fine-art tradition, not of our popular composers such as Emmett and Foster.)"

While one may not agree with Chase's opinions, I have always found students easily engaged with Chase.

Daniel Kingman's *America's Music: A Panorama* (1979 and 1990)[24] rejects even more completely than Chase a traditional chronological/historical approach in favor of what he terms "streams." Kingman is adept at constructing intelligible but intricate contrapuntal relationships within his six main streams ("Folk and Ethnic Musics," "Popular Sacred Music," "Three Prodigious Offspring of the Rural South," "Popular Secular Music," "Jazz and Its Forerunners," and "Classical Music"). The nature of Kingman's vertical thinking is evident in the large diagram included in the back of the book, where his six topical "streams" are stacked up as a visualization of the counterpoint of American musical styles. Kingman not only encourages the use of his topics to produce a depth of thinking within each of the six streams, but the chart illustrates how lines cross and mix together to form new voices or syncreticized musical styles. It is readily seen that early rock 'n' roll joins voices from Anglo-Celtic ballads through country music and rockabilly with voices from boogie woogie, urban blues, and rhythm-and-blues, and that rhythm and blues joined with Creole elements to produce Zydeco in yet another interaction.

In the Epilogue to *Music in the New World*.[25] Charles Hamm explains that when planning a book of manageable size, he made the decision to include music that was changed in its New World surroundings by what he terms a process of "contaminated" acculturation (as in jazz, country-western, and various stages of American popular song), and omit that which was not changed (such as Moravian music, music in late 19th-century ethnic communities, and Catholic and Jewish liturgical music). Hamm infuses his discussion with a sense of ideological and musical conflict that encourages the counterpoint of topics. When summarizing the debate over regular singing during the 1720s, for example, Hamm states that the controversy "was in essence a confrontation between literate, urban people who preferred literal performances from musical notation, and rural, nonliterate folk who were quite content with oral-tradition music."[26]

---

[24] New York: Schirmer Books, 1979; second ed., 1990.

[25] New York: W. W. Norton & Co., 1983.

[26] Ibid., 46. The other American music text in wide use is the third edition of H. Wiley Hitchcock's *Music in the United States: An Historical Introduction* (Englewood Cliffs, N.J.: Prentice Hall, 1988). Hitchcock's work is organized in clear chronological divisions, with separate coverage of sacred and secular in music to 1820, cultivated and vernacular from 1820-1920, and a chronological/topical approach to the twentieth century. Hitchcock does not deal with folk music, since it is covered by Bruno Nettl in another volume of the Prentice-Hall series. This,

CULTURAL COUNTERPOINT IN THE VISUAL ARTS

Cultural counterpoint is first and foremost a mindset, stemming from the desire to view different ideas and layers of activity simultaneously, rather than in disjunct compartments. This polyphonic view may involve envisioning all layers of a single society, such as the economic and social facets of the musical lives of northern free blacks in the nineteenth century in combination with music of slaves and free southern blacks. It may also involve consideration of how blacks interacted with ruling white musicians, such as popular white lyceum managers, black musicians playing in white bands, black protests against the segregation of entertainment facilities and organizations, and how black performers were promoted by the elite white infrastructure.

Contrasting works of visual art is an equally effective way of viewing cultural counterpoint. The juxtaposition of four or five paintings, architectural structures, or sculptures allows simultaneous comparison of subject matter, technique, and viewpoint. To visually grasp cultural counterpoint in the late nineteenth century, for example, a portrait by John Singer Sargent (such as his 1889 depiction of the conductor George Henschel), an image of industrial realism (such as Thomas P. Anschutz's "Steamboat on the Ohio," ca. 1896), a photograph of urban poverty by Jacob Riis, and "The Thankful Poor" (1894) by black artist Henry O. Tanner offer immediate and startling ideological and social contrasts.[27] Regional differences, ethnic perspectives, economic and class diversity, medium, and artistic vantage point present a rich collage. For recent art, Lucy Lippard's *Mixed Blessings: New Art in a Multicultural America* is a milestone for seeing images as counterpoints of ideologies.[28]

---

compounded by the equal but nonetheless separate treatment of cultivated and vernacular traditions, does make the perception of musical interaction from the bottom up quite difficult. Nonetheless, Hitchcock writes in an extremely clear and informative style with much stylistic commentary. His direct approach is appreciated by students who need to work upward from detail to concept before tackling the kind of contrapuntal simultaneity and expression of opinion offered by Chase.

[27] Sargent's and Tanner's paintings are widely available in monographs and catalogues. The Anschutz may be found (along with many other fine examples) in Marianne Doezema's *American Realism and the Industrial Age* (Bloomington: Indiana University Press, 1980). Several of Riis' photographs are available in Paul von Blum's *The Critical Vision: A History of Social and Political Art in the U.S.* (Boston: South End Press, 1982).

[28] New York: Pantheon Books, 1990.

Thus, cultural counterpoint is a useful approach toward synthesis, whether we are viewing Woodward's matrix of ideologies, hearing a variety of musical styles and viewing their lines of interaction in Kingman's diagram, or seeing contrasting artistic images in close juxtaposition. The ultimate goal of fostering cultural counterpoint returns to the question of what the *unum and pluribus* owe each other. Stanley Aronowitz and Henry A. Giroux suggest the complexity of depth and self-knowing that the fostering of voice affords:

> "Voice" refers to the ways in which students produce meaning through the various subject positions that are available to them in the wider society. . . . It is important to stress that students do not have a singular voice, which suggests a static notion of identity and subjectivity. The concept of voice, in the most radical sense, points to the ways in which one's voice as an elaboration of location, experience, and history constitutes forms of subjectivity that are multilayered, mobile, complex, and shifting. The category of voice can only be constituted in differences, and it is in and through these multiple layers of meaning that students are positioned and position themselves in order to be the subject rather than merely the object of history.[29]

Lawrence Fuchs concludes that this type of knowledge will "build a stronger and more humane multi-ethnic society, one in which individuals are free to express their ethnic traditions and interests within the framework of a civil culture," where the *pluribus* — the many of ethnic diversity — become the *unum* of civic culture.[30]

==

[29] *Postmodern Education*, 100.

[30] Lawrence H. Fuchs, *The American Kaleidoscope: Race, Ethnicity, and the Civic Culture* (Hanover, N.H.: The University Press of New England, 1990), xviii.

THE "ALL-IN-ONE":

AMERICA AS CATALOG IN POETRY, MURAL PAINTING AND

MUSIC

by **Annette M. Hansen and Betty Ch'maj**[1]

California State University, Sacramento

> *"I believe it was his vision—the peculiarly American vision of the all-in-one--that led him [Ives] to present mixtures as special insights. As in the case of Whitman it could sometimes lead him to catalogues of opposites, as if by naming all, he might assimilate all into the melting pot."* —Robert Dumm on Charles Ives *(Clavier*, Oct.,1974)

Was it Ralph Waldo.Emerson who started it all? In his famous American Scholar address of 1837, Emerson instructed Harvard graduates on how to create an "American" scholar—not through a study of the ancient past but through the study of everyday life itself, life as a catalog of ordinary images: "What would we know the meaning of? The meal in the firkin; the milk in the pan; the ballad in the street; the news of the boat; the glance of the eye; the form and the gait of the body— ..." Was it Emerson who passed on to Walt Whitman not only the catalog habit, with its expectation that in naming all he might assimilate all into a melting pot called Nation, but also his transcendentalist faith in an ultimate unity—if only the scholar could find the "ultimate reason of these matters," the "eternal law," the "highest spiritual cause lurking ... in these suburbs and extremities of nature?"[2]

---

[1]The idea for this essay was mine, but Annette wrote the first two parts of it, up to Baca. I wrote the rest and edited the whole.--BC

[2] Just after the familiar "meal in the firkin, milk in the pan" passage, Emerson had added: "show me the ultimate reason of these matters; show me the sublime presence of the highest spiritual cause lurking, as always it does lurk, in these suburbs and extremities of nature; let me see every eternal law . . . ." In the preface to *Leaves of Grass*, Whitman identified the "genius" of the "common people" as the place to find the ultimate reason, spiritual presence, and eternal law Emerson had called for. Charles Ives, subject of the epigraph to this chapter, also acknowledged Emerson's direct influence upon him. It is along these two primary routes--through Whitman and Ives--that the process of creating the "All-in-One" can be traced back to the Sage of Concord. See Betty E. Chmaj, "The Journey and the Mirror: Emerson and the American Arts," *PROSPECTS V: An Annual of American Culture Studies*, ed. Jack Salzman (Cambridge University Press, 1986).

   In any event, teachers seeking to demonstrate the importance of American diversity, whether or not they wish to emphasize Emerson's influence, do well to begin with Whitman. From Whitman, they can easily trace outward not only to other authors in the Whitman tradition but also to mural painters and composers who adopted the catalog habit, complete with its expectation—to use Robert Dumm's phrase—that simply by naming (or picturing, or sounding) the multiple separate images that were part of the American experience, they could somehow assimilate the All into the One.

   It is precisely in this direction that the recent focus on the "multi" of American multiculturalism is leading those looking for models to affirm American pluralism. Teachers seeking ways to portray the full spectrum of American diversity are led to Whitman as the poet who took up Emerson's call and turned it into a celebration of individuality within the national whole. In Whitman's poetry they find cataloged not only ethnic diversity, but also diversity of occupations, geography, hardships— America's sense of itself as possessed of democratic variety in all things.

I Hear America Singing[3]

I hear America singing, the varied carols I hear,

Those of mechanics, each one singing his as it should be blithe and strong,

The carpenter singing his as he measures his plank or beam,

The mason singing his as he makes ready for work, or leaves off work,

The boatman singing what belongs to him in his boat,

   the deck-hand singing on the steamboat deck,

The shoemaker singing as he sits on his bench, the hatter singing as he stands,

The wood-cutter's song, the ploughboy's on his way in the morning,

   or at noon intermission or at sundown,

The delicious singing of the mother, or of the young wife at work,

   or of the girl sewing or washing,

Each singing what belongs to him or her and to none else,

---

   [3]*ED. NOTE: Some documents should be part of anybody's multicultural course. This is one of them. So is Emma Lazarus's poem for the Statue of Liberty (p. 69, above), Langston Hughes' "Let America Be America Again," (p. 160, below) and Woody Guthrie's "This Land is Your Land" (p. 171, below). Scot Guenther uses "I Hear America Singing" as the connective linking American Civ 1 to American Civ 2 at San Jose State (see syllabus #18 in Part I and Essay #9 in Part II.--BC*

The day that belongs to the day--at night the party of young fellows, robust, friendly,

Singing with open mouths their strong melodious songs.

While the line of descent from Whitman through writers in the Whitman tradition—such as Carl Sandburg, Hart Crane, Thomas Wolfe, Langston Hughes, Allen Ginsberg, Lawrence Ferlinghetti, Jack Kerouac—may be well known to teachers of literature, there are also painters and composers in whose work may be found not only the catalog habit, but also the attempt to construct, through art, images that impose some kind of order upon a clutter of diversity forever threatening to overleap its boundaries—that is, images that will pull a "Unum" out of the unruly "Pluribus."

A. POETRY

Whitman

In "Song of Myself," Whitman's longest poem, there are at least fifty catalogs, short and long. For Whitman, the idea of Self or Soul served as the unifier, the Oneness into which he incorporated his multitudes. "In all people I see myself, none more and not one barley corn less/ And the good or bad I say of myself I say of them." (stanza 20) His purpose for the poem itself was to define America, not in terms of geography or history but in terms of consciousness, and teachers may wish to quote from the Preface to *Leaves of Grass* to provide the keynote to his "song." Among the catalogs I like best in "Song of Myself" are these:

The little one sleeps in its cradle,

I lift the gauze and look a long time, and silently brush away flies with my hand.

The youngster and the red faced girl turn aside up the bushy hill,

I peeringly view them from the top.

The suicide sprawls on the bloody floor of the bedroom,

I witness the corpse with its dabbled hair, I note where the pistol has fallen.
    (stanza 8)

The pure contralto sings in the organ loft,

The carpenter dresses his plank, the tongue of his foreplane whistles its wild ascending lisp.

The married and unmarried children ride home to their Thanksgiving dinner,

The pilot seizes the king-pin, he heaves down with a strong arm,

The mate stands braced in the whale-boat, lance and harpoon are ready.

The duck shooter walks by silent and cautious stretches,

The deacons are ordain'd with cross'd hands at the altar,

The spinning-girl retreats and advances to the hum of the big wheel,

The farmer stops by the bars as he walks on a First-day loafe and looks at the oats and rye,

The lunatic is carried at last to the asylum a confirm'd case,

(He will never sleep any more as he did in the cot in his mother's bedroom) . . . (stanza 15)

And these lines:

I am of old and young, of the foolish as much as the wise,

Regardless of others, ever regardful of others,

Maternal as well as paternal, a child as well as a man,

Stuff'd with the stuff that is coarse and stuff'd with the stuff that is fine,

One of the Nation of many nations, the smallest the same,
the largest the same, ...

Comrade of Californians, comrade of free North-Westerners (loving their big proportions,)

Comrade of raftsmen and coalmen, comrade of all who shake hands . . .

Of every hue and caste am I, of every rank and religion,

A farmer, mechanic, artist, gentleman, sailor, quaker,

Prisoner, fancy-man, rowdy, lawyer, physician, priest. (stanza 16)

In "Starting from Paumanok," Whitman adopted another device for cataloging America, the image of the journey. In this motif teachers have a strategy for introducing the ideas of American migration and immigration as journeys out of the Self:

Starting from fish-shaped Paumanok where I was born

Well-begotten, and rais'd by a perfect mother,

After roaming many lands, lover of populous pavements,

Dweller in Manhattan my city, or on southern savannas,

Or a soldier camp'd or carrying my knapsack and gun, or a miner in California,

Or rude in my home in Dakota's woods, my diet meat, my drink from the spring,

Or withdrawn to muse and meditate in some deep recess,

Far from the clank of crowds intervals passing rapt and happy,

Aware of the fresh free giver the flowing Missouri, aware of mighty Niagara,

Solitary, singing in the West, I strike up for a New World. . . .

Splashing my bare feet in the edge of the summer ripples on Paumanok's sands,

Crossing the prairies, dwelling again in Chicago, dwelling in every town,

Observing shows, births, improvements, structures, arts,

Listening to orators and oratresses in public halls,

Of and through the States as during life, each man and woman my neighbor,

The Louisianian, the Georgian, as near to me, and I as near to him and her,

The Mississippian and Arkansian yet with me, and I yet with any of them . . .

Yet upon the plains west of the spinal river, yet in my house of adobe,

Yet sailing to other shores to annex the same, yet welcoming every brother.
(stanza 14)

Thus does Whitman give equal validity, democratic validity, to each experience, each geographical location, each life style, each personality. Focusing on place, with no mention of race, sex, ethnic background, economic advantage or hierarchy of leadership, he celebrates regional diversity with appreciation and fervor.

Sandburg

Carl Sandburg continued the Whitman tradition in seeking to be a poet of the people during the hard-hit 1930s. He used cataloging to portray vividly the unrefined reality of the common folk, respecting their innate dignity. For instance, in his book-length *The People, Yes,* (1936), he wrote:

The people, yes, the people,

Everyone who got a letter today,   And those the mail-carrier missed,

The women at the cookstoves preparing meals, in a sewing corner mending, in a basement, laundering, woman the homemaker,

The women at the factory tending a stitching machine, some of them the mainstay of the jobless man at home cooking, laundering,

Streetwalking jobhunters, walkers alive and keen, sleepwalkers drifting along, the stupefied and hopeless down-and-outs, the game fighters who will die fighting,

Walkers reading signs and stopping to study windows, the signs and windows
   aimed straight at their eyes, their wants,

Women in and out of doors to look and feel, to try on, to buy and take away, to
   order and have it charged and delivered, to pass by on account of price and
   conditions,

The shopping crowds, the newspaper circulation, the bystanders who witness
   parades, who meet the boat, the train, who throng in wavelines to a fire, an
   explosion, an accident –

   The people, yes – (stanza 19)

and, on the same theme:

Who knows the people, the migratory harvest hands and berry pickers,
   the loan shark victims, the installment house wolves,

The jugglers in sand and wood who smooth their hands along
   the mold that casts the frame of your motor-car engine, . . .

The riveters and bolt-catchers, the cowboys of the air in the big city, the
   cowhands of the Great Plains, the ex-convicts, the bellhops, redcaps,
   lavatory men –

The union organizer with his list of those ready to join and those hesitating,
   the secret paid informers who report every move toward organizing,

The house to house canvassers, the doorbell ringers,
   the good-morning-have-you-heard boys, the strike pickets,
   the strike-breakers, the hired sluggers, the ambulance crew,
   the ambulance chasers, the meter readers,
   the oysterboat crews, the harborlight tenders –

Who knows the people? (stanza 21)

Here issues of class are foremost, as they are in the writings of Studs Terkel,
who also uses the catalog style, although in prose, and whose works are frequently
linked to Sandburg's (both were from Chicago). From both, teachers can draw
illustrations of working class life and the labor movement. Like Whitman,
Sandburg affirms democracy. He does not support one experience over another,
nor—although his politics are ever present—does he attempt to justify all the
experiences. Rather he says: here it is, look, all of this is America. That is the
quintessential catalog style--to list, to name, to document, and assume that the
images will speak for themselves.

Hughes.

As Sandburg tends to foreground class, Langston Hughes, who drew on both Whitman and Sandburg as models, foregrounds race. Continuing Whitman's emphasis on the ordinary citizen, he created a new audience for poetry—the African American community—by writing of their struggle for dignity in direct, frank, open verse. In his 1932 poem, "I, Too," he speaks to the need for his community to be a part of Whitman's America; the "I" Whitman inhabited when he heard America singing needed to acknowledge another "I":

I, too, sing America.

I am the darker brother.

They send me to eat in the kitchen

When company comes,

But I laugh,

And eat well,

And grow strong.

Tomorrow,

I'll be at the table

When company comes.

Nobody'll dare

Say to me,

Eat in the kitchen

Then.

Besides

They'll see how beautiful I am

And be ashamed.

I, too, am America.

In "Freedom's Plow," Hughes praised the laborers' hands that built America:

Free hands and slave hands

Indentured hands, adventurous hands,

White hands and black hands

Held the plow handles,

Ax handles, hammer handles . . .

All these hands made America.

Labor! Out of labor came the villages

And the towns that grew to cities.

Labor! Out of labor came the
  rowboats

And the sailboats and the steamboats

Out of labor came the factories,

Came the foundries, came the
  railroads,

Came the mighty products moulded,
  manufactured,

Sold in shops, piled in warehouses,

Shipped the wide world over:

Out of labor—white hands and black
  hands--

Came the dream, the strength, the
  will,

And the way to build America.

Now it's Manhattan, Chicago,
  Boston and El Paso —

Now it is the U.S.A.

In 1938 Hughes took that theme further, in a poem that provides a paradigm for contemporary explorations of the tension between unity and diversity, equality and difference: "Let America Be America Again." It is a poem that speaks to the issues facing us today as we struggle to rediscover the meaning of America. The "America" Hughes offers is a dream, a hope, a possibility that has not yet been achieved but, over the years, has remained alive in the hearts of believers. Before using the poem in the classroom, it may be useful to point out the role Hughes had played during the Harlem Renaissance of the 1920s, affirming black identity and seeking to free blacks from what he then called "the urge to whiteness in the race." As might be guessed, the "PC-bashers" of his day accused him of separatism at the time. When he wrote "Let America Be America Again" in 1938, in the depths of the Great Depression, he had transcended separatism in favor of a more daring stance. Buttressed by the belief of his literary mentors Whitman and Sandburg that poets, like scholars, must assume responsibility for *creating* America, and in opposition to the idea of twoness DuBois had described three decades before, Hughes offered in this poem a conundrum, a riddle directly relevant to our own multicultural times.

Let America be America Again

Let America be America again.
Let it be the dream it used to be.
Let it be the pioneer on the plain
Seeking a home where he is free.

(America never was America to me.)

Let America be the dream the
    dreamers dreamed

Let it be that great strong land of love
Where never kings connive nor
    tyrants scheme
That any man be crushed by one
    above.

(It never was America to me.) . . .

*Say who are you that mumbles in the
    dark?*
*And who are you that draws your veil
    across the stars?*

I am the poor white, fooled and
    pushed apart,

I am the Negro bearing slavery's
    scars.
I am the red man driven from the
    land,
I am the immigrant clutching the hope
    I seek – . . .

I am the farmer, bondsman to the
    soil.
I am the worker sold to the machine.
I am the Negro, servant to you all.
I am the people, worried, hungry,
    mean –
Hungry yet today despite the dream.
Beaten yet today – O Pioneers!
I am the man who never got ahead,
the poorest worker bartered through
    the years.

Yet I'm the one who dreamt our basic
    dream
In that Old World while still a serf of
    kings,

Who dreamt a dream so strong, so
brave, so true,

That even yet its mighty daring sings
In every brick and stone, in every
furrow turned
That's made America the land it has
become.
O, I'm the man who sailed those early
seas
In search of what I meant to be my
home –
For I'm the one who left dark
Ireland's shore,
And Poland's plain, and England's
grassy lea,
And torn from Black Africa's strand I
came
To build a "homeland of the free."
The free? A dream –
Still beckoning to me!

O, let America be America again –
The land that never has been yet –
and yet must be –
The land where every man is free.

The land that's mine –
The poor man's, Indian's, Negro's,
ME—
Who made America,
Whose sweat and blood,
whose faith and pain,
Whose hand at the foundry,
whose plow in the rain,
Must bring back our mighty dream
again. . . .

O, yes, I say it plain,
America never was America to me,
And yet I swear this oath –
America will be!
An ever-living seed,
Its dream
Lies deep in the heart of me.

We, the people, must redeem
Our land, the mines, the plants, the
rivers,
The mountains and the endless plain—
All, all the stretch of these great green
states-
And make America again!

Ginsberg

Allen Ginsberg, associated with the Beat Generation poets of the 1950s, most directly continued Whitman's poetic style. "Howl" is a recognizable descendant of *Leaves of Grass*. "The Fall of America," dedicated to Whitman, catalogs Ginsberg's journeys back and forth across the states between 1965 and 1971. Although it lacks Whitman's optimism and sense of spiritual causes, it is in the Whitman tradition of geographic cataloguing. It begins:

Beginning of a Poem of These States

Under the bluffs of Oroville, blue cloud September skies, entering U.S.
border, red red apples bend their tree boughs propt with sticks –

At Omak a fat girl in dungarees leads her big brown
horse by asphalt highway.

Thru lodgepole pine hills Coleville near Moses' Mountain—a white horse
standing back of a 2 ton truck moving forward between trees.

At Nespelem, in the yellow sun, a marker for Chief
Joseph's grave under rilled brown hills – white cross overhighway.

At Grand Coulee under leaden sky, giant red generators
humm thru granite & concrete to materialize onions –

And grey water laps against the grey sides of Steamboat Mesa.

The poem continues under such headings as: "Continuation Of A Long Poem Of
These States: San Francisco Southward," "These States Into Los Angeles,"
"Kansas City To St, Louis," "Cleveland, The Flats," "An Open Window On
Chicago," "Manhattan 'Thirties Flash" and others. Such titles alone catalog
American geography.

Much of Ginsberg's writing is protest poetry. Speaking from and for people on
the margins of society, those at the bottom of the social pyramid, he rails against the
inequities of the American system in a voice of accusation. His "Howl" is an
insightful catalog of the radical dissent of the 1950s. It begins:

I saw the best minds of my generation destroyed by madness, starving,
        hysterical, naked,

    dragging themselves through the negro streets at dawn looking for an angry fix,

angelheaded hipsters burning for the ancient heavenly connection
        to the starry dynamo in the machinery of night,

who poverty and tatters and hollow-eyed and high sat up smoking
        in the supernatural darkness of cold-water flats floating
        across the tops of cities contemplating jazz,

who bared their brains to Heaven under the El and saw Mohammedan angels
        staggering on tenement roofs illuminated,

who passed through universities with radiant cool eyes hallucinating
        Arkansas and Blake-light tragedy among the scholars of war,

who were expelled from the academies for crazy & publishing obscene odes on
        the windows of the skull,

who cowered in unshaven rooms in underwear, burning their money in
        wastebaskets and listening to the Terror through the wall . . .

who talked continuously seventy hours from park to pad to bar to Bellevue
        to museum to the Brooklyn Bridge,

a lost battalion of platonic conversationalists jumping down the stoops off
 fire escapes off windowsills off Empire State out of the moon,

yacketayakking screaming vomiting whispering facts and memories and
 anecdotes and eyeball kicks and shocks of hospitals and jails and wars ...

There is a relentlessness to Ginsberg's "Howl"—his "alienated assault on
culture and society"[4]—that mesmerizes us into acknowledging the depth of his
generation's sense of grief as they contemplated what America has meant to them.

Chiang

Like Hughes and Ginsberg, who use specific segments of American society as
representative of the American experience they catalog (racial in Hughes' case,
generational in Ginsberg's), women writers and artists have also been drawn to
represent their views of America in long lists. In 1939, Faye Chiang used
America's daily habit, the six o'clock news and the headlines of the daily
newspaper, to portray American life in wrenching images, as in this excerpt from
"It Was As If":

headlines:

woman jumps off brooklyn bridge clutching her raggedy ann doll.

son kills mom and dad in outer suburbia in fit of rage.

miss america crowned in fairbanks alaska.

more than half the world population dying of starvation.

the unemployed masses marched toward the sea on both

coasts of the nation in the formation of lemmings. asked

one participating in this remarkable sight (by this

reporter) the reasoning behind such an exodus, he replied:

for lack of something better to do. unquote.

teenaged youngsters rampaged through the national parks in

their annual outburst of destruction, while our elderly

---

[4]Peter Clecak, *America's Quest for the Ideal Self* (Oxford University Press, 1988), p.163-167,
who argues that the propensity of Ginsberg, like other Beat generation poets and post World War II
dissenters, to catalog so relentlessly America's faults was a way of demanding "a place on the
American turf rather than inclusion in any of its severally socially contrived hierarchies of wealth,
power, influence or authority."

continue contemplating the nutritional value of bird seeds.

purina's warehouses have since been depleted of dog and cat food.

heads of state gathered on the white house lawn in search

of easter eggs carefully camouflaged in the bushes;

united nations members continued playing monopoly far

into the night: this is the six o'clock news.

Lim

As Whitman presumed to incarnate all Americans into his Soul or Self in "Song of Myself," so poet Genny Lim today wonders if she is not part of all women in the multicultural world she inhabits. As "Wonder Woman," she contemplates her world in Whitmanesque accents:

Sometimes I stare longingly at women
   who I will never know

Generous, laughing women with
   wrinkled cheeks and white teeth

Dragging along chubby, rosy-cheeked
   babies on fat, wobbly legs

Sometimes I stare at Chinese
   grandmothers

Getting on #30 Stockton with
   shopping bags

Japanese women tourists in European
   hats

Middle-aged mothers with laundry
   carts

Young wives holding hands in coffee-
   houses

Smiling debutantes with bouquets of
   yellow daffodils

Silvered-haired matrons with silver
   rhinestoned poodles

Painted prostitutes posing along
   MacArthur Boulevard

Giddy teenage girls snapping gum in
   fast cars

Widows clutching bibles, crucifixes

I wonder if the woman in mink is
   content

If the stockbroker's wife is afraid of
   growing old

If the professor's wife is an alcoholic

If the woman in prison is me.

There are copper-tanned women in
   Hyannis Port playing tennis

Women who eat with finger bowls

There are women in factories
   punching time clocks

Women tired every waking hour of
   the day

I wonder why there are women born
   with silver spoons in their mouths

Women who have never known a day
   of hunger

Women who have never changed their
   own bed linen

And I wonder why there are women
   who must work

Women who must clean other
   women's houses

Women who must shell shrimps for
   pennies a day

Women who must sew other
   women's clothes

Who must cook

Who must die

In childbirth

In dreams

Short, tall, skinny, fat

Pregnant, married, white, yellow,
   black, brown, red

Professional, working-class,
   aristocrat

Women cooking over coals in
   sampans

Women shining tiffany spoons in
   glass houses

Women stretching their arms way
   above the clouds

In Samarkand, in San Francisco

Along the Mekong.

Thus the journey that started out from Whitman's fish-shaped Paumanok, having passed through Sandburg's populist affirmations and Hughes' impassioned pleas, beyond Ginsberg's chronicles of a dropout society and Chiang's headlines of everyday events, has taken us to Samarkand, to San Francisco, and along the Mekong. Here Lim's women stretch their arms above the clouds to connect with one another much as Whitman's American soul once sought to make its "Passage to India." In these examples and others, we can recognize the same insistent need among poets to inventory images, the same assumption that by naming all one can assimilate all, the same "peculiarly American" vision of the all-in-one.[5]

B. MURAL PAINTING

> *A truly 'public' art provides society with the symbolic representation of its collective beliefs.*--Preface, *"Signs from the Heart": California Chicano Murals, 1990.*

Writers have not been alone among those compelled to catalog America. Among painters, muralists have been especially adept at designing forms of public art to

---

[5]Chiang and Lim quoted from Dexter Fisher, *The Third Woman: Minority Woman Writers in the United States* (Houghton Mifflin, 1980), and Cherrie Moraga and Gloria Anzaldua, *This Bridge Called My Back: Writings of American Women of Color* (Persephone Press, 1981).

give symbolic representation of "collective beliefs." Mural-painting as a means of communicating multiple visions came into its own in the United States with the WPA projects of the New Deal period (thanks partly to the influence in America of the pioneer Mexican muralist Diego Rivera) and again with the contemporary mural movement that began in the 1960s. Both are closely tied to multicultural sentiments.

During the 1930s, Thomas Hart Benton and Ben Shahn created murals that embodied American diversity in visual catalogs that reached beyond the decade. During the 1960s and 70s, the collages of Romare Beardon, like Langston Hughes' poetry, focussed on the distinctiveness of the African American experience. More recently, the Chicano mural movement has expressed the frustrations and celebrated the achievements of Chicanos as they struggle to define and maintain their culture. There are murals by many other artists and groups to be found all across the country—in post offices (see the essay by John Carlisle), libraries, banks, and other buildings students can visit. But even when students cannot see the murals themselves, teachers can make slides from books for classroom use, and videotapes are available of mural works, many of which are being discussed on public television. The following is a sampling.

Benton

A nine-panel series entitled "America Today," painted by Thomas Hart Benton for the New School of Social Research in New York City attempted, like Whitman's catalogs, to include everything significant Benton saw as American. Under the titles, "City Activities," "City Building," "Instruments of Power," "The Changing West," and the like, the individual panels sought to give a comprehensive picture of the development of industrial America and its effects on rural America, and to portray city life. Matthew Baigell characterizes the series as "a panoramic treatment of competing motifs" in which Benton sought to show "the abundance of energy and the variety and confusion of everyday existence by presenting the uniquely American fusion of a rural and frontier psychology and an advanced technological system."[6]

In other murals, Benton mixed American folk legends with real-life incidents to portray American regions (he was central to the group known as "Regionalists" and

---

[6]Benton painted three sets of panels between 1930 and 1933. The first two were commissioned for the New School for Social Research and the Whitney Museum of Modern Art, both in New York City. The third was commissioned for the State of Indiana Pavilion at the Century of Progress International Exposition held in Chicago in 1933-1934 as a history of the state. Matthew Baigell, *Thomas Hart Benton* (Harry Abrams, 1973), pp. 111-112. This book has good reproductions for making slides.

"American Scene" painters during the 1930s). Examples are the two murals, easily located in books about Benton, titled "Arts of the West" and "Arts of the South," while the mural "City Life" provides an example of the subtle anti-city bias that can be found among some of America's most enthusiastic catalogers.

Shahn

As Benton's murals use cataloging to fulfill the motives of the 1930s Regionalist school of thought, Ben Shahn's murals illustrate a left-wing perspective of the same era, the attitudes of social realists and social protest painters. The story of American immigration is the theme of one of Ben Shahn's murals, originally called "Jersey Homestead" (now "Roosevelt Homestead"), painted in 1936 for the Community Center in Roosevelt, New Jersey. Shahn portrays a crowd of refugees, still wearing numbers pinned to their clothing, streaming over a bridge, with the Statue of Liberty, an American flag, and the waiting room for processing immigrants seen in the background. The immigrants flow into a crowded gallery of garment industry scenes—sewing rooms, ironing rooms, employment lines – and then move on to join in a union organization rally, a back room political meeting, and into a scene with city planners and row houses. They then walk across a bridge into what we realize will be their more individualized separate lives. The mural is a natural for use in relation to units focusing on immigration, especially through Ellis Island at the turn of the century.[7]

Bearden

Romare Bearden's four-foot by eighteen-foot collage, "The Block," is an installation rather than a mural, but as a form of public art that draws upon a similar region of experience, it fulfills a similar purpose. Completed in 1971, "The Block" was exhibited with a tape recording of street sounds to help depict the activities of a city block in the black section of any major American city. Through the windows, Bearden gives us glimpses of life inside the multi-storied buildings as well as showing us life at sidewalk level, in the churches, apartments, barber shop, corner liquor store and, beyond, the traffic of the street leading uptown. Painted on the side of one building is the kind of fanciful mural that began to appear on the walls in black urban neighborhoods during the 1960s and 70s.

After travelling the roads of America, Bearden said he found that in order to describe truthfully the human experience as he knew it, he had to project "black truth upon white consciousness." His need, similar to Langston Hughes's, was to "redefine the image of man in terms of the Negro experience," which led him during the 1960s to create collages (collage as a form lends itself to cataloging) in

---

[7]Bernardo Bryson Shahn, *Ben Shahn*, (Harry N. Abrams, 1972).

which he juxtaposed fragments of.black-and-white photographs to portray aspects of black American life. These crowded "photomontages," as he called them, were, collectively, a catalog of black experience, leading logically to "The Block.".[8]

Baca

As a Chicana, both ethnic and female, Judith Baca provides us with an example of a muralist in the contemporary world of multicultural experience. An activist who has become a leading voice of the Chicano community, Baca, like Sandburg, Hughes, Shahn, and Guthrie, has used her art to make political statements, but like Judy Chicago, she has also made a point of involving others in the projects she directs.[9] Baca became a muralist because she had difficulty fitting the image of

FIGURE #1. Judy Baca with her team for the "Great Wall of Los Angeles" Project. Photo: Linda Eber. © Social & Public Art Resource Center, 1981. Used with permission..

---

[8]Quoted in M. Bunch Washington, *The Art of Romare Bearden: The Prevalence of Ritual.* (Harry N. Abrams, 1972), p. 9.

[9] During the 1970s and 1980s, artist Judy Chicago led the way in affirming the idea of cooperative art as female, in contrast to the individualism of the "artist as hero" to which male artists had become accustomed and which women artists were expected to embrace in their art-school training In her Dinner Party project and Birth Project, Chicago worked with other women to validate women's traditional and collective forms (needlework, china painting, quilting) at the same time that she advanced the argument in her writings that collectivity, working together, is a female way of working superior to the usual male way of making art.

artist she encountered in art schools. She wanted to work collectively with others and create a public art that would make a difference to the larger society. She became the leader of a collective public art movement that sought to bring together artists from different racial and ethnic backgrounds, women and men, and--most interestingly--the very teenagers who hung out in the streets of the city, often in gangs, and made a ritual of decorating its walls with the code language of graffiti.

Figure #2. GREAT WALL OF LOS ANGELES, 1940's section, 1981. Acrylic on cast concrete, 13'x350', by Judith Baca.. © Social & Public Art Resource Center. Used with permission..

"The Great Wall of Los Angeles," a history of California (Califia) told from a "minority" or "counter-hegemonic" point of view, was begun in 1976 by a racially and ethnically mixed group of ten artists and eighty-some teenagers. Directed by Baca and completed in 1983, it is over a half-mile long; Lucy Lippard thinks it may be the longest mural in the world. It is located not in the barrio where local mural art by and for Chicanos might be expected to flourish, but in a flood control channel in the San Fernando Valley, a suburban locale settled by those who moved there to escape from the barrio as it grew. Since the history of California is the Wall's subject, catalogs of historical images are to be expected, but they are images of conflict, division, and battle as the history unfolds, decade by decade, from the points of view of America's rasquaches--images of Mexican American deportation, Japanese American internment, Zoot Suiters rioting, women transformed from Rosie the

Riveters into housewives, poor families divided in order that freeways can service the well-to-do, and so on.[10]

But to Baca, the most important "focus" of the Great Wall project is not the subjects it catalogs but the way the mural was made, the "cooperation in the process underlying its creation." "The thing about muralism is that collaboration is a requirement," she explains. Such a view updates the vision of the all-in-one. "Presenting mixtures as special insights" comes to describe the agents as well as the subjects of these murals.[11]

This is only a sampling of the catalog impulse to be found in muralism, past and present. The Chicano muralist movement in the Los Angeles area is the strongest trend in the nation at present but other examples may soon appear. As more and more multicultural artists emerge to claim our attention, seeking ways to create a public art that will serve a social purpose, and as more volumes like Lippard's appear which acknowledge that emergence, the impulse to record diversity promises to get stronger, the catalogs of images longer.

C. MUSIC

Turning from visual arts to music, the most obvious place to look for examples of cataloging is in song lyrics. The most conspicuous trait in the lyrics of American patriotic song has been its impulse to catalog the reach of national scenery. From Samuel Ward (1848-1903) in "America the Beautiful," lauding the nation for its "spacious skies and amber fields of grain,/ for purple mountain majesties above the fruited plain," to Woody Guthrie during the 1930s, telling the common people, "This land is your land, this land is my land,/ from California to the New York Island,/ from the redwood forests to the Gulf Stream waters," to Irving Berlin during World War II, asking God to bless America "from the mountains/ to the prairies/ to the oceans white with foam," Americans have laid claim to nationality by

---

[10] When the Chicano mural movement began, in fact, its artists found inspiration from a whole array of influences. "They looked to Los Tres Grandes--the Mexican muralists Diego Rivera, José Clemente Orozco, and especially David Alfaro Siqueiros; to the all-important family structures of their communities; to the *rasquache* (underdog) worldview; to *corridos*, the popular arts, *milagros, monitos,* home altars, low-riders, and decorated cars, and they began to see them all as subjects for art, as works of art in themselves." Lippard, *Mixed Blessings* p. 170.

[11] Lippard, pp. 170-71, plate 28. See also *Signs from the Heart: California Chicano Murals* (Venice, California: Social and Public Art Research Center, 1990), pp. 76-82. For information about slides on recent murals in California focussing on Chicano and other groups, contact Social and Public Art Research Center, 685 Venice Blvd., Venice, CA 90291. (213) 822-9560.

equating Nation with Nature, cataloging landscape images from sea to shining sea. In the lyrics not only of patriotic songs but also political songs, protest songs, nonsense songs, sentimental songs, work songs, freedom songs, folk ballads, household laments, country and rock and rap music, there are catalogs of many kinds. Among these, Guthrie's may be taken as example.

Woody Guthrie

Guthrie acknowledged a debt to Whitman and Sandburg in his autobiography, but at the same time insisted that his people spoke a different language: "Whitman makes glorious the works, labors, hopes, dreams, and feelings of my people, but he does not do this in the sorts of words my people think, talk, and dance and sing," Guthrie wrote. "Sandburg tosses in grammar words that I never do hear my kind of folks talk. They praise, describe, they pay their thanks and tributes to my people, but not in words my kind of people think. So I've got to keep on plugging away."[12] The several verses of "This Land is Your Land" show what Guthrie saw and felt in America on his journey through its natural and social landscapes:

1. As I went walking, that ribbon of highway

   I saw above me that endless skyway

   I saw before me that golden valley

   This land is made for you and me. CHORUS

2. I roamed and I rambled, and I followed my footsteps

   To the sparkling sand of her diamond deserts

   While all around me, a voice was sounding,

   Saying this land was made for you and me. CHORUS

3. The sun came shining and I was strolling

   And the wheatfields waving and the dust clouds rolling

   As the fog was lifting, a voice was chanting

   This land was made for you and me. CHORUS

4. In the square of the city, by the shadow of the steeple

   By the welfare office I saw my people

   As they stood hungry, I stood there wondering if

   This land was made for you and me. CHORUS

---

[12] Guthrie, *Pastures of Plenty*, ed. David Marsh and Harold Leaventhal (Harper-Collins, 1980)

5. As I went rambling that dirty old highway

    I saw a sign sayin, This is private property

    But on the other side, it didn't say nothin'

    This land was made for you and me. CHORUS

In Guthrie's "Pastures of Plenty," by contrast, a migrant farm worker addresses a different America with accusation and anger in his voice, tallying up in his catalog the places he has worked and the crops he has picked in the course of a lifetime of working the land:

1. It's a mighty hard row that my poor hands has hoed

    My poor feet has traveled a hot dusty road

    Out of your dust bowl and westward we rolled

    And your deserts was hot and your mountains was cold.

2. I work in your orchards of peaches and prunes

    And I sleep on the ground 'neath the light of your moon

    On the edge of your city you'll see us, and then

    We come with the dust and we go with the wind.

3 California, Arizona, I made all your crops

    Then its north up to Oregon to gather your hops

    Dig beets from your ground, cut the grapes from your vine

    To set on your table your light sparkling wine.

4. Green pastures of plenty from dry desert ground

    From the Grand Coulee Dam where the waters run down

    Every state in this union us migrants has been

    We'll work in this flight and we'll fight till we win.

5. It's always we ramble, that river and I

    All along your green valley I'll work till I die

    My land I'll defend with my life if needs be

    'Cause my pastures of plenty must always be free.

Images from John Steinbeck's classic *Grapes of Wrath* provide the catalog content for Guthrie's "That Old Dust Bowl" and other songs in his album Dust

Bowl Ballads. "That old dust bowl/ Kilt my baby," the song begins, "But it can't kill me, boys, it can't kill me"; "that old tractor/ tore my house down," "that old pawnshop/ took my furniture," and so on. Clearly the America of the migrant farmer and the Dust Bowl balladeer are as far from purple mountain majesties above the fruited plains as Sandburg's and Hughes's catalogs are from Whitman's.

But lyrics alone, after all, are literature--not the only way American music has used catalogs to represent American diversity. Three examples will illustrate three very different uses of music: (1) the popular musical *West Side Story*; (2) the works of Charles Ives, in particular his *Fourth Symphony*; and (3) a new lyric opera about the California gold rush by Daniel Kingman called *The Golden Gyre*.

West Side Story

Jerome Robbins' 1957 musical *West Side Story* (music by Leonard Bernstein, lyrics by Stephen Sondheim, choreography by Robbins) was a milestone in the history of musical theatre for its use of modern music and dance to represent the reality of American cultural conflict as experienced by the young on the streets of our cities. The conflict is between two street gangs, the Jets, made up of white youths whose grandparents may well have been immigrants at the turn of the century, and the Sharks, a gang of newly-arrived Puerto Ricans. The setting for working out the conflict, as the title announces, is New York City, the metropolitan inner city having displaced the American small town as the locale for telling the American story. One example of cataloging appears in the successive stanzas to the song "Gee, Officer Krupke," in which the Jets deride, in succession, the solutions offered by the courts, the police, psychologists, and sociologists to the problems of juvenile delinquency.

A second, more important catalog is the list of attractions as against the list of failures of "America," a song sung to accompany a brilliant dance number. During the course of the song, in the movie version of the musical, the opportunities that attract Puerto Rican *women* to America--namely, the freedom from the limitations and drudgery that are so often a part of immigrant women's lives in their homeland—are counterpointed to the disappointments of Puerto Rican *men* who discount such opportunities and material advantages as intended mainly for well-to-do whites. The dialogue includes exchanges like this:

WOMEN: Buying on credit is so nice--!

MEN: One look at us and they charge twice!

WOMAN: I'll have my own washing machine!

MAN: What will you have, though, to keep clean?

and again, in a continuing satire of America's promise to immigrants:

> *WOMEN:* Life can be bright in America!   *MEN:* If you can fight in America!
>
> *WOMEN:* Life is all right in America--   *MEN:* If you are white in America!
>
> *WOMEN:* Here you are free and you have pride!
>
> *MEN:* 'Long as you stay on your own side!
>
> *WOMEN:* Free to be anything you choose--
>
> *MEN:* Free to wait tables and shine shoes!

More subtle in terms of purely musical cataloguing is a moment in the musical that has been widely remarked upon by musicologists—the reprieve of the song "Tonight," in which five quite different voices retain their distinction as they sing together, expressing their different desires. The example offers a musical paradigm for an alternative to the image of the melting pot—or for what is sometimes taken to be the same thing, a symphony orchestra that has diverse instruments "blending" to create "harmony." Although the movie version of *West Side Story* has its flaws, it has the advantage in the classroom of making it is easy for students to identify the five separate voices in the "Tonight" reprieve, since the camera focuses on the five different presences as they sing. There is even a moment during the sequence when Lieutenant Shrank, a sixth presence representing hegemonic adult authority, drives by, ominously watching and waiting—but Shrank does not sing. In the sequence, each person or group articulates the promise "Tonight" holds, but each sings a different song—some to the same melody, all to different words. Tony and Maria sing the ballad-like *melody*, although with different words, and it is in this melody that the hope of sweet fulfillment through musical resolution seems to be promised. Their expectation of a happy ending (consonance) points up the importance of the American love mystique in sustaining multicultural unity. By contrast, the Jets and Sharks sing the *countermelody* in angry accents (dissonance), looking forward to their forthcoming "rumble," with no interest in happy endings—only in triumph. Most interesting of all, in terms of contemporary significance, is Anita, who sings her tune forthrightly and boldly, but in a different key:

> Anita's going to get her kicks tonight,
>
> We'll have our private little mix tonight —

The same capacity for affirmation that enabled Anita to lead the Puerto Rican women to embrace the promise of "America" allows her here to affirm her sexuality (if only to herself) in a tone and manner more usual to such modern performers as Madonna and Tina Turner than to the "trapped" women of the conformist 1950s. (Whether these affirmations of her sexual interests make Anita a stereotype when viewed from an older perspective or a feminist when viewed from a newer one, or both, is a relevant subject for debate.) The overall picture of this passage is of a catalog of five separate musical ideas, five expectations, each hoping for fulfillment. In terms of the plot, what actually happens is different from everyone's expectations, but for the duration of the reprieve, we are given an astonishing musical image of diversity in which separateness is never compromised.

Charles Ives

Among composers of fine-art music, Charles Ives, profoundly influenced by Emerson, probably comes the closest to achieving in music what Whitman did in poetry—namely, including all of America in his works of art. Ives did not try to detach music from everyday reality; his subject matter often focused on everyday, middle-class New England, which, geographically, represented America to him. Some of his titles reflect as much: "Three Places in New England" features the Boston Common, Putnam's Camp, and the River Housatonic as it flows past Stockbridge; the four movements of "Orchestra Set No. 2" are entitled "An Elegy to Our Forefathers," "The Rockstrewn Hills Join in the People's Outdoor Meeting," "From Hanover Square North at the End of a Tragic Day" and "Central Park in the Dark, " and so on. Many of Ives's works quote liberally and sometimes simul- taneously from American popular musics—hymn tunes, patriotic songs, ragtime, band music, Stephen Foster melodies, and sentimental ballads. He might quote a phrase directly from these or, in Lou Harrison's phrase, decompose and recompose a melody taken from the popular repertoire. Like Whitman's poetry, much of Ives's entire *oeuvre* can be characterized as a catalog—a portrait, as Robert Dumm would have it, of the American All-in-One.

Rosalie Sandra Perry has rightly described Ives's technique as "patch-work"— collections of fragments, motifs, genre scenes, scraps, and pieces." Since his attempt was to present more than one idea at a time, formal transitions were not appropriate. At times this created passages with so much "diversity" crammed into them that they were virtually impossible to play—and, some thought, equally impossible to hear.[13]

In his song "The Majority," also titled "The Masses" (1914), we see Ives's effort to invent musical forms that would put his political views into music. The text of the song expresses his faith in the people and in direct democracy:

> The Masses! The Masses! The Masses have toiled
>
> Behold the works of the World!

---

[13]Perry, *Charles Ives and the American Mind* (Kent State University Press, 1974), p. 59.

> The Masses are thinking,
>
> Whence comes the thought of the World!
>
> The Masses are singing, are singing, singing,
>
> Whence comes the Art of the World! [etc.]

We may examine the introduction to the song in order to see in purely visual terms how this innovative composer sought to translate the political idea of validating multiplicity--the masses, the diverse American "majority"--into abstract musical notation."[14]   To study this single page of sheet music is to recognize the tension between unity and diversity as a very real struggle in Ives's thought. His use of multiple voices (diversity) is conspicuous here, and so is the way he has the "will" of the majority respond to individual voices--i.e., in the accents given to the 14-voice clusters. Such emphases are apt. In an essay called "The Majority," Ives called for a 20th Amendment to the Constitution that would transfer power directly to the masses,

a plan for direct government he championed vociferously, especially after the failure of the Treaty of Versailles. In "The Majority" and other works, we see his effort to use purely musical forms to put those political views into music.[15]

---

[14]Perry, p. 63. I am indebted to Perry for reproducing this page of the score.

[15]J. Peter Burkholder calls *The Majority* (1914-15) "a testimony to Ives's faith in the masses and the song that perhaps comes nearest to expressing his political credo." *Charles Ives: The Ideas Behind the Music* (Yale University Press, 1985), 106. Daniel Kingman calls the piece "a startling work, big in conception," expressing Ives's "complex and sometimes contradictory idealism--a

An excellent aural example to use with students to illustrate how Ives translated the myth of America's unity and diversity into musical form appears in his magesterial Fourth Symphony. A general explanation of Ives's overall program for the work (which will likely appear on liner notes) should precede the playing of the example, a segment about three minutes long from near the very end of the second movement. It is the moment when a solo violin can be heard rising up out of a sweep of sound, playing a familiar hymn tune with great assurance and fervor, only to be rudely interrupted in mid-phrase by the orchestra, which gives us the full impact of what Ives identified as "reality"--"the 4th of July in Concord, brass band, drum corps, etc." Ives' "reality" is, in effect, a multi-layered musical catalog.[16] Two theoretical approaches representing two schools of thought in American Studies may be used to explain to students what happens in this example. Both will be of interest to multiculturalists today:

Now for older Ives scholars like myself (the myth-and-image American Studies scholars), it is impossible *not to* hear the myth of America in such music: the violin gives us the familiar, hegemonic, hymn-singing, white-picket-fence America. This is Grover's Corners' America, Norman Rockwell's America, self-assuredly playing its sentimental hymns as the pilgrims, in Ives' words, make "their journey through the swamps and the rough country." I take Ives at his word when he says these sentimental episodes are constantly being "crowded out" by "reality"--the loud multiple conflicting strands that speak of the other America: the masses, the brash and dissonant democratic majority. One way or another, what I hear in Ives again and again is the dialectic between the one and the many, the unum and the pluribus, individualism and democracy often pulling in opposite directions. I don't hear Ives pronouncing judgement, saying that one direction is better than the other but rather, like Emerson, constantly musing over the continuing conflict between them.

A poststructuralist listening to that same passage, however, will hear something else. The sentimental violin is "Rollo," effeminate or feminized, a kissing cousin to those audiences with "lily-ladybird ears" for whom Ives had such contempt. When the Concord band moves in like a juggernaut, it shuts

---

deep faith in democracy." *American Music: A Panorama.* 2nd ed. (Schirmer Books, 1990), pp. 511-12. Frank Rossiter has the best discussion of Ives's politics, and he comments also on his use of dissonance in music addressing the issue of direct government, in *Charles Ives and His America* (New York: Liveright, 1975), pp. 136-40.

[16]In fact, it is his favorite catalog, for the passage used here also appears in the "Hawthorne" movement of the *Concord Sonata* and in his *Three Places in New England.*

Rollo up, triumphally rolls right over him, and what is revealed, says the new
theorist, deconstructing Ives' intent (new theorists tend to focus, as the New
Critics once did, more on the work itself than what the author said he meant)—
what is unveiled, says the theorist, is Ives' misogyny, his "masculine protest"—
i.e., "the obsession with virility based on the dread of being feminized in
relation to other men." All that "innovative energy [is] fringed by a certain
panic" (it has been called Ives' "homosexual panic"). Thus identity politics
pronounces Ives guilty—politically incorrect, his work becoming one more tool
of Western oppression.[17]

Whether or not those two positions are compatible, without question, Ives's music
is bound to offer the richest vein of material to mine for examples not only of
cataloging as such but of catalogs that somehow attempt, as Emerson himself
always did, to insist on unity even as they acknowledge diversity and conflict.

The Golden Gyre

Daniel Kingman's *The Golden Gyre* is a one-hundred minute epic cantata
based on letters and diaries of those who participated in the California Gold Rush.
This work brings us full circle to the point at which this essay began—Whitman's
conviction that America in the mid-nineteenth century could be defined as its
people's collective experience, their emotional experience in their journey through
the land. At the same time, Kingman's work is revisionist history—very much a
voice of the "post-Columbian" 1990s, for the same impulse that questioned popular
interpretations of how Columbus "discovered" America has come to question how
the West was "won"—in this case, how the discovery of gold in California made
America a success. As Kingman wrote in his program notes, although no other
event besides the Civil War had "so riveted the attention, enlisted the man and
womanpower, tested the courage and endurance, or had such a lasting effect" as
had the discovery of gold in California in 1848, "the popular images of the ensuing
Gold Rush . . . do not begin to convey the vastness of this turbulent adventure.
Nor can these conventional images give any feeling for the impact the experience
had on individual human beings."[18] Making use of the "new social history,"

---

[17] Betty Ch'maj delivered this polemic against the excesses of theory in a paper, "American
Music and the PC Debate," at the 1992 meeting of the Sonneck Society for American Music. The
poststructuralist "theorist" quoted is Lawrence Kramer, who had delivered a paper critical of Ives at
a conference on "Feminist Theory and Music" in Minneapolis the previous June. His paper will
appear in a forthcoming collection edited by J. Peter Burkholder.

[18] Program notes for the premiere performance, Festival of New American Music, Crocker Art
Museum, November 17, 1991. Kingman explains that he thinks of "gyre" as a large circle or
circular motion, as in the pattern traced by the Gulf Stream, or as in the word *gyroscope*.

Kingman bases his text on actual accounts by those who made the trip and those they left behind (largely taken from J. S. Holliday's *The World Rushed In, An Eyewitness Account of a Nation Heading West*). The words are sung or spoken by soprano and baritone, in order to reveal the "emotional essence of each of the scenes" in this "restless and prodigious American Odyssey."[19]

As Kingman presents the saga, of a nation heading West is not a story with a happy ending—and this too is typical of revisionist perspectives. The journey ends where it began (thus the title) after Easterners have crossed the country overland to California, then sailed down and through the Isthmus of Panama, then back up to New York City. But what makes Kingman's work compelling is the music—a startling, unrelenting post-Ivesian catalog of dissonance, multiple rhythms, and abrupt declarations. It is the combination of the modern and the "multi" (multivocal, multirhythmic, multilayered) that make the work especially arresting as an example for use in classes on multiculturalism.[20] Some sense of the "multi" may be gained from the text, as in these descriptions of the streets of San Francisco, whose music the composer himself described to me as "probably the most venturesome and 'far out' in the piece":[21]

---

[19]Kingman, Program notes. Kingman enthusiastically acknowledges Holliday's volume, which teachers might wish to assign along with the tape. However, Kingman's score is more modern and "multi" than Holliday's book, more unrelenting, lending force to the narrative.

[20]After its premiere November 17, 1991, *The Golden Gyre* was recorded on November 19, 1991 and January 19, 1992, with Kingman conducting. A recording of the performance on two cassettes, plus a copy of the text, may be obtained from the composer by sending $15.00 to "Golden Gyre," 600 Shangri Lane, Sacramento CA 95825.

About my interpretation of his work, the composer wrote: "I found your 'reading' interesting, and in general not at all at odds with what I might consider a valid 'extension of meaning,' if I were to think about it. (In actuality, I don't think 'multiculturalism' ever occurred to me at the time, but it certainly is inherent in both the experience and the material.)" Letter from Daniel Kingman to Betty Ch'maj, April 13, 1992.

[21]Here is what he said about this section of the cantata: "You quoted some lines from the San Francisco scene. This scene is probably the most venturesome and 'far out' in the piece. It is experimental, in a way, and I'm not sure it wholly succeeds. What I was trying to achieve was the *simultaneous* expression of two views of the city--which could be *any* frontier city, or really *any* city, when you get right down to it. The baritone and percussion celebrate, even glorify, the material aspects of 'progress'--pride in the booming construction, the teeming populace (a typical real estate developer's view). The soprano, viola and piano, on the other hand, deplore the lack of anything that ministers to deeper human needs--the lack of friends, the commercialization of affection represented by the whores, and so on. All this is symbolized by the absence of flowers: 'Yes, tell me of fresh flowers, the old familiar faces: here all are strangers.' Interestingly, both of

Here you can step out of your house and see the whole world spread out before you in every shape and form. Your ears are filled with the most delightful music, your eyes are dazzled with every thing that is beautiful, the streets are crowded–the whole city are in the street. . . .--*Megquier, Apron Full of Gold.*

Pass through Kearney Street, to the head of Commercial Street, and look down through a portion of the town. . . . What a sea of heads, what a moving mass of human beings meets the view . . . . A congregation of all nations, creeds and tongues – English and Spanish, German, French, Chinese, Sandwich Islands, Indian . . . and in passing through, one hears their jargon at every corner, and sees the strange and peculiar costume of each nation. . . .--*Delano, Chips.*

Soon after this passage, a caterwauling "quodlibet" describes the streets at night in Sacramento. This astonishing musical catalog (see example from the score, next page)[22] illustrates the following passage taken from Bayard Taylor's *Eldorado, or Adventures in the Path of Empire:*

There is . . . a large floating community of overland emigrants, miners, and sporting characters who prolong the wakefulness of the streets far into the nights. The door of many a gambling-hell on the levee and in J and K Streets stands invitingly open; the wail of torture from innumerable musical instruments peals from all quarters through the fog and darkness. *Full bands, each playing different tunes discordantly, are stationed in front of the principal establishments, and as these happen to be near together, the mingling of the sounds in one horrid, ear-splitting, brazen chaos would drive frantic a man of delicate nerve.* . . . The very strength, loudness, and confusion of the noises, which, heard at a little distance, have the effect of one scattering performance, marvelously takes the fancy of the rough mountain men. [Italics added.]

In the course of representing a single sentence--above, in italics--with appropriate musical form, Kingman inserts fragments from several Western popular songs-- "Wait for the Wagon," "Sweet Betsy from Pike," "Ol' Rosin the Beau," "Pike Country Miner," "Used-up Man," and "Money Musk," with "O Susanna" making its appearance at the end of the passage. These tunes compete with one another in the woodwinds and strings--flute, clarinet, violin, cello--with piano and percussion aiding and abetting, or defying, or both. The passage from the score, taken from the very middle of the italicized sentence, illustrates this complexity. It will be noted

---

your excerpts (chosen to support your 'multi' interpretation) are from the 'progress' side." Letter from Daniel Kingman to Betty Ch'maj, April 13, 1992.

[22]© Copyright Daniel Kingman 1992. Used with the permission of the composer.

that no two of the tunes are played by the same instrument in the same key and same meter. The two vocalists shout out the words in unison, trying to be heard over the percussion, which continues to surge loose and loud, in different rhythms from different cultural styles--all in order to create the "ear-splitting brazen chaos" that so offended Taylor and so delighted the "rough mountain men." The result is startling, overwhelming, exuberant, even a little frightening.

ILLUSTRATION: *"Bra-zen Chaos"--The Birth of Multiculturalism in California*

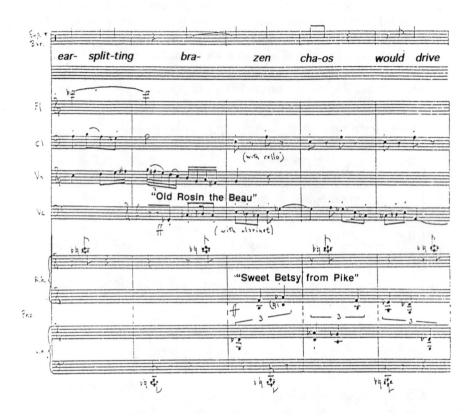

And so on. Just such "noises" would certainly have pleased Whitman, and they
would have enraptured Ives—for both would have heard in them the sound of
democracy, the sound of America itself.

****

Whether or not Emerson's words were the catalyst for Whitman's attempts at
naming, his poetic catalogs have continued to serve as models for defining America
as that "congregation of all nations, creeds and tongues" Kingman's music gives
us. Over the years, from Whitman to Kingman, American artists in many fields
have produced a rich and exciting portrait of a diverse people in fervent pursuit of a
Dream, a portrait of multiple meanings and conflicting creeds—a portrait of America
as catalog.

Multiculturalism in California Post Office Murals-- "The People and the Land"

by John C. Carlisle

Purdue University at Calumet
Director, Interphase II Productions

#1: *"Preaching and Farming at Mission Delores."*[1]

Introduction

During the economically bitter days of the Great Depression, many programs were developed by the federal government to assist unemployed workers. One program accelerated construction of federal buildings, especially hundreds of post offices throughout the country. The Treasury Department, which administered the federal buildings program under its Public Buildings Branch, established a plan to reserve up to one percent of the cost of a new building for "artistic embellishments," that is, for the commission of decorative sculptures or murals.

---

[1]This is the first of six details from a large mural at the Rincon Annex Post Office, San Francisco, by Anton Refreiger. All photographs are by John C. Carlisle, used with permission.

When the Civil Works Administration was established in November, 1933, by executive order of President Roosevelt, its goal was to provide work relief during the coming winter months. One such program was the PWAP, the Publics Works of Art Project, which hired artists and craftsmen to produce art works for public places. PWAP lasted only until the following spring, but it gave employment and several hundred thousands of dollars in wages to artists, who, in turn, spent that money in their local communities.

In 1979, I began to search for the extant murals in California locations in order to produce a slide/tape program for use by teachers. Completed some years later, this program highlights the artists and the thematic content of the murals in more than forty towns and cities, ranging from St. Helena and Ukiah in the north to Culver City, San Pedro, and Calexico in the south. *THE PEOPLE AND THE LAND: The California Post Office Murals* is the title for a series of slides with text on tape (or filmstrip with tape) which presents the multifaceted story of our most populous state as it was told by the artists in their murals for post office lobbies, painted under the auspices of the Section of Fine Art and Treasury Relief Art Project between 1934 and 1943.[2]

CALIFORNIA AS MULTICULTURAL MOSAIC

These murals can be viewed today as portraying California as a multicultural mosaic, a state which is reflective of the American mosaic. At least three of the murals, in Berkeley, Compton, and East Los Angeles, portray Native Americans, both before and after the arrival of the Spanish settlers. Both missionaries and rancheros are depicted in half a dozen of the locations, including Los Banos, Merced, San Francisco's Rincon Annex, and South Pasadena--where the artist presents a humorous figure, a priest with his gown hiked above his ankles leading a herd of goats across the forefront of the painting. Nineteenth century immigrants, especially those from the eastern United States, are shown in another half-dozen or

---

[2]AudioVisual Programs available from Interphase II Productions, P.O. Box 10132, Merrillville IN, 46411-0132.

1. *THE PEOPLE AND THE LAND: The California Post Office Murals.* Slide/tape package $50.00. Filmstrip/tape package $37.50.

2. *IMAGES OF PAST AND PRESENT: The Texas Post Office Murals.* Slide/tape package $75.00. Slide/tape package for VHS $50.00. Slide/tape package for Beta $25.00. Filmstrip/tape package $37.50.

3. *ART FOR MAIN STREET: The Indiana Post Office Murals.* 16mm film, 22 minutes $375.00, VHS videotape $50.00.

so locations, including Maynard Dixon's "Road to El Dorado" in Martinez. This work portrays a mixed bag of newcomers, ranging from sailors who may just have jumped ship when they arrived for the gold rush to dandies in frock coats and women in long gowns and bonnets, all dreamers, all seeking fame and fortune.

THE STORY OF VENICE

The story of another California dreamer receives graphic presentation in Edward Biberman's "The Story of Venice." The center of the mural contains a portrait of Abbott Kinney with his original 1905 layout for the city in the background, complete with canals and beautiful homes. When that venture proved unprofitable, he built an amusement part, shown in the mural's left section. Later in the century, oil brought new profits, and the cluster of workmen on the right in the mural completes 'the story of Venice.'

IMAGES OF LABOR

In many respects, the portrayal of workers in the California murals makes the strongest multicultural statement of any in the works. The laborers on farms and fishing boats and in factories and vineyards are pictured in more than a dozen cities.

#2. "Building the Railroad." Detail #2 from Rincon Annex, by Anton Refreiger. In the foreground, white men flanked by non-white workers; in the background, Chinese stoop labor.

Healthy, muscular workers are exalted in Henry Varnum Poor's "Grape Harvest" in Fresno, Lew Keller's "Grape Pickers" in St. Helena, and in Barse Miller's "Airplane Factory" in Burbank. Stoop labor is given dignity and value in George Samerjian's "Lettuce Workers" in Calexico and in Moya del Pino's "Flower Farming and Vegetable Picking" in Selma. Even the Hollywood subculture is represented in Miller's other Burbank work, showing a "Dance Scene" being filmed, and in Samerjian's depiction in Culver City,"Studio Lot," which depicts a lot full of leftover artifacts from old movies.

CHALLENGING THE CANON?

These New Deal art works also can be discussed in terms of contemporary concerns about propriety, what is "acceptable" in public murals officially sponsored by the government. Anton Refregier's Rincon Annex work, "Hardships of the Emigrant Trail," depicts several dead settlers, one killed by an arrow, another by bad weather. In his time, Refregier was, in our contemporary terms, attacking the canon, for such "negative" images would normally not have been allowed by the decision-makers in the Section on Fine Arts in Washington, D.C.

#3. "Hardships of the Emigrant Trail," from Rincon Annex.
Post Office mural by Anton Refrieger.

It was the staff of the Fine Arts Section that decided what was appropriate and what was not; Washington set the standard and the artists either met it--both in terms of iconography and style--or they were asked to make changes until they did. The Rincon Annex commission was awarded in 1941, but the mural was not executed and installed until 1946-1948, years after the Section officially had ceased to exist, which is probably the reason Refregier was able to complete this series of murals, which also depicts riots and the infamous Tom Mooney case. Usually, only the advent of World War II and the demise of the Washington agency allowed such artists to complete their works as intended.

SELF-CENSORSHIP?

Another slide in the package, a detail of Fletcher Martin's 8' x 42' mural in San Pedro, was also involved in the issue of censorship of the arts. Shortly after *THE PEOPLE AND THE LAND* was published, a major high school textbook publisher contacted me and asked to use this slide to illustrate New Deal art in its history of the United States under preparation. I was delighted, as the mural is one of my favorites. The detail, taken from the center of the work, shows a mail carrier, a delivery boy, and a newspaper boy, among others. Eventually the editor called me to say the slide had been replaced. Several staff members felt it would never pass the censors in Texas because the delivery boy is shown jumping up on his bike with his uniform stretched tightly across his buttocks. The publisher feared the image would be attacked as pornographic!

THE MURALS

 # 4. "Indians by the Golden Gate." Detail #4, from RinconAnnex Post Office mural.

Berkeley, California-- "Incidents in California History," by Susan Scheuer

Beverly Hills-- "Payments Help Trade," by Charles Kassler

Burbank-- "Aircraft Workers and Movie Scene," by Barse Miller

Calexico-- "Lettuce Workers," by George Samerjian

Canoga Park-- "Palomino Ponies," by Maynard Dixon

Claremont-- "California Landscape," by Milford Zornes

Compton-- "Indians and Missionaries--Early California" by James Redmond

Culver City-- "Studio Lot" by George Samerjian

East Los Angeles-- "World War II Theme," by Boris Deutsch

Fresno-- "Grape Harvest," by Henry Varnum Poor

Fullerton-- "Fruit Picking," by Paul Julian

Hayward-- "Rural Landscape," by Tom Lewis

Huntington Park-- "History of California," by Norman Chamberlain

La Jolla -- "California Landscape," by Belle Baranceneau

Lancaster-- "Hauling Water Pipe Through Antelope Valley," by Jose Moya del
Pino. Even though the gold rush brought wealth from the land, irrigation
allowed settlers to develop a continuing bounty from the soil. Moya del Pino
commemorates this technological change.

Los Baños--"Early Spanish Caballeros," by Lew E. Davis. The first non-Native
American inhabitants are shown--five cowboys on spirited palominos are

depicted on the open
plain with rugged hills of
the Los Baños region in
the background.

Martinez-- "Road to El Dorado," by Maynard Dixon

Merced-- "Vacheros," by
Dorothy Puccinelli. In
1806, Lt. Gabriel Mor-
aga and his soldiers
found a river after
several hot, dry days of
pursuit of Indian war-
riors in the San Joachin
Valley. The Soldiers
named the river El Rio
de la Neustra Senora de
Mercedes (Our Lady of
the Mercies River).

#5. "Water!" Horses, vacheros, and desert--
the romance of California conquest.

This name, shortened by time and non-Spanish-speaking settlers, became the Merced River and gave the town its name.

Merced-- "Early Settlers," by Helen Forbes. One hundred years after the events depicted in the previous mural, the trapper and explorer Jedediah Smith and his party ford the Merced River, carrying their pelts for the spring rendezvous. They get named the "early settlers."

Modesto-- "Mining, Agriculture, Irrigation," by Ray Boynton

Oceanside-- "Air Mail," by Elise Seeds

Ontario-- "The Dream and The Reality," by Nellie Best

Oxnard-- "Oxnard Panorama," by Daniel M. Mendelowitz

Pacific Grove-- "Lover's Point," by Victor Arnautoff

Placerville -- "Forest Genetics," by Tom Lewis

Redondo Beach-- "Excursion Train and Picknickers in the Nineties" and "Sheep Farming," by Jose Moya del Pino

Redwood City-- "Flower Farming and Vegetable Raising," by Jose Moya del Pino

Reedley-- "Pickers," by Boris Deutsch

San Francisco-- "Hardships of the Emigrant Trail," by Anton Refregier *(See detail of this and other images by Refregier from the Rincon Annex mural, San Francisco, throughout this chapter.--BC)*

San Gabriel-- "Gabriel County," by Ray Strong. Jedediah Smith and his scouts are shown on their first trip to the San Gabriel Valley and mission. The men are dominated by the dry, eastern slopes of the Sierras as they head for Cajon Pass.

San Pedro-- "Transportation of the Mail," by Fletcher Martin

San Rafael-- "San Rafael Creek--1851," by Oscar Galgiani

Santa Cruz-- "Fishing," by Henrietta Shore

Sebastopol-- "Agriculture," by Mallette Dean

Selma-- "Land of Irrigation," by Norman Chamberlain

South Pasadena-- "The Stage Coach," by John Law Walker

South San Francisco-- "South San Francisco in Past and Present," by Victor Arnautoff

St. Helena--"Grape Pickers," by Lew Keller

Stockton--"Modern Transportation of the Mail," by Frank Boynton

       "Mail and Travel by Stagecoach," by Jose Moya del Pino

Susanville-- "Deer," by Helen Forbes

Ukiah-- "Resources of the Soil," by Benjamin Curmingham

Venice-- "Story of Venice," by Edward Biberman

Ventura-- "Agriculture and Industries of Ventura," by Gordon Grant

Woodland-- "Farm Life," by George Harris.

#6. "Preaching and Farming at Mission Delores," with the preaching set into context
(compare to Figure #1)

USING EMOTIONS IN THE CLASSROOM
by Peter Frederick,
Wabash College

EDITOR'S NOTE: The three short pieces below were written by Peter Frederick to address different audiences, but together they give voice to an issue that needs to be addressed by teachers of courses on American multiculturalism--namely, the uses and abuses of emotion in their classrooms. Readers may wish to consider Frederick's argument in relation to his own syllabus and commentary on Syllabus #1, the commentary by Rosenmeier and Gouse on Syllabus #13, and my own Essay #5, on using media to introduce courses on American multiculturalism, and Essay #10 on the Roots Project, during which emotion in the classroom is a normal event.--BC

1. THE MEDICINE WHEEL AND USING EMOTIONS IN TEACHING

In order to increase our students' motivation and involvement in their own learning, we should consider the power of using emotions in the classroom. Emotions are taboo in higher education. The paradigm that governs how we are supposed to know and learn is rational, logical, empirical, analytic, competitive and objective. Students learn to think that emotions, such as anxiety, fear, joy, shame, anger, boredom, and excitement, are not supposed to be present in the classroom in some form all the time. Our challenge is not to stifle feelings, and therefore block learning, but to harness or connect them to the subjects we love to teach.

Parker Palmer, the authors of *Women's Ways of Knowing,* and others have recently been describing new epistemologies and their implications for learning. In this new model of knowing, the teaching/learning process is more connected, synthetic, intuitive, interactive, empathic, collaborative, subjective, and even spiritual. By this model, as Palmer puts it, students "see the connection between subject and self." Their understanding of reality and their motivation to learn is enhanced by the intersection, Palmer says, of "knowledge and autobiography."

The North American Indian tradition has long understood this holistic approach to learning. The Medicine Wheel, an ancient sacred symbol, represents (among other things) four interconnected dimensions of holistic growth. The mental, emotional, physical and spiritual. These are also recognizable as Jungian (and Myers-Briggs) indices of thinking-feeling and sensation-intuition. Nothing arouses more faculty or student interest than considering the implications of the Medicine Wheel for teaching and learning, especially finding strategies for focusing on the long-ignored emotional and spiritual aspects of the classroom. This workshop will explore such strategies as story-telling, role-playing, guided imagery, auto-biographical connections, and the emotional impact of using music and visual images in the classroom.

There are, of course, dangers in arousing feelings in class but these are outweighed by what is gained. Teaching to emotions is motivational. It focuses student attention and builds community. Emotions trigger memories and serve as a retrieval cue of retention. More important, emotional experience leads to cognitive insight; affect deepens understanding. Teaching to emotions, however, is not only a means to traditional ends but has value as a goal in its own right. We urge students to think critically, write and speak fluently, reason logically and compute correctly. Should we not also help them to feel authentically and thus validate a hidden world full of learning potential? In our effort to motivate and involve students more in their own learning, nothing has as much potential as finding strategies for connecting their emotions to our learning goals. The symbol of the Indian Medicine Wheel suggests how.

The Medicine Wheel

There are four dimensions of "true learning." These four aspects of every person's nature are reflected in the four cardinal points of the medicine wheel. These four aspects of our being are developed through the use of our volition. It cannot be said that a person has totally learned in a whole and balanced manner unless all four dimensions of her being have been involved in the process.

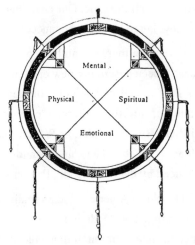

2. AFFECTIVE LEARNING THROUGH THE USE OF MEDIA

No account of actively engaging students in learning about American culture is complete without acknowledging the power of media. Much has been written on the use of films and other audio-visual techniques. My focus is on the role of media in evoking students' affective emotional learning, a woefully neglected but crucial area of teaching and learning. Emotions have surely played an enormous role in history; therefore, they belong in the classroom. Emotions focus attention and are motivating, to be sure, but teaching to emotions is also appropriate because affective experience leads to cognitive insights.

Here are some examples. First, as students enter the classroom it is an opportune time to establish a mood to ready them for the content for a particular class period. At the beginning of class, show some slides of war scenes, say, or of farm life in the Great Plains during the 1930s, or of men and women performing gender-distinct roles, or of American Indian cultures. Or, as they walk in, they hear an inspiring speech--FDR, or Malcolm X or Maya Angelou. Or, music is playing, say, Civil War, labor movement, or civil rights songs. Or, place several objects around the lecture hall. Each of these openings makes clear the tone and content of the day, and hooks student interest right away.

Even more emotionally engaging is to combine a piece of music with some slides. Imagine, for example, walking into a course listening to Dvorak's New World Symphony while looking at slides of Native American Indians. This is how I generally begin my United States history survey course, and it makes the obvious point, although few students these days know Dvorak. Within the hour I shift to Neil Diamond singing about "America," as students view slides of immigrants streaming to the United States from all over the world. The combination leads to a discussion of who "Americans" are and whether we are a "melting pot," "stew," "salad," "quilt," or "mosaic." Imagine a collage of slides of slave life while listening to spirituals. Or of looking at Civil War battlefield scenes while listening to "We are Coming, Father Abraham" or George Frederick Root's "Battle Cry of Freedom." Students understand the Civil War with their hearts and emotions as well as with their heads and reason.

The possibilities for the twentieth century are obviously much more extensive. For example, imagine the effect of listening to Billy Joel's "Goodnight, Saigon" while viewing slides of American soldiers and Vietnamese peasants. There are many effective combinations of labor songs and labor struggles, or of civil rights songs with scenes of the movement and the resistance against it. Even more powerful, put some slides together synchronized with the visual images suggested by Martin Luther King's "I Have a Dream" speech or his Memphis speech the evening of April 3, 1968 ("I've been to the mountaintop, and I've seen the Promised Land ..."). To illustrate the shift in mood of the black liberation struggle in the 1960s, put slides together with Malcolm X's "Message to the Grass Roots," delivered in November, 1963.

Harry Chapin, who died tragically young a few years ago, created songs that told compelling stories of ordinary people's everyday struggles and tragedies. He also sang of the changes from the 1960s to the 1970s. One such song, "She is Always Seventeen," presents a metaphoric and ambiguous account of broken and persisting dreams while moving historically through the period from 1961 ("When we went to Washington/ And said, 'Camelot's begun'") to 1975 ("when the crooked king was gone,/ {we were} sayin, 'the dream must go on.'"). . . . After exploring students' emotional and cognitive responses to songs such as Chapin's, it is helpful to go back through again slowly, discussing the historical context and meaning of each line of the lyrics and how it is further illuminated (and interpreted--perhaps overly so!) by the visual images that have accompanied it. Lines such as the following might be rather obvious:

> *It was 1965, and we were marchin once more*
> *From the burnin cities, against the crazy war,*
> *Memphis, L.A., and Chicago, we bled though sixty-eight*
> *'Til she took me up to Woodstock sayin, "With love it's not too late."*

But consider the possibilities to express an interpretive point of view with the lines that immediately follow:

> *We started out in the seventies, livin' off the land*
> *She was sowin' seeds in Denver, tryin' to make me understand.*
> *Then mankind is woman. And woman is man,*
> *And until we free each other, we cannot free the land.*

It should be obvious that the use of music and slides, even though presentational, is far from a passive learning experience for students. Indeed, they are actively involved with their whole beings.

It should also be obvious that the use of powerful emotion in class raises delicate questions of professorial power and student freedom. The emotions that are evoked as students hear Dr. King conclude his "Mountaintop" speech with the words, "Mine eyes have seen the glory of the coming of the Lord," while the slides change from a picture of King standing at a lectern to lying on the balcony of the Memphis motel where he was shot are overwhelming. I have done that presentation numerous times and the intensity of emotion is palpable; I am aware that, after an excruciatingly long moment of silence to let the image sink in, whatever I choose to say next has enormous power to be deeply heard and retained. It is a humbling responsibility, and I almost always feel a need to make comments at a level of morality and justice appropriate to the meaning of Dr. King's life.

I am also aware of the potential to abuse that responsibility. We must be thoroughly cognizant of the affective effect of the use of media in the classroom, and learn how to deal with student feelings as well as thoughts. Much active learning results from an exploration of the visual images and verbal lyrics of the examples cited here. But sometimes, particularly with emotionally powerful presentations, it is best to let the music and slides make the whole point, without comment, and simply conclude the class with whatever each individual student carries away in his or her heart and head from the experience. In this way, students own their own feelings and insights.

3. EMOTIONS AND MULTICULTURAL AMERICA

I frequently use music and slides in various combinations to engage students' emotions as well as their intellect in learning about multiculturalism in America. Emotions (and music) have surely played an enormous role in the history of cultural pluralism in America and therefore belong in our classrooms. Emotions focus attention, motivate students, and affective experience often leads to cognitive understanding and insight. Following are two or three examples.

I often use a piece of music and a collage of visual images appropriate to the topic or text for the day as a way of setting the tone at the beginning of class. The slide/song presentation that I have had the most success with in teaching about multicultural America in a variety of contexts is Neil Diamond's "America," admittedly not our students' favorite artist yet still an effective and powerful piece of music. To accompany Diamond's account of the journey of various peoples to this country ("we come to America," "got a dream they come to share"), I have put together an always-changing slide set of about 40 visual images of many "boat people": the "Mayflower," a slave ship, 19th century immigrant steamers, 20th century Southeast Asian or Haitians on rickety boats, scenes of the lower East side of New York, Chicano migrant workers in California, slaves, white and black farm workers, and various family portraits of the many faces of America. No matter what audience experiences it, everyone's "grandmother" is there. Intermixed with these images of people are slides of important American icons: the Statue of Liberty, the flag, Mount Rushmore, and some pro- and anti-immigration cartoons. The presentation ends with a poster of Black Elk's son, Ben, with the word "FIRST" on it, or with a scene from "Do the Right Thing."

Students are prepared for the 5-minute "show" by being asked to be aware of "words, images, and feelings" as they experience it. I give them a moment to write down their immediate reactions, and usually to talk with the person next to them. The discussion begins by inviting and writing down all the "words, images and feelings" that the presentation evoked. We fill the board or an overhead transparency. Then I ask, simply, "what themes, patterns and issues do you see in our list?" What follows is invariably a highly-charged exploration of what an "American" is, and whether our history has been a "melting pot," "stew," "salad," "quilt," "mosaic," or the newest one, a "kaleidoscope." There is almost no issue of the contradictions, successes and ironies of American multiculturalism that does not result from this experience.

==

"emotion strenthens the bond of association"--Aristotle
Tell me, and I'll listen
Show me, and I'll understand
Involve me, and I'll learn."--Lakota
"emotion triggers memories, which in turn lead to more emotions, which [bring] more
memories"--William James

WHO ARE WE — AS AMERICANS?
TWO IDEAS FOR INTRODUCING COURSES ON AMERICAN MULTICULTURALISM

by Betty Ch'maj

Since 1965, I have taught introductory American Studies courses in which what we now call multiculturalism has been an integral part. I have always incorporated the arts – literature, painting, music, film, and architecture — into the courses for use in conjunction with the other course material. The following are two kinds of introduction I have developed for these courses which seem to me well-suited for adaptation to courses on American multiculturalism.

I. AN INTRODUCTORY "QUIZ"

On the first day of class, I announce that in this class we have a "quiz" at the *beginning* rather than the end of the term. (We will have quizzes in the middle and the end, too, but not like this one.) I invite students to participate in a "free-association" exercise, jotting down on half-sheets of paper what immediately comes to mind when I ask them a series of questions about matters that may seem obvious to them — so obvious they may never have stopped to think about them. I tell them their papers will not be graded, and I urge them not to tell me what they think they *ought* to believe but what they really do believe, or have believed, in relation to the questions. If nothing comes to mind, rather than try to fake it, they should leave the space blank. Still, they should try their best to come up with some kind of answer through free association. Here are the questions I use:

1. What mental image or mental picture comes to mind when you hear the words "the American"? (It might be a person, a character, a cartoon, a movie figure – whatever jumps to mind. Take your time. Think about it.)

2. Now try describing the image you are struggling to identify. For example, what does the person look like? what clothes do you see this person wearing? what facial expression? Jot down anything that comes to mind.

3. Can you go further and picture an occupation? hobbies? politics? How about region or locale – that is, *where* do you see this person, in what context?

4. To go at it another way, try filling in the blank on this sentence: "Among the peoples of the world, the American could be described as the_____."

5. Next: what mental image comes to mind with the term "the American Dream"? Again, describe as best you can, using images and as much detail as you need.

6. How about "the American way of life"? "American individualism"?

7. Do you have a mental picture associated with the very word "America"?

8. Suppose you heard someone say that Americans generally fall into two different groups – what might you assume those two main groups would be?

9. Suppose you heard someone refer to "the American paradox," or an American "contradiction," or a "dilemma" central to American life – what might you guess that paradox or contradiction or dilemma might be or be about?

10. Now, based on your answers, how would you describe *your own* attitude toward "the American"? Like or dislike? Did you include yourself when thinking about "the American"? If not, why not? Name two or three factors you think influenced your attitudes about "the American" the most.

At this point, I interrupt and invite students to share a few of their answers orally, just long enough to demonstrate the variety and conflicts in the answers they are bound to give. Often, a few students will find themselves in heated disagreement even at this point, and "political correctness" will surface as they defend their views. Then I ask the class as a whole: how many saw the American as tall or tallish? as white or Anglo? as male? Most have raised their hands for all three, at which point I tell them that when I interviewed fourteen experts in 1965 and asked the same questions, those were the *only* points of agreement – i.e., that the American was tall, white, and male (although only James Farmer, himself black, bothered to use the word "white"). I invite students to compare their answers to those given by these experts, as heard on the first program in the audio series, "Portrait of the American."[1] Generally speaking, I have found this introduction not only piques interest but it helps to establish the atmosphere of openness to disagreement which I feel should be encouraged as early as possible in any class dealing with multiculturalism.

----

[1] © Betty E. Chmaj, 1965, all rights reserved. A tape with a transcript of this program is still available--write to me c/o Department of Humanities, California State University, Sacramento 95819. Instructors who wish to use the program might focus first on the descriptions given by James Farmer, William H. Whyte, Jr., John Higham and Irving Howe before citing the "Thirteen Answers" used by other respondents, who include John Dos Passos, Alfred Kelly, Alfred Kazin, R.W.B.Lewis, Ihab Hassan, Victoria Shuck, Alan Harrington, Robert Cooley Angell, and Marshall Fishwick. Please state in a letter that you want the material for classroom use only (any other use is forbidden by copyright laws) and include $10.00 for shipping and handling.

II. A MULTI-MEDIA INTRODUCTION

Another way to introduce such a course is with a collection of slides, video images, tapes, and handouts of literature — that is, art works that set out quite deliberately to define or comment on what "the American," "America," "the American Dream," and "the American way of life" are presumed to be. Images from advertising, book covers, and the like that more subtly aim at definition can effectively be juxtaposed to selected works of art. A collection of images might be put together that focus on a single icon – the American flag or the Statue of Liberty, for example — as seen by different cultural groups or different eras.

The advantage of this approach is that it can anticipate the variety of attitudes from a variety of people that will surface in the course. The disadvantage is that artists do tend to make their statements in ways that may seem too deep or daring for the first week of class, requiring more *explication du texte* than students are able to take in. Still, I like using multi-media introductions in my Humanities courses; I find they are terrific as attention-getters and mind-bogglers, even when they require imaginative leaps that may at first seem too challenging for beginners.[2]

EXAMPLES TO CONSIDER FOR THE FIRST WEEK OF CLASS

I. Music: *"America the Beautiful"* (sung in class, from memory)
"Stars and Stripes Forever" (Sousa march, on record or tape)
"This Land is Your Land" (sung in class, from lyrics on handout)
"America" from *WEST SIDE STORY* (video, with lyrics on a handout)
"The Fourth of July" by Charles Ives (from *HOLIDAYS SYMPHONY*)

II. Slides: A selection of paintings, sculpture & photographs from this list:

"Pilgrims Going to Church," by George Boughton (1930s); *"Kindred Spirits,"* by Asher Durand (1849); *"Historical Monument to the American Republic,"* by Erasmus Salisbury Field (1876); *The Statue of Liberty,* by Bartholdi, in the painting by Edward Moran; *"America,"* sculpture by Daniel French;

---

[2]Teachers who wish to build up slide collections are wise to learn how to photograph images found in texts, newspapers, ads, etc. at campus photography labs. Among recent texts on American art, the one I would recommend first for the theme of multiculturalism is Lippard's *Mixed Blessings: New Art in a Multicultural America* (Pantheon Books, 1990). As its book jacket says: "In America today there is a little-known explosion of creative art by women and men from many different ethnic backgrounds. . . *Mixed Blessings* is the first book to discuss the crosscultural process taking place in the work of Latino, Native-, African-, and Asian-American artists." For many more suggestions, see Essay #4 and Checklists A-D in Part III of this book.

"The Steerage" *(1907),* photograph by Alfred Steiglitz; *"American Gothic,"* by Grant Wood (1930); *"American Tragedy,"* by Philip Evergood (1937); *"American Landscape"* by Charles Sheeler; *"The American Way of Life,"* by Margaret Bourke-White; *"The American Dream,"* by Luis Jiminez; *"Manchild in the Promised Land,"* by Phillip Mason; *"Thousands of Girls Vie for the Title of Miss America on National Television Tonight,"* by Ellen Lampert; *"Nightmare in the American Dream Factory,"* installation art by Ellen Lampert; *"The Block,"* installation art by Romare Bearden. And so on.

III. Images using the American Flag:

Flags in imagery related to "patriotism narratives" in the war against Iraq. Flags in protest imagery of Vietnam paintings & artifacts. Flags in paintings by Jasper Johns. *"Flag for the Moon: Die Nigger,"* by Faith Ringgold. *"Pax Americana,"* by May Stevens. *"Yes, Leroi,"* by David P. Bradford.*&**[3] *"My Country Right or Wrong,"* by Joseph Cliff.* *"Stars, Bars and Bones,"* by Bertrand Phillips.* *"Alternative,"* by Marion Epting.* *"America the Beautiful"* and *"American Hang-up"* (body prints) and others from *Mixed Blessings.*

IV. Literature:

A. *FOUR SCENES FROM AMERICAN FICTION:* [4] 1. Reading by a typical "Gamecock of the Wilderness" (1700s), from *American Humor* by Constance Rourke. 2. Excerpt from *The American* (1876) by Henry James. 3. Excerpt from *Babbitt* (1920) by Sinclair Lewis. 4. Scene from *The American Dream* (1960) by Edward Albee.

B. *THREE POEMS READ ALOUD IN CLASS:*[5] 1. Whitman, "I Hear America Singing." 2. Hughes, "I Too Sing America." 3. Ginsberg, from "America"

V. Multi-Media Performance Art, MTV, Film: 1. *Laurie Anderson,* performance art from her video, "Home of the Brave." 2. *Michael Jackson* in concert in Asia (MTV). 3. Selected scenes from *Yankee Doodle Dandy* (on the video, AMERICA AT THE MOVIES) compared to scenes from Oliver Stone's *Born on the Fourth of July* or *JFK.*

---

[3]Works with one asterisk (*) may be found in Samella S. Lewis, *Art: African American* (1978), under "The Flag: A Symbol of Repression." Works with two asterisks (**) are in David Hammer, *Black Artists on Art* (vol.1). Both volumes have explanations by the black artists.

[4]Excerpts from these four works are dramatized on the same program (#1) of PORTRAIT OF THE AMERICAN that has the interviews used for the first-day "quiz." See footnote #1, above.

[5]See these poems and others in our survey of American "catalogs," Essay #2, above.

Essay #6

TRANSFORMING THE AMERICAN

LITERATURE SURVEY CLASS

by Sherry Sullivan
Department of English,
University of Alabama at Birmingham

When the debate over the American literary canon first began to heat up several years ago, I was delighted. The kinds of changes being called for seemed to me entirely legitimate and long overdue, and I welcomed the opportunity to overhaul my old course syllabi to include more works by women, people of color, and working-class writers. The task would be made easier, I thought, by my experience in American Studies. Having helped to found the American Studies program (a minor) at the University of Alabama at Birmingham, and having co-taught several times one of the required core courses in the program, I was accustomed to using non-traditional course materials – including literary works. And I had learned to teach such materials in sociocultural context and from various disciplinary perspectives. Some of these materials and this contextual, interdisciplinary approach, in fact, had already become a part of my American literature survey classes.

Despite such advantages, however, I had no idea how difficult and how disorienting it would be to implement very significant changes; or how profoundly transforming these changes would prove to be. Moreover, there was at the time relatively little written on the practical implications of the canon debate for teachers in the classroom. Even now pedagogical help, though it exists, is often hard to find.[1] My purpose here, therefore, is to offer to others philosophically committed to or already engaged in the struggle to implement these changes, some encouragement, some direction, and some practical advice. This is less a "how to"

---

[1] The most fruitful sources of help include *Radical Teacher* 37, a special issue on "Balancing the Curriculum"; *Women's Studies Quarterly* XV (Fall/Winter 1987), a special issue on Feminist Pedagogy; Susan Gushee O'Malley, Robert C. Rosen, & Leonard Vogt, eds., *Politics of Education: Essays from Radical Teacher* (New York, 1990); and (most recently), Paul Lauter, *Canons and Contexts* (New York, 1991).

paper, though, than part of an ongoing exploration of ideas and possibilities for radically reconstructing a course that continues to be (along with composition courses) the mainstay of most undergraduate English departments.

A major difficulty, as many who embark on this path soon discover, is how to teach works most of us have not studied in graduate school, have not read or taught since, and which often do not readily lend themselves to the formal (especially new critical) literary analysis in which we were trained. Many of these works fall well outside the boundaries of what has traditionally defined "great" American literature.[2]   How do we teach, for example, *The Coquette*, the *Autobiography of Black Hawk*, or *The Woman Warrior*?

My own first response was to avoid the more problematic and select works which more or less fit traditional criteria for literary excellence, and thus lent themselves to the literary analysis with which I was most familiar.[3]   This approach – a kind of "add-and-stir pluralism" – was the least disruptive kind of change I could make. Though my syllabus was altered to accommodate new writers (I had to eliminate somebody to fit them in), the basic structure of the course and the way the material was taught remained essentially the same.

The approach was a legitimate first step, I think, but eventually I was obliged to come to grips with its limitations. Much more is at stake in the canon debate than simply making room in the syllabus for works by women, ethnic writers, and writers of color. The traditional syllabus – even integrated – continues to privilege writing by a white, anglo-American, mostly Protestant, mostly male elite. As long as their works continue to dominate the syllabus, their ideas, values, beliefs, and cultural practices are positioned at the center of the course and made implicitly the norm. Works by members of various non-dominant groups are consequently rendered secondary or exceptions; their ideas, values, beliefs, and cultural practices speak from the margin, implicitly "other." Those hierarchical distinctions (of class, race, ethnicity, gender, region) which mark the traditional American literature course and had excluded these writers from serious consideration in the first place,

---

[2]They may not, for example, adhere to the prevailing features of a particular genre (say, the novel); or embody dominant values and ideas (individualism, personal development, success); or display certain aesthetic qualities of form and style (allusive language, irony and paradox, completeness), while avoiding others (didacticism, sentimentality, incompleteness, grossly improbable or formulaic or static plots and characters).

[3]Examples are found in older editions of *Norton* or other standard anthologies: Ralph Ellison, say, rather then Zora Neale Hurston, Edith Wharton rather than Anzia Yiezierska, Langston Hughes rather than Mourning Dove.

are left intact and unchallenged. In fact, they are reinforced.[4] This was not at all what I wanted my American literature classes to do.

What I had to consider, therefore, was a much more ambitious and comprehensive reconstruction of the course. Such a move is particularly daunting in a survey course, where one is presumed to be introducing students to the basic (and sacrosanct) premises of a discipline.[5] In order to prepare myself, I read books and articles that placed the teaching of literature and the production of literary canons in historical perspective.[6] These works enabled me to let go of my illusions about the timeless nature of "great" literature, the absolute necessity of including (or the crime of omitting) a particular work or author, and the inherent superiority of any one approach to teaching literature. They encouraged me to question traditional notions of what makes a text "literary."

Now, unencumbered by ties that bound me to a particular canon, I began to make more substantial changes in my syllabus. I added still less familiar works by a greater diversity of writers – women, blacks, native Americans, hispanics, and working class. More significantly in terms of how the course evolved, for the first I time placed these works at the center of the course, where they gained new legitimacy and power.[7] At the same time, I retained canonical texts which worked well with these other selections. My aim was not to substitute a new canon of non-traditional works for the old, but to bring a wider range of works, representing different cultural perspectives, into better balance. Now canonical texts no longer

---

[4]See Johnnella Butler and Betty Schmitz, "Different Voices: A Model for Integrating Women of Color into Undergraduate American Literature and History Courses," *Radical Teacher* 37, 4-9.

[5]See Marilyn Schuster and Susan R. Van Dyne, *Feminist Transformation of the Curriculum: Working Paper #125*, Wellesley College Center for Research on Women (1983).

[6]See, for example, the first chapters of Terry Eagleton's *Literary Theory: An Introduction* (Minneapolis, 1983); Paul Lauter's "Race and Gender in the Shaping of the American Literature Canon: A Case Study from the Twenties" in *Canons*; Jane Tompkin's "Masterpiece Theater: The Politics of Hawthorne's Literary Reputation" in her *Sensational Designs: The Cultural Work of American Fiction, 1790-1860*; Nina Baym's "Melodramas of Beset Manhood: How Theories of American Fiction Exclude Women Authors" in Elaine Showalter's *Feminist Criticism* (New York, 1985); and Henry Louis Gates' "Tell Me Sir, . . . What Is Black Literature?" *PMLA* 105: Jan. 1990, 11-22. These works explain just how literary studies became a legitimate part of university curricula; why particular writers and works were made the focus of study; how they were researched and taught; and the ways in which these conventions have changed over time.

[7]See Butler, 4-9.

controlled the syllabus. And the single act of their displacement from the center set into motion a sequence of other changes I had not anticipated.

First, because of their new prominence in the syllabus, these non-canonical works obliged me to re-think the ways I usually organized and presented my material. I strove now to integrate the canonical with the non-canonical (rather than the reverse). Traditional devices, such as genre or chronological periods, and "fountainhead" paradigms (where the syllabus is founded on sameness), simply fail to do this well.[8]   Thus I chose an organizing theme such as "Ethnicity and Diversity in American Literature" rather than, say, "The Puritan Heritage"; or "Patterns of Emigration and Migration in American Literature" rather than "The Westward Movement," and so on.[9] My underlying paradigm, similarly, suggested a mosaic or kaleidoscope rather than a linear construction like the evolution or decline of a particular tradition or movement.

Second, I also had to reconsider my goals for the course. Certainly, I no longer was committed to presenting students with a more or less homogeneous body of knowledge (in the form of great ideas from "great works" by great men) – knowledge they needed in order to consider themselves "educated." Now I was committed to engaging students in an exploration of a diverse and fragmented, contradictory and complex American cultural reality – as this was reflected in and shaped by all kinds of literary texts. This is American literature speaking in tongues (Bakhtin's "heteroglossia"), from different cultural perspectives and experiences, and revealing both overlapping and competing "ways of knowing." My immediate goal was parity and dialogue (or "dialogics," in Bakhtin's sense of different meanings operating on different levels of discourse) across and within the boundaries of gender, race, ethnicity and class.[10]   My long-range (and more

---

[8]The "fountainhead" or analogy paradigm is the controlling structural device for many academic disciplines. It stresses similarity among selected works and plays down difference, particularly when differences are multiple rather than simply dualistic (Schuster and Van Dyne, 8). See for further discussion Deborah S. Rosenfelt, "Integrating Cross-Cultural Perspectives in the Curriculum: Working for Change in the California State Universities," *Radical Teacher* 37, 10-13; and Lauter's *Canons and Contexts* on the similar negative effects of the "mainstream" paradigm.

[9]See also my syllabus *(Syllabus #15A & B, with its appendix on the first-day activity.--BC)* At UAB, survey courses are listed in the Class Schedule with a generic title, in this case "American Literature, 1865-Present." Individual classes consequently are distinguished from one another only at the first class meeting, when the syllabus is distributed and the special focus or theme of the course (if any) is discussed. (See my Appendix on first day activity.)

[10]M. M. Bakhtin, *The Dialogic Imagination*, ed. by Michael Holquist (Austin, 1981).

ambitious) goal was to encourage students to regard knowledge itself as process, not product: open-ended and incomplete, dynamic and multi-faceted, above all problematic.

Third, I had to change the way I presented non-canonical works and their relationship to traditional texts. Both the number and prominence of different cultural perspectives now represented in my syllabus meant that I could no longer simply lump them together as "other" (in contrast to a presumed norm), nor as "the" voice of the victims of dominant oppression. They had become much more demanding and complex texts to reckon with, each with its own peculiar teaching challenges. How, then, to get inside them? How to give students access to them? Drawing here upon my American Studies experience, I knew that like all "texts" they had to be approached quite self-consciously as cultural products of a particular time and place and individual – as well as group – consciousness. With this in mind, I could discuss with my students familiar literary questions of voice, audience, and function. We could then pursue less traditional questions of ethnography and context: What group or cultural values, ideas, and belief systems does this text express? What social, political, and economic factors might have influenced its production and reception?[11]

Finally, these changes in the syllabus forced me to begin the process of transforming my classroom practice (by which I mean the way I conduct my class, the activities and assignments I design, and the kinds of classroom relations I try to foster among students and between students and myself). I wanted to promote a class that was in practice as well as in content less hierarchical, less patriarchal, more egalitarian.[12] I wanted to facilitate through class activities, as well as through the private act of reading, the making of connections across traditional boundaries of class, race and ethnicity, gender and sexual preference, generation, region – and

---

[11] Supplementary course materials may be in order here, unless one is using an anthology, such as the new *Heath Anthology of American Literature*, which provides adequate historical and sociocultural information. The idea of organizing class discussion around these five questions comes from Paul Lauter, in the recent *Heath Newsletter* IV (Fall, 1990). Lauter observes that these questions also help students better understand why they may respond sympathetically to some works and be put off by others ("Is this writer addressing me or readers like me? Who then, and why?"). See Butler for additional strategies of approach to non-traditional material.

[12] See feminist pedagogy articles on this subject, particularly Carolyn M. Shrewsbury, "What Is Feminist Pedagogy?" *Women's Studies Quarterly* XV, 6-13; Schuster & Van Dyne, 13-15; and Nancy Schneidewind, "Feminist Values: Guidelines for Teaching Methodology in Women's Studies," *Politics of Education*, 11-22.

so on. I wanted students to experience in class, cognitively and emotionally, what they had in common with members of different cultural groups; and at the same time, to recognize and respect cultural and individual differences.

This is a tall order, and well beyond the scope of this paper to discuss in detail. But I may note briefly here my discovery that the first step in making class dynamics less hierarchical had already been taken. By virtue of placing at the center of my syllabus non-canonical and (to me) unfamiliar texts, I had given up some of my authority and control as presumed expert on all course materials. Like giving up the ordered hierarchy of the canon, this was at first unsettling. It meant often coming to class "unprepared" (from a traditional point of view), with incomplete or uncertain readings, fragmentary background information, and purely speculative conclusions.

In response I decided not to disguise my lack of specific expertise, but to openly acknowledge and use it from the first day to pedagogical advantage. Letting go of this type of control over the material and (by extension) over classroom procedure, I reasoned, might have benefits. Students might be stimulated to participate more actively in class discussion and to engage more deeply with course readings than they typically do in required literature survey courses.

The process of course transformation I've described here is a kind of leap into the void – with all the anxiety, discomfort, and conflict such a leap can entail. Because we were not trained to teach like this and most of us have had no models to follow, we must through trial and error train ourselves. On the other hand, our education generally has given us the ability to make these personal and professional changes. (Part of our job, as I see it, is to foster this ability as well in our students.) The ultimate goal of a multicultural education in particular is to encourage openness to liberating, non-repressive social change – in ourselves, in our students, and in society at large. In the rather rarefied and privileged space of the college classroom, we can act on this goal by constantly attending to the content, form, and process of what we teach.

ED. NOTE: For illustration of the changes in her own classes, see also Sullivan's Before and After syllabi in Part I, with her "Ground Rules for Discussion" and commentary on first-day activity appended.

Essay #7

TRANSFORMING THE AMERICAN
MUSIC SURVEY COURSE: "BEYOND THE CANON"

*ED. NOTE: This is Professor Willoughby's "progress report" after her first
attempt at teaching Music 129 as a Target course for the "Beyond the Canon"
Project at California State University at Sacramento. It is in the form of a memo
to the college committee assigned to evaluate how well such courses are
fulfilling the new Ethnic Studies requirement in the General Education program.
The samples from student papers which follow Willoughby's report exemplify
kinds of research likely to emerge from the new emphases on multculturalism.
I found them fascinating to read, illustrating both strengths and potential weak-
nesses of multiculturalim's first phase; I have had to edit them down drastically
due to space limitations. See p. 111 for my general introduction.--BC*

January 29, 1991

To: "Beyond the Canon" Committee
From: Susan Willoughby
Target Class: American Society and its Music (Music 129)

I am working on the first of the *Beyond the Canon* objectives: *Increasing the
multicultural content of the curriculum* of my Music 129 class. Since this class has
always included music of cultures other than European based American culture, I
have not added any categories or topics (other than the two noted as numbers 5 and
6 below), but have increased the class time spent on music of some cultures and
have directed writing assignments to projects on music of cultural minority groups
in the U.S. Time changes are roughly as follows:

1. Decrease Anglo-American folk music by two class periods: 4 to 2.

2. Increase Afro-American folk, blues and jazz by four class periods: 6 to 10.

3. Increase Native American music by two class periods: 1 to 3

4. Increase Hispanic music by one class period: 2 to 3.

5. Include one class period on Cajun music.

6. Included a guest presentation on the Sikh (Indian) community of Yuba City.

7. Decrease introduction and overview time by one or two class periods.

8. Decrease American fine art music by three or four class periods.

Assignments and Schedule Changes

Assignments have been adjusted to include 1) a running journal of commentaries on the ideas presented on music of cultural minorities, 2) a review of a live performance by a cultural minority group, 3) a research paper on an aspect of music of an ethnic minority group in U.S.

For Fall, 1990, the changes were successful, although my introduction of the "Beyond the Canon" project seemed to scare off some; I had many more students drop than I normally have. Others waiting were added, however, and the makeup of the class then included more students of color and other cultural backgrounds.

Assignments were interesting and productive, with the exception of the long-term journal on multiculturalism: I did not have time to check their writings or assign new ones, and so cancelled the assignment halfway through the semester. This semester I have again instituted the journal, giving it greater grade percentage and reducing the wordage on another assignment. The review of a live performance of a cultural minority seemed to get students out to concert experiences they would not otherwise have had. Much of the writing was vivid, with new information for the students and for me; they seemed to enjoy the new concert experiences.

The research papers were particularly rewarding. With the help of the humanities librarian, I put extra books on reserve dealing with music of other cultural groups; she isolated many volumes to show the class during a special library presentation. I was pleasantly surprised that despite what seemed to be initial concern and fear of the project, students developed interesting topics and were able to take active personal interest in them. At the end of the semester I compiled a composite of their research papers, giving each student about half a page, and made copies for the class members. I also took photographs of class members and mounted them on a board in commemoration of their pioneering roles as a target class. This seemed to be very pleasing and meaningful to them.

Materials

Fall semester 1990 was the first time we had the new (second) edition of Dan Kingman's *American Music, A Panorama*, and he has included a chapter on music of other cultures in the U.S.: "Regionalism and Diversity." I have assigned this chapter as a first reading, following introduction of the course.

Besides the many films I have used for years in Music 129, I incorporated new videos which were particularly useful in the study of American folk music. Alan Lomax's *American Patchwork* series includes filmed performances of white and black folk music from the southern Appalachians, blues from the south and west, and jazz traditions showing direct linking with West African musical characteristics.

This series is the best of its kind I have seen and has the added advantage, especially for foreign students, of presenting most of the text in subtitles; it does not assume that all Americans can understand southern folk dialects. I was able to use from five to twenty-five minutes of these videos in almost every class session on folk music. In addition, the class saw many portions during different class periods of the Bill Moyers special *Amazing Grace,* enabling them to compare styles of black and white Americans from folk to professional and operatic performers.

Professor Joaquin Fernandez, specialist in Mexican and South American Music, provided lists of bibliography on Mexican-American music, vocabulary lists and articles which were reproduced for the students. Professor Jim Chopyak, our Department of Music's change agent, kept me well supplied with articles on multiculturalism, films and videos, publishers' catalogs on music of other cultures and information on local concerts of non-Western music.

Guest Lecturers

(1) Professor Joaquin Fernandez visited my class and lectured on the Mexican *corrido* ballad and other forms and played an exciting sampling of Mexican music on the piano. His lecture was preceded and followed by preparation and follow-up on Mexican American and Latin-influenced music.

(2) A Mexican American student, Rosemary Martinez, who has studied dance in Mexico since the age of five, taught the class a Mexican folk dance to taped music she brought from her large collection.

(3) Joyce Middlebrook, a graduate student in the music department, gave a guest presentation on the music of the Indian Sikh community of Yuba City. She included a television news special on them and a video she made herself of a Sikh wedding celebration. Joyce came dressed in Sikh costume, brought along a drum, and stressed to the students the fact that the Sikh culture has existed in our midst in its original form for years, uninfluenced by or assimilated into American culture.

(4) A Black student I happened to meet accepted my invitation to come into class with his guitar and sing his own folkish and contemporary Christian songs. The class noticed immediately that his style was not very "black," but based on white hymn tradition. They appreciated his willingness to sing for them.

SPRING 1991: The syllabus is mostly the same as last term with a few changes.

(1) The multicultural journal, as noted, has more weight and is given more time.

(2) The Journal of Listening Experiences assignment is smaller by one review to allow for the multicultural journal assignment.

(3) Professor Fernandez will lecture on music of the Caribbean & its influence, rather than on music of Mexico.

(4) I am spending less introduction time explaining and justifying the *Beyond the Canon* project.

(5) I will include Jerome Kern's *Showboat* to provide more historical background on issues of racism.

(6) The first piece of journal writing, "My experience with music of other cultures in the U.S.," will be excerpted and presented to the class along with statistics and issues of multiculturalism.

(7) We will have more guest lecturers than last semester.

===

EXCERPTS FROM STUDENT RESEARCH PAPERS
ON MUSIC OF CULTURAL MINORITIES IN THE UNITED STATES

1. STUDENT PAPERS ON NATIVE AMERICANS

BYRON STANLEY, "MUSIC OF THE AMERICAN INDIAN":

Although Native songs could be categorized in a number of ways – privately owned or publicly owned, sacred or secular, and old or new, (6) —the majority of them have a similar theme. This is that matter and spirit are not antithetical, but in fact interwoven. This means that, to the Indians, man not only shared his physical world with his natural surroundings, but he also shared a spiritual one. They regarded themselves as a part of one great living whole. (7) To an outsider, the Hopi Ceremony would look like an attempt to imitate animals; however, the songs and dances are not intended to emulate, but to transform. This transformation was from the material world to the spiritual one where direct interaction with the spirits took place. (10) Thus music and songs were a vital link with the spiritual world. . . . Although the Indian life of the past will never return, the spirit of oneness with the earth must return or mankind will eventually lose the battle he foolishly waged on nature. Their songs of the past may point us in the right direction for our future.

BRADFORD THORNBERRY, "PERCUSSION INSTRUMENTS OF THE NATIVE AMERICANS"

The drum is sounded for all important events in the Indian's life. The drum in many Native American societies is treated with respect and care. The Menominee tribe of the Great Lakes region is described as having the following attitude toward the drum: "Well, we treat (the Drum) as a person. That is the way we (Menominee) was preached (by the Ojibwa) . . . they even make special beds for that Drum. Keep it as a person. We Indians do that just for the sake of God; appreciate, take care of that Drum good, because that's his power. That is why we decorate that drum, make it look pretty, clean, because it is from God." (Vennum 61) In many societies the drum is the center of attention in the rituals of the tribe. In the Yuki tribe the drum is promised "much to eat" (Kroeber 190) during the construction process if the wood produces a good sound. Tobacco is offered to the drum in some societies to help its tone. The drum is treated as though it were alive. Although I did not find any mention of this in my research, I would think that this is so because the drum is constructed from objects of nature that were once alive and the sounds produced were the objects speaking again. This observation is supported by the Native Americans' strong tie with nature in their religion and their belief that a spirit resides in all things of nature.

KAY J. SPLER, "NATIVE AMERICAN MUSIC [FOR MENSTRUATION CEREMONY]"

Native Californians traditionally lived in small tribal groups where the roles each person played were well defined. Men were the hunters and women the gatherers. But the world of dreams and spirit world contacts were the most important and individual parts of their lives. There are songs for almost every occasion: ceremonial dances, social dances, songs for gathering, songs for games, songs for initiation rites, songs for animals, war songs, love, birth and death songs, songs for planting, songs to and from the spirits, and songs from dreams. Ceremonial life as well as daily life was filled with music and sacredness. A child was born into a tightly woven family in a small tribal group. It was swaddled tightly in a basket-type cradle. As a child grew, many family members took part in educating her. The child learned skills and the attitudes and ways of doing things from those around her, as children do nowadays. A girl's childhood ended with her first menstruation. The girl's family, and in some cases the entire tribal group, would hold a coming-of-age feast and maybe a dance. The following is a puberty dance song from the Wintu: "Thou art a girl no more, Thou art a girl no more; The chief, the chief, the chief, the chief, Honors thee In the dance, in the dance, In the long and double line of the dance, Dance, dance, Dance, dance."

2. STUDENT PAPERS ON MUSIC OF BLACK AMERICANS:

CANDY JACKSON, "LIFE IN THE SEA ISLANDS"

Africans . . . were captured in their homeland of West Africa, thrust onto ships and brought to America to assume the position of slaves. . . . Now they were slaves, and their primary function was to make their masters happy. There was, however, a place along the east coast of the United States that slavery was very different. . . . The Sea Islands stretch from Maryland to Florida and could only be reached by boat. . . . unsuitable for the British because they were not used to that climate. Therefore, it was common for plantations consisting of six to seven hundred slaves to have only one, no more than two, whites living on it. . . . Thus it was possible for them to keep their African culture alive. . . . The Georgia Sea Island songs are very depressing to me. They focus on the reality [of slavery] that most African Americans long to forget. . . . [but] in all my readings I have formulated the impression that the blacks on the Sea Islands were basically content there because it reminded them of home. With little outside influence or interference, the people on those islands had created a little Africa. I feel that the name should be changed to the "Africans' Sea Islands."

GLEN AOKL, "MUSIC OF THE GEORGIA SEA ISLANDS"

The musical styles influencing American music came from a number of cultures, such as the African and Caribbean. The African influences were characterized by a constant overlapping, part crossing, and polyrhythms between leader and chorus, by clapped accompaniment, by improvisation, syncopation, and shifting vocal qualities (Lomax). The African styles allowed the slaves to transform a dreary spiritual from the whites into something excitedly syncopated with tricky parts and accompanied with clapping, fife and banjo playing. . . . Today the responsibility of carrying on the Island heritage belongs to Frankie and Doug Quimby . . . who are both Georgia Sea Islanders. They have collected chants, work songs, and games from the Island oldtimers, and . . . have performed at the White House, Carnegie Hall and the Smithsonian. . . . Jump for Joy, a slave dance, involves rhythmically slapping the knees, then sliding the hands from knee to knee and back, giving the illusion that one is crossing the legs. The slaves used the illusion to fool their owners...because of the belief that crossing the legs was sinful . . . Quimby explains that with a few more steps and gestures added; this knee slapping routine led to the Charleston, a white dance craze of the 1920's. (Grogan).

DEBBIE PUGH, "SLAVE SONGS"

When I think of work songs, I picture slaves working in the fields and chanting. What I never realized before was that these chants and songs had an important purpose . . . to help keep the beat to a swinging hoe or a rowing oar. According to Kingman, this singing was used to "coordinate and lighten physical work, acting as both a stimulus and a lifter of spirits." (48) The slave owners loved when the slaves sang in this manner. The beat and rhythm tended to make the slaves more productive. The owners actually encouraged the singing by paying extra wages to those slaves who had the ability to lead the other slaves in song. (Krehbiel 32) Spirituals came about when the slaves learned of Christianity. . . . they drove the slave owners to church services on Sundays [and] . . . would sit and listen to the sermons, prayers, and hymns . . . but felt compelled to change them to suit their own styles and needs. Spirituals not only expressed the slaves' love for their new-found Christian faith, but also their hate for slavery and their hopes and plans for escape. For example, (the song, "Let my people go") . . . Through my readings, I've come to truly appreciate what I have and what these people were put through. For us to forget their trials and tribulations is wrong; to learn from their experiences is crucial.

MIKE ACUFF, "THE BANJO"

Black citizens have made several contributions to the American music world. Their (single most significant contribution) *(questionable: S. W.)* to American music is the creation of the banjo. Our black citizens were very quick to learn any instrument that would produce rhythm. Such instruments ranged from sticks . . . to guitars. There is much speculation as to where the idea of combining percussion features with a string instrument originated. Africans have always had a deep interest in percussion sounds. On the plantations, blacks were forbidden the use of loud and provoking musical instruments such as drums and wind instruments. Possibly these conditions had created a demand for such an instrument. Africans still use a primitive instrument, the *banju,* made of strings stretched over a shallow tray. In the early 1700s the banjo emerged in the black community. . . . They called this instrument a 'banjar.' Most were made out of old furniture.

JIM MINUN, "THE LIFE AND MUSIC OF ROBERT JOHNSON, KING OF THE DELTA BLUES SINGERS"

Robert Palmer, a Blues scholar, wrote that "Fellow guitarists would watch him with unabashed, open-mouthed wonder. They were watching the Delta's first modern bluesman at work" (Barlow 47). Robert Johnson's life was short, although, in those short twenty-six years, he not only shaped and influenced the music of his own generation, but also every generation that has followed since. . . . He connected the gap between the rural beginnings and the modern urban manifestations that the Delta blues style would eventually lead to. It was the world's loss when he was poisoned by a jealous boyfriend, in August of 1938.

CAROL RAMMING, "EARLY COUNTRY BLUES"

Country blues is often said to have its ancestry in the field of cries and hollers of the nineteenth century. These cries and hollers were solitary, highly personal means by which black workmen expressed feelings and relieved loneliness. Sociologically, country blues was born in the wake of a number of important changes. After the Emancipation, blacks suddenly had the new solitude of their little farms in place of the communal bond of slavery. This complimented the highly individualized nature of the blues, as opposed to the social nature of the work song, for example. Additionally, blacks developed new mobility as they were forced to migrate to big cities outside of the Deep South. (Oster 46) Some blacks even chose to make a living as itinerant blues musicians, wandering the streets of the city. . . . So, the country blues provided a way for black Americans--troubled by poverty, racism, and broken families--to express feelings of loneliness, unhappy love relationships, and alienation in a highly personalized way. However, to see only poverty and statements of despair in blues is to miss the ultimate joy as a way to get relief from one's misery. While many blues songs have gloomy text and moody music, Harry Oster points out that "their burden of woe and melancholy is dialectically redeemed through sheer force of sensuality into an almost exultant affirmation of life, of love, of sex, of movement, of hope."

MELLISSA MCCLENDON, "JAZZ DURING THE 20S IN AMERICA"

Jazz in the 1920's evolved from the mixture of African rhythm and European instruments and techniques. This evolution was not static and jazz continued to change until some of its forms did not resemble the original art. Jazz was the result of the blending of different cultures in such a way as to capture the best of two worlds. Some elements of jazz come straight from African culture, such as the call and response. Dixieland uses this to a great extent as each instrument plays a solo after a general introduction. Emphasis on rhythm was primarily due to the importance of religion. African religion is oriented toward ritual, and African ritual always involved a lot of dancing. . . .

JULIE PRINCE, "THE ORIGINS AND HISTORY OF JAZZ MUSIC"

I have found many similarities and patterns between modern day jazz and its ancestry that have helped me to better understand its content. . . . the African was not accustomed to distinguishing his personal life from his public one. Many activities that Americans would consider to be "private" or "family" matters, such as a birth, death, marriage, and even sex, were considered to be a concern for the entire group in Africa and were celebrated by the community as a whole. Music was a major device used by the African to affirm his bond with the group, and was almost as common as the use of everyday speech in our lives. "Language and speech were not strictly divided"; "His music was woven as thickly through his life as a rose vine through a trellis" (Collier 7) . . . most importantly, there were a few certain characteristics that are true of African music that have carried over to the United States in the form of the beginning roots of jazz. Probably the most obvious characteristic was rhythm . . .Another trait [was] call-and-response patterns . . .Another [was] a rough tonal quality, meaning that the sound of a distinct pitch is not easily deciphered on a regular note scale. This trait came to be called a "dirty" tone, or the "blue" note in jazz music. In singing, Africans did not strive for some ideal tone . . . ; instead they deliberately tried to add texture of the sound by using vocal buzzing, rasps, shouts and cries . . . .

PILAR N. FUNES, "AFRO-AMERICAN GOSPEL TRADITION"

. . . After Emancipation there was a general revival of this "Old-time" religion. Because Afro Americans were released from restrictions on religious activity, they held worship services more often and for longer periods of time (Stillman 65); services which in the past were held for just a few hours were now extended for weeks and even months, the behavior was intensely emotional since there were no longer restrictions on noise. The excitement, shouting, and dancing could often be heard at a great distance. (Waterman 63) The successful growth of the "old-time" religion was due in large part to the satisfaction of the emotional needs of the Afro-American congregation by Afro-American ministers who knew what kind of religion their people wanted and were capable of providing it. . . In its early beginning in the 1920s, the gospel style was outlawed by most churches of orthodox tradition. It gradually gained acceptance, first as solos in the home and in churches and later by endorsement by the National Baptist Convention in Chicago in 1930.

KAREN L. BARBEE, "MAHALIA JACKSON: THE GOSPEL QUEEN"

. . . And if logic were consistently logical, the existence of black Americans during this time period would result in extreme unhappiness and unproductive lives. Yet, observation of Mahalia's life and the contributions thereof would disprove this seemingly clear logic. . . . One need only to refer to the history of the Apostles, Abraham Lincoln, George Washington Carver, and the one who had the greatest impact on Mahalia's life, Jesus Christ. . . . Would that "the whole world", in like manner, selflessly chose to use hardship and trials as fertilizer for barren ground, yielding fruitful, productive lives for the benefit of all mankind . . . Mahalia Jackson had many opportunities to take a God-given talent and use it for her own selfish ambition [to sing] in nightclubs, or even on Broadway, for the main purpose of making a living. (Wylie 73) But she chose instead to selflessly follow what she believed God would have her do--sing to His Glory.

E. ANDREW GAMBLE JR., "BLUES AND ROCK AND ROLL--THE BLUE NOTE CONNECTION"

. . . But the most important effect created on the guitar and the one that has the greatest effect on rock and roll is the ability to bend the strings to reach notes that are not on the scale. These 'blue notes' are the trademark of the rock and roll guitarist as well as the bluesman. The next big step towards rock and roll was taken when the guitar was electrified to make the instrument louder so it could be heard in large jazz ensembles. What this also did was to create two effects that would have a profound effect on rock and roll. The first of these effects is distortion--this is simply when the volume is played too loud for the speaker to handle--. . . Many of today's major rock bands use this technique to change the sound of the music--. . . The second effect is feedback: . . .electrical interference between the guitar's pickup and amplifier. This effect was used to its fullest in the 1960's and early 1970's by the great guitarist, Jimi Hendrix.

MICHELE REIFFER, "BLUES ROCKS ON IN THE 50'S"

. . . As civil rights were a main issue in the 1950s, so was the new craze of rock and roll. Both had strong connections and integration with the blues. The fifties were the era of the bus boycotts in Montgomery, Alabama, and of freedom rides for the desegregation of transport, of sit-ins, of lunch counters, and of education (61). . . It was about this time that rhythm and blues simultaneously was hitting the charts. Rhythm and blues inspired a group sound in a time when voices of many were needed to bring solidarity. . . . In the 1950s there was much racial tension. One situation that did not help ease the pain was that white singers were "stealing" songs from the black singers. Elvis was climbing the charts through racial ambiguity. Elvis's wild, "honky tonk", blues style awakened many white people. However, he did not please everyone. Many Southern blacks resented the success Elvis won with music that black artists had originated but could not sell beyond the "race record" market of a segregated commercial world.

LAWRENCE MASSEY, "AFRO-AMERICAN SOCIAL CONSCIOUSNESS THROUGH MUSIC TAKEN FROM THE SOUL (THE 1960'S - 1970'S)"

. . . In 1965 black message music seemed to take off exponentially, first through American's ghettos via the use of Rhythm and Blues, from which *soul* evolved, into other types of popular black American music as well. . . .Known as "Soul Brother Number One alias 'the Godfather of Soul,'.James Brown created many cuts that leaned toward social implications instead of the normal boy-girl love relationships. In 1965, I believe he started it off with "Don't Be a Drop-Out", a cut that, as implied, encouraged young Afro-Americans to receive and get an education. In 1967, he released what I would term the biggest selling song that reflected the black consciousness movement, entitled, "Say it Loud, I'm Black and I'm Proud". . . This fantastic, eyebrow raising, highly vocalized, ten year (1965-75) era of prevalent Afro-American social consciousness in music finally ended with a recording which I will call a secular sermon, "Wake up Everybody."

MARK BLANKENSHIP, "RAP MUSIC: THE NEW FORM OF MUSIC"

I will never forget the first time my parents heard it. . . . Boom, Boom, Boom, roaring from his car speakers. My parents joked and yelled "What is that?" I responded by telling them that was rap music—a new form of music my parents had never heard of, even though it had been around for a few years. Needless to say, they were not impressed, and they proceeded to change the subject.

Rap was born in the late 1970's on the east coast. This form of music originated in the ghetto of New York City by the poor, crafty black folks. It is the latest inner city language, born of street smart vibes and ghetto geniuses. (Horne 9) As we enter the nineties rap is as popular as ever. Television shows such as The Prince of Bel Air, Living Color, and Yo MTV Raps are being watched by millions of people. Rappers such as MC Hammer, who endorses British Knights shoes, and Young MC, who endorses Pepsi, are making millions of dollars from their songs. . . Hopefully more people will start to realize that rap is a very worthwhile form of music. . . . One of the main attractions of rap to the black youth of the Bronx was that rap gave them an outlet to show how good their gangs were. Since most of gang members were male, rap served as a way to boost their egos. Rhymes were made to . . . create an assertion by a gang about its dominance within the neighborhood. In no time, dancing was integrated with rap. One of these dances was breaking. . . . They claimed that the energy expended in break dancing is the same as fighting, and the end result is beneficial for all parties participating.

How did rap overcome its shortcomings during its early stage? First, the image of the uneducated inner city youth of the ghettos has been eliminated. . . . Secondly, the bad boy image of gang bangers has been replaced with socially conscious artists. . . . One thing is sure: when rap music is played, bodies sway, dancing shoes move and spirits flow. Not bad for a music that was born within the hearts of the black youth living in the slums of a forgotten part of the nation.

3. *MUSIC OF HISPANIC CULTURES IN THE UNITED STATES*

ROSEMARY MARTINEZ, "TEX-MEX MUSIC: ITS ASSIMILATION INTO AMERICA"

The Texas-Mexican music has been in existence in the United States for half a century. The music was brought over by the Mexican people during the time the Revolutionary War took place in Mexico. The increased migration of Mexicans into Texas after the turn of the century ensured that Norteno (Northern) culture was constantly reinforced in an already Mexicanized Tejano (Texan) society. (Pena, 1985) Ensembles congregated for the enjoyment of upper-class folks who enjoyed the variety of "orquesta typica" (string orchestra) which consisted of violin, psaltery, guitars, mandolins, and contrabass. These instruments originated from the orchestra-like ensembles that were typically played in postcolonial Mexico during the French and Spanish occupations. Yet, the working-class people of Texas could not afford, or were not used to, this kind of music and developed their own type of music called the conjunto (Pena 1985) . . . . After WWII, the music of the Tex-Mex conjunto was being dominated by the big bands of the United States, such as Tommy Dorsey and Glenn Miller, which were very popular during that time. There was a strong sense that the Mexicans had to adapt to the cultural and social domination of the American way of life.

JULIE MCCLENDON, "MARIACHI BANDS IN THE UNITED STATES"

Mariachi music has its origins in the Roman Empire: Spain, North Africa, French and PreColumbian Indian Civilizations of Meso-America. (Anton et al. 57) . . . Mariachi music is perhaps the best known type of Mexican folk music..Brightly-costumed, strolling musicians sing and play violins, guitars, and trumpets. This style of music originally came from Guadalajara in the state of Jalisco but more recently has spread throughout Mexico and the American Southwest (Anton et al. 57) . . . Perhaps the most famous mariachi song is "Guadalajara". Every Mexican restaurant I've been into in the United States is familiar with this song. A few years ago . . . , our family took a boat ride on Lake Patzcuaro. Mariachi bands were on all the boats; when asked if they would play "Guadalajara" they just looked at us and substituted another song in its place. . . . In the United States, the mariachi bands tend to play songs from the "old country," songs that they remember from their youth. To me, mariachi music seems a vital, evolving part of the music scene in Mexico, while in the United States it is part of the nostalgic look at a person's roots.

DAVE NORWOOD, "THE MUSICAL TRADITIONS OF LATIN AMERICA"

The music of Latin America, or salsa as we call it, takes its roots in Cuba. This Latin sound is a unique mix of folkloric music with tastes of jazz texture. We find that the name 'salsa' emerged in the late 1960's and early '70s, and simply means 'sauce.' (Gerard 3) The evolution of salsa amongst these people is an attempt to capture the musical tradition of jazz and rock, while keeping a politically-motivated desire to create a pan-Latin American sound. . . . we find the joining of post Cuban Revolution dances and musical traits in the Puerto Rican community (the Nuyoricans) . . . Before the revolution occurred, the mambo, the cha cha and the pachanga were among the favorite dances of Cuban Salsa. . . . Brazil has also had its hand in on the formation of salsa. Willie Colon . . . is able to perform songs by combining Cuban mambo, Puerto Rican bomba, and Brazilian samba . . . This type of salsa is an interpretation of Latin pride, and a cry for all Latin people to rise above impoverished beginnings and discrimination.

4. MUSIC OF LESSER KNOWN MINORITY GROUPS

JOY L. HOLMES, "HAWAIIAN MUSIC IN THE UNITED STATES TODAY"

The impact of western-influenced music on traditional Hawaiian music is tremendous, and the way it exists in the United States today is phony—intended to promote tourism to Hawai. . . . Hawaii had a flourishing Polynesian culture when discovered by Captain Cook in 1778. Since then, there has been an addition of Polynesians from other island groups, such as Asians, Samoans, and Caucasians . . . The Hawaiian people believed that everyone has "mana", spiritual power, and the amount of mana one had determined one's place in society. . . "Mana is cumulative and becomes greater, generation by generation, only through its conscious preservation and strengthening" (Kanahele 53) . . . They believed in many gods, and to honor those gods, they performed hula and chant. The hula was originally performed by men, taken to the temple and used in worship. The dance movements were connected with nature's movements. Later, the hula engulfed all of Hawaiian society and became a way of teaching, a form of entertainment, and a foundation for self-defense.

JENNIFER GEORGE, "DANISH-AMERICAN BALLADS AND SONGS"

In many respects, the emigration from Europe to American was the major social movement of the nineteenth century. More than 300,000 Danes left their native land in search of a better home. Despite the relatively small number, the exodus to American was a prominent topic in popular songs (Wright). "There is a consensus in all the existing studies that the Danes were among the most rapid assimilators of the American ethnic groups." (Nielsen) This might explain why much of the Danish American emigration history and music is not recorded. . . . Danish songs did not necessarily give a realistic picture of the New World. An early song gets right to the point. The title is "Do you Want to be Rich?" Others cite freedom, as in "Til pennen jeg tager": "There is no distinction between rich and poor,/ Between young and old, they are all equal,/ Here the disdain of pride is not known,/ One loves everyone who wanders that path." Many songs are sprinkled with humorous phrases or satire and mock the gullibility of the emigrants . . . Christian Winter's poem, "Flugten til Amerika," is still recited by Danish school children, an example of . . . the stereotype of America as paradise (Bertelsen): "The horses' hooves are shod with silver,/And the wagon wheel silver-mounted,/ The gold just lies there at your feet, /You merely bend down to get it."

JAMES F. ROBERTS, JR., "THE HINDU JOURNEY TO WESTERN CULTURE"

I am co-illustrating an Electrical Engineering textbook written by a Hindu professor, which provided me with an excellent opportunity to find out more about this culture. Dr. Lahti allowed me to accompany him to a religious gathering at his home to learn more about Hinduism and the music associated with this religion. I suppose that my Christian background paved the way for most of my bias, for I found the music very difficult to listen to. If I could understand the language I might have appreciated what sounded like screeching to the untrained ear. As for the actual ceremony, I found the sitting position very uncomfortable, but somehow I felt a certain peace as I concentrated on the unidentifiable chanting and what sounded like gargling. Another aspect . . . [I] found strange was that there were no women present. After the event Dr. Lahti . . . explained that the music provided something of a matrix for our souls to cling to in order to take a step closer to Brahman. Reflecting on my Hindu music experience as a whole, my overall opinion is much the same as my opinion of the modern atonal works heard at the New Music Festival. That is, I find it hard to sit back, relax and listen to these types of music. It seems to take a certain cultural or religious connection to really understand and appreciate Hindu music.

Essay #8

TEACHING AMERICAN CULTURE THROUGH MUSIC: A TRIALOGUE

WITH PROFESSORS SUSAN WILLOUGHBY,
JAMES MCCORMICK AND JAMES CHOPYAK
California State University, Sacramento
JAN PETRIE, interviewer

ED. NOTE: See p. 111, above, for my general introduction to this essay.--BC

PETRIE: The title Ch'maj chose for this trialogue was not "Using American music to teach *about* American culture" but using music to teach Culture itself. That is, in the case of American music, she feels it won't do to speak of "minorities" and "subcultures," because minority implies there's a majority somewhere, and subculture implies there's a "main" culture out there. But when you look at American music--as distinct from other arts—anything you actually call American already mixes material from the so-called minorities and subcultures, especially black culture. As teachers of American music, how do you respond to that idea?

CHOPYAK: I still like the terms "mainstream" and "non-mainstream." You can make a good argument that not everything is a part of mainstream American culture, but there are streams that interact and are constantly changing. What is "non-mainstream" today becomes part of the "mainstream" tomorrow.

WILLOUGHBY: I am discovering a way to teach that to my students. Since we have so many cultures already well integrated into our society, students who grew up in this context do not realize they are living in a multicultural society to the extent they are. What I do is take music that is already representative of several cultures, take it apart and show them, for example, that this came from African culture, this idea came from the Germans who came in the eighteenth century, and so on. My experience is that the students are surprised. I think showing them where things came from will tend, in the long run, without my making any direct statement, to reduce racist attitudes that might exist. I do believe that simple education, explaining to them what is actually there and what actually happened, will give a more comprehensive view of the world they live in and reduce prejudice.

CHOPYAK: I agree. Most students don't realize all the different strands that contributed to our society. There is a tendency to think that only in recent history with jet planes have peoples from different cultures come into contact. Nonsense! For thousands of years there has been contact between different cultures and mixing of musics. Of course, this is very focused in the United States. I agree with Susan that the study of music could very well lead to better racial understanding. For many students it is a shock to consider that mainstream American music has been so heavily influenced by what *they* think of as minority, "non-mainstream" cultures. This is an important thing for them to learn.

McCORMICK: Let me cite specifically one technique to portray this. Ballad scholars will take a ballad from the British Isles of the seventeenth or eighteenth century, and follow it across the states to show how a folk idiom became a country expression as it reached the frontier, where the occupation itself changed the lyrics, and the oral tradition may well have changed the melody. You can show how with technology in the twentieth century, and "folk" going "country," it changes again. Then when Black influence adds energy and rhythm, the ballad will move into a rock experience. That one simple ballad then has taken on many new forms as the new melody gives meaning to people's lives. The lyrics change drastically, as well as the actual musical content.

CHOPYAK: This is a good way to reinforce for students that the idea of mixing is not a brand new thing. Some people act as if the whole multicultural movement is a new concept. It is not new. What has changed is the speed with which it is happening, and some of the component parts are different. But the mingling of different races has been going on for a long time. Some of the interaction is beneath people's consciousness. Musically, some people hear something and say, "I am going to try that at home" and multicultural music happens automatically. You also get some people who say consciously, "I am going to write multicultural music."

Look at what is happening in broadcasting now, with global programs playing pop music from all over the world. International pop music, for lack of a better term, is rooted in American pop music, which is already a mixture of African, South American, Western, European all mixed in together. Then it moves out to other parts of the world, recombines with their traditional music, and it is now coming back here —whether it is Paul Simon doing things with African musicians and Brazilian musicians, or New Age music opening up a whole other category, with musicians taking concepts from traditional musics in China, Indonesia, Africa and so forth and then combining it with synthesizers or acoustic instruments.

McCORMICK: And we say, "Wow. Isn't this neat. It's new." But it is just the marriage of technology with some older idea we embrace in a contemporary idiom.

CHOPYAK: To put it in an international context, most of the origins of instruments we call Western instruments can be traced to Africa, the Middle East and Asia This kind of interconnection between cultures and peoples is not new. It is just faster and more intense, with satellite transmissions and cassette tapes.

WILLOUGHBY: In the section of our American music class in which I am trying to infuse multiculturalism, the class was given an assignment to do a short research paper on music of an American ethnic minority. A student asked if she could do her paper on the songs of Danish-Americans. I said No, and thought it over for a few days and came back and said she could. The point is that when we talk about multiculturalism, we have to let students know that the multiculturalism in themselves has been going on for a long time. The paper was very interesting.

PETRIE: Why did you say no initially?

WILLOUGHBY: Because I felt when we started out we were basically dealing with racism, and I told the students I didn't think there was a lot of difference between a Danish-American or a French-American or a German-American. They were White people. So we have to expand the term multiculturalism in our work, in our discussions, and in our understanding.

McCORMICK: Many of your students, as I recall, found it meaningful.

WILLOUGHBY: I think some of the most significant reactions were from a couple of Black students in the class who said they learned a lot about themselves because even they did not realize the extent to which Black American culture is infused into all our popular music. They also have not had that much education about early music of Black Americans in the United States, so they were able to understand their essential selves better.

CHOPYAK: That gets to one of the erroneous assumptions that people of a particular ethnicity are going to have some particular knowledge of that culture. It doesn't work that way.

McCORMICK: As a concrete example to show cultures in transition, I use the Cajun experience. I show Cajuns in transition in Arcadia, coming down through Nova Scotia to Louisiana, and there you had the marriage of fiddle tunes (which were fairly similar yet took on a Cajun spice). Then the big change came with the Creole--the mixture of Spanish and French elements--and that changed to Zydeco music with the blues influence. And then they added the accordion. We did not have the accordion in Arcadia, French Canada, or Nova Scotia. We had the fiddle, but the accordion could cut right through the din, the loudness of people enjoying themselves. This is a clear example for my students of cultures in transition.

PETRIE: I am wondering about the idea that there really isn't any "majority" when we talk about music.

CHOPYAK: American music, by definition, is a mixture, a mainstream that gets influenced by components within it. But if you are talking about *academic* study and teaching of music, that has very clearly had a mainstream, a canon.

PETRIE: Is that the majority then?

CHOPYAK: In Academia, yes, it is. For American society, no, that is not what it is. As each new kind of American music has developed, it has been influenced by one of the "minority" or "non-mainstream" groups. Jazz became mainstream because of the interaction between black and white American cultures. Rap music began as Black American, African American, music. It was not accepted at first by mainstream society, but it quickly became accepted. These things get accepted much more rapidly now than ever before because of the money in it.

McCORMICK: In this morning's paper (3/5/91), an article on "Sacramento's Changing Face" stated, "Sacramento's experience mirrors the population shift across the state, one that has been evident for some time in California's schools. The rapidly growing number of minority students has made the white majority a minority since the mid 1980s." Statistics dictate that sooner or later this is going to infiltrate into the teaching and the content of our courses, including music courses.

CHOPYAK: The musical influences may take more time to set in. Asian Americans are the second or third biggest group in California. There are more Asians than African Americans. But the musical influences may be diluted because so many people are not bringing their own classical or traditional musics with them. The fact that we have a rapidly growing Asian population does not mean that traditional Chinese and Vietnamese music will start creeping into American pop music. I don't think that will happen. For one thing, there is already Vietnamese and Chinese pop music. There will be influences, but exactly what, who knows?

WILLOUGHBY: The question is, *when* is it going to start happening? I have been watching for that too. We know there are no books in our library about this kind of popular music in the United States.

CHOPYAK: There are a few articles coming out in some journals. To me it is interesting that the same bias we have seen in the study of Western music against pop music still exists in ethnomusicology, but this is beginning to change. Ethno-musicologists are beginning to look at popular musics--at some of the conferences now--as a legitimate topic. For a time they thought all popular music was Western. In the past, when I presented papers on Asian popular music, I have had people get angry because they thought it was Western music.

McCORMICK: In New Orleans I was at a Popular Culture Association meeting and a man stood up and banged the table and said, "Popular culture is here to stay. The sooner we understand that, the better."

PETRIE: Isn't that how we can see multiculturalism best--in popular culture?

CHOPYAK: Yes. I think in many ways we can. The only problem in looking at it that way is that when you talk about popular culture, you are talking about the business interests and how much they are controlling where the big money lies. This is one of the arguments among people looking at popular music in different parts of the world: how much of this is what people really want to listen to and how much of it is big American, European or Japanese companies pushing this stuff? If you have a multibillion dollar industry promoting certain things, with the capabilities of selling these tapes at low prices, people will tend to buy that. On the other hand, you can't force people to listen to stuff they don't want to listen to either.

If you do listen to the global beat, there are some fascinating mixtures. With synthesizers, you can have electronic sounds with all kinds of different tunes. The technology of recording is in some ways detrimental to traditional music and in other ways it helps them. It provides a way for music that would die off anyway to survive. If it is recorded, even if people don't pass it on to the next generation, you've got it. By the same token things become standardized. Technology has spread Western music to other countries and maybe dominated them to some extent, but it allows us to hear those musics, too.

McCORMICK: We are a very mobile society, and we have made a quantum leap in technology. Think of Leonard Bernstein back in the 1960's talking about Roy Harris and saying, "American music is wide open music because it reflects the spaces of the West." We have come a long way from that sort of generalization.

CHOPYAK: There are many other multiethnic countries in the world going through change even more rapidly than we are and they have the same questions. What is Malaysian music? You find the same arguments going on in many parts of the world. What makes it unique in the United States is that we have so many different groups of people. What happens here affects what happens everywhere.

WILLOUGHBY: I want to point out that this process of integrating— allowing the musicians to integrate, rather than business interests--I think happens with jazz musicians. They are one of the avant garde groups who will hear something and immediately absorb it intentionally into their art. By contrast a couple of projects were done on subcultures in the United States who preserve their culture intact and do not dilute it with American music, particularly the Sikhs. They keep their culture intact. It has not combined, or Vietnamese cultures as far as I can tell, or the Hmongs. They have their festivals with their music and their music doesn't mix, whereas Mexican culture has its festivals and they play Mexican music, but we also have a huge repertoire of American popular music that has been influenced by, or is a translation from, Mexican-American songs.

CHOPYAK: People definitely hold on to ethnic music. This is related to the argument about a multicultural education, whether you should have separate streams of education teaching separate things about each ethnic or cultural group. You have many people in the United States, especially academics in ethnomusicology, interested in the traditional musics of other parts of the world, and we may be moving toward a point where some of it will be preserved more purely in the United States than anywhere else. Last semester our Indonesian students here put on an Indonesian cultural night. They did what from their perspective is traditional music. Some people who are academically oriented said it was not traditional--it was influenced by pop. For a young person in any part of the world, old music to them is what their parents listened to. But purists, cultural specialists, are very likely to try to preserve the traditions intact. We can all learn a lot from that, but they also have to be open to the modernization in the "home society."

This gets us to another big argument, the constant argument in some circles over westernization and modernization. Very often what seems to us like westernization in someone else's culture from *their* perspective is modernization. They say, "We drive cars and go to work in tall office buildings just like you. Do you just listen to the music of medieval Europe? Why should we have to listen only to the music from our history of that period?"

McCORMICK: Another point: You can teach geography through American music. You have in tunes historical, racial, sociological implications, such as "Down in Alabam'," subtitled "Ain't I Glad I Got Out of the Wilderness." You have "The Arkansas Traveler" and "Camptown Races." You can see how they tried to put our history in music, you can see stereotypes, and you can see this whole idea of multiculturalism and how to use music to teach about aspects of culture.

CHOPYAK: Music can also be used to teach about a new group of immigrants coming from a totally different culture. Get a recording from the Smithsonian and play it as an example of their traditional music. That will make a dramatic impact on the students. Their culture is very different from American culture. You can try to explain it, but the *sound* of different music makes the point better than lecturing.

McCORMICK: The film, "Discovering American Indian Music" is one of my favorites to show the love of tradition. It walks through a variety of elderly Indians and shows the pride they take in their rituals. At one point they show young people around the campfire, and suddenly that rather immortal chant becomes a little more contemporary/folk. It almost has a melody that you and I would be accustomed to.

CHOPYAK: To see young people getting into their own cultural traditional music is a reflection of what is happening in society when people get interested in their cultural roots, their own ethnic heritage. Compared with 25 or 30 years ago when that film was made, now many young Native Americans are actively involved in their traditional music and dance, albeit with some changes. You do not find this across the whole spectrum of different ethnic groups, in many instances. People are taking an interest in tradition whereas previous generations did not want to. They wanted to assimilate so did not want to be tied to traditions.

PETRIE: Why do you think that is? Is it a popular thing or a political thing?

CHOPYAK: I think it is part political, a reflection of our society right now. We seem to be moving in that direction. People are taking more interest and making a statement. They say, "I am proud of my heritage." I don't want to have to blend into the mainstream and be like everyone else and be ashamed of my past.

PETRIE: Did any of you see this article in *Newsweek* (cited 12/24/90) about being politically correct?

CHOPYAK: There are lots of things being written about this idea. Some people are comparing it to the Red-baiting that went on during the 1950's. I think there is hysteria on both sides, quite honestly. Some people involved in multicultural education are reacting a bit hysterically to the attack from the right wing. That is too bad because it impedes doing something constructive. There is hysteria from both sides.

McCORMICK: We are concerned about prejudice, but not just racial prejudice. A lot of rock and rollers snub country music, yet when you tell them that country music and rhythm and blues with a backbeat are your basic rock and roll, they are shocked and surprised. Introducing rock vis-a-vis country music shows that we should not harbor prejudice against any style or group. Then they change their attitude toward the guy sitting beside them who happens to enjoy country music.

WILLOUGHBY: I have discovered in the last year or so that more and more students are turning in well-written papers about country music. And that reveals an attitude, because usually people who liked country music did not write very well. A lot of students have told me this semester that country music has really changed and is becoming very popular with the younger people.

PETRIE: I want to ask next about assignments that worked particularly well for you in the classroom.

CHOPYAK: One of the things I find works is encouraging students to attend performances and cultural events that involve music and dance performances of different cultures. I do this for many reasons. Part of it is just to expose them to live music. Some of it has to do with the fact that one reason for racism is ignorance and lack of contact with other people. For instance, I suggested to students that they attend a Persian cultural night. They were terrified at first. They think, "Oh, the Iranians!" The Persian students here know that I often send students there so they are on the lookout for people who look bewildered, and they usually have someone come up and say, please come in and have a seat and we will explain to you what is going on. I have had so many reports from events like this where students will say, "I was terrified, but in the end I had a wonderful experience and I have a different impression of these people now." My main purpose is for them to experience the music and write about it, but the ulterior motive is to have them experience a culture they have never had to deal with. Not everybody reacts positively. I have had students go to Mexican performances and come back complaining that all they heard was sung in Spanish. You don't always win that way, but it is still important to have them approach another culture and have that common experience.

WILLOUGHBY: I require them to write a review on a live performance by an ethnic minority group. That has been successful. They also do a research paper on music of a cultural minority. *[See Essay #7.--BC]*

One of my most successful efforts working with multiculturalism has been with the TV series, "American Patchwork"—in particular when Alan Lomax deals with the music of the Appalachians, the white music and the black. He shows pictures of an old white man playing a fiddle in the South. He points out the way he is moving his hand, the way he is able to slide from one note to another--something he would have picked up from the Blacks in the South, who picked up the fiddle originally from the English people who came over, and then fed back their little slant on fiddle playing, so that now the white fiddlers play with a certain fluidity in their bodies that they did not have earlier, that one does not hear in, say, Scottish fiddling. He does the same with the dancing. He shows how some of the white dancers in the South are now able to have a middle body rhythmic response, which is typical of Black Americans. He does it very well and convincingly and with a lot of graciousness and understanding of the Black culture.

CHOPYAK: That ["American Patchwork"] was a five-part series on PBS.

WILLOUGHBY: The one on New Orleans jazz shows a picture of people dancing in the street at a festival. Then the film footage shifts immediately to an African village where they are doing almost exactly the same movement.

McCORMICK: Also "Black Music in America from Then Until Now," made in 1971, and selections from "The American Experience" are good videos. Something I tried this semester is "100 Years of Music at Carnegie Hall," recently on PBS. What I love about the video is that it explores the premieres and debuts of every style of music and as many colors as you can imagine. It brings us right up to the present. *[See Checklist D, Part III, for all these videos.--BC.]*

==

TEAM TEACHING A
MULTICULTURAL AM CIV COURSE

by Scot Guenter
American Studies, San Jose State University

At San Jose State University, a twelve-unit, year-long, multiculturally sensitive, team-taught overview of American culture is an integral foundation of our American Studies program. Since the course was designed to meet an array of lower division undergraduate requirements, the enrollment draws students from a wide range of backgrounds, with a wide range of majors and career goals. The structure is of a large group lecture followed immediately by small group seminar/discussion. There are many opportunities in this arrangement, not only for passing on to students information vital to their future roles as citizens and leaders but also for developing their skills in critical analysis and several methodologies. Although such a course requires constant sensitivity to a dynamic relationship among its elements, it is useful here to separate out three aspects of our approach: multiculturalism, team teaching, and interdisciplinarity (as opposed to multidisciplinarity).

1. MULTICULTURALISM--Given the demographics of San Jose State University's student population and the surrounding communities we serve, the faculty in the American Studies program at San Jose State firmly believe that multicultural and multiperspective awareness must become part of our students' working repertoire of interpretive modes. We are already a vibrant and exciting mix of races, ethnicities, and cultural legacies that will become the norm in the state of California in the next twenty years, and this transition is in the process of becoming a national phenomenon. The city of San Jose, according to recent census data, is one of three cities in the state which is "non-majority": with an overall population of 782,248 our ethnic distribution is 49.6% Anglo; 26.6% Latino; 19.5% Asian and 4.7% African-American. Our student body reflects this culturally diverse population. Students of color comprise forty percent of our students, and studies indicate that white students will comprise less than fifty percent of the student body by the late 1990s. Fifty-two percent of our students are women. In such a situation, the need for multicultural sensitivity and knowledge is imperative – which is not to suggest that homogeneous campuses do not require such awareness; of course they do (perhaps more so) but learning to appreciate each others' legacies is something our students must come to terms with both inside and outside the classroom *now*.

In his commencement address at Duke University in 1991, George F. Will complained, "Some policies instituted in the name of 'multiculturalism' are not celebrations of the pluralism from which American unity is woven." He was wary of fragmentation, claiming that "America's increasing diversity increases the importance of universities as transmitters of the cultural legacy that defines and determines national unity." (Will, "Commencement at Duke," AMERICAN SCHOLAR 60 [Autumn 1991], p. 501.) I agree that our job is, in part, to transmit our cultural legacies and the rich pluralism of this society both past and present, which is not to say we must all agree on and preach a consensus view of history. Perhaps a key element in our approach to multiculturalism is a strong commitment to multiperspectives. I want my Hispanic students to experience the emotions of life at a Japanese internment camp during World War II, my Asian-American students to understand the struggles of a runaway slave girl, my African-American students to grasp Emerson's sensitivity to nature. I teach (and I believe) that each student should become aware of his or her own group's history and achievements, but that our goal is to learn how we *share* these legacies. By learning to see the world from a wide range of perspectives we are not only sensitized but empowered; with knowledge comes responsibility not only to ourselves but to our larger communities. Throughout the year, as our syllabi indicate, the experiences and cultural creations of Native Americans, European-Americans, African-Americans, Latino-Americans, and Asian-Americans are studied. Issues of gender, race, ethnicity, and class are addressed, for clearly these groups should not be studied in isolation but in their interactions. Given the high cost of many texts, we have found the multicultural collection of sources in the Heath Anthology, when combined with the multicultural social history (including a taste of original documents) to be found in the reader THE WAY WE LIVED, will meet almost all of our reading needs without emptying our students' wallets.

A FINAL NOTE: I tend to use Whitman's "I Hear America Singing" as a bridge -- chronological and philosophical – between American Studies 1A and IB to keep intact the multicultural theme between the two halves of the course.

2. TEAM TEACHING--The true success or failure of the course depends largely on the cohesiveness and common vision of the faculty members who make up the team. Generally, one will be a specialist in American history, another in American Literature, and the third in political science, sociology, ethnic studies, or interdisciplinary studies. The team members meet to discuss their philosophies and goals the semester before the course is taught, design the course through mutual agreement, and meet together regularly throughout the school year to monitor the success of their strategies and interactions. The team represented in the sample syllabi *(#18, in Part I)* included a specialist in women's history and popular culture, an expert on the American Renaissance in literature, and an American Studies Ph.D. interested in cultural rituals and icons. From the start we shared a commitment to teach critical thinking skills, maintain an openness to alternative perspectives, and engage in reflexive self-examination of cultural identity and stance.

Of course the instructors will have different views, draw on different methodologies, and demonstrate different styles of teaching in the lecture hall. All attend each others' lectures, sitting among the students and taking notes and learning along with them. All must be the best kind of teacher — the kind that never stops being a student. As the course develops, the instructors not only address the students but refer back and forth to each other's assertions and presentations. They become three different voices engaged in conversation with the students and each other, and the students, through their journals and their seminar discussions, are encouraged to develop their own sense of Voice in the ongoing conversation that is the study of American culture.

INTERDISCIPLINARITY--An important foundation for this course is its commitment to interdisciplinary analysis. If a student comes to think of one day as "history day," another as "literature day" or "political science day," the class is failing its fundamental purpose. The goal must be to demonstrate by example what Gene Wise called "connecting minds" in the lecture presentations, and then help the students to build skills of analysis and integration, developing their own connecting minds in seminar. The daily journal is a wonderful tool in this process. Although it requires a lot of instructor time reading and writing responses and suggesting avenues of cultural inquiry, it helps the students become more personally involved in the living culture whose diverse and complex history they are studying.

A dynamic way to stress the insights gained from interdisciplinary analysis is to use music and visual aids in combination when focusing on complex levels of interaction occurring at any particular cultural moment. For instance, in teaching about the American Revolution, I focus one lecture on the use of editorial cartoons (engravings) to delineate political and social views in England and America before and during the war. This study of the cartoon both as art form and as propaganda opens the door for discussions of iconography, civil religion, rhetoric, and political science that continue throughout the course. Incorporated also are patriotic ballads of the period, sometimes performed live by a folk singer I am lucky enough to know. Similarly, the study of consumer culture in the age of tail fins and Elvis is presented through slides of advertising and pop culture, augmented by theme songs from television situation comedies that portray the suburban myth of the family. Students discuss how media not only reflect but affect cultural values and perceptions. Near the end of the course, they are exposed to the evolution of MTV aesthetics and asked to evaluate procedures the network follows in selling to corporate sponsors seeking to reach the youth market.

One interdisciplinary avenue of inquiry that belongs in every American Civilization course is an examination of American "civil religion," since this constellation of symbols, values, myths, and rituals is vital in binding a diverse, multicultural people together. One can introduce this analysis at many different points—at the sanctification of George Washington early in the Federalist period, in the rise of manifest destiny, in the music and poetry of the Civil War, in the flag-raising at Iwo Jima as transformed through photography and sculpture, in the counterculture's appropriation of the national banner during the turbulent 60s, or in the cultural responses to the Gulf War. As a topic, "civil religion" requires the teacher to draw on art history, music, political science, and literature to demonstrate the power of the media and the influence of institutions.

Since my own research has centered on the American flag, I use slide lectures to illustrate the use of the flag as symbol to provoke questions about how cultural values and beliefs are transmitted and how they change. Helping students realize how such a process works empowers them, and at the same time, seeing the interdisciplinary process at work leads them back to integrating and synthesizing their knowledge of the world around them. Both goals are admirable, especially in a multicultural society.

Essay #10

GOOD INDIANS LIVE, BAD INDIANS DIE
A Critique of *Dances with Wolves*

by Shoots the Ghost

ED. NOTE: "Shoots the Ghost" was an undergraduate at the University of California, Santa Cruz, when he wrote this essay in 1991 as a paper for American Studies 101, taught by Marilyn Patton. He is Oglala Lakota, born in a log cabin near Kyle, South Dakota, on the Pine Ridge Indian Reservation. The name he was born with is Marlon Sherman; Shoots the Ghost was his grandfather's grandfather's name.

Dances with Wolves is a marvelous piece of propaganda, a pacifier shoved into Indian mouths, a balm to soothe White guilt. It exemplifies the strength of the American Myth of the Frontier in which white males dominate their surroundings, and Indians and women are present only as props, as means to an end.

This is an extremely difficult movie to critique: I became far too involved in the story. I left the theater emotionally exhausted. People were crowding in on all sides, prodding cheerfully: "How did you like it?" "What did you think?" "Explain that scene where...," as if it should be such an easy thing to pick my heart up off the ground. If we were at their mother's funeral, would I ask them to describe for me how they were feeling? I had to see the movie again. The first time I was too immersed in the warm comfortable flow of the Lakota language, mesmerized by the broad sweeping view of my homeland. I found myself contrasting the high nasal speech of Kevin Costner with the rich throatiness of Floyd Westerman, rather than concentrating on the plot. Detachment finally prevailed, somewhat.

Kevin Costner would probably be shocked to hear that he was just another gear in imperial America's myth-making machine. He undoubtedly believes he has made a thoughtful, sensitive movie about a man who escapes the savagery of civilization to experience the civility of the savages. While it does portray the Lakota more fairly than any movie in recent past, it is still a white man's movie about white males choices. The movie follows John Dunbar (Costner) from Civil War battlefield to a Sioux village on the plains. The characters are all either noble or barbaric—there is no in-between. The land is unfailingly beautiful, as are the protagonists. With the exception of the essential plot twist, the story follows classic western plot lines. Richard Slotkin says our adherence to the "myth of the frontier, the conception of America as a wide-open land of unlimited opportunity, has blinded us to the consequences of the industrial and urban revolutions and to the need for social reform." *Dances with Wolves* fosters the same idea. By dumb luck, Dunbar becomes a hero while trying to commit suicide. His reward for his "heroic" act is to be assigned to the military. He chooses the West, because, he says, "I want to see the frontier before it's gone." The first we see of the frontier is miles of waving grass, hills that seem to roll on forever, badlands that dwarf the team and wagon. Music swells as the camera pans. The wilderness is perfect, untouched, a place where a man can lose himself or find himself.

The rolling prairie represents Slotkin's land of unlimited opportunity. This is supposed to be our vision of America, and of the world. We should be able to take our political, economic or spiritual opportunity and enrich ourselves accordingly. According to the elements of the myth displayed here our possibilities are limitless. Later "versions of the myth showed the hero growing closer to the Indian and the wild land. New versions of the hero emerged, characters whose role was that of mediating between civilization and savagery, white and red." Dunbar proves himself a modern-day ecologist by cleaning out the abandoned fort and nearby pond. He befriends a wolf, which comes to symbolize not only Dunbar's Lakota neighbors, but all American Indian tribes. In growing closer to the Euro-American form of civilization the wolf seals his fate. The implication is that had the Indians remained "wild" they would be thriving today. . . .

Through the course of the year, Dunbar becomes closer to the Lakota people. He gifts them with coffee, finds their first buffalo of the season, even hunts with them. Dunbar's first meeting with an Indian shows us what their relationship will be. Kicking Bird, is out sightseeing, finely clothed in quilled buckskins, and Dunbar bursts upon him, stark naked and shouting. Kicking Bird flees in panic. The white man's nakedness illustrates not only his loneliness, but also his openness, his ability to lay new experiences upon his open soul without prejudice.

Dunbar is always in control, always the hero. When he comes upon a grieving Indian woman, catching her unaware, he subdues her and takes her back to her village, managing to ride right past the sentries and enter the village unnoticed from above. Later, it is Dunbar who finds the buffalo herd, and who saves a young hunter from certain death during the hunt. During the attack by the Pawnees, it is Dunbar who saves the village, by unearthing his cache of firearms. Near the end of the movie Dunbar displays great knowledge of White ways and wisdom when he advises the tribe to move further into the wilderness. These incidents show that our hero is extremely competent in all situations, and we have to wonder how the Indians got as far as they did without him. These are, of course, essential elements of the American myth. The white male must be at ease in the wilderness and among lesser peoples. He must journey through the wilderness into the "kingdom of death for the purpose of extracting some power or secret which will enable man to

The message of the movie is dimmed somewhat by the screenwriter's attempt to make a contemporary point. Dunbar is unfailingly good, pleasant and patient. The Sioux are noble, almost childlike. With one exception, whites are dirty beasts. The Pawnee are red savages, louts at least. The Bad Guys are so bad that they are not believable. If they were more true to life, they could be our alter egos, and we might be warned about becoming like them. Unfortunately, these are only caricatures. The only lasting image is that of the good white man who attempted to save his Indian friends from the inevitable onrushing stampede of civilization.

Edward Said says that men make their own history--in our case a "Western style of dominating, restructuring, and having authority over" the wilderness. What we see in *Dances with Wolves* is a retelling and a continuation of American history, made more palatable by the lovable personality of the hero and the use of romantic imagery. Said writes that "the things to look at are style, figures of speech, setting, narrative devices, historical and social circumstances, not the correctness of the representation nor its fidelity to some great original." Even though the Lakota are portrayed as intelligent, the tribe is still only a vehicle, a means by which Dunbar can make his spiritual journey through the wilderness and emerge a better man.

Historically, the movie is often incorrect. There are no real badlands between Kansas and South Dakota, where the Pawnee and Sioux territories would overlap. Also, the Pawnee were never such a threat to the Lakota. They were a more seden-tary people who lived in earth lodges and only followed the buffalo herd briefly each year. If anything, the Lakota terrorized them, pushing them ever southward. One scene in particular bothered me: the hunters lying on a hill over-looking the buffalo herd, while the wind was blowing across their backs toward the herd.

The grand settings and emotional dialogue blind the audience to the underlying theme. We see a white man on a hardy steed galloping across endless prairies, and believe this is America for the taking. We patriotically see bad white men and savage Indians, not as our possible selves, but as the Others. The wolf and the Lakota are subordinate to the hero. Even the woman he eventually marries barely exists because she is, after all, a white woman raised by Indians, and it is only natural that he should take her away from all that. (Pygmalion revisited--!)

Toni Morrison says, "canon building is empire building." Dunbar is just another cannonball fired at non-white, non-male peoples. For all his environmental friendliness, his straight-arrow altruism, his gallant patience, his anthropologically correct technique, he is still a symbol of male supremacy. Through him, the Indian is seen as a noble but doomed race of people soon to be wiped from the face of the continent. This is a sad fact, we are told. We are not told that these same people are alive today, with a whole new set of problems, but with a whole set of solutions, if

alive today, with a whole new set of problems, but with a whole set of solutions, if anyone would care to listen to them. The problem is that nobody wants to listen. Everybody has their own ideas about how Indians should be handled. These ideas are, of course, gleaned from the volumes of the Imperial Canon.

People tend to think, as Said put it, that "if the (Indian) could represent itself, it would." Colonized peoples, whether they are categorized by race, gender or class, are thought unable to understand their own role in the world, incompetent to decide their own fate. When they vocalize their own solutions they are labelled radicals, and relegated further out on the periphery of society. Those in power socially and economically tend not to hear articulate voices of the underclasses. Sports are acceptable and beauty pageants are fine and Tonto is a nice guy in the funny clothes, but anything more that that threatens the hierarchy. *Dances with Wolves* is nothing more than the Lone Ranger and Tonto, dressed up in 1990 fashions.

There is a potentially rich story to be told about Stands with a Fist, the white woman raised by the Indians, and how she reweaves the threads of her life to make herself a whole person. Likewise, the encounter of the Lakota with the soldier, if told from the Indian perspective, could have shocking impact (and would probably be considered a foreign film). These things should be considered in the telling of any story. As Morrison says, "it is no longer acceptable merely to imagine us and imagine for us. We have always been imagining ourselves. We are not Isak Dinesen's "aspects of nature," nor Conrad's unspeaking. We are the subjects of our own narrative, witnesses to and participants in our own experience."

Unfortunately, however much we might want to tell our own story, Indians are poor box office draw. *Dances with Wolves* was made and distributed because of Costner's superstar status. *Pow Pow Highway*, on the other hand, was never a mainstream hit. Even though *Black Elk Speaks* surely made money for Neihardt, the book and the philosophies contained within it had no impact on government policies or public opinion. The American majority, whatever their political opinions, are fine-tuned to the American myth, in which the white male is the wise decision maker. Any story that does not fit the myth is suspect, likely to be ignored, if not ridiculed outright.

This is a movie Americans can feel good about. The good Indians live, the bad Indians die, the white hero marries a white woman and the wolf is howling on the cliff, still wild, still beautiful.

======================================

WORKS CITED: Toni Morrison, "Unspeakable Things Unspoken: The Afro-American Presence in American Literature." *Michigan Quarterly Review*, 28, 1989 (Winter), 8-9. Edward Said, *Orientalism* (Pantheon, 1978), 3, 21, 27. Richard Slotkin, *Regeneration Through Violence: The Myth of the American Frontier, 1600-1860.* (Wesleyan University Press, 1973), pp. 5, 21.

ONCE UPON A NIGHTMARE:
GROWING UP GAY IN AMERICA

by the Rev. Douglas Morgan Strong, Minister
A sermon at the Unitarian Universalist Society of Sacramento, June 9, 1991

I was born late and I was born fat and I was born gay. Three realities of my existence, none of which I would fully understand for years. When I first met my mother I was wearing a paper crown on my head, or so the family story is always retold, because I was the fattest baby in the nursery, ten pounds eight ounces. Even then I didn't want mom thinking I was a wimp. When I first met my mother I had no more idea that I was gay than I knew that she was my mom. It would be many years before either of us came to understand my sexual truth, and the powerful feelings which sexuality – any sexuality – brings to life. Before I came to understand and celebrate my personhood, I would venture through a long, disturbing, traumatic and excruciating nightmare called growing up.

My purpose this morning is not to attempt to explain or justify homosexuality. I don't want to give you statistics and quotes from medical, social, psychological, religious or political people – all of whom have pontificated about the pros and cons of same-gender love in abundant and sundry ways. Rather I want to share with you some of my life. And I want to start by assuring you of four things: (1) I am not atypical. My history, my story, is repeated by gay men everywhere. There may be minor variations, but trust me, the painful path to personal prophecy is repeated by countless gay men. (2) Gay men and lesbians are not necessarily alike. I cannot speak for lesbians, for many lesbian friends tell me their approach to their sexual truth is much different from men. I don't know one gay man who hasn't always known--in some dark recesses of his inner being--that he is gay, while I know many women who, discovering their lesbianism, were truly surprised at the revelation and feel it to be a sexual *preference*. (3) I feel no call to justify or explain why I am gay--it just is. Homosexuality is a minority, not a pathology. I belong to a minority group and as we all know, minority groups across our culture are realizing their own potential, celebrating their roots, rejoicing in their own power and demanding equality from archaic attitudes. And (4) for gay men, homosexuality is not a preference, it is a given, a truth. I never actively chose to be gay. It never was an option, I never voted to be a homosexual. It just is. It is as much a part of me as my height, my eye color, my left handedness and my obsession for Mexican food, talking too much, searching for the perfect room arrangement, and high energy. I have always resented the use of "preference"; it is regularly used to indicate that if one can prefer this, one can prefer that, that sexuality is somehow a choice. For me, it just is.

I hate pain, believe me. I am a committed coward, just ask my dentist. I cannot imagine any man actively choosing a life style that is, if current social definitions continue to persist, doomed to be riddled with sorrow, and even, in a growing number of instances, dangerous to your life and health. With the avalanche of hate from the religious right, William Buckley, the Sacramento *Union*, and other political conservatives, with the hysterical need for the general public to blame gay men for AIDS and the unconscionable way people treat gays and lesbians, I am convinced that I wouldn't have wanted myself to be gay. It just is.

I didn't catch it from a toilet seat or get it by eating too many eggs, as one medical report suggests. I was never converted by that mythical monster—the dirty old man forcing unnatural acts upon me. No one taught me to be gay. It just is.

I grew up essentially just like anyone else in middle America. Wholesome parents, an affirming liberal religious community (I am a sixth generation Unitarian Universalist), the regular assortment of friends and foes, lots of brothers and sisters, three parents, many wholesome relatives. I grew up in middle America in the 50s, where John Wayne taught boys how to be men, and no one had ever heard of quiche. Very early, I knew my lot in life was to be strong, self-sufficient, in control and tough. Big boys don't cry, that's sissy (i.e., girl) stuff. Yet, I was afraid of the dark and when my sister hit me (a regular occurrence until I grew taller), I bawled. I grew up admiring Tom Sawyer and the Hardy Boys. Tim was my favorite Mouseketeer. For you see, I grew up learning boys were different than girls, and better. I grew up knowing when it hurt, there was no hug; when I was mad, there was no soothing; when I was scared, there must be no hint of fright. "A little pain builds character," my dad would tell me. I grew up knowing that a hero is the guy who stays in the game even after his leg gets crushed in a stampede of feet. I grew up hating worlds like "scared-y cat," "gutless" and "no balls."

A regular kid – just like any other boy. By the time I was six or seven I knew that dad could hug, hold and kiss my sisters but if a kiss touched my lips from him, it would send shivers of discomfort down both our spines. By the time I was six or seven, affection from my older brothers meant rough-housing, being tossed around or part of a mock fight. So there was I, a regular kid, growing up, following and believing all those messages every other kid is given. yet deep inside there were other messages – powerful and emotional – which contradicted everything. I grew up looking, longing and later even lusting for other boys.

At puberty came "guy talk," always in a whisper, never in the presence of teachers or girls. I believe the process is referred to as male bonding. The talk was intense, and only public in the locker room, where I first learned that girls were somehow involved with sex. We used code words--then it was a baseball language – something about bases, hits, and scoring, with dreams of the ever-distant goal of a home run. I remember Peter Scott yelling out once, from inside the shower, that he had scored with Lila Somebody or other. Everyone else was impressed, eager to hear more. I was afraid, confused and ashamed. Guy talk left me perplexed and worried. I learned in the locker room that breasts (or knockers, grapefruits, boobs) turned guys on. I learned the sole purpose of life, at the age of sixteen, was to make it sexually. And everyone, including me, knew the other half of the experiment was a girl. No one ever mentioned same gender love, let alone endorsed or approved of it.

I listened and became frightened. For me, girls were delightful companions, easy to know and trust. I became puzzled. For me, girls aroused little if any sensual feelings. I became petrified. I knew what caused the rumble deep in the bowels of my being. I knew what excited me, and honey, it wasn't grapefruits! I knew what I felt and I grew more and more distraught and discouraged. I became increasingly withdrawn (imagine me withdrawn!), wanting desperately to have some locker talk of my own, to prove my manhood, to be one of the guys. I lived in total panic for years. What were these feelings? why did I have them? how could they be made to go away? when was I going to be normal? what was wrong with me?

All through my adolescence I lived with a gnawing and growing fear that someone would call me "queer." (I don't think "faggot" was the term of choice in Madison, Wisconsin, back then--it was "queer.") I cried in opaque silence, forcing myself to notice girls, to date girls, to kiss girls. I subscribed to *Playboy* when I was eighteen for one year, desperately praying that the models would excite my hormones and get the juices flowing. Nothing stirred, nothing flowed. There were precious few references to homosexuality in *Playboy*. The only cartoons depicting gays were always demeaning, showing men only as ultra-feminine.

All throughout college I suffered. I avoided looking at men, dropped out of swimming, and rushed some fraternity in a search to be normal. I continued to date women but always found myself looking at men and feeling the stirrings within. Now, as we all know, sexual stirrings trigger messages in our loins. Hormones secrete chemicals which elicit strange but exciting feelings. Each time I found myself getting excited, I suffered. Go away, feelings! I am not supposed to think, see, notice, feel. These rumblings, these yearnings are wicked, dirty, sinful. They mean that I am a sissy, a failure, a fairy, a disgrace. And as we all know, because we each somehow managed to live through them, those years of adolescence and early adulthood are the years of men's greatest prowess, when our stirrings are nearly constant. The inner conflict for me was beyond comprehension. I became convinced that something dreadful was wrong. I must be suffering from some incurable mental disease. I drove myself to despair. I wondered. I worried. I waited. Minute after minute, day after day, month after month I struggled and I cried, "Why was I different?"

When I was a sophomore in prep school, one Tuesday someone took a Hershey chocolate bar label, folded it to read "HERS" and taped it to my back. I wore it all day. The entire high school enjoyed the joke, and for the next two and a half years, I scratched my back eight to ten times a day! So much energy eaten away, so much agony and so much pain. I became so self-conscious that in one two-week period, in chemistry class alone, I broke four graduated cylinders and six beakers, spilled the entire tray of chemicals, and fell into three students' science project – decimating it totally. I had become the school klutz. In gym I was always the last guy chosen for a team. Once when I unintentionally caught the football, I ran like fury toward the goal, . . . only to learn I had inadvertently run the wrong way and made the winning touchdown for the other side. Then, when I was a senior, the varsity team elected me homecoming queen and made sure the entire school knew. Today I would attend proudly and take John along as my "king," but in 1961 I went home, wept, and two weeks later attempted suicide – and nearly succeeded.

I had been called sissy, queer, and later faggot so many times growing up that I couldn't count them all. Yes, I knew that I was somehow different, yet I never conceived that I might be homosexual. I concluded that I was too "sissy" and that was why I was different. I developed a systemic approach to becoming more macho, more male. I began smoking a pipe, went out for sports, and studied men's actions – how they moved, their arm gestures, their stances. Men, I concluded, pointed with their whole arm, using a deliberate and stern motion. Men did not point with one finger like I did. Men cross their leg and place their hand over the upper thigh by twisting the hand backwards, thumb on the outside. Men did not delicately and daintily cross their legs and quietly fold their hands on their lap like I did. Men hold the phone like it is a baseball bat. Men don't hold the phone with their index finger resting comfortably along the outside of the receiver like I did. I studied, mimicked, imitated and copied. I methodically reviewed my vocabulary, removing certain words I deemed too feminine – words like "marvelous," "divine," "delightful." I borrowed a key to the language lab and went in late at night to listen to my voice, watching the green intonation line on the oscilloscope and practiced developing modulated male tones.

I lived in constant fear someone would see me as "queer," by dint of my gestures, my dress (I *never* wore yellow on Thursdays) or my voice. I died a little each time someone on the other end of the phone would say, "Just a minute ma'am." I crossed streets to avoid a tough-looking guy and changed my route if there were more than one. I dropped out of Scouts, and I refused to pursue my studies in classical piano and, later, interior design because they were "sissy" activities. My behavior modification plan dominated my life for more than eight years. Eight years of daily review, looking over my words, my actions. I was hell-bent for an election to rid myself of being a "sissy."

What is incredible about those years is that I never identified myself as a homosexual. I guess we all have powerful psychic defense systems. Mine protected me from myself. It would be thirty before I would come to terms with my sexual identity. What is even more incredible about those years is that I had no one in whom I could confide. Not once during those thirty years did I ever share my pain, my fear, my burden, my anguish with anyone. I suffered and by god I suffered alone. I was so ashamed that I could no more muster the courage to confess what happened inside when a hunk walked by that I could speak Greek.

I carried my burden in cloistered silence. For thirty years I never knew anyone who was identified as gay or lesbian. I never told my buddies in high school or college that the feelings they had when they saw a good-looking woman were the same feelings I had when I saw a good-looking man. The irony of it all was that while the guys bragged in the locker room, I stumbled upon the men's room at the library and then the woods behind the zoo and became sexually active but never could tell anyone. I had brief, anonymous sexual experiences after which, while they left me physically relieved, I was emotionally tortured. In those encounters, none of which lasted more than a few minutes, I never spoke with my partner, nor did I meet the same man more than once. There was never the warmth of a smile, the touch of a hug, the affirmation of cuddling, or even a thank you. While others were learning traditional courting practices, endorsed and encouraged by parents, schools and society, I was growing more and more schizoid. Then came the mental gymnastics with which I successfully divorced my activity from my reality and grew increasingly hostile towards gays.

As I think about those years, the one outstanding and remarkable thing is that I endured it. I have no idea if you can fathom the pain of that life, the incredible suffering. . . . I suffered in silence. Outwardly my life was a cascade of successes. As I matured, friendships flourished. In college I was "boy therapist," the shoulder upon which many guys wailed out the woes of becoming adults. Later as a national officer for the American Red Cross, I excelled constantly. Filled with glowing praise, I ascended the corporate ladder at a rate which astonished many. Flanked with the protection of time and the gift of good therapy, I can now look back at that life. There is new clarity now—and it leads me to wonder, IF ONLY:

IF ONLY someone who loved and nurtured me (like my family) had reached out to help, to say something, to say anything. My family now confesses they always "suspected" but I guess felt inadequate to start a conversation, preferring simply to avoid the entire topic and thus let me suffer in silence. IF ONLY they had made the plunge, I could have stood proudly earlier. IF ONLY I could have trusted someone enough to have shared the burden. But I remember every nasty anti-gay comment ever uttered by anyone, which only reinforced my misery and walled me off more. IF ONLY I could have seen or even known a real live homosexual, a role model to quietly assure me that being gay is, for me, normal. If only Anita Bryant had done her service of bringing gayness out of obscurity and into American homes twenty years earlier, I might have had the boldness to scream for help. IF ONLY I had met a caring, loving man who could have taught me that love is more than meeting behind the zoo, that one can respect sexuality rather than exploit it, I could have suffered less. But those things didn't occur.

What did happen was a long, slow, hard, growing process, accented with moments of despair yet flavored with the reassurance that I too have a song to sing. That I too have worth, that I too can love.

It happened for me during seminary – the coming out process. I didn't come out to make waves, or as a political statement. I came out because I was tired, tired of the double game, tired of hiding, weary of the pain. I know exactly what Rosa Parks meant when she explained her refusal to walk to the back of the bus. You just reach the point of total psychic exhaustion.

During seminary, I learned that one Don Clark had written a book called *Loving Somebody Gay*. While serving as a student minister in Santa Monica, I went to the UCLA bookstore in search of it. There, under the banner GAY STUDIES, was the book. I will never forget the moment. The cover of the damn book was white with bold, bright, 64-point, red lettering:

L O V I N G   S O M E B O D Y   G A Y

The letters were so big that I couldn't hide them with my fingers. I paced up and down the aisle for twenty minutes. With shaking hands I reached out for the book and promptly dropped it on the floor. Everyone in West L.A. heard that book drop, and they all looked. I was mortified. I knew I never could take the book to the cashier. I couldn't even bend down to pick it up off the floor. So I left. The next day, in different clothes and wearing dark glasses, I slipped back into the store and stole the book. I read it intently and was astonished to see a misprint, right there on page 28. It said "celebrate" being gay. Surely that was a misprint. One celebrates joyful things. To celebrate gayness was an oxymoron.

The book was terrific. And it was the beginning of rebuilding my identity, filling my worth with understanding and compassion. I have come to realize that I am not an "admitted" homosexual, as an article in the *New York Times* once called me. I am what I am, nothing more, nothing less. . . . Often lesbians and gays hear people talk about the "problem of homosexuality." Being gay isn't the problem—I'm too tired to carry that torch for society—it's your problem. I have come to rejoice in who I am because there simply have been too many years, too much grief, I am drained. There is no more suffering I can do—I am all suffered out.

The last seventeen years have been radically different. I discovered my energy knows no limits and I abound with enthusiasm for life and for people. I lost forty pounds, I stand taller, and I think I smile more. By comparison to *those* years, my life today is sheer joy. I am proud to say that my family is overwhelmingly supportive in affirming my gayness. John is welcomed into our family as an "in-law" and we are seen as a couple.

Yet there are still time of pain. . . . Recently while attending a conference, I happened to take a local bus. The driver muttered to me as I got on, "Where are your pearls, honey?" I looked right at him and in my well-modulated male tone, I said, "Pearls, with corduroy? Are you mad?" and walked to my seat. While I enjoyed my reply, there are still times of pain. . . . That pain is by no means restricted to gay men and lesbians. Every woman here this morning has experienced the pain of having your personhood diminished because of prejudices against women. Those of you who are older and looking for a job know what it feels like to be overlooked because you are perceived as too ancient. All members of racial minorities have lived the same pain and know the agony. All of us as religious liberals are subject to potential mistreatment at the hands of the "moral" majority.

The pain of being different touches many, if not most, of us. It is mitigated by the degree of social acceptance and understanding which accompanies how we are viewed. There is a hierarchy of discrimination out there, and the painful truth is that gays and lesbians are at the bottom. Nearly sixty years ago, in 1928, Radclyffe Hall, author of *The Well of Loneliness,* wrote, "You are neither unnatural nor abominable, nor mad; you're as much a part of what people call natural as anyone else; only you're unexplained as yet—you've got your niche in creation." I have found my niche—in the caring affirmation of my religious movement, in the profoundly affirming acceptance I have received . . . and most importantly, my friends, in the loving arms of my John, whose devotion and love permits me the strength to minister . . . I have found my niche—as a gentle pioneer who somehow found the strength to leave the agony behind, bringing to those whose hearts long for understanding a real-live-come-and-touch-'em faggot whose pride for life outweighs the painful past.

While I served our church in Norfolk, Virginia, the congregation had suffered for years over the question of abortion. So I invited the congregation to an evening of healing, a time to listen, reflect, identify blocks, and then move on. Phyllis Stein, a member, attended and wrote me this letter afterwards:

> *Dear Douglas,*
>
> *You done good tonight.*
>
> *I'm grateful to you for giving so much of yourself in the short time I have known you. It would have been so easy to have copped out on this abortion issue, but you didn't and I want to thank you for caring enough to go through with it.*
>
> *God, we are all so vulnerable, shooting quills like threatened porcupines to protect our soft little underbellies. And the more scarred we get, the fiercer we get with the stickers. But the first time is always the hardest. I am sure that being gay in a straight world has been hard as hell. But it has also probably had a great deal to do with giving you your greatest gifts. In your refusing to stay in a closet you have demonstrated to all the rest of us that we don't have to stay in our particular closets.*
>
> *And everybody's private little closet door was opened up tonight. If we don't have the courage to examine the contents and throw out the garbage, it's our own fault. You showed us how and that's all a body can do.*
>
> *I hope you find Peace and Joy wherever you go.*

I will cherish that letter forever because it affirms my niche. Maybe by being who I am and what I am, you are invited to be who you are and what you are, and together we can touch hearts, mend minds, and make our lives more holy.

It is a worthy adventure and I feel blessed to be a small part of it with you.

Amen, friends, amen.

Essay #12

WHEN I GROW UP I WANT TO BE A LESBIAN

by Karin Kawelmacher
Author for *Naiad Press* and Contributing Editor,
Uncommon Voices, Bay Area Career Women[1]

Dear Folks,
Dear Folks Back Home,
Dear Co-Workers and Friends of my Past:

I have probably started this letter to you a dozen or more times on paper, and hundreds of times in my head. There's this guilt I've been carrying around since I last saw you. I feel guilty because I never told you what I wanted to be when I grew up. Oh, I talked about being rich and famous and having a wonderful career. What I never said was that when I grow up I want to be a Lesbian.

I Know What You're Thinking

You're a little shocked. I understand that. Put your head between your knees if you need to. Take it slow. Now that you're breathing okay, I know exactly what you're focussed on. Sex. Being a lesbian is all about sex, right? Well, yes and no. Yes, it is about sex. But the sex part seems so natural that it's practically the last thing I think about when I think of myself as a lesbian.

If having sex with other women was all that was required to be a lesbian, then why are we writing books such as *Odd Girls and Twilight Lovers: A History of Lesbian Life in Twentieth-Century America* or *Safe Sea of Women: Lesbian Fiction 1969 –1989*? Why did *Out of Time*, a novel about discovering lesbians of the 1920s, win the 1991 Lambda Rising Lesbian Fiction Award? If being a lesbian was just about sex, would we be so preoccupied with the past? I think not. I think we're trying to document our past to have a history of our lives in America and the world.

There must be more than the sex part of being a lesbian. There's the political, legal and equal rights part. The family, career and friends part. The in, out and on the fence part. There's the guilt, fear and pride part. As I grow older I grow

---

[1]An earlier version of this article appeared in *Uncommon Voices,* Newsletter of the Bay Area Career Women, vol 11, no. 4 (August-Sept 1991). Reprinted by permission of the author.

impatient with my lack of self-assurance. And I keeping thinking that if I ever finish growing up then I'll be a lesbian.

Conflict, Conflict

So much of what I want to say to you is about feeling and thinking two conflicting ways simultaneously. Two kinds of guilt, for instance. I know you respected me — I respected you. But I never trusted you enough to tell you about the lesbian part of me. I withheld that information from you when I spent eight or more hours a day with you for eleven years. The entire time I knew you I considered myself "married" but if you asked about the gold band I wore I was evasive. Of course I feel guilty about that now.

The other kind of guilt is guilt over being afraid. I count myself as a proud member of the gay community here, and by not speaking out when I might have to you, who knows how many of you have cast ballots against me, never knowing you were voting against a friend? I've since learned that most people who discover someone they care about is gay *change* their attitudes dramatically because gay people are no longer a frightening unknown.

I was most afraid of what you would say and how my difference would make you feel. It still seems unfair that you won't know unless I tell you, since we're the minority you can't see unless you look for us. I was afraid of losing your respect and affection, and afraid you would treat me differently. I was also afraid of how I would react to your reaction. What if I found myself retreating to the "well of loneliness" and begging you for mere tolerance? It's hard to admit even to myself, but I've had times when I thought all I had a right to was tolerance. It didn't help that, at the time I was coming to terms with my sexuality, Harvey Milk, my only hero, was assassinated.

I tell myself I don't know when I could have told you. At first our boss was someone I knew would fire me on the spot like the "good Christian" he was. I didn't have any protection under the law and I still don't. And then, later, when the new guard came in — how could I have told you then? The perfect moment never arrived — the years flew by, then we entered the Reagan years, and human rights everywhere were cut off for lack of funds. The fear kept growing while I didn't.

Your No-Win Proposition

If I had "come out" to you and you had said no big deal, I would have thought: (a) you didn't understand how important it was to me; (b) you were lying; and/or (c) you had no appreciation for how unique and wonderful gay men and lesbians are. If you had shown some flash of terror or disgust, I would have had proof that I was right to keep it to myself. And if you had said, "Gee, that's wonderful," I would have thought you were loony — don't you know how hard it is to be different?

There was no way you could have responded appropriately and therefore I had every reason not to tell you. I found excuses not to tell you and you helped me out. Every joke and bigoted remark you made about gay people (usually in ignorance, not in malice) justified my reticence, inflamed my fears and increased my guilt. I'm "out" where I work now. I feel confident and proud. But if for some reason I found myself living in Helmsville USA, I know the fear would come right back and into the closet I'd go. Knowing I could regress to lesbian infancy once again, I know I'm not grown up yet.

So What Else Would You Like to Know?

I'll gladly talk about myself, but please remember I can only speak for myself. I can't speak for lesbians of color, low-income lesbians or single lesbians or lesbians older or younger than me. I can't even speak as a lesbian who has made love with more than one woman.

I certainly can't speak for gay men. Lesbians and gay men have different outlooks and needs. For example, it appears most gay men see their homosexuality as something they were born with. Apparently, most lesbians see it as a choice. This difference intrigues me because men have choice in their lives where women do not. Yet when it comes to this they feel they had no choice and speak of sexual "orientation." Women, who have fewer options in life, feel they have *chosen* to be with women and speak of sexual "preference." As I grow up, I know my preference is becoming an orientation. If I had to choose again, there would be no choice: I will always turn to women for emotional sustenance and sex.

So What is a Lesbian?

If I had an answer to that I'd tell you. But I don't. Nobody does. The only safe thing I can say is that if you have a Y chromosome you're probably never going to be a lesbian. *Generally,* as I said above, a lesbian is a woman who turns to other women for emotional sustenance and sex. That's it for generalities. We don't agree on much else.

I know you have preconceived notions about what lesbians are like. Forget them. You may have heard of the "lesbian nation," but we are a divided one. Our ten percent cuts across all women — every type of woman is represented in our community, each with her own needs and perceptions of what the unified whole should be like. Part of me knows how frustrated each minority community within our minority community is. I know that some of us are more disenfranchised than others, and most of us are disenfranchised to some extent. And all of us have our own political agendas.

Sometimes it seems, as one reporter from the National Lesbian Conference concludes, we've confused lesbian politics with ritual humiliation of other lesbians. The conference, held in March of 1991, took years and a half million dollars to plan. It was held in Atlanta to show defiance of Georgia's sodomy laws. During the course of this three day event, many minority groups within the conference protested the involvement and participation of other minority groups. The fat dykes protested others' preference for skinny women; lesbians over fifty want to be called old lesbians. Lesbians of color took over the only voting session in an attempt to force white lesbian conference organizers to sign a letter of apology because the conference did not achieve 50% racial parity. The American tradition of voicing our differences is evident here: we treasure diversity at the cost of unity, *pluribus* over *unum*.

Three days later, a lot of intelligent, committed women were very angry — poorer by hundreds of dollars in expenses, yet not one issue had emerged as a single cohesive factor. As I think about it, I come up with an image in the back of my mind: if a fundamentalist group had taken over the podium during a voting session, 2,500 lesbians would have made their will known with a single, unified roar of determination and anger. I've observed it in other minority communities: we'll be more rude, childish, unfair and brutish to each other than we would ever permit any "outsider" to be and we believe it's perfectly acceptable to do so because we're "family."[2] No wonder some of my lesbian friends have given up politics, coalition building and searching for mutually beneficial goals.

---

[2]*ED. NOTE: The situation Kawelmacher describes at the National Lesbian Conference in 1991 was replicated in the National Women's Studies Association, when 100 women walked out of the 1990 convention to protest the firing of a black employee on the staff, after which five members of the NWSA national staff resigned and the 1991 annual meeting had to be cancelled. Attempting to rebuild in 1992, new leaders urged members to find common ground, but at the conference itself, the same dynamics Kawelmacher reports led to problems. It was reported that some lesbians attending complained that the keynote speaker had made "heterosexist" remarks; other members said a white woman should not have been chosen as keynoter. Ecofeminists protested that every meal served at the conference included meat, and one participant asked that conferees in the future not use hair spray and perfume. Despite such disagreements among diverse factions, the NWSA membership did achieve consensus in approving a new constitution, which steering board members hope will put to rest "competing expectations." See "Women's-Studies Group, Hoping to Heal Wounds, Finds More Conflict,"*

Such an irrational situation probably makes no sense to you, but then you're not afraid for your rights every day of your life. Who will walk into your bedroom and say, "You can't do that"? Who says to you, "We don't care how long you've been in love, you can't have a joint <fill in the blank> and that's it"? Would any of your "in-laws"— with the backing of the law behind them — keep you from visiting your loved one in the hospital? It happens to us every day. If it doesn't happen we still know it *could* happen, which is just as effective at keeping us from growing and taking the rights and privileges that should be ours.

Me vs. Them

There's a whole generation of women only a few years younger than I (I'm 31) who wear leather jackets with stickers that say "Promote Homosexuality" and "L.A.B.I.A." and "DYKE." Right out in public. When I see Them on the streets I smile. They're very political and although I sometimes don't agree with their methods or aims, usually I get a charge of proud energy when I see them. I wish I knew some of Them because I'm sure we both could learn and grow if we shared. There's one reaction I have to Them that reminds me I have a lot of growing up to do. It doesn't happen often — usually on days when I'm feeling that tolerance is the only thing I can hope for. On those days I'm glad those outrageously provocative women are there for you to see. Compared to them, I must be "normal."

Even as I think it I know I'm saying, "Don't hate me, hate Them instead." Fear makes all of us do irrational things, like being willing to sacrifice a little liberty — especially somebody else's — in exchange for a little safety. I know that They are me, or at least what I might have aspired to, if I'd been born a little later. I'll be grown up when I stop thinking of Them with a capital T. I'll be

---

The Chronicle of Higher Education, *July 1, 1992, A13-14. But see also the protest against the* Chronicle's *coverage in a letter to the editor by the national director of NWSA, pointing out that in fact the conference had succeeded in "forging an exquisite compromise on major structural change within the organization, culminating in dramatic consensus among myriad constituent groups," and had achieved a "reclamation of community and common purpose."* Chronicle of Higher Education, *August 5, 1991, p. B2.*

The dissension at both national conferences typifies the current tension between unity and diversity--betweeen the desire to affirm common ground as against the desire to concede the right to differ--that is discussed elsewhere in this volume, among other places, in my introduction. We can expect that tension to surface often in coming years.---BC

grown up when I'm free of my own homophobia. I'll be grown up when I don't flinch at the L-word anymore.

Something to Lose

So maybe you can understand why I kept silent all those years. But if I had it to do over again, I wish I could say of course I'd trust you. My heart feels every gay person in America should come out, right now, but my head knows we can all do it only if we separately have nothing to lose. Gay people with angry ex-spouses have children to lose. Gay workers have jobs to lose. Gay tenants have their homes to lose. It's apparent from the rising tide of hate crimes that many of us have our personal safety to lose.

Personally, I always felt I had my unique personality in your eyes to lose. I was never sure you could see me as different parts without losing sight of my whole. To paraphrase Afro-American poet Pat Parker, to be my friend you have to do two things. First, forget that I am a lesbian. Second, never forget that I am a lesbian. But I can't expect you to do this if I can't do it myself.

As a middle-class white person, I wasn't raised with multiple self-images. I've had to adjust to seeing the whole of myself made up of parts: the lesbian part, the woman part, the worker part, and so on. I'm one-half of an urban, upwardly mobile, homeowning, mortgage-holding, tax-paying American couple and sometimes I still can't spell lesbian to save my life.

When I grow up I want to know I've grown up. And I want to be a lesbian.

Essay #13

"UPWARD" MOBILITY AND THE WORKING CLASS STUDENT IN THE UNIVERSITY

by Renny Christopher,
University of California, Santa Cruz

Class is almost too difficult and painful a subject to think about for me. I want to blank out what I have discovered. I would like to hide the bad parts of my years here and tell everyone I had a "wonderful time at college." People will not expect anything but a glowing recount of my "college years." I suppose I'll have to burst a lot of people's bubbles.–Sheri Lea Randolph

One version of the American Dream is that of "upward" mobility. But when a working-class student moves "upward" into the academy, what is the price of that mobility? I will be examining the experiences of some working class students, including myself. It is important to note at the outset that these students are all in the humanities, and that the experiences of working-class students in the sciences may be different. In fact, working-class students may be drawn to the sciences precisely because of their supposed "objectivity." All the student experiences discussed here are from so-called "elite" universities in California. It is possible that class bias may vary by region, and that experiences in state universities may differ. I received my BA from an elite private college (on a scholarship!), my MA from San Jose State University, and my advancement to PhD Candidacy at the University of California. (My experiences at SJSU did differ somewhat, although I did experience subtle forms of class bias there as well, especially in that I was discouraged to write a thesis, rather than taking exams. I believe that my professors thought I would embarrass them—despite the fact that I was a straight A student, I came to class in workboots, straight from my construction job.)

One other note before proceeding: this essay is laced with quotes. Unionization and collectivity have been the traditional tools of the working class; I have tried to make this a polyvocal text, to the extent that I can in so short as space.

"[T]he more I've come to understand about education, the more I've come to believe in the power of invitation," writes Mike Rose in his account of so-called "underprepared" students in the academy, *Lives on the Boundary* (132). But what is it that academic institutions are inviting working class students into? As Rose's and other accounts show, working class students are being invited into an academic world that demands that they deny their world of origin. This demand for denial of the working-class world of origin is stated clearly by a working-class woman who dropped out of a PhD program in sociology for class-related reasons:

> *The problem with letting academics make the definitions is that they can say this is the better world and yours is a worse world; they can say working class people can't talk, can't think, and although you and I know that's bullshit, we're being asked to accept the whole thing, definitions and all, and therefore to reject our old world, rather than changing their definitions* (Cheryl Gomez).

Sheri Lea Randolph, a white working class student from Barstow, California, who received a BA in Women's Studies from UC Santa Cruz, writes in her autobiographical senior thesis:

> *I remember the first time I took a Women's Studies course. I felt so wonderful. It was the first class I had where I felt accepted. However, I soon began to pull away and keep my mouth shut in class, not because I didn't have anything I wanted to say, but because I felt, again, stupid. Here were women who spoke so eloquently, who knew so much, and who used such large words – how could I live up to that? I felt silly whenever I ventured my opinion. I felt like a stupid oaf with no class who didn't know anything. No class. What a phrase. But that's exactly how I feel (9).*

Randolph's thesis is a catalogue of classist attacks she suffered during her five years as undergraduate, including meeting with incredulity from fellow students about her summer job at McDonald's, and incredulity because as a freshperson she didn't know what an AP course was —her high school hadn't offered any.

Randolph is not alone. A student in the course I taught in 1991 at UCSC on Working Class Literature told of a fellow student who derided her cruelly upon finding a Reader's Digest Condensed Book in her dorm room. The assumption is that a job at McDonald's and a Reader's Digest Book are inferior, to be ridiculed. But as Randolph explains, in Barstow, the McDonald's job was the only job available to her. And many uneducated people seek out the Reader's Digest books to try to expand their educations. To deride anyone for such an attempt is arrogant.

Jessie Virago, a white working-class re-entry student at UCSC, writes,

> *During lunch with a professor of literature with a PhD from Yale, I mentioned my social background and the years I had spent as a secretary prior to attending school. He replied, "But you always knew you were smart, right?" Hear how the conjunction "but" juxtaposes smart with secretary or smart with working class. I consider the equating of social*

class position with intelligence to be one of the most common, egregious, and offensive examples of classism in America. It does insidious damage to working class people's sense of intellectual and academic entitlement, and it is particularly galling to hear it from one's professors (Virago, "Structural," 6).

I believe that these types of incidents are quite common for working-class students in the University, and they serve to undercut those students' selfhood. I have many such stories myself. I will tell one, the most recent.

I was talking with two fellow graduate students, friends. One of them started telling the other how good I was at literary theory. "She can talk about all that stuff like nobody else. And she's always talking about her working-class background, and how deprived she was. I bet none of that is true." She turned to me. "I bet one of these days we'll meet your parents, and it'll turn out that your father is a professor of Philosophy at Harvard!" Both of them laughed. I laughed, too, but my hands were shaking in my jacket pockets. The reasoning goes like this: if my father really is a carpenter, I couldn't possibly be as smart as I am. So, in order for me to be as smart as I am, my father must be a professor at Harvard. That means that we have not a class system, but a caste system--no working class kid can be smart, and upper middle class kids will always be smart. Meanwhile, I feel doubly undercut—either I'm not really working-class and am faking it, for reasons I can't imagine, or I'm a phony in school, and I don't belong. Either way, I lose.

This identity choice is the one that working-class students are faced with by the structure of the academy, and the naively classist attitudes of faculty and fellow-students. In the United States we really believe that the poor lack virtue (and the underprivileged often believe this as firmly as the overprivileged, that somehow we as individuals have done wrong, or we'd be middle-class like everybody else). The middle-class institution sees itself as doing a favor to working-class students by inviting them to become middle-class. But accepting that invitation means denying one's past, changing one's identity, being ashamed of one's relatives, and concealing one's origins. This is too high a price to pay for entry into the academic world, which does not supply enough spiritual rewards to meet the loss.

A professor I know told me she once spoke at a faculty party about her working-class origins, and was taken aside by a well-meaning senior colleague who told her she might not want to reveal her background like that. It's usually not so clear as that [but] . . . the message from the University is: you can be here, but not the way you are now; you can be here if you become one of us.

Randolph writes about this pressure:

Almost everything that I was in Barstow is considered "bad" or "wrong" here, and I have learned to disavow or hide those parts of myself. Doing this has made me feel disconnected; I have a hard time remembering who I really am. College has forced me to split myself in a way that was very painful. The worst thing about that split is that it was done in a subtle way, in a way that made me think I was to blame for the pain (98).

One thing that working-class students carry with them is a sense of guilt, or a knowledge of their connection to a world of structural inequality, which they, as individuals, have moved out of, leaving others behind. This knowledge can be both strength and debility; it is always, for us, a source of pain, and something that sets us apart from our middle-class colleagues. Randolph writes of this feeling,

I have been given a chance to move out of the working-class. I know I cannot throw this opportunity away. If I did, I would be letting down the people who count on me to show them that it can be done. If I failed, they would have to face the reality of America, which is that there is no hope for most of them. I am one of the exceptions which help to perpetuate the myth of an easy upward mobility in the U.S.A. I feel this hope whenever I go home. The people who will never experience this mobility are the ones who ask me about college with a wistfulness that is painful to witness. I do not want to burst their bubble. I remember that feeling – five years at the University has killed it in me. This feeling was a belief in the rightness of our society, a belief that somehow you were responsible for your economic situation. Who am I to destroy their hopes? (99)

Marcus Mabry, a Black student from the slums of New Jersey attending Stanford, writes in an essay entitled "Living in Two Worlds,"

Even though I know that education is the right thing to do, I can't help but feel, sometimes, that I have it too good. More than my sense of guilt, my sense of helplessness increases each time I return home. As my success leads me further away for longer periods of time, poverty becomes harder to conceptualize and feels that much more oppressive when I visit with it (126).

Most eloquently, Jessie Virago says of her experience:

I've consistently received excellent evaluations and been asked to be a teaching assistant or tutor. While I deeply appreciate this validation and encouragement, I am also made acutely uncomfortable by it; I know I am no brighter now than I ever was. What that means is that I was this bright when I was a nurse's aide; this bright when all my books fit into the headboard of my bed; this bright when I spent over half a decade in a windowless office filling in little blanks in insurance claim forms; this bright when my boss sexually harassed me and put his dirty spoon in his out-basket for me to wash. . . .

More than that, it means that my sister and cousins, and legions of other
working-class sisters and cousins, are every bit as bright as I am and remain
just as trapped as I was – trapped not in the working class but in what we are
taught it means to be working-class and female in this country (Staub 6).

Are there other models available for working-class students? Is it possible to
move from the working classes into "higher education" in such a way that one is
not obligated to renounce one's world of origin to succeed in the academy? As it
stands now, I don't think so. One can be an activist, and talk about the issues, but
one must do it in the "proper" way or one will not be heard. When I give papers at
conferences I don't chew gum while I talk, I don't wear blue eyeshadow and a
polyester flower-print dress, and I don't use "fucking" as an adjective. If this were
my image, academic audiences would, I'm quite certain, fail to take me seriously.

But I want to take a moment here to make an impassioned plea about academic
writing style. Although my grammar in this essay is quite correct, you will note that
mostly I use simple, declarative sentences. I have not used jargon, nor have I made
allusion to hopelessly abstract, arcane theories. In other words, I have endeavored
to write a paper that my mother could read. I believe that my generation of scholars
has it in our power to democratize the academy simply by writing clear prose. One
can couch quite complicated ideas in quite straightforward language. (I stand fast by
this position although I have been punished for doing so; recently a paper that was
accepted by one co-editor of an anthology was rejected by the other on the grounds
that it sounded like "it was written by a first-year graduate student.") . . .

What are the implications of all this so far? First, we should acknowledge that
white working-class students are an unrecognized minority among our students,
and that the class dimension of the experience of non-white students is also
ignored, to their detriment (that is, working-class black students have an additional
set of problems that middle-class black students do not face). The great triad of
debate these days, Race, Class and Gender, presumes to include Class but it
seldom does. Discussions of class often move off into the direction of Race or
Gender, or simply do not begin in the first place. Class is very difficult to talk
about, and there is little contemporary off-campus working-class activism for the
academic world to learn from, as there have been strong civil rights, feminist, and
gay/lesbian movements in the recent past.

There are also implications for teaching. Carol Whitehill, a UCSC counseling
psychologist, produced a dissertation that examines the intellectual experiences of
24 re-entry working-class women. Her research shows that these students are
"academically empowered in classes where they discuss issues of structural power
and in which the instructor is non-authoritarian" (Staub 6). This sounds like good
pedagogy to me, but it is still the exception, not the norm, even at the supposedly

liberal and progressive UCSC. Michael Nettles, Vice President at the University of Tennessee, reported at a conference on Class Bias in Higher Education on a study which identified a number of factors that affect academic success for non-traditional students: close involvement and relationship with the faculty; opportunities to develop peer relationships and engage in cooperative learning experiences; adequate study time; on-campus rather than off-campus work; and reasons to feel involved with and committed to the college (Virago, "Dismissed").

These factors go beyond pedagogy to suggest necessary changes in the structure of the institution itself. Let's make them.

There is another reason the topic of class is important, beyond the pedagogical implications. That reason concerns the failure of the Left in America. In a 1939 essay, "Boys' Weeklies," George Orwell pointed out that the popular press had a conservative cast, because the conservatives were willing to woo the "common people," in forms they were interested in, and the leftists were not. The situation in America today is much the same. The conservatives in academia invite non-traditional students to leave behind their heritages, and join the so-called "great tradition." Leftist academics, on the other hand, tend to pay lip service to the working classes, even while they deny the perspectives, experiences, and potential contributions of the working class students in their classrooms. And until the American left enlists the American working classes, it is doomed always to fail.

And that failure is something unacceptable to students who, like Randolph, Mabry, Virago, and me, still have that working-class experience lying behind us, sending us ghost-feelings like an amputated limb. It is impossible to be a working class student and to live with the knowledge of real, ongoing economic and cultural oppression that we bring to the academy with us without also experiencing the desire to change the structural inequality of the system. A modest beginning is simply to acknowledge the existence of classism on campus, and move to end it.

WORKS CITED:

Cheryl Gomez, Personal interview, 10-8-89.

Marcus Mabry. "Living in Two Worlds." *Crossing Cultures.* NY: Macmillan, 1991.

Sheri Lea Randolph, *Victim of Circumstance: The Effects of Gender and Class Roles in my Life.* Women's Studies Senior Thesis, UCSC, 1988.

Elaine Marie Staub, "Pressure Points: Money, Class & Stress on Campus." *Matrix,* March, 1990: 6; 24.

Jessie Virago, "Class Dismissed," *Matrix* Nov. 1990, and "Structural Power, Academic Entitlement, and Peer Teaching Assistants in Writing Classes for Late-Entry Women" (Paper presented at the Class Bias in Higher Education conference, Center for Labor and Society, Queens College, 1990).

Essay #14

THE ROOTS PROJECT: "IT CHANGED MY LIFE"
by Betty Ch'maj

Over the course of twenty years of teaching courses in American Studies, I have watched as an assignment I now call the Roots Project has literally changed my students' lives and perspectives. To begin with, here is the way I present the assignment to students in the course syllabus:

THE ASSIGNMENT: Each of you is to give an oral (8-10 min.) or written (6-7 page) report tracing your own roots, not by recounting genealogy as such (that kind of report may mean a lot to you and your family but it can be a bore for others to listen to), but by putting together a story to illustrate significant migrations, issues involving identity (racial, religious, regional, gender and/or generational identity), stereotypes, conflicts, the experience of marginality, intermarriages and other interactions. Do not limit yourself to the "positive" aspects of your history--tell the whole story you uncover, whatever it is.

Each of you will prepare a one-page outline for the whole class, with whatever appendices are interesting or relevant (maps, for instance, or photographs, or family trees with unique labels). As guidelines for what to include, begin with the themes introduced in the class lectures so far. Choose some particular slant to use as an organizing principle for your report--use that as a theme for your title. You may need to narrow your focus to one generation, one set of experiences, one side of your family, even a single person. If you need help on deciding how to focus, make an appointment with Dr. Ch'maj during office hours. After you have produced a preliminary outline, if you are giving an oral report, you must have an interview, at which time you will be assigned the date of your report.

All students will evaluate and grade the oral reports on the "reactions sheets" provided. You'll see--the system works really well. Oral reports will be heard the 5th to 7th weeks. Written reports are due the first day of the 5th week.

What has mattered, what this essay is about, has been the response of the students themselves to the challenge, how they have seen it, year after year, as a transformative moment in their lives--that is what has made the Roots assignment unique. Listen to what some of them said the last two years alone when asked to

evaluate the experience (I have translated their distinctive handwriting styles into
different font styles to convey some sense of the variety in their voices):

THE ROOTS PROJECT WAS THE REAL CLINCHER FOR ME IN THIS
CLASS. I MEAN BY THAT THE CLASS HELPED ME FIND A PART OF ME
THAT I HAD NO IDEA EVER EXISTED.

The roots project demonstrated to me that people have
backgrounds which they care about very much. This was good for me
to see because I know and care very little about my own genealogy,
lives of ancestors, etc. It was good to hear the sincerity and
devotion in the speakers' voices. The project really opens up
members of the class. It was good that some were so willing to tell us
very emotional tales--it means they were comfortable with the
audience . . . I am glad that I was here.

VERY FASCINATING FOR ME FIRST TO LEARN ABOUT
MY PAST AND THEN TO BE ABLE TO PRESENT THE
INFORMATION TO THE CLASS--A TRANSFORMATIVE
PROCESS, IT CHANGED ME FOREVER!

*Listening to all the reports, it was a lot to digest, but everyone's
reports were so fascinating and different that it made it exciting to go
to class each day.*

As a listener I learned a lot from all the reports. At first I thought the whole
project was going to be in a way 'BLAND.' In fact it turned out to be a great PLUS
in my learning about history.

The Roots Project broadened my
views. When looking at another person
now, in my mind I say, there is something
unique about this person that I should
respect. This project is the first and
only one in college that has changed me
when dealing with another person.

*You have opened my eyes onto a whole different world. I
was going through life with blinders on. You have helped me
remove them. I wasn't aware of multiculturalism until now.*

*The roots project turned out to teach me more than I thought it would.
It made me dig down deep and find things that my family ordinarily would
not tell me. I had to think through my own identity.*

To answer your question, NO!, 5 speeches a day 5 days in a row did not bother me one bit. Each day I could listen to people and learn and picture their relatives and homelands from the speeches students gave. This was really incredible.

5 days of reports @ 5 per day? I was fascinated. It was a lot of information and rapid switching of gears but a tremendous overview of American ethnicity & also a way of getting to know the class. This kind of sharing promotes a kind of understanding and acceptance not achieved in other ways.

WOW! THE "AMERICAN HEGEMONIC IDEAL" EXISTS NOWHERE IN THIS CLASS OF FORTY STUDENTS!

I learned the history, values, expectations, and ways of life of my family's generations. I loved learning how the changes occurred through the history of my family. Therefore, I liked to hear other's presentations. It helped me to understand more about them and also changed my perceptions about others.

Due to a tremendous, screaming anger that seemed to grow inside as I did my research and then as I spoke to my mother, I felt it would be more effective to avoid the emotional issues as much as possible when reporting so I could make sense and maintain my composure.

Learning about my ancestors reaffirmed the independence and the good ol' hard work ethic which is instilled in my roots and values.

Researching my family history made me think of my parents more as people. I never really got along with my parents very well, so I know I sound shallow not knowing anything about my family history--this is because I never before asked them about it.

The nervousness and anxiety of waiting for my turn to report was overwhelming--WHEW! It wasn't so bad after all. It helped me find out for myself where I come from and why I feel so strongly about my culture. **PRIDE** is what I felt when I had a chance to share my information as well as my thoughts and feelings.

The big issue brought out by my experience was my incredible apathy toward the Japanese internment in World War II. I do feel badly about what my parents went through, but I didn't want to get emotional in public.

*I LOVED the Roots Project, but I felt cheated that
we did not discuss MINE in greater detail.*

**I was amazed at the amount of cultural baggage (preconceptions)
I carry. I learned more about myself--the way I view people.**

THE VIDEOS WE SAW ON THE DAYS THERE WAS TIME
FOR THEM ALL SEEMED TO GO ALONG GREAT WITH
THE REPORTS--DID YOU RIG THAT UP FOR OUR
BENEFIT OR DID IT JUST HAPPEN THAT WAY?

*What I admired most was what happened at the end, when you
quoted from so many of the written reports!!! Just when we
though we had grasped all the major ideas, some student too
shy to give an oral report surprised us by unveiling an
entirely different point of view It made us think again.*

==================

It is the authenticity of these personal voices that provides the evidence of the
Roots Project's transformative power. My students have testified year after year
that doing the assignment for themselves first and then listening to the reports of
their classmates has an impact upon them that can be *powerful.* They don't always
know why, but they know their attitudes have been changed, their biases
challenged, their lives redirected. The Roots Project provides them with a unique
avenue to identity and history. It is the closest I have ever come to a "never-fail
formula" to help students understand themselves, understand each other, and
understand the culture they have in common.

The success of the project depends, first, on how the assignment is given.
"Straight" genealogy should be prohibited,[1] and students should be encouraged
beforehand to tell the whole story in their pasts as they find it--its negative as well
as positive side, the failures as well as the glory. Family members (parents,
grandparents) whom students are likely to interview for the project typically assume
family history should be charted in terms of standard genealogy; they will likely
stress events and lineage the family can be proud of. Over the years, my students

---

[1]I do provide genealogy charts for those who wish to use them, if only to get started, citing as
model the charts provided in the Appendix to James Watt and Allen Davis, eds. *Generations: Your
Family in Modern American History* (Alfred A. Knopf, 1974, 1978). The charts urge attention to
ethnicity, place of birth, occupations, migrations, religion, political affiliations, views of
homeland and America, education/training, etc. for the student's forebears on both father's and
mother's sides of the family. Since so many students now have divorced, adoptive, or single
parents, however, teachers do well to alert the class not to take the chart as a model of normality.

have told of having slave and Indian ancestry, but I have yet to hear about an ancestor who was a slave *owner* or an Indian *killer*. On the other hand, some students have enjoyed reporting on relatives who were criminals, culprits, and ne'er-do-wells, some highlighting negative histories with such titles as "This is Not the Brady Bunch" and "We Didn't Exactly Come on the Mayflower."

Secondly, a classroom atmosphere must be established that is respectful of privacy yet permissive of unexpected emotional display. During each of the past three years, students--male and female--have broken into tears (to their own dismay) while giving oral reports. At the beginning of each day of oral reports, I pass out "reaction sheets"--a half-page on which each class member evaluates each speaker with comments and a grade. The class member signs his/her own name on the bottom half and adds any comments intended for my eyes only. I read all the reaction sheets before passing them on to the speaker (the next class period) having cut off the bottom half for my files. These evaluations serve a marvelous purpose, providing students with more than simply one reaction (the professor's) and transposing any emotional outbursts into part of the academic experience; the class members' comments inevitably reassure when reassurance is needed but still evaluate the content of the report on its academic merits (since they are required to grade). When students think the speaker has failed to meet the assignment, or when the evaluators are uncomfortable with the process, they are able to complain directly to me at the bottom of the sheet, and I do not need to spend class time discussing the emotions as such--or discussing the process. After each report, rather, time and class size permitting, I use the opportunity to draw out whatever patterns have emerged and connect them to the larger themes of the class.

After the oral reports have ended, the whole class atmosphere has changed. I then take time to call on those whose written reports I have read by then, asking them to explain or expand on some topic they have raised. This way their voices are also heard by their classmates and some part of their stories told aloud. Not only does this serve to embrace them in the new atmosphere, but inevitably examples from their papers serve to introduce themes, peoples, and points of view the oral reports did not--sometimes quite remarkably. By the time the Roots Project ends, the class is never the same. Students have a new perception of who they are and who their classmates are.

It is helpful to invite written evaluation of the project as it proceeds. The students' voices are worth listening to, not only as testimony to the power of the assignment but as answers to questions the teacher did not ask. Not all evaluations are positive. There are always students who don't like to grade--and since students collectively tend to grade higher than I do, there are always some who would rather have their classmates' grades than mine. (I joke about this, saying grading is what they pay me for, and I have to earn my paycheck.) I definitely recommend grading the projects, however difficult to do so; the year I tried a Credit/No Credit system, the quality of the reports dropped substantially.

Students typically want to ask questions after each oral report. I am reluctant to let that happen, not only because of the time it takes, or to guard the speaker's privacy, but also out of a nagging suspicion that prolonged open discussion might turn my classroom into the Sally Jessy Raphael show! There is a certain risk in "using emotion in the classroom," as Peter Frederick puts it in his essay, and I do not have the luxury Jesper Rosenmeier has at Tufts of limiting the class to ten graduate students. (Given California's budget crunch in 1992, I allowed in 40 students despite the official class limit of 25.) I agree wholeheartedly with Frederick and Rosenmeier that this kind of learning experience is essential to multicultural education, but I think it should be accessible to *all* students, not only an elite--to large classes, undergraduate classes, and "101" classes full of new students (for students new to universities often include members of the "new immigrant" generation). The secret to making the assignment work despite large classes and less sophisticated students, I believe, is careful control over the way it is conducted.

STUDENTS TALK ABOUT THEIR ROOTS

From titles to snippets to longer examples, here are how my students have reported on their roots over the course of three years. To begin, here are some titles:

Robert E. Lee Meets Ellis Island

MOMMY, WHERE DO REDNECKS COME FROM?

Just Because Everything Has Changed, Why Should Anything Be Different? IF YOU AIN'T DUTCH, YOU AIN'T MUCH

The Beginning of the Rest of My Life. **In Mom We Trust.**

Roots of a Pacific Islander. *Just a Country Boy at Heart*

PORTUGUESE

PO~~RTU~~GEE

PROUD TO BE PR~~XT~~UGE

THE MAFIA AT MY WEDDING. My Grandmother and I

TRIUMPH OF WILL! *Sino-Americanization.*

JAMAICAN, BLACK, OR JUST ME? Will I Ever Leave California?

It's Amazing Knowing the Grief that is Out There!

Being Norwegian-American: From <u>Vaer Så God</u> to <u>Uff Da</u>!
"In proportion to its population, Norway has sent more of its
people to live in America than any other country except Ireland."

My Probable Past
Reconstructing My Cherokee Ancestry

around 1830 : great-great-grandmother born--no recorded birth, name unknown

1838-1839: Great March, Trail of Tears--removal to Indian Territory   (In 1906,
              federal government pays each Cherokee $31 for each relative who
              marched The Trail of Tears!!)

around 1860: great-grandmother A-nih-kih born

around 1868: A-nih-kih begins living in Indian Schools in Arkansas and Oklahoma

1872: A-nih-kih baptised "Eliza" in a Methodist Church in Centerview, Missouri

1874: As Eliza, A-nih-kih hired out to a family in Centerview, Mo. . . .

**"Many people were hurt in the process of fighting for
equal   rights, but it did not stop them from trying."**

"For the black race, music played an important part in relieving the
pressures of society. It was the reviving and assurance of a better day in times of
sorrow, anger, protest, and hatred."

"In 1982, through the streets of Saigon, Hue To and her husband made a mad dash for freedom in the middle of the night. The young couple had tried unsuccessfully to escape four times before, with nothing more than the clothes on their backs and the hope of a better life for their unborn baby."

"Four generations of women, each the eldest daughter and eldest child, each hard-working, independent, self-taught but longing for widened horizons through education. Each a pioneer in her era, each living the words from the Statue of Liberty in her home . . . and today my family includes a Vietnamese refugee, a black woman from Denmark, and racially-mixed grandchildren."

"A black woman told me her story of being beaten and raped by some white men of the KKK."

"When an American song was played, the young people took to the dance floor, but when a Spanish song was played, the older couples came on the dance floor and the younger ones sat down."

=================

SELF-IMPOSED MARGINALITY (Excerpt from a written report, 1991)
by Lisa McKinnon

Self-imposed marginality may be both harrowing and enlightening, depending on one's frame of reference. Theoretically it is easy to sympathize with an outsider, to pledge fidelity to the fringe while standing firmly rooted in the center. My experience at La Piñata exposed the racial reality hidden beneath my "Humanities major" seemliness. Never was I more aware of my racial bias than that Saturday my husband decided to go cruising for authentic Mexican cuisine.

"Del Paso Y el Camino, antes de McDonald's," Nicholas had replied in Americanized Spanish. And so we drove to La Piñata. My husband babbled of carnitas and chili verde bursting with jalepiño and hand-tossed tortillas. Through their food and language, we established perceived connection with the Mexican people. As tourists in Mazatlan, we had enrobed them in nobility, firmly believing that they lived the "true life." Decked with this frame of reference, we rolled into the Mercado, its parking lot littered with Vegas, low-rider Caminos, battered Ford pickups with rosary beads dangling from the rear-view windows. Hombres slouched on the hoods, slurping meñudos and Pacifico beer. Their women dragged on ultra-slim cigarettes, flicked their ashes, and gazed at me through kohl-lined eyes. I became colorless against this Little Mexico, an unwanted tourist in their town.

I could not go in, you see; I am blonde and white and grossly American, even armored with my Mexophile sentiments. My husband, dark-skinned through years of construction labor in the sun, brown-eyed and determined to munch on those tacos carnitas, marched through the Mercado door. I sat in my dwarfed Geo Metro, and in Humanities-major fashion, relished the culture surrounding me. Hombres poured out the Mercado in twos and threes. They swaggered to their sleaze queens, slipping their calloused hands over their women's thighs, slurping beer and singing to Ranchero music pouring from their stereos. I devoured the panoply of culture throbbing around me; unseen I blended into the white interior of my little American car.

The first man sauntered past, nicking my fender with his knees. I smiled feebly, waved and mumbled, "Buenos dias, señor." He stopped and stared, bared a mouth of gold-capped rotted and broken teeth surrounded by brown, cracked lips. I am a Humanities major; I appreciate and embrace culture. I am not marginal because I grasp no center. I cannot lock the door. He slapped the hood of my Geo, breathed "blanca puta" and swaggered on. My fading blue eyes bored into the door of La Piñata. It flicked and swung open. Three hombres followed by chicas dressed in Sunday frill balanced styrofoam containers steaming with menudo. A bambino toddled behind, followed by two low-riders clinking Dos Equis bottles. A Sunday Catholic family burst out with burritos, tacos, and quesadilla wrapped in waxed paper and foil.

The second man slung himself into my rear view mirror, whistled and waved. I feigned sleep and burrowed into the seat. He eased around to my window and stared. Does he really see me? Does he see the stereo, my purse, our tapes? Impulsively my fingers rambled over the lock. I am a Humanities major. I cannot lock the door. He grinned, mouthed "Bueñas dias," and swaggered to his Nova. My husband tapped on the glass, smiled his perfect orthodontal smile, and waved for me to unlock the door. His arms overflowed with brown paper bags steaming with carñitas, chili verde, cilantro, and chiuaua queso. I could not budge. He had to open the door to assure me I had not locked it.

Frequenting the margin, if only for twenty minutes on a Saturday afternoon, makes one aware of the conscious and unconscious ways we alienate others. . . .

"THEY SEEMED MORE AMERICAN THAN I"

by M. Kathleen Hanson

Although a native Californian, I come from a white Southern family. Like most Southerners, my family are great story-tellers and the best stories are based in facts and fantasies that deal with kinship accomplishments. I was luckier than most of my classmates in having this tradition to draw on. Most of the true family stories had already been well-documented and provided me with little challenge for original research. But there was one story that no one had seemed interested in pursuing. In a family of Anglophiles, the story of twin sisters who came from Ireland in the years before the Civil War had attracted little attention or curiosity. Snippets of their story surfaced from time to time, tantalizingly, mysteriously, but no one had ever followed up on these fragments.

Since I had only a few weeks to research their stories, I had to make long-distance phone calls to enlist the aid of family members on both coasts. It promptly became an active and popular family project. Using the basic data, dates, places, and historical events, I was able to reconstruct the framework of a credible story. From my research into travel conditions, wedding customs, architecture of middle Georgia, and the records of railroad building in DeKalb County, Georgia, I was able to flesh out their tale with interesting details. I learned about a wedding feast where the groom and all male guests were served a sumptuous meal in the dining room while the bride and female guests sat on small chairs lining the halls and served themselves from a buffet; of a trip that couples made on a complicated system of river travel, allowing me to imagine how the sisters must have felt as they looked out on the "wild and primitive country" through which they travelled. Wonderful books by the Georgia Architectural Foundation provided me with facts about the kind of hand-hewn houses that would have been their homes. Railroad research records accounted for the changes in lifestyle that would have affected their daily existence as the Georgia interior was opened and civilized during the thirty-year period before the Civil War.

But all this research did not answer why they came to the new world. Why did one sister remain loving and giving and the other become, according to those close to her, bitter and cruel, known for her caustic tongue? While I never did find out for sure why the two sixteen-year olds either ran away or were sent to the Americas, with no apparent destination and no one to receive them, I was led to speculate on the answer--to "reconstruct" their tale.

I discovered that in "Roots" stories, the history of the families is often colored as much by the information they choose to omit as by explanations passed from one generation to the next. In the story of the twin sisters, some of the omissions created interesting settings for speculation. ...*Economics*: I learned that both sisters were able to read and write, were musically-trained, and were skilled in farm management--a very unusual combination of skills for immigrant women from Ireland. ...*Religion*: They came from a country where most were Catholic, but they married in the Baptist church. Neither sister ever attended services--at a time when social custom decreed that good Christian women were devout church-goers. They used their own "funny" Bibles for personal devotion and only opened the King James family Bibles for public family occasions. ...*Family Connections*: There is no evidence that they ever wrote to or received letters from Ireland. Their skills and training lead one to assume that they came from a family of some means and position, yet visitors never came from the old country. There is also some discrepancy about the age of the oldest child of one of the sisters; the family Bible shows one date but rumor says the date in the "funny Bible" was different. Could one sister have been pregnant? Were both turned out or forced to run away? These were the conclusions I found difficult to resist as explanations for their enigmatic tale. This was "the shadow over Stone Mountain" (the title I gave my Roots report), a shadow in our family history.

I was among the first presenters in giving this report orally to the class. As I then listened to other reports, something began to happen. I was more and more moved and touched. I had been told all my life that my family had been "Americans" before there even was a United States. My mother's family is descended from James Oglethorpe, founder of the colony of Georgia. My father's family were merchants in the Baltimore tidal basin when that body of water was still uncharted. My sister and I bear the dubious distinction of eligibility for the Daughters of the American Revolution *and* the Daughters of the Confederacy.

But as I listened to my classmates' stories, I often felt I was the outsider, the "immigrant." They seemed more "American" than I because of their multicultural backgrounds. These feelings caused me to reevaluate my concepts of America as a multicultural nation. I doubt that I would have experienced that startling "marginality" if the teacher had simply lectured on the subject. It was a dawning realization that emerged when listening day after day to the other students who chanced to enroll that term which made possible that shock of recognition.

--Kathleen Hanson

=====================================

These are scraps of stories, snippets taken out of context, at most, a few paragraphs, but perhaps they are enough to make my point. Perhaps they will help to persuade some reticent "traditionally-trained" scholar to try out the Roots Project as a classroom experience in American Studies courses seeking to respond to the challenge of multiculturalism. There are risks involved in trying it. There are mistakes to be made, awkward moments to be overcome. But there are also opportunities to redefine America through the students who take our classes, to alter their perspectives in ways no other assignment can, and with a little luck, to change their lives.

Essay #15

"TWONESS" TALES — AND OTHERS

THE TABLE OF CONTENTS FOR
CROSSING CULTURES: READINGS FOR COMPOSITION
(THIRD EDITION)
edited by Henry Knepler and Myrna Knepler[1]

EDITOR'S INTRODUCTION:

With the surge of interest in multiculturalism in the 1990s, "readers" with such titles as American Mosaic, Imagining America *and* Crossing Cultures *began rolling off the presses. They included stories, poems, and essays selected to represent the response to America by various racial and ethnic groups, men and women, working-class and middle-class, and sometimes gays and lesbians. Readers are commonly used in English classes where composition is taught, or Speech classes where rhetoric is taught, but they are also serving courses in Ethnic Studies (see syllabus #9 by Otis Scott) for the obvious reason that they can offer a great deal of variety within the covers of a single affordable text. They are also structured at times to offer divergent points of view, to aim at philosophical balance. Inevitably, however, they are bound to favor the short poem, the short story, the short essay, or the easily understood excerpt from a longer work.*

What is compelling about the reader Crossing Cultures *is its Table of Contents, in which vivid passages (usually a sentence) from each chapter are presented in order to convey the essence of its contents. The result is that the Table of Contents itself is an artifact, a barometer useful for measuring the zeitgeist.*

I was struck by the recurrence of polarity in the chapter titles of this anthology and the passages chosen to explain them. Again and again, the voices in the collection present the issue, what does it mean to be American? as a story of oppositions. For example, there is Elizabeth Wong's story of a Chinese mother's desire to preserve language VERSUS her daughter's desire to be "the all-American girl." There is a chapter titled "Anglo VERSUS Chicano: Why?" Another, on

---

[1]I am grateful to Macmillan Publishing Company for permission to reprint the Table of Contents. In the 3rd edition (1991, the first was in 1981), thirty percent of the selections are new. More selections were added that cross the Pacific rather than the Atlantic Ocean, due to increased interest in the Pacific Rim, especially Japan and China.

class difference, is called *"Living in Two Worlds." These are variations on the theme of "twoness," to cite W E B DuBois' classic definition of this polarity ("One ever feels one's twoness--A Negro, an American, two souls, two thoughts, two unreconciled strivings . . .") Indeed the very title of the Kneplers' book, "Crossing Cultures," points toward twoness, assuming as it does that crossings occur between discrete cultures with boundaries.[2]*

But what happens when voices present American culture in this way? Take the entry from the Table of Contents called "Halfway to Dick and Jane: A Puerto Rican Pilgrimage":

> "When you got to the top of the hill, something strange happened: America began, because from the hill south was where the 'Americans' lived. Dick and Jane were not dead; they were alive and well in a better neighborhood."

The question teachers are invited to ask is, Who gave America to Dick and Jane? How does such an approach reify the notion that America has all along belonged to middle-class suburban WASPs, rather than having been intended all along as the haven for the many--many nationalities, races, religions, classes, cultures? How does the assignment of such passages encourage students to construct (or reconstruct) their own life histories as Twoness Tales, interpreted in terms of conflicts between groups? How do they also implicitly encourage students to embrace identity politics?

Other questions rise out of the chapter themes: how has the drama of migration shaped our expectations and our lives? how does the journey motif, whether the journey is to or within America, encourage identification with the classic "hero's quest"? why are the "coming of age" stories so compelling--and so similar? how are family structures challenged by the American experience, and how is resistance to "Americanization" mounted by families? what role does education play in dividing generations and defining American dreams? how are our students affected by reading so many stories in the first person, told "from the inside out"? To be sensitive to such questions, even when reading a Table of Contents, is to recognize emerging patterns in the study of multiculturalism.--BC

===================================

---

[2]So does the cover image of the book, a painting done in 1969 called "Across the River" by Ralph Fasanella (identified on the back cover as the "son of Italian immigrants and native of New York City's Greenwich Village"). The image counterpoints an inner-city vista of tenement houses in the foreground--with clothes hanging on the lines, people walking, and children playing--against a stark suburban scene across the river, where a shopping mall, intersecting freeways, and a wooded knoll are visible, with a solitary bicyclist the only human being to be seen.

CROSSING CULTURES Table of Contents

of the treadle against the linoleum floor, by the patient twist of her right shoulder as she automatically pushed at the wheel with one hand."

PART FOUR: IDENTITIES

Part III: Checklists

===

THE VISUAL ARTS AND MULTICULTURAL AMERICA

AN ANNOTATED BIBLIOGRAPHY OF BOOKS

by Jackie R. Donath
California State University at Sacramento

The visual arts both reflect and illuminate the world around us. Visual depictions and ideas break through the barriers of language in ways which allow for new sorts of communication and understandings of different lifestyles and cultures. Images are increasingly important in our expanding world culture, and can offer important insights into America's multicultural society.

This bibliography is intended to make instructors aware of books with high quality reproductions, or particularly useful texts, which deal with the visual arts of the cultures of the United States. While my central focus has been to search out images which illuminate works of art by members of various groups, I've also included some resource material on the images of ethnic groups in the popular and elite arts and media. [Please note that this bibliography does not generally focus on individual artists nor does it include citations from periodicals.]

--Jackie R. Donath

I. ARCHITECTURE:

Adams, Robert. *The Architecture and Art of Early Hispanic Colorado.* Boulder, CO: Colorado Associated University Press, 1974. The first extensive survey of Spanish American art and architecture on the Colorado frontier. Eighty-five sepia and cream photographs. Suggested readings list.

Lancaster, Clay. *The Japanese Influence in America.* NY: Abbeville Press, 1983. 2nd ed. Discusses adoption and assimilation of "Japanese manner" in American arts from colonial period to the twentieth century. Focuses on architecture, both elite and vernacular, and does a bit with decorative arts as well. Good quality b&w illustrations. Bibliography.

Nabokov, Peter and Robert Easton. *Native American Architecture.* NY: Oxford University Press, 1989. This is the first book length, illustrated study of North American Indian architecture in one hundred years. A collaborative effort between an architect (Nabokov) and an anthropologist (Easton), it divides the the nation into nine geographic areas. The chapter-essays and bibliographies are first rate. There are disappointingly few color plates, but the black and white images are of generally good quality.

Upton, Dell, ed. *America's Architectural Roots: Ethnic Groups Built America.* Washington, D.C.: Preservation Press. A pocket handbook with black and white illustrations. Introduces the contributions of various groups to the American vernacular landscape. Jam-packed with interesting and important information. Superior bibliography and list of information sources arranged, as are the chapters, by ethnic group.

II. BIBLIOGRAPHIES AND RESEARCH GUIDES:

Included in this category are sources generally found in the reference section of the library.

Asians in America: A Selected Annotated Bibliography. Davis: Asian American Studies, University of California, 1983. A small but important resource.

Bogle, Donald, ed. *Black Arts Annual.* NY: Garland Publishers, Inc., 1990. A yearly report and analysis of events/ works in the Afro American artistic community. Divided into nine annotated sections: Art, Literature, Photography, Music/Jazz and Classical, Music/Popular, Dance, Theater, Movies, Television. Each section begins with an overview essay, occasionally quite intriguing. Plenty of b&w photos.

Cederholm, Theresa Dickason. *Afro-American Artists: a Bio-Bibliographic Directory.* Boston: Trustees of the Boston Public Library, 1973. Alphabetical listings of artists include media, titles of works, collections, and sources of information on each artist profiled. Useful, but dated.

Goldman, Shifra M. and Tomas Ybarra-Frausto. *Arte Chicano: A Comprehensive Annotated Bibliography of Chicano Art, 1965-1981.* Chicano Studies Library Publication, University of California, Berkeley, 1985. In addition to subject, author, and title, this bibliography begins with a chronological essay framed by a significant theoretical model. Alphabetically lists the Chicano artists and periodicals cited.

Grigsby, J. Eugene, Jr. *Art and Ethnics; Background for Teaching Youth in a Pluralistic Society*. Dubuque, Iowa: Wm. C. Brown Co., Publishers, 1977. Though dated, and basically an art education text, this book has first-rate introductory material on ethnic resources; on modeling; on protest and religion as components of ethnic arts; and on the subjects of folk, academic, and international ethnic arts. Good bibliography. B & W illustrations.

Haseltine, Patricia, compiler. *East and Southeast Asian Material Culture in North America: Collections, Historical Sites, and Festivals*. Westport, CT: Greenwood Press, 1989. Useful and informative collection of information about seriously underrepresented groups.

Holmes, Oakley N., Jr. *The Complete Annotated Resource Guide to Black American Art. (Spine title: Resource Guide to Black American Art.)* Spring Valley, N.Y.: Black Artists in America, 1978. An annotated catalog of books, dissertations, periodicals, video, audio, motion pictures, slides, prints and organizations of Afro-American visual artists. Still an excellent guide, although begs for updating.

Igoe, Lynn and James Igoe. *250 Years of Afro-American Art: An Annotated Bibliography*. NY: Bowker, 1981. An encyclopedic reference work, arranged in three sections: basic references to more than one artist or Afro-American art in general; subject; and artist.

Tribal and Ethnic Art. Santa Barbara, California: Clio Press, 1982. Nine hundred abstracts of books, dissertations, exhibition catalogs, articles published between 1972 and 1979. Of most interest in the context of American multicultural arts are the sections on theory, the Americas, and a small section on Eskimos.

Yochim, Louise Dunn. *Harvest of Freedom: A Survey of Jewish American Artists in America*. Chicago: References, Inc., 1989. Centrally focused on American art by Jews since WWII, with some discussion of 19th century artists. For the most part, treats artworks from a biographical perspective. Appendix organizes artists discussed into alphabetical chart and includes information on media of choice, place of birth and dates. A few color reproductions.

III. EXHIBITION CATALOGS:

Often a bountiful source of high production-quality images and, increasingly, fine essays, most are directed to a literate, but unscholarly, audience.

San Francisco Art Institute. *Other Sources: An American Essay*. San Francisco: San Francisco Art Institute, 1976. This Bicentennial exhibition highlighted the works of Bay Area artists whose "ancestral origins and artistic sources are different from the mainstream of European culture." Three interesting essays, "Third World as a State of Mind," "On Understanding Third Word Art," and "Sources" accompany statements by artists, a directory of works, and a collection of poetry. B &W illustrations and photographs. A rough and amateur product which nonetheless maintains a kind of raw power even after fifteen years.

A. Afro-American:

Adele, Lynne. *Black History/Black Vision: The Visionary Image in Texas*. Austin: Archer M. Huntington Art Gallery, University of Texas at Austin, 1989. Arranged by artist, focuses on six "self-taught" (folk) African Americans whose subject matter is primarily religious. Some color prints and a bibliography.

Anacostia Neighborhood Museum. *The Barnett-Aden Collection*. Washington, D. C.: Smithsonian Institution Press, 1974. A catalog of the gallery's holdings in Afro-American art. Most of the reproductions are in black and white, but this collection is one of the most significant in the nation. Short biographies of represented artists increase the usefulness of this small volume.

Campbell, Mary Schmidt and The Studio Museum in Harlem. *Tradition and Conflict: Images of a Turbulent Decade, 1963-1973*. NY: The Studio Museum in Harlem, 1985. A melange of essays accompany images from this exhibition: Campbell does her usual excellent job in the introductory essay and writes about images from the period 1963-1973; Vincent Harding discusses the Freedom Movement from 1955-1972; Lucy Lippard compares the Black, Women's and Anti-War Movements; and Benny Andrew's journal is excerpted. A chronology of events and a catalog of the exhibition are also included. Mostly b&w photos.

Driskell, David. *Contemporary Visual Expressions; The Art of Sam Gilliam, Martha Jackson-Jarvis, Keith Morrison, William T. Williams*. Washington, D.C.: The Anacostia Museum, 1987. The inaugural exhibition of the new museum building was the occasion to show the work of four contemporary Afro-American artists whose works draw on urban settings of New York and the District of Columbia. Each artist's profile is illustrated with color plates of some of the works on exhibit. Exhibition chronologies and a selective bibliography are also included for each.

----------*Hidden Heritage: Afro-American Art 1800-1950*. San Francisco: Art Museum Association of America, 1985. Catalog of exhibition held at Bellvue Art Museum, Bellvue, Washington, which offered "encapsulated history" of Afro-American fine art from early in the nineteenth century until the middle of the twentieth century. Some excellent color plates.

---------- *Two Centuries of Black American Art*. NY: Alfred A. Knopf, 1976. This ground-breaking exhibit, mounted as part of the Bicentennial celebration, was the first major historical survey of Afro-American art history. Excellent introductory essays on "Black Artists and Craftsmen from 1750-1920," and "The Evolution of a Black Aesthetic 1920-1950." A good bibliography and catalog of the exhibit which includes accession and biographical information are also included. Twenty-three color plates.

Gaither, Edmund D. *Aspects of the 70's Spiral: Afro-American Art of the Seventies.* Roxbury, MA: The Museum of the National Center of Afro-American Artists, 1980. This small catalog has a very short (2 page), but informative, introductory essay, b&w illustrations, and biographies of the artists included in the show.

Hartigan, Lynda Roscoe. *Sharing Traditions; Five Black Artists in Nineteenth Century America.* Washington, D.C.: Smithsonian Institution Press, 1985. Catalog of a SITES exhibit with an excellent essay by James O. Horton on African American identity in the nineteenth century. Hartigan profiles the lives and works of the exhibition's subjects: Joshua Johnson, Robert Scott Duncanson, Edward Mitchell Bannister, Edmonia Lewis, Henry Ossawa Tanner.

Johnson, William H. *Novae: William H. Johnson and Bob Thompson.* Los Angeles: California Afro-American Museum Foundation, 1990. The "similarities and differences in lives, artistic choices and styles of work" of two Afro-American painters are treated in three essays accompanying excellent reproductions of material in the exhibition. A small bibliography whets the appetite for more.

Livingston, Jane and John Beardsley. *Black Folk Art in America 1930-1980.* Jackson, MI: University of Mississippi Press, 1980. Designed to enhance an exhibit at the Cocoran Gallery of Art, Washington D.C. Three excellent essays define Black folk art (Jane Livingston), discuss its origins and early expressions (Regina A. Perry) and focus on its spiritual components (John Beardsley). Twenty artists and their works are profiled and photographed. A fine short bibliography of general texts on Afro-American folk arts and art history is supplemented with a bibliography of material on the artists featured in the exhibit.

McElroy, Guy C., Richard Powell, Sharon Patton. *African-American Artists 1880-1987: Selections from the Evans-Tibbs Collection.* Washington, D.C.: Smithsonian Traveling Exhibit Service, 1989. Introduction by David Driskell and excellent essays enliven text which divides period into three parts. Beautiful color plates.

Rozelle, Robert V., Alvia Wardlaw, and Maureen A. McKenna, eds. *Black Art: Ancestral Legacy; The African Impulse in African-American Art.* NY: Harry N. Abrams, 1990. This oversized, glossy book combines a fine color catalog of the traveling exhibition organized by the Dallas Museum of Art with six excellent essays on the relationships between African arts and African-American expressions. Essays and biographical sketches are accompanied by good quality black and white photographs. A short bibliography completes the volume.

Studio Museum in Harlem. *Harlem Renaissance: Art of Black America.* NY: Harry N. Abrams, Inc., 1987. This beautiful illustrated and designed volume has an introductory piece by Mary Schmidt Campbell and scholarly, readable essays by David Driskell, David Levering Lewis, and Deborah Willis Ryan. There is a chronology of the Harlem Renaissance, but most of the information comes by way of the exhibit's focus on Aaron Douglas, Meta Vaux Warwick Fuller, Palmer Hayden, William Henry Johnson, and James Van Der Zee. Supplementary materials include a bibliography of books and exhibition catalogs.

B. Chicano/Hispanic/Latino:

Beardsley, John and Jane Livingston. *Hispanic Art in the United States.* NY: Abbeville Press, 1987. Published in conjunction with an exhibition held at the Museum of Fine Arts, Houston, and other museums, in 1987. The color plates are magnificent and the three excellent essays: "Art and Identity: Hispanics in the United States," by Octavio Paz; John Beardsley's "And/Or: Hispanic Art, American Culture;" and a piece on "Recent Hispanic Art: Style and Influence," by Jane Livingston are supplemented by short biographies of contemporary Hispanic artists. A modest general bibliography focuses on contemporary Hispanic arts and the continuing tradition and influence of religious art in the Southwest. Highly recommended.

Bronx Museum of the Arts. *The Latin Spirit: Art and Artists in the United States 1920-1970.* NY: Harry N. Abrams, Inc., 1988. Provocative informative essays treat uniquely Hispanic materials and the larger contributions of Latinos to American Art movements like surrealism and conceptual art. The 100 excellent color prints and 130 b&w images are enhanced by short biographies of the artists in the exhibit and a bibliography including sources in both English and Spanish.

Contemporary Arts Museum, Houston, and Santos Martinez. *Dale gas: Chicano Art of Texas.* Houston, TX: Contemporary Museum of Art, 1977. It's quite dated, but there is still a marvelous vitality to this first major museum "assessment" of visual and literary works by Chicano/Chicana Texans. Some works are in Spanish.

Eldridge, Charles C., Julie Schimmel, William C. Treuttner. *Art in New Mexico 1900-1945; Paths to Taos and Santa Fe.* NY: Abbeville Press, 1986. Glossy exhibition catalog with several chapters of potential interest, all accompanied by gorgeous color reproductions: William Treuttner's essays on "Science and Sentiment: Indian Images at the Turn of the Century," and "The Art of Pueblo Life," and Julie Schimmel's "The Hispanic Southwest." A bibliography and biographies of the artists included in the show are useful addenda.

Wroth, William, ed. *Hispanic Crafts of the Southwest*. Taylor Museum of Colorado Springs Fine Arts Center, 1977. Fine essays on, and illustrations of, weaving, furniture and jewelry-making make this catalog of an exhibit of twentieth century manifestations of Hispanic Southwestern craft traditions.worth a second glance, despite the disappointment of black-and-white photographs.

C. Native American:

Coe, Ralph T. *Lost and Found Traditions: Native American Art 1965-1985*. Seattle, WA: University of Washington Press, 1986. Published in conjunction with an exhibition organized by The American Federation of the Arts. Highlights the richness and diversity of a twenty year period's work in traditional American Indian forms. All the 403 pieces in the exhibit are illustrated and annotated, unfortunately only 48 in (excellent) color (355 b&w). Maps and a small glossary enhance a well-written and personable foreword and introductory text by Coe.

---------- *Sacred Circles: Two Thousand Years of North American Indian Art*. London: Arts Council of Great Britain, 1980. A well-conceived survey of Native American art produced for British exhibition. Good reproductions and Coe's usual cogent and readable text.

Conn, Richard. *Robes of White and Sunrise: Personal Decorative Arts of the Native American*. Denver Art Museum, 1974. This small, well-illustrated catalog provides a shallow, but useful survey of costume and domestic arts.

Seymour, Tryntje Van Ness. *When the Rainbow Touches Down; The Artists and Stories Behind the Apache, Navaho, Rio-Grande Pueblo and Hopi Paintings in the William and Leslie Van Ness Denman Collection*. Phoenix, AR: Heard Museum, 1988. This catalog is organized by tribe, and the essays accompanying photographs of collection and other illustrative materials involve interviews and useful information about tribal ways of life, religions, and artways. Individual artists profiled; some specific paintings described and illustrated with color. The appendices include sources, select bibliography, orthographic notes and glossary.

Silberman, Arthur. *100 Years of Native American Painting*. Oklahoma City: Oklahoma Museum of Art, 1978. Introduction by Jamake Highwater. Slim volume organized by artist. Some color illustrations. Short suggested reading list.

Walker Art Center. *American Indian Art: Form and Tradition*. NY: E. P. Dutton, 1972. Informative and evocative essays by Gerald Vizenor, David Gebhard, Martin Friedman, and Vincent Scully stand out among thirteen essays which accompany this catalog of an exhibition sponsored by the Walker Art Center and the Minneapolis Institute of Arts. While the illustrations are generally black and white, the text is first rate, even after almost twenty years. The bibliography follows the order of the essays (a useful device) and includes references to California and the Southwest, geographic areas not considered in the text.

D. White Ethnics:

Garvan, Beatrice B. and Charles F. Hummel. *The Pennsylvania Germans, A Celebration of Their Arts, 1683-1850.* Philadelphia Museum of Art, 1982. This exhibit was organized by the Philadelphia and Winterthur museums.The catalog has good color illustrations and the text is organized by topics such as "marketplace" and "religion and education." Bibliography also included.

Milwaukee Art Center. *From Foreign Shores; 3 Centuries of Art by Foreign-Born American Masters.* 1976. Profiles of mostly "artistically significant" European men, but offers interesting sense of American context/influence. Touches briefly on provocative issue of immigration and the arts. B&W photographs predominate, but a good resource for citing images which may be found elsewhere in color.

IV. FINE ARTS:

Cockcroft, Eva, John Weber, James Cockcroft. *Toward a People's Art; The Contemporary Mural Movement.* NY: E. P. Dutton and Co., 1971. Written by two muralists and a political sociologist. Murals are discussed as expressions of community sensibility and tools for social change. Though dated, bibliography and information on murals are still basically useful. Some color photographs.

Lippard, Lucy R. *Mixed Blessings; New Art in a Multicultural America.* NY: Pantheon Books, 1990. This book is so important it deserves a category of its own. Centering her text on the processes of contemporary multi-cultural "naming," "telling," "landing," "mixing," "turning around," and "dreaming," Lippard discusses and illuminates the contemporary arts of various ethnic groups in the Americas. Provocative essays, black and white, and color plates, and, her "eclectic (and eccentric) bibliography," make this a valuable addition to any scholar's library. *See Checklist F in this volume.--BC*

A. Afro-American:

Butcher, Margaret Just. *The Negro in American Culture.* NY: Alfred A. Knopf, 1972. 2nd edition. "Based on materials left by Alain Locke," it offers introductory information on African-American creative culture. Arranged historically and topically.

Dover, Cedric. *American Negro Art.* Greenwich, Conn.: New York Graphic Society, 1960. A classic historical study of Black American painters, sculptors and craftsmen. 400 illustrations, few color.

Fax, Elton C. *Black Artists of the New Generation.* NY: Dodd, Mead Inc., 1977. Foreword by Romare Bearden. Biographical approach to twenty Black artists, most of the late Sixties. A few b&w photographs of artists and works.

Fine, Elsa Honig. *The Afro-American Artist: A Search For Identity.* NY: Holt, Rhinehart & Winston, 1973. Central, basic text for students of Afro-American art history. Includes historical, biographical and critical information. Some indifferent color plates.

Gay, Geneva and Willi Baber, eds. *Expressively Black; The Cultural Basis of Ethnic Identity.* NY: Praeger Publishers, 1987. A multidisciplinary look at Black cultural experiences. Particularly valuable essay by Gladstone L. Yearwood on "Expressive Traditions in Afro-American Visual Arts."

Gayle, Addison Jr., ed. *The Black Aesthetic.* NY: Doubleday, 1971. The opening chapter on "Theory" provides useful categories for examining the (visual) arts of non-white and non-mainstream groups.

Lewis, Samella S. *Art: African-American* .NY: Harcourt, Brace, Jovanovich, 1978. Chronologically organized study of history and issues in Afro-American art history, 1619-1970's. Lots of illustrations, though disappointingly poor quality and few in color. Bibliography.

----------and Ruth S. Waddy. *Black Artists on Art.* Los Angeles: Contemporary Craft Publishers, 1969. First-person comments by contemporary Black .artists. Illustrated with mostly b&w reproductions. Some pungent quotes.

Locke, Alain Leroy, ed. *The Negro in Art: A Pictorial Record of the Negro Artist and of the Negro Theme in Art.* NY: Hacker Art Books, 1968. Divided into three sections: "Negro as Artist," "Negro in Art," and "Ancestral Arts," each with commentary, biographical information, and some (mostly b & w) plates. Good as general introduction to visual materials to locate in other sources. Very short, dated bibliography.

B. Asian-American:

Cochran, Jo, et al., eds. *Gathering Ground: New Writing and Art by Northwest Women of Color.* Seattle, WA: Seal Press, 1984. Collection includes drawings & literary work by Asian-American women and others.

The Hawk's Well: A Collection of Japanese-American Art and Literature. San Jose: Asian American Arts Project, 1985. One of first and few books to include visual materials by Asian Americans.

C. Chicano/Hispanic/Latino:

Boyd, E. *Popular Arts of Spanish New Mexico*. Santa Fe: Museum of New Mexico Press, 1974. Comprehensive, scholarly treatment of Spanish colonial arts and crafts in northern New Mexico from 17th century to modern period. No color.

Cockcroft, Eva Sperling and Holly Barnet-Sanchez, eds. *Signs from the Heart: California Chicano Murals*. Venice, CA: Social and Public Art Resource Center, 1990. Published by clearing house for information on and action in social and public arts. Good general introduction. Informative essays: Shifra Goldman, "How, Why, Where and When It All Happened: Chicano Murals of California;" Tomas Ybarra-Frausto, "Arte Chicano: Images of a Community;" Amalia Mesa-Bains,"Quest for Identity: Profile of Two Chicana Muralists based on interviews with Judith Baca and Patricia Rodriguez;" Marcos Sanchez-Tranquilino, "Murales del Movimiento: Chicano Murals and the Discourses of Art and Americanization." Thirty-six excellent color plates, suggestions for further reading. Highly recommended. *[See Essay #2 for one use of this volume.]*

Quirarte, Jacinto, ed. *Chicano Art History: A Book of Selected Readings*. Research Center for the Arts and Humanities, University of Texas, San Antonio, TX, 1984. Significant collection of primary and secondary sources.

Quirarte, Jacinto, ed. *Mexican American Artists*. Austin: University of Texas Press, 1973. Attempt to "describe and define" work of Mexican-American artists according to culturally relevant, but not particularly developed, criteria. Text includes information on Mexican antecedents as well as focus on Mexican-American art in the twentieth century (to 1946). Twenty-six good color plates, one hundred and eleven b&w illustrations; short, somewhat useful bibliography.

D. Native American:

Broder, Patricia Janis. *American Indian Painting and Sculpture*. NY: Abbeville Press, 1981. Gigantic, oversized collection of color reproductions of seventy-four works by trans-Mississippi Native artists and commentaries by art historian Broder.

Feder, Norman. *American Indian Art*. NY: Harry N. Abrams, Inc., 1965. Although dated, this huge (445 pages) volume still offers a fine introduction to the subject. Chapters on general topics in Indian art are followed by mostly black and white plates, and short essays on the arts of different geo-cultural areas.

Feest, Christine F. *Native Arts of North America*. NY: Oxford University Press, 1980. Survey (excluding architecture) of "major" tribes of North America. Part I includes essays on history of Native arts and impact of Europeans on traditional forms. Part II offers more specific treatments of genres, techniques and styles. Ten page bibliography is quite comprehensive and partially annotated.

Highwater, Jamake. *Song From the Earth: American Indian Painting.* Greenwich, Conn: New York Graphic Society, 1976. This first history of Native American painting for the general public begins with pre-1900 art forms and ends with works of the 1970's. Illustrations include 32 color and 130 b&w plates. A very short general bibliography and a useful basic chronology complete the volume.

----------*The Sweet Grass Lives On: Fifty Contemporary North American Artists.* NY: Lippincott and Crowell, 1980. Companion volume to *Song of the Earth* offers biographical profiles of contemporary Native American painters and sculptors. A coffee table sized book with excellent color reproductions. Highwater's texts are always informative; introductory essay contrasts Western European and Native American artistic concepts.

Mather, Christine. *Native America: Arts, Traditions, and Celebrations.* NY: Clarkson N. Potter, 1990. A glossy, but compelling collection of artifacts.

Matthews, Zena Pearlstone and Aldona Jonaitis. *Native North American Art History: Selected Readings.* Palo Alto, CA: Peek Publications, Inc., 1982. Informative & useful collection. Excellent bibliography.

E. Jewish:

Thompson, Vivian. *A Mission in Art: Recent Holocaust Works in America.* Mercer University Press, 1978. Based on author's dissertation. Personal, historical, and psychological perspectives on arguably the most significant event in modern American Jewish history. Works by survivors, their children, and those empathetic to themes of holocaust. Focuses on artists themselves and what they have to say about works. Some fine color reproductions. Selected bibliography of primary and secondary sources.

V. FOLK ARTS:

A rich source of images and information about different American cultures and subcultural groups whose access to more mainstream channels of communication and information may otherwise be rather limited.

Dewhurst, C. Kurt, Betty MacDowell, Marsha MacDowell. *Religious Folk Art in America; Reflections of Faith.* Disappointing b&w photographs, but a superior text treats a wide variety of religion-related artifacts in an introductory, but sophisticated fashion. Includes material on Puritan, African American, Native American, Hispanic, women and denominational experiences. Rich source of images to search for in color reproductions.

Ferris, William R. *Afro-American Folk Arts and Crafts.* Jackson: University Press of Mississippi, 1983. Folkloric study of African-American quiltmakers, sculptors, instrument-makers, basket-makers, blacksmiths and potters. Also includes important analytical essays and two significant bibliographies: Simon Bronner and Christopher Lornell's seminal collection of material on folklore and art history and an historical bibliography of Black artisans and craftsmen. Volume also includes a list of films on the subject of Black folk arts.

Glassie, Henry. *The Spirit of Folk Art; The Girard Collection at the Museum of International Folk Art.* NY: Harry N. Abrams, Inc., 1989. Three hundred objects drawn from the world's largest collection of cross-cultural folk art are illustrated in glowing color. A number of American examples are used, and this gem also includes superior essays by Glassie on the nature of folk art, and the relationship between folk and other arts.

Hartigan, Lynda Roscoe. *Made with Passion: The Hemphill Folk Art Collection.* High quality color photographs and an excellent bibliography enhance this volume, which includes works by, and portraying, Afro-Americans, Native Americans, and European ethnics. Of particular interest are pieces from the collection categorized under "communal expressions." (Unfortunately, 1930's Pueblo/Hopi Mickey Mouse kachina is photographed in black and white.)

Lipman, Jean, Robert Bishop, Elizabeth V. Warren, Sharon L. Eisenstadt. *Five-Star Folk Art: One Hundred American Masterpieces.* NY: Harry N. Abrams, 1990. The grand mavens of the "collectable" pick their choices of the most artistically excellent examples of four hundred years of American folk art. Michelin-style rating and elite criteria do not prevent this from being useful. Beautifully photographed, with the artifacts arranged according to genre, and accompanied by short, informative essays. Quite a good bibliography.

Mayerson-Ungerleider, Joy. *Jewish Folk Art; From Bible Days to Modern Times.* While relatively little in this book is specifically American, it provides a fine introduction to, and illustrations of, Jewish cultural continuities across time and space. Folk artifacts are arranged according to their association with different areas in Jewish life. Chapters deal with marriage, home, birth, sabbath, synagogue, and holidays. Glossary, bibliography, good color photographs.

Rumford, Beatrix and Carolyn J. Weekly. *Treasures from the Abby Aldrich Rockefeller Folk Art Center.* Boston: Little, Brown & Co., 1989. Not many works here are identified with specific ethnic or racial groups, but a number of interesting artifacts made by Afro- and Euro-Americans are contextualized by their American experiences. Beautiful photographs and a readable, informative text.

Vlach, John Michael. *The Afro-American Tradition in the Decorative Arts.* Cleveland Museum of Art, 1978. As adjunct to museum exhibition, folk art expert provides first-rate introduction to Afro-American basketry, musical instrument, wood carvings, quilting, pottery, boatbuilding, blacksmithy, architecture and graveyard decoration. Many illustrations, some color. Excellent bibliography.

Wilder, Mitchell A. *Santos: The Religious Folk Art of New Mexico.* NY Hacker Art Books, 1976. A good introduction to an important Hispanic folk art form. Unfortunately, poor quality b&w photographs.

VI. PHOTOGRAPHY:

Bolton, Richard, ed. *The Contest of Meaning; Critical Histories of Photography.* Cambridge, MA: M.I.T. Press, 1989. Of interest are introductory essay and those in sections titled "how does photography construct sexual difference?" and "how is photography used to promote class and national interests?" Geared to readers with previous exposure to these issues, there is a disappointing lack of basic bibliographic information on the subject of critical approaches to photography.

Moutoussamy-Ashe, Jean. *Viewfinders: Black Women Photographers.* NY: Dodd, Mead, 1986. Treats period from 1839-1985 with historical overviews followed by focus on individual artists. Includes bio-bibliographic, geographic and bibliographic material. Good b&w photographs.

Willis-Thomas, Deborah. *Black Photographers 1840-1940: An Illustrated Bio-Bibliography.* NY: Garland Publishers, 1985. Significant contribution to under-developed area. Alphabetical arrangement of artists within three chronological divisions. Information on each photographer includes dates, principal subjects, photographic processes employed (introduction includes information about this subject), collections, short biographical information and a selective bibliography.

VII. MULTICULTURAL IMAGES IN VISUAL ARTS AND MASS MEDIA:

Bataille, Gretchen and Charles L.P. Silet, eds. *Images of American Indians on Film: An Annotated Bibliography.* NY: Garland Publishing, Inc., 1985. An invaluable resource for information on the portrayal of Native Americans in the movies. The book is divided into four sections and an index: general background books and articles, books and articles on Native Americans in films, reviews of individual films, and a filmography of sound films dealing with American Indians. Brief but clear annotations.

----------*The Pretend Indians: Images of Native Americans in the Movies.* Ames: Iowa State University Press, 1980. A polemic on the treatment and stereotyping of Natives in classic Hollywood cinema.

Cripps, Thomas. *Slow Fade to Black: The Negro in America Film, 1890-1942.* NY: Oxford University Press, 1977. A seminal work on this subject. Some b&w photographs.

Honour, Hugh. *The Image of the Black in Western Art.* Cambridge, MA: Harvard University Press, volumes 1-4, 1976-1989. Most germane is vol. 4: *From Revolution to World War I,* which is in two books: Part I: *Slaves and Liberators* and Part II: *Black Models and White Myths.* Lavishly illustrated. Contextualizes images which are part of both European and American painting and sculpture.

McElroy, Guy C. *Facing History: Black Image in American Art 1710-1940.* San Francisco: Bedford Arts, 1990. An extraordinary exhibition catalog. Essay by Henry Louis Gates, Jr. on "The Face and Voice of Blackness," and McElroy's introductory piece on "Race and Representation" are first-rate. All images are high quality, exhibit material reproductions are all in color and well-annotated. Useful bibliography. Highly recommended.

Parry, Ellwood. *The Image of the Indian and the Black Man in American Art 1590-1900.* Discussion of the iconography of the New World in terms of Blacks and Natives. Begins with "European Interest in New World" and concludes with period "From the Centennial to the Turn of the Century." B&W reproductions of artworks. Selected bibliography arranged according to subject: Indians, Blacks, and American Art and Artists.

Stedman, Raymond William. *Shadows of the Indians: Stereotypes in American Culture.* Norman, OK: University of Oklahoma Press, 1982. An examination of the common stereotypes of Native Americans present in all types of popular culture throughout American history. Despite some factual errors and a condescending bias against some of the popular culture artifacts under discussion, Stedman's able demonstration that quasi-sympathetic treatments of Native peoples in film, on stage, and in literature often mask stereotypic portrayals, makes this a worthwhile volume. There are also dozens of useful illustrations, a literary/historical chronology, a bibliography, and a general and title index.

Steinland, Sally. *Unequal Picture: Black, Hispanic, Asian and Native American Characters on Television.* Washington, D.C.: National Commission on Wider Opportunities for Working Women, 1989. Paper discusses biased portrayals of ethnic and racial minorities on television in recent seasons.

Woll, Allen and Randall M. Miller. *Ethnic and Racial Images in American Film and Television: Historical Essays and Bibliography.* NY: Garland Publishers, 1987. Analytical essays improve the value of this listing of books, dissertations, reports, and scholarly and popular articles on the subject.

==

MULTICULTURAL AMERICAN ARTS:
A RESOURCE GUIDE
TO I. AFRICAN-AMERICAN, II. NATIVE AMERICAN, III. MEXICAN AMERICAN, IV. ASIAN AMERICAN ARTS, AND V. SOURCES ON FORCED MIGRATION– JAPANESE & NATIVE AMERICAN

by Keith Atwater

ED. NOTE: See also Atwater's syllabus, #3 in Part I.--BC

General Reference:

Baker, Houston A., ed: *Three American Literatures*. MLA Association, 1982. This valuable introduction to multicultural literature includes useful and informative essays on Native American, Asian American, and Chicano literature. Well-researched, scholarly, and readable, this fills a need in literary criticism.

Simonson, Rick, and Walker, Scott, ed.: *Multicultural Literacy: Opening the American Mind*. Graywolf Press, 1988. Taking its title from two recent studies of American higher education, this collection of thoughtful essays by James Baldwin, Paula Gunn Allen, Wendell Berry, Carlos Fuentes, and Ishmael Reed provide thoughtful, forceful, and timely responses to current educational issues.

Tiedt, Pamela and Iris: *Multicultural Teaching: A Handbook of Activities, Information, and Resources*. 3rd ed., Simon & Schuster, 1990. Designed for elementary and secondary teachers, but with interesting classroom projects and, more important, a look at what's going on in some classrooms in America. Useful statistics and booklists on linguistics, stereotypes, and ethnic groups from Egyptian to Swedish.

I. AFRICAN-AMERICAN ARTS

General Reference:

Southern, Eileen: *The Music of Black Americans*. Norton, 1977. This exhaustive treatment provides good background for studies of jazz, blues, spirituals, ragtime, and gospel traditions. Thorough, but occasionally musically technical, this is still a standard reference.

Lanker, Brian: *I Dream A World: Portraits of Black Women Who Changed America*. Stewart, Tabori, & Chang, 1989. Powerful b&w portraits make a strong visual accompaniment to this bio/photo book of significant African-American women, from Maya Angelou to Shirley Chisholm, Coretta Scott

King, Alice Walker, and a host of lesser known social workers, teachers, poets, musicians, and artists.

Autobiography/Biography

Angelou, Maya: *I Know Why the Caged Bird Sings.* Bantam, 1970. The first of several volumes of autobiography, this look at Angelou's formative years in a small southern town remains forceful and accessible, with a sharp eye for detail.

Carter, Vincent: *All God's Dangers: The Life of Nate Shaw.* 1974. This text provides a valuable look at the world of the cotton-raising South and the black experience there; moreover, it's a fine example of oral literature, using the transcribed stories of an aged sharecropper.

Haley, Alex: *Autobiography of Malcolm X.* Grove Press, 1965. A major book that connects students to the anger of civil rights era American black life--to the politics of race, religion, self.

Novels:

Baldwin, James: *Go Tell It On the Mountain.* Laurel 1953. Baldwin's fine novel reveals in moving eloquent prose the dark corners of Harlem, the black church experience, and the struggle for identity and self-respect. This is a powerful novel.

Ellison Ralph: *Invisible Man.* Signet, 1952. The intensity, violence, comedy, pain, and soul-searching of the black American are all here in this important work of fiction, though this novel is quite a bit longer than Baldwin's.

Morrison, Toni: *Beloved.* New American Library, 1987. This Pulitzer Prize winner is contemporary fiction at its best, a powerful study of the psychic scars of slavery, but very challenging for the undergraduate not majoring in English. Shorter and more accessible are *The Bluest Eye* (1970) and *Sula.*

Short Stories/Essays:

Baldwin, James: *Notes of a Native Son.* 1955. Short essays on various issues in black American life and culture. See also *Nobody Knows My Name* (1960) and *The Fire Next Time* (1963).

Ellison, Ralph: *Shadow and Act.* 1964. Ellison's short pieces of criticism on literature, jazz, and black culture have value more as background than exciting literature.

Chambers, Bradford, ed.: *Right On! An Anthology of Black Literature.* New American Library, 1970. This very handy paperback collection includes poetry and prose of the Harlem Renaissance--Jean Toomer, Countee Cullen, Langston Hughes; works from the '50's and '60's --Gwendolyn Brooks, Wendell Hines, and LeRoi Jones; and an introduction.

Poetry: These poets are widely anthologized:

Maya Angelou; Imamu Amiri Baraka; Gwendolyn Brooks; Nikki Giovanni; Langston Hughes; Sonia Sanchez

Films/ Documentaries:

LANGSTON HUGHES: THE DREAM KEEPER, 1988, 60 minutes. This retrospective of Hughes' work includes scenes of Harlem, Paris, readings of his works, and his connections to jazz & blues.

AMAZING GRACE WITH BILL MOYERS, PBS, 1989. 60 min. About 20 min. of lively black gospel style renditions of this hymn in several settings provides vivid insight into this musical style. See also "Goin' Home to Gospel" (PBS).

DO THE RIGHT THING (1988), MO BETTER BLUES (1990), JUNGLE FEVER (1991)--major films by important black filmmaker Spike Lee.

Music/ Plays: Significant playwrights include:

Lorraine Hansberry: "A Raisin in the Sun" (1959)

LeRoi Jones (Imamau Amiri Baraka): "Dutchman" (1964) "The Slave" (1969)

Short List of "Classic Jazz" Albums by African American artists::

"The Louis Armstrong Story"--Columbia; "Jazz I, II, III" (early jazz)--Folkways. "This is Duke Ellington"--RCA; "The Best of Count Basie"--Decca; "The Charlie Parker Story"--Savoy; "Piano Starts Here" (Art Tatum)--Columbia; "Strictly Bebop" (Dizzy Gillespie)--Capitol; "Giant Steps" (John Coltrane)-- Atlantic; "Bitches Brew" (Miles Davis); "Modern Jazz Quartet"--Prestige

II. NATIVE AMERICAN ARTS

General Reference:

Allen, Paula Gunn: *Studies in American Indian Literature.* MLA, 1983. Allen's critical analysis provides a good introduction and insightful studies of contemporary and traditional materials. A Laguna Pueblo writer and teacher, she has published fiction and non-fiction, notably *The Sacred Hoop* (Beacon, 1986) an important look at the feminine, spirituality, and women's roles.

Brown, Joseph Epes: *The Spiritual Legacy of the American Indian.* Ten lucid and interesting essays provide a thoughtful look at the key ideas in many Native Americans' perceptions of time, the earth, spirituality, dance, and the arts as related to their world views.

Lincoln, Kenneth: *Native American Renaissance.* Harper & Row, 1985. Lincoln's critical study provides a thorough and wide ranging study of written and oral traditions from the nineteenth century to Black Elk to Welch, Momaday, and significant contemporary novelists and poets.

Autobiography/Biography:

Blackman, Margaret: *During My Time: A Haida Woman.* University of Washington, 1982. Adding a much-needed study of woman's experience, this traces the life of Florence Edenshaw Davidson (b.1896) and her life on a remote Puget Sound island through puberty ceremony, arranged marriage, and major social upheavals of this century.

Eastman, Charles A., M.D.: *From the Deep Woods to Civilization.* Little, Brown, 1916. A converted Christian, educated in eastern colleges, Dr. Eastman's memoirs provide interesting material for discussion about the clash of two cultures, issues of identity and assimilation, Christianity, and American values and earlier views of Native Americans. See *Soul of the Indian* and *Indian Boyhood* (1911, 1902).

Lame Deer, John (Fire) and Richard Erdoes: *Lame Deer Seeker of Visions.* Simon, 1972. In contrast to Eastman, Lame Deer's often feisty and humorous accounts of his many activities provide useful insights into Lakota tradition, ceremony, dance, sacred lifeways and 'medicine', and the effects of prolonged contact with the dominant Anglo society.

Neihardt, John G., ed.: *Black Elk Speaks.* University of Nebraska Press, 1932, 1961. A perennial classic, still in paperback and still worth close study, albeit now with the awareness of critical questions about Neihardt's role and Black Elk's possible blending of Christian and Lakota spirituality.

Novels:

Allen, Paula Gunn: *The Woman Who Owned the Shadows.* Spinsters, 1983. This provocative and probing novel works with images and ideas of healing, wholeness, tradition and the contemporary world as it probes creatively issues of friendship, sexism, feminism, and racism. An anthology of several Native American women writers working with similar themes in literature and oral tales, edited by Allen, is valuable as well. See *Spider Woman's Granddaughters,* Fawcett, 1989.

Momaday, N. Scott: *House Made of Dawn.* Signet, 1968. A Pulitzer Prize Winner, this bleak yet richly textured and engrossing novel contains important and profound ideas about past and present, peyote and spirituality, despair and redemption, identity and the meaning of history, ritual, ceremony, and roots.

Silko, Leslie: *Ceremony.* Viking, 1977. A perennial favorite in many classrooms, this novel of a mixed-blood war veteran's search for meaning and ways to survive probes the clash of cultures, myth and magic, and healing power of ceremony, visions, roots, and place.

Waters, Frank: *The Man Who Killed the Deer.* Pocket Books, 1971 [1941]. The grandaddy of serious fiction on Native American themes and lifeways.

Though Waters is a bit of a romantic and not Native American, this book has been well received by Native scholars, and successfully taught to diverse students in college classrooms. Good material on cosmology, dance, Indian-Mexican-White relations, creation stories, and conflict. His noteworthy nonfiction studies of arts and lifeways are *Book of the Hopi* and *Masked Gods*.

Welch, James. *Winter in the Blood*. Bantam, 1974. Terse, dark, and very well crafted, this short novel has an existential and Hemingwayesque feel. Thought-provoking literature, it stands with other Welch novels, notably *The Death of Jim Loney* and *Fools Crow*. Welch, a fine poet as well, has recently been criticized by some Native Americans for allegedly catering to Anglo commercial fiction tastes.

Short Stories/Essays:

Green, Reyna, ed.: *The Remembered Earth* (1981) and *That's What She Said: An Anthology of American Indian Women's Writings* (1983)

Ortiz, Simon J., ed.: *Earth Power Coming* (1983)

Rosen, Kenneth, ed.: *The Man to Send Rain Clouds* (1974)

Silko, Leslie: *Storyteller* (prose and poems) (1981)

Poetry:

Bierhorst, John, ed.: *In the Trail of the Wind* (1971)

Ortiz, Simon J.: *Going for the Rain* (1976); *A Good Journey* (1977)

Rosen, Kenneth, ed., *Voices of the Rainbow* (1975)

Rothenberg, Jerome, ed., *Shaking the Pumpkin: Traditional Poetry* (1972)

Silko, Leslie: *Laguna Woman* (1974)

Welch James: *Riding the Earthboy 40* (1971, rpt. 1976)

Films/Documentaries:

HOPI: SONGS OF THE FOURTH WORLD, PBS video, 60 min. 1987. Explores Hopi spirituality creation stories, Corn Mother, pottery, weaving, painting, dance, connectedness to the land, kachinas, and cultural survival, using interviews.

FRITZ SCHOLDER, PBS video, 30 min. 1976. This documentary follows noted California Mission Indian artist Scholder through the painting, photographing, and lithograph-making process. On Indian problems in Gallup, New Mexico.

IN THE SPIRIT OF CRAZY HORSE. Frontline (order from PBS), 1989. Most of this study of Lakota tribal ways and conflicts with the government is political, but includes footage of dances, funerals, and bloody protests in the early 70's;

useful background to culture study that must deal with divisive battles of recent decades.

Music/ Drama/ Dance:

Austin, Mary: *The Path of the Rainbow: An Anthology of Songs & Chants from Indians of North America.* (Liveright, 1934) This book is representative of an entire genre of 'first generation' American ethnologists and music collectors, many women: Natalie Curtis, Frances Densmore, Alice C. Fletcher, and others. Despite some ethnocentrism and problems of translation and interpretation, these noteworthy pioneers make a good starting point for a thorough overview.

New World Records (albums): *Songs of Earth, Water, Fire, and Sky; Songs of Love, Luck, Animals, and Magic; Turtle Dance Songs of the San Juan Pueblo.* Good audio quality, concise and accurate liner notes by Alfonso Ortiz and others, a respected scholarly record label make these music samples very worthwhile.

Black Bear, Ben, Sr., and Theisz, R. D.: *Songs and Dances of the Lakota.* North Plains, 1976. A welcome resource by a Lakota elder.

Canyon Records, Phoenix, Arizona (albums): *Gallup Intertribal Ceremonial Dances*: Live recordings available on cassette from several of the recent annual intertribal dances provide a broad spectrum of tribal music. Canyon has extensive catalog of Native American music of the Southwest.

Art:

Adams, Clinton: *Fritz Scholder: Lithographs.* (1975) Good source for making slides of Scholder's lithographs of the 60's and early 70's.

Berkhofer, Robert E.: *The White Man's Indian: Images of the American Indian From Columbus to the Present.* Vintage, 1979. Useful and comprehensive illustrated look at mythic portrayals & stereotypes in various media, and the prejudices and approaches of recorder/interpreters through American history.

Curtis, Edward S.: *The North American Indian.* An exhaustive and important photographic record of Native Americans from the early 1900's, these volumes have been reprinted in the 1970's. Portrayal of Indian lifeways, clothing, spirituality, and differing interpretations of a 'dying' race, a changing/unchanging people, etc. Note also 1991 studies of other photographers by Patricia Broder and M. K. Keegan, and photo essays of Ansel Adams, Kate Cory, & Laura Gilpin.

Dockstader, Frederick J.: *Song of the Loom: New Traditions in Navaho Weaving.* Hudson, 1987. A close careful study of rug patterns, styles, & changes, this well-illustrated text yields some useful color slides.

Northland Press, Flagstaff, AZ: *Beyond Tradition: Contemporary Indian Art and its Evolution* (1988) and other works. This small, high-quality publishing house has put out distinguished art books that provide sources for excellent color slides. Also available in a VHS video; *Artistry in Clay; Our Voices, Our Land; Hopi Silver; Hopi Kachinas; The Weavers Pathway;* also available are books of legends, photography, and literature.

Trimble, Stephen: *Talking With the Clay: The Art of Pueblo Pottery.* School of American Research Press, 1987. In-depth and well illustrated, this is a good source dealing with many aspects of Pueblo clay artistry.

NOTE: The art critic and anthropologist Jamake Highwater has offended many Native American peoples by claiming to be Blackfeet Indian when he apparently is not. While his significant written output is insightful, as are his film documentaries, in my opinion, including him in a guide to authentic resource materials would be inappropriate at this time.--Keith Atwater. ED. NOTE: Contrast this opionion to Donath's in Checklist A.--BC

III. MEXICAN-AMERICAN ARTS

General Reference:

Bruce-Novoa, Juan: *Chicano Authors: Inquiry by Interview.* University of Texas Press, 1980. A series of oral interviews, transcribed, and in some cases translated from Spanish, reveal the thoughts and influences of 14 authors, including Rivera, Anaya, Arias, Mendez-M, and Portillo. Candid and insightful.

Pettit, Arthur: *Images of the Mexican American in Fiction and Film.* Texas A&M Press, 1980. Useful overview of Anglo stereotypes and images of Mexicans and Mexican-Americans from the early 1800's through mid-1970's film and television reveals Anglo interpretations of Greaser and bandito and everything in between, from *Viva Zapata* to TV westerns to *Milagro Beanfield War.*

Trejo, Arnulfo, ed.: *The Chicanos as We See Ourselves.* University of Arizona Press, 1979. A variety of important voices in Chicano studies provide insights into Chicano heritage, identity, political activism, women's roles, Spanish language in culture and education, and literature and drama.

Valdez, Luis and Steiner, Stan, ed.: *Aztlan: An Anthology of Mexican American Literature.* Knopf, 1973. Wide-ranging, inclusive collection includes early texts and reflections of Aztec heritage, poetry, the growth of the Chicano movement, historical roots of Anglo-Mexican tension as revealed in the arts, drama, the role of the church, la Tierra (the earth), women, and migrant workers. Other similar collections are *We Are Chicanos* (1973) edited by Philip Ortego, *Voices of Aztlan* (1974) edited by Harth and Baldwin, and *Mestizo,* (1978) edited by Jose Arman.

West, John O.: *Mexican-American Folklore*. August House, 1988. Helpful all-purpose reference provides background on folk tales, religion, herbal remedies, arts, especially mural art, traditional holidays, dance, architecture, foods, games. Illustrated.

Autobiography/Biography:

Galarza, Ernesto: *Barrio Boy*. University of Notre Dame Press, 1971. Like Kingston, some Chicano authors use a novelistic approach to explore their formative years, in this case, a boy growing up in a corner of an American city.

Acosta, Oscar Zeta: *The Autobiography of a Brown Buffalo,* 1972. Another novel as autobiography. Concerned with recovering authentic Mexican-American identity.

Rodriguez, Richard: *Hunger of Memory: The Education of Richard Rodriquez*. Bantam, 1982. Many Chicanos feel Rodriguez "sold out" his ethnicity with his unpopular stand on bilingual education. But despite, or perhaps because of the sharp conflict, this book deserves a look. The sections on family and Catholicism are poignant and well done.

Novels:

Anaya, Rudolfo: *Bless Me, Ultima*. Tonatiuh-Quinto, 1972. A justifiably acclaimed novel, one of the few taught in college literature classes. It's all there: coming-of-age, folk religion, spirituality, symbolism, family, and nature. More accessible, mythical and political is his novel *Heart of Aztlan* (1976), a good introductory text for lower division, community college, or even high school classes.

Brito, Aristeo: *The Devil in Texas*. Bilingual Press, Tempe, AZ, 1990. This fascinating and dense short novel, published in Spanish and English in the same edition, weaves small-town U.S.-Mexico border politics, clashes and racism with a mythical and allegorical exploration of cultural past & present.

Short Stories/Essays:

Romano V, Octavio ed.: *El Espejo: the Mirror--Selected Chicano Literature*. 1972

Portillo-T, Estela: *Rain of Scorpions and other Writings*. Tonatiuh. 1975

Poetry:

Gonzales, Rudolfo (Corky): *I Am Joaquin!* (Bantam, 1972)

Soto, Gary: *The Elements of San Joaquin* (University of Pittsburgh, 1977) *The Tale of Sunlight* (University of Pittsburgh, 1978), *Who Will Know Us?* (Chronicle, 1990), *Home Course in Religion* (Chronicle, 1991).

Zamora, Bernice: *Restless Serpents*. (Disenos Literarios 1976)

Films/Documentaries:

Valdez, Luis: LA BAMBA; PBS television: MI OTRO YO ("My Other Self")

Music/Plays:

Valdez, Luis: *Actos, Zoot Suit,* "Huelga en General" (UFW Songs album)

Los Lobos: *Pistola y el Corazon.* Linda Ronstadt: *Canciones de mi Padres*

IV. ASIAN-AMERICAN ARTS

General Reference:

Chin, Frank, et al: *AIIIEEEEE! An Anthology of Asian-American Writers.* Doubleday, 1975. Significant collection of representative fiction as valuable for its critical commentary and cogent introduction as it is for its fine cross-section of Chinese-, Japanese-, and Filipino-American literature samplings.

Chin, Frank, et al: *The Big Aiiieeeee!: Chinese-American and Japanese-American History and Literature.* Howard University Press. Coming out eight years after their first study, this probing critical commentary takes advantage of recent scholarship as it reveals stereotypes and misconceptions in Asian-American letters and Anglo-American responses.

Hsu, Francis L.K.: *Challenge of the American Dream: The Chinese in the United States.* Wadsworth Press, 1971. Offers some cogent and useful observations of assimilation, migration, prejudice, and identity in American life.

Kim, Elaine H.: *Asian-American Literature: An Introduction to the Writings and their Social Context.* Temple University Press, 1982. Thorough and balanced criticism offers insights into the work of Okada, Kingston, Bulosan, Mori, and others as it clarifies reactions, misinterpretations, and key meanings of these texts in connection with identity, community, & dominant culture.

Autobiography/Biography:

Bulosan, Carlos: *America is in the Heart,* 1946. Excerpted in *Aiiieeee,* this lesser known work by a Filipino immigrant who worked in the fields and gambled in the back rooms of California ethnic neighborhoods shows compellingly the pains and problems of life as a 'hyphenated American.'

Kingston, Maxine Hong: *Woman Warrior: Memoirs of a Girlhood Among Ghosts.* Random House, 1975. Beautifully written, this memorable book is already a minor classic in multicultural studies. Also notable is her *China Men* (1980).

Novels:

Chu, Louis: *Eat A Bowl of Tea,* 1961. Considered the first major Chinese-American novel, this well-crafted blend of comedy and pathos led to a fine film version. Issues of generational conflict and domestic life in America are developed here.

Kadohata, Cynthia: *Floating World*, Viking, 1989. About an adolescent girl's experiences following family and work across western America and her relationship with her feisty grandmother. An enjoyable and thought-provoking contemporary novel.

Kogawa, Joy: *Obasan,* David R. Godine, 1982. Kogawa's wry, luminous, touching prose marks this autobiographical novel, taught in Asian-American literature courses with success.

Okada, John: *No-No Boy,* Univ. of Washington Press, 1976. Originally brought out and ignored by Japanese-Americans and critics in 1957, this intense, searing novel has reemerged as the significant fictional voice for the World War Two internee experience. Profound thoughts and emotions concerning what it means to be a loyal American, a dutiful child, a Japanese make this early novel essential reading.

Tan, Amy: *The Joy Luck Club,* Ballantine, 1989. Used in many college literature courses; probes mother-daughter relationships and, like Kingston, the power of story in cultural life.

Short Stories/ Essay:

Mori, Toshio: *Yokohama, California* 1949.

Poetry:

Garret Kaoru Hongo: *Yellow Light* (1982), *Bridge of Heaven* (1988).

Lim, Genny: *This Bridge Called My Back* (1981).

Bruchac, Joseph, ed: *Breaking Silence: An Anthology of Contemporary Asian American Poets.* Greenfield Review Press, 1983. 50 poets' work.

Films/Documentaries:

MAXINE HONG KINGSTON: TALKING STORY, PBS, 1990, 60 minutes

Music/Plays:

Chin, Frank (plays): "The Chicken Coop Chinaman" (1971), and "Year of the Dragon" (1974)

Gotanda, Philip Kan (plays): "Yankee Dawg You Die" (1989)

V. SOURCES FOR A COMPARATIVE STUDY: "FORCED MIGRATIONS: A CHRONICLE OF JAPANESE AND NATIVE AMERICAN DISPLACEMENT"

NOTE: For both Japanese-American artists (whether or not they were personally involved in the internment) and Native American artists (writers and poets), reflecting on forced migration has been absolutely central, a seminal experience to their art. This list favors works that are "primary" in the sense that they confront the migrations and their meanings.--KA

Armor, John, and Wright, Peter. *Manzanar.* NY: Times Books, 1988.

Bruchac, Joseph, ed. *Breaking Silence: An Anthology of Contemporary Asian American Poets.* Greenfield, N.Y.: Greenfield Review Press, 1984.

Conrat, Maisie and Richard. *Executive Order 9066: The Internment of 110,000 Japanese Americans.* Cambridge, Mass.: MIT Press, 1972.

Crow Dog, Mary/ Erdoes, Richard. *Lakota Woman.* 1990. NY: Harper Perrenial, 1991.

Deloria, Vine, Jr. *Custer Died for Your Sins.* 1969. NY: Avon, 1972.

Eastman, Charles A. (Ohiyesa). *From Deep Woods to Civilization.* Lincoln and London: University of Nebraska Press, 1916.

Houston, Jeanne Wakatasuki: *Farewell to Manzanar.* 1973. NY: Bantam Books, 1973.

Inouye, Daniel: *Journey to Washington.* NY: Prentice-Hall, 1967.

Kim, Elaine. *Asian American Literature: An Introduction to the Writings and their Social Context.* Philadelphia: Temple University Press, 1982.

Kogawa, Joy. *Obasan.* Boston: David R. Godine, 1981.

LePena, Frank. *The World's a Gift.* Exhibit catalogue, 1988.

McGaa, Ed (Eagle Man). *Mother Earth Spirituality.* NY: Harper & Row, 1990.

Mirikitani, Janice. *Breaking Silence.* San Francisco: Celestial Press, 1982

Miyakawa, Edward. *Tule Lake.* Seattle: House by the Sea Press, 1979.

Momaday, N. Scott. *House Made of Dawn.* NY: Harper & Row, 1968.

--------. *The Way to Rainy Mountain.* 1969. NY: Ballantine Books, 1970.

Mori, Toshio. *The Chauvinist and other Stories.* Asian American Studies Center, UCLA, 1979.

--------. *Yokohama, California.* Caldwell, Idaho: The Caxton Printers, 1949.

Neihardt, John G., trans. *Black Elk Speaks: Being the Life Story of a Holy Man of the Oglala Sioux.* 1932. NY: Pocket Books, 1972.

Niatum, Duane, ed. *Harper's Anthology of 20th Century Native American Poetry.* NY: Harper & Row, 1988.

Oishi, Gene. *In Search of Hiroshi*. Rutland, Vt: Charles E. Tuttle Company, 1988.

Okada, John. *No No Boy*, 1957. Seattle: University of Washington, 1957.

Okubo, Mine. *Citizen*, 13660. Seattle: University of Washington, 1983.

Ortiz, Simon. *Going for the Rain*. NY: Harper & Row, 1976.

--------. *A Good Journey*. Berkeley: Turtle Island, 1977.

--------. *Fight Back: For the Sake of the People, For the Sake of the Land*. Albuquerque: University of New Mexico Press, 1980.

Rosen, Kenneth, ed. *The Man to Send Rain Clouds: Contemporary Stories by American Indians*. NY: Vintage Books, 1975.

Scholder, Fritz. *Lithographs*. Exhibit catalogue, 1975.

Silko, Leslie Marmon. *Ceremony*. NY: Viking Press, 1977.

--------. *Laguna Woman*. Greenfield, N.Y.: Greenfield Review Press, 1974.

--------. *Storyteller*. NY: Seaver, 1981.

Simmons, Leo. *Sun Chief: Autobiography of a Hopi Indian*. New Haven, Conn.: Yale University Press, 1942.

Sone, Monica. *Nisei Daughter*. 1953. Seattle: University of Washington Press, 1979.

Takashima, Shizuye. *A Child in Prison Camp*. Tundra Books, 1971.

Velie, Alan R., ed. *American Indian Literature: An Anthology*. University of Oklahoma Press, 1979.

--------. *Four American Indian Literary Masters: N. Scott Momaday, James Welch, Leslie Marmon Silko, Gerald Vizenor*. University of Oklahoma Press, 1982.

Welch, James. *Riding the Earthboy 40*. NY: Harper & Row, 1971.

--------. *Winter in the Blood*. 1974. NY: Bantam Books, 1975.

Wood, Forrest G. *The Arrogance of Faith: Christianity and Race in America*. Boston: Northeastern University Press, 1991.

Yamamoto, Hisaye. *Seventeen Syllables and Other Stories*. Latham, New York.: Kitchen Table: Womer of Color Press, Inc., 1988.

Checklist C

AN AMERICAN VIDEOGRAPHY
AN ANNOTATED LISTS OF VIDEOTAPES, 16MM FILMS, AND MOVIES

compiled by Annette Hansen,
with occasional comment by Betty Ch'maj

ED. NOTE: This checklist has three sections. The selections in the first two sections, Videotapes and 16mm Films, give information (where known) on running time, year produced, and producer. Except for a few instances, I have cited the source with an abbreviation on the title line. A key to the abbreviations appears below. Unless otherwise noted, I have quoted explanatory material from the brochures or catalogs put out by the distributors cited in the Key. To update the lists and obtain more titles, write for the catalogs.--AH

Key to Sources - 16mm film and video catalogs

(CA)=Color Adjustment, Resolution Inc./California Newsreel, 149 Ninth Street, San Francisco, CA 94103

(CG) =The Cinema Guild, 1697 Broadway, New York, NY 10019, Tel.(212) 246-5522

(CON)=Context: Southeast Asians in California, ed. Judy Lewis Folsom Cordova Unified School District, 2460 Cordova Lane, Rancho Cordova, CA 95670

(FFHS)=Films For The Humanities & Sciences, Princeton, NJ

(FL)=Filmakers Library, 124 East 40th Street, New York, NY 10016, Tel.(212) 808-4980

(LCA)=Learning Corporation of America, Deerfield, IL

(OWM)=One West Media, P.O. 5766, Santa Fe, NM 87502-5766, Tel.(505) 983-8685

(PBS)=Public Broadcasting Service, 1320 Braddock Place, Alexandria, VA 22314-3337, Tel.(800) 344-3337

(VSB)=The Video Source Book, Vol I & II. Ed. David J. Weiner. Gale Research Inc., Detroit, Michigan. 1991

I. VIDEOTAPES (VHS OR BETA INDICATED):

A DAY ON THE BAY. 1989. Derry, NH: Chip Taylor Communications. 27 min; VHS. Documentary chronicles the history of Santa Cruz's Italian fishing community, from colorful 1880's beginnings through assimilation into mainstream American culture a century later.

A WRITER'S WORK WITH TONI MORRISON, PARTS I & II. Bill Moyers' A World of Ideas. (PBS) 30 min. each. Part I: Pulitzer Prize-winner Morrison discusses the characters in her work, the people in her life, and the power of love to illuminate both. Part II: She discusses the African-American presence in American literature, from the 19th century work to today.

AARON LOVES ANGELA, 1975 (VSB) 99 min; Beta, VHS. A Puerto Rican girl falls in love with a black boy amidst harsh realities of the Harlem ghetto. Directed by Gordon Parks, Jr. MPAA. RCA/Columbia Pictures Home Video.

AFTER SOLIDARITY: THREE POLISH FAMILIES IN AMERICA, 1988 (VSB) 58 min; VHS, 3/4U. Emotional chronicle of two years in the lives of three Solidarity activists forced to leave Poland and emigrate to the United States. Dist: Filmakers Library, Inc.

ALEX HALEY: THE SEARCH FOR ROOTS, 198? (VSB). 18 min; Beta, VHS, 3/4U. Haley discusses his background, his own life, and his journey to Africa. Ancillary materials available. Dist: Films for the Humanities.

ALICE WALKER: A PORTRAIT IN THE FIRST PERSON, 1988. Chicago, IL: Films Incorporated. 30 min; VHS. Topics include family violence and the position of black women in America.

ALL ORIENTALS LOOK THE SAME, 1986 (VSB) 20 min; Beta, VHS, 3/4U. Confronts the prejudices and inconsistencies of the title phrase. Dist: The Cinema Guild.

AMERICA, 1973 (VSB) 52 min; Beta, VHS, 3/4U. Special order formats. In this well-known 13-program series, Alistair Cooke digs up America's roots, finding reason and order in our past. Narrated by Cooke. RELEVANT TITLES INCLUDE: 4. Inventing A Nation, 5. Gone West, 9. The Huddled Masses, 10. The Promise Fulfilled and the Promise Broken, 13. The More Abundant Life. Ancillary materials available. Prod: BBC. Dist: Time-Life Video.

AMERICA AND THE AMERICANS, 1968 (VSB) 54 min; Beta, VHS, 3/4U; 2 programs. Two-part series based on narrator John Steinbeck's insight into what America is and what it will be. Several controversial areas covered-- conservation, civil rights, destructive use of natural assets, political systems, and corporate image. Dist: CRM/McGraw-Hill.

AMERICA AT THE MOVIES, 1976 (VSB) 116 min; Beta, VHS. Scenes from over eighty motion pictures tell the story of America in the movies under such headings as "The Land," "The Cities," "Families," "War," and "The Dream." Includes scenes from "The Birth of a Nation," "Citizen Kane," "Yankee Doodle

Dandy," "Dr. Strangelove," "East of Eden," Charlie Chaplin and Buster Keaton films, new and old westerns. Dist: RCA/Columbia Picture Home Video.

AMERICA BECOMING,1991 (PBS) 90 min. Director Charles Burnett captures the dynamic of a changing America, where great waves of newcomers are once again seeking the land of opportunity. Feelings and stories of ordinary people in everyday context in interviews from across the country Features songs, poetry, dance, & language from the diverse nationalities. Dist: WETA

AMERICA: A PICTURE IN THE MIND, 1976 (VSB) 10 min; Beta, VHS, 3/4U. Documents America's vision of personal freedom through art and historical footage, and through the words of John F. Kennedy and Martin Luther King, Jr. Dist: Media Guild.

AMERICAN EXPERIENCE, THE. 1988-91. (PBS) A 29-part series which provides compelling introductions to critical issues; each 60 min. The following seem the most pertinent (see others in Musicography):

A FAMILY GATHERING. The dramatic story of the consequences of the U.S. internment policy on the Yasui family. Masua Yasui emigrated from Japan to Oregon in the early 1900's, established a dry goods store and sent for his fiancee. He was a respected figure in the community until December 12, 1941, after Pearl Harbor, when he was arrested as a "potentially dangerous" enemy alien and interned along with many other Japanese-Americans.

GOD BLESS AMERICA AND POLAND TOO. Humorous and moving story of 94-year old Frank Popiolek, who arrived in America from Poland on a steamship in 1911 at age 15.

JOURNEY TO AMERICA. The personal story of people who came to America between 1890 and 1920, during the largest single recorded migration in human history. Rare archival materials are interlaced with oral interviews to capture the excitement and drama of this momentous journey.

LOS MINEROS .The story of Mexican-American miners and their struggles to shape the course of Arizona history. Recounts the rise and fall of the sister cities of Clifton-Morenci, where the mining of copper ore governed the lives of all the inhabitants. Rare film, interviews and contemporary footage of the towns and miners tell the story.

==

AMERICAN SHORT STORY, THE. Video series. (PBS) VHS. Relevant titles:

THE BLUE HOTEL by Stephen Crane. 55 min. The story of a Swedish immigrant and a tragedy he may or may not have caused.

THE DISPLACED PERSON by Flannery O'Connor 58 min. Set in Georgia in the late 1940's. A Polish family comes to America to work on a farm and meets with tragedy. A poignant picture of how the fragile balance of relationships between a white landowner and the blacks and poor whites who work for her is tipped when a foreigner unfamiliar with the Southern system enters the picture.

NOON WINE by Katharine Anne Porter. 81min. Story of a Swedish immigrant who starts a job on a farm and causes the downfall of his new employer.

THE SKY IS GRAY by Ernest J. Gaines. 46 min. In Louisiana in the 1940's, a young boy becomes aware of what it means to black in a white world.

===

AMISH; NOT TO BE MODERN, THE. 1985 (FL) 57 min; VHS An exclusive portrait of day-to-day life in a rarely-filmed religious community that separates itself from the world. Stirring Amish hymns, composed in the 1500's and handed down orally, complete the soundtrack.

AN AMERICAN STORY WITH RICHARD RODRIGUEZ, 1990. (WNET and WTTV) Two 30 min. VHS. Bill Moyers' A World of Ideas. The author of *Hunger of Memory*, the controversial volume on many reading lists, shares experiences of growing up in America as the son of immigrants, the loss of his "Mexican soul," and his first exposure to American culture. Includes his observations on America's growing sense of loss and American society today.

ANCESTRAL VOICES, 1989 (PBS) 60 min. Bill Moyers' Power of the Word, a six-part series featuring poets. Episode includes poets who turn to the past and their own cultural heritage to understand the present. Garrett Kaoru Hongo's poetry reflects his Japanese-American heritage, his desire "more than anything to belong to the history of Asians in America." Joy Harjo, a member of the Creek tribe, writes poetry influenced by her Native American heritage, emphasizing the oral traditional and sacred imagery of her people. Mary Tall Mountain's poetry reflects her Native American and Anglo heritage. And so on.

BLOODLINES AND BRIDGES: THE AFRICAN CONNECTION, 1986. (WTYS/ PBS) 30 min. Marian Crawford, an orphan searching for her family's lineage, traces her roots back to Africa. Personal commitment to African values is the focus. An unusual program; also features a traditional African dance troupe and the Aisha Shule school, where children learn both social consciousness and the history of Africans and African-Americans.

BLUE COLLAR AND BUDDHA, 1987 (CON) Taggart Siegel and Kati Johnston, Siegel Productions, P.O. Box 6123, Evanston,IL 6202 Tel. (312) 528-6563.

VHS. Juxtaposes the Lao refugee community, building a Buddhist temple in Rockford, Illinois, with the locals at a neighborhood drinking establishment. Contains unedited language, possibly too profane for classroom use, but it illustrates all the usual stereotypes and derogatory statements.

COLOR ADJUSTMENT: BLACKS IN PRIME TIME, 1991 Dir. Marlon Riggs. 90 min. "A broadcast quality documentary that traces the development of images of blacks on prime-time TV from the 1950's to the late 1980's. Footage from programs such as 'Beulah,' 'All in the Family,' 'The Jeffersons,' and 'Frank's Place.' Interviews with producers and stars."--ASA Program, 1991.

ETHNIC NOTIONS, 1986 (CA) Dir: Marlon Riggs. 56 min; VHS. Traces the evolution of the deeply rooted stereotypes which have fueled anti-black prejudice. Loyal Toms, carefree Sambos, faithful Mammies, grinning Coons, savage Brutes and wide-eyed Pickanninies roll across the screen in cartoons, feature films, popular songs, advertisements, household artifacts, even children's rhymes. Narration by Esther Rolle and commentary by respected scholars shed light on the origins and consequences of a 150-year-long parade of bigotry, situating each stereotype historically in white society's shifting needs to justify racist oppression from slavery to the present.

FAMILY ACROSS THE SEA, 1991 (CA) 56 min. VHS This film shows how scholars have uncovered the connection between the Gullah people of South Carolina and the people of Sierra Leone, a powerful demonstration of how African Americans kept ties with their homeland in speech, songs and customs through centuries of oppression.

FAMILY ALBUM,THE. 1987 (FL) 60 min. VHS Utilizing a vast collection of rare 16mm home movies from the 1920's through the 1950's Alan Berliner has skillfully created an intimate composite portrait of American family life.

FROM MY GRANDMOTHER'S GRANDMOTHER UNTO ME, 1990. (CG) Dir: John David Allen. 52 min. VHS The storytelling tradition of the southern Appalachians comes vividly to life through actress/writer Clarinda Ross's portrayal of four generations of her maternal ancestors.

GIRL WHO SPELLED FREEDOM, THE. (CON) Disney Movie, about 2 hours, [n.d.] The story of a Cambodian mother and six children who were sponsored by a Kentucky family; Lin Yann went on to be the national spelling bee winner.

GREAT BRANCHES, NEW ROOTS; THE HMONG FAMILY, 1984 .(CON) Hmong Film Project, 2258 Commonwealth Avenue, St.Paul, MN 55108. 52 min. VHS Opens with animated "Flood" folktale; explains and documents the Hmong concept of "family," and how the family is faring in the United States.

HAPPY BIRTHDAY MRS. CRAIG. (FL) 55 min. VHS Five generations of a black family and their role in the American experience are celebrated at Mrs. Lulu Sadler Craig's 102nd birthday party.

HERO STREET, U.S.A., 1984. Atlanta, GA: Modern Talking Picture Service. 28 min. VHS. Tells of eight Mexican-Americans boys whose families emigrated to the U.S. from Mexico about 1910 who grew up in the U.S.A. and fought and died in World War II.

HIDDEN HERITAGE; THE ROOTS OF BLACK AMERICAN PAINTING, 1990 Falls Church, VA: Landmark Films. 52 min; VHS. Traces works of Black American artists from the American Revolution to World War II, placing artists' individual achievements in the context of social change, abolition of slavery, Jim Crow laws, racial violence and segregation.

JAMES BALDWIN; THE PRICE OF THE TICKET, 1990. (CA) 87 min. VHS Captures the passionate intellect and courageous writing of a man (Baldwin) who was born black, impoverished, gay, and gifted. Archival footage evokes the atmosphere of Baldwin's formative years, newsreel clips record his running commentary on the Civil Rights movement, and writers Maya Angelou, Amiri Baraka, Ishmael Reed, William Styron and biographer David Leeming place Baldwin's work in the African-American literary tradition. The film skillfully links excerpts from his major books to different stages in black-white dialogue.

JEWS AND AMERICANS, 1989. Boston: CineResearch Assoc. 30 min. VHS. Jews speak out about their sense of identity & how they are seen by non-Jews.

LA OFRENDA, 1989. Los Angeles: Direct Cinema, Ltd. 50 min. VHS. A non-traditional look at Mexican ceremonies and rituals observed in both Mexico and the U.S. to celebrate the Days of the Dead.

LORRAINE HANSBERRY: THE BLACK EXPERIENCE IN THE CREATION OF DRAMA, 1975. (FFHS) Traces the artistic growth of playwright Lorraine Hansberry, largely in her own words and own voice.

LOUISE ERDRICH & MICHAEL DORRIS, 1989 (WNET and WTTV/ PBS). 30 min. VHS. Bill Moyers' A World of Idea. Louise Erdrich and Michael Dorris talk about American Indians' status and condition in modern America.

MAKO, 1979 Annandale, VA: Educational Film Center. 29 min. VHS. A Hollywood actor takes the viewer on a detailed excursion into the world of Asian movie stereotypes.

MAYA ANGELOU. (PBS) 60 min.VHS Bill Moyers' Creativity series. Moyers accompanies Maya Angelou on her return to her home town, noting the ways that memory and experience impinge upon art.

MY YIDDISHE MOMME McCOY 1991 (CG) Dir: Bob Giges. 20 min. VHS An intimate portrait of 90-year-old Belle Demner McCoy. Her story reflects eighty years of change in America--the loosening of Jewish tradition, the strengthening and adaptation of Jewish culture in a new world, and the growing idea of marriage as an institution for love rather than a means to preserve tradition.

NATIVE AMERICAN IMAGES, 1980. (VSB) 25 min; Beta, VHS, 3/4U. Peace pipe symbolism, the religious ceremony of the sweat lodge, and the spiritual significance of group dancing are featured. Taken from 1979 World Symposium on Humanity. Dist: Lionel Television Productions.

NATIVE LAND, THE. 1976 (VSB) 25 min; Beta, VHS, 3/4U. An insight into Indian life and thoughts about land and heritage, told from the Indian's point of view. Dist: Atlantis Productions.

ON MY OWN: THE TRADITIONS OF DAISY TURNER, 1987. (FL) The University of Vermont and Vermont Folklife Center. 28 min. VHS Stories of a 102-year-old black woman who grew up in rural Vermont show us how a black family could flourish in a New England town.

OTHER VOICES, OTHER SONGS: THE GREEKS, and OTHER VOICES OTHER SONGS: THE ARMENIANS. (FL) 30 min each. Sapphire Productions. Traditional music and dance brought by immigrants to America helped newcomers bridge the gap between their old and new homes. THE GREEKS examines the roots of Hellenic music. Authentic songs and dances by several Greek-American companies. THE ARMENIANS celebrates the survival of a people despite persecution. Performances by several folk music and dance companies, including the Sayat Nova Armenian Folk Dance Company.

OURSELVES, 1979. Annandale, VA: Educational Film Center. 29 min; VHS. Five women share what it is like to grow up Asian and female in America.

PRIMAL MIND, THE. 1987 (PBS) 60min. VHS Superbly written and narrated by noted art historian Jamake Highwater, this multidisciplinary, multicultural show reveals key ideas, similarities, and differences between Anglo-European and Native American architecture, dance, sculpture, painting, views of nature and time, using skillful interplay of materials by California Indians, Fritz Scholder, Jackson Pollock, Martha Graham, Navajo art, Medieval and Celtic arts, etc.

SPIRIT TO SPIRIT; NIKKI GIOVANNI, 1987 .Los Angeles: Direct Cinema, Ltd. 28 min. VHS. Poet Nikki Giovanni reads from her work. Performance footage, excerpts from interviews, archival film footage and stills.

STORIES OF MAXINE HONG KINGSTON, THE. Parts I & II. Bill Moyers' A World of Ideas (PBS). Two 30 min. programs. Kingston offers new images of America as a "melting pot" where the dutiful notions of the Puritans blend with the Monkey Spirit of the Orient to produce a new American consciousness.

SUBVERSION? 1970. Washington, D.C.: Public Television Library. 27 min; 3/4 VHS. Narrated personal experiences and the tragic images in Dorothea Lange's photos give an intimate view of the Japanese American detainment camps.

SUSUMU, [n.d.], a film by Gei Zantzinger. Constant Springs Productions. 22D Hollywood Avenue, Ho-Ho-Kus, NJ 07423. Tel.(201)652-1989. Fax.(201) 652-1973. A musical dedication to the Japanese Americans interned during WWII, featuring Sumi Tonooka's Tone Poem in Three Movements. A deeply personal look at one family's experiences in internment camps is captured in Tonooka's music, family photographs, archival footage and interviews.

TONGUES UNTIED. Marlon Riggs, director. Award-winning PBS documentary on black gay men.

TROUBLE BEHIND, 1991. (CA) 56 min. VHS. A powerful 2-part documentary. Part I uncovers the origins of today's racism in the history of a seemingly typical American small town. Includes new clips from "Birth of a Nation." Part II explores how the town's present citizens evade and deny their town's "whites only" reputation. Beautifully shot and imaginatively edited, the film uses oral history to show how memory both preserves and represses the past.

VOICES OF MEMORY[n.d.] From Bill Moyers' The Power of the Word (PBS). 60 min. Interviews with two poets. Gerald Stern's poems resurrect and reconstruct past experience, and his Jewish heritage provides him with inspiration and direction for his search. Li-Young Lee's poetry reflects his struggle with his Chinese heritage.

WOMEN OF SUMMER, THE : AN UNKNOWN CHAPTER OF AMERICAN SOCIAL HISTORY, 1986 (FL) 55 min. VHS Award-winning NEH documentary captures an historic moment when feminists, unionists, and educators came together to pursue a common social ideal from 1921 to 1938. Folksingers Holly Near and Ronnie Gilbert help to celebrate with the alumnae.

WHERE THE SPIRIT LIVES, 1989 The American Playhouse series. (PBS) Amazing Spirit Productions/ order from Atlantis Releasing, distributor. "A young native girl is lured from her home, torn from her family and carried off to a world she can't understand. Based on true events, it is a story of courage, hope and deviance."--Leader to the PBS showing, which is followed by a documentary film, GOING BACK TO THE BLANKET, which includes footage on location of WHERE THE SPIRIT LIVES, interviews with those who actually attended "residential schools for Indians" such as the drama portrays, and Native American commentators. 120 min. *Excellect film to pair not only with the documentary footage provided but also another on the Carlisle School for Indians (PBS) and to* Dances with Wolves. *Although it has the same Good guys/Bad guys dichotomy--in reverse--that Shoots the Ghost rejects (see Essay #10), this is an effective antidote to the movie and teaches well.--BC*

YELLOW TALE BLUES: TWO AMERICAN FAMILIES .(FL) 30 min. VHS. An innovative documentary on ethnic stereotypes. Clips from Hollywood movies reveal nearly a century of disparaging images of Asians. These familiar images are juxtaposed with portraits of the Choys, an immigrant, working class family, and Tajimas, a fourth-generation middle class California family, whose efforts to establish themselves in America make the celluloid images seem both laughable and sad.

POSTSCRIPT: In addition to YELLOW TALE BLUES, these titles of Asian-American films and plays should be added: 1000 PIECES OF GOLD, EAT A BOWL OF TEA, COME SEE THE PARADISE, & PACIFIC OVERTURES.

II. 16 MM FILMS:

A SLAVE'S STORY; RUNNING A THOUSAND MILES TO FREEDOM, 1972. Oberon Communications. 26 min. Dramatizes the true story of William and Ellen Craft's escape from slavery in 1848, including their flight from Macon, Georgia, to Philadelphia, Pennsylvania. Features Ossie Davis.

BILL COSBY ON PREJUDICE, 1971 Pyramid Film and Video. 25 min. Cosby in a satiric diatribe: a super bigot sees himself as the common man on the street. Discusses stereotyping of old people, Blacks, Italians, Scots, Midwesterners, women and others, as lazy, aggressive, irreligious, and overly religious.

BLACK ARTISTS IN AMERICA, 1975. Los Angeles: Handel Film Corp. 20 min. Prominent Black artists talk about their backgrounds, art, and role in society. Charles Alston, Romare Bearden, Ernest Cricholow, Sam Gilliam, Jr., Hughie Lee-Smith, Norman Lewis, Merton Simpson and others. Music by Ahmad Jamal, Billy Taylor.

BLACK WOMAN, THE. 1970. Bloomington, IN: National Educational TV. 51 min. Nikki Giovanni, Lena Horne, Bibi Amina Baraka and other Black women discuss their role in contemporary society. Includes performances by singer Roberta Flack, dancer Lorretta Abbott, and poet Giovanni.

DISCOVERING AMERICAN INDIAN MUSIC, 1971. 29 min. BFA Films and Video, Inc. 24 min. Introduces the rich and varied musical traditions of the American Indian in the songs and dances of tribes from various parts of the country. EMI, 1979. Annandale, VA: Educational Film Center.

FROM THESE ROOTS, [n.d.] William Greaves Productions, Inc. 28 min. Explores the extraordinary artistic cultural and political flowering that took place in Harlem during the "Roaring 20's." This vivid portrait of life during the Harlem Renaissance is created with period photographs. Narrated by Brock Peters. Original music by Eubie Blake. Winner of 22 film festival awards.

HENRY: BOY OF THE BARRIO, 1968. Atlantis Productions. 30 min. Documents two years in the life of a Mexican-American youth in the ghetto of a major city; depicts conflicts with society, economic conditions in Henry's home, his attitude towards school, the death of his father, his mother's alcoholism, loss of interest in school, and his drifting towards drugs and crime.

HOPI KACHINAS, 1961. North Hollywood, CA: FilmFair Communications. 9 min. The Hopi Kachina doll is intended primarily to teach Hopi children to see meaning in the religious rituals and dances of their people.

HUPA INDIAN WHITE DEERSKIN DANCE, 1958. Irwindale, CA: Barr Films. 11 min. Shows how ancient cultural patterns are still followed by the Hupa Indians in their ceremony.

I AM JOAQUIN, 1970. George Ballis Associates. 20 min. Dramatizes the Chicano poem by Corky Gonzales about the Mexican-American experience from Cortez to the farm workers' struggle, emphasizing problems of suppressed Mexicans.

LOON'S NECKLACE, 1949. Ontario, Canada: Crawley Films, Ltd. 10 min. Dramatizes Indian legend of how the loon received its distinguished neckband.

MI VIDA: THE THREE WORLDS OF MARIA GUTIERREZ. (OWM) 28 min. 16mm or VHS, 3/4U. At age fourteen, Maria Gutierrez was illiterate, unable to read Spanish or English, entering school for the first time in a California migrant labor camp. Four years later she won a four-year scholarship to the University of California. The film chronicles a life of hardship and ambition.

MY HANDS ARE THE TOOLS OF MY SOUL, 1977. Chicago, IL: Texture Films. 54 min. A moving film illuminating the cultural landscapes of the American Indian; permeated by the Indian sense of harmony of nature, the intimate relationship between man and his environment.

NO MAPS ON MY TAPS, 1979. Los Angeles: Direct Cinema, Ltd. 58 min. An intimate portrait of three jazz dancers, combined with film clips of the heyday of tap dancing; fascinating and entertaining part of Black culture.

OSCAR HOWE: THE SIOUX PAINTER, 1973. South Dakota Arts Council. 29 min. A contemporary American artist participates in this study of his life and work, analyzing the symbolic meanings of forms and their cultural significance in relation to his Sioux heritage.

RIGHT ON/ BE FREE, 1971. Hollywood FilmFair Communications. 15 min. Portrays experiences of African-Americans through their art, poetry and music.

STRANGE FRUIT, 1979. Washington, D.C.: American Film Institute. 33 min. Inspired by Lillian Smith's famous novel of the same name and set in Georgia in 1948, this film tells the story of Henry Brown, a Black painter who is moved to action by the "accidental" death of a voter registration organizer.

TEATRO CAMPESINO, 1979. Bloomington, IN: National Educational Television. 61 min. A history of El Teatro Campesino from its beginning in the fields to its present role as theater committed to social change on a broad front.

TOTEM POLE, 1963. Berkeley: University of California Extension Media Center. 27 min. The Northwest Pacific Coast between Puget Sound and Alaska was inhabited by many Indian tribes with complex social systems, arts and mythologies. One of their achievements was a highly sophisticated wood carving art that found its highest expression in the totem pole.

III. MOVIES ON VIDEO --"60 TEACHABLE FLICKS"

*ED. NOTE: This section lists movies that can be rented at any good video store, mostly Hollywood or television films. Out of the hundreds of possible choices, we chose sixty sample films--some old, a few new, some box office hits, some unknowns, from "Meet John Doe" to "Boyz N the Hood," from Chaplin's "The Immigrant" to Sweden's "The Emigrants"--an altogether idiosyncratic selection. The ratings (from * to *****), data, and descriptions, unless otherwise indicated, are quoted from two commercially-available catalogs,* **Video Movie Guide 1990** *(Ballantine) and* **Movies on TV and Videocassette, 1990-91** *(Bantam). The name immediately after each title is that of author, where known; the name after the rating is that of the director; next is the comment from the catalog (if any), date, and playing time. Only occasionally are actors listed. The italicized comments at the end of the citations are our own [mainly mine--*

BC]. Musicals, rock concerts, and the like which are rated by the two sources will be found in the next section, under Musicography--BC & AH.

A WEDDING. *** PG. Robert Altman. ". . . this is a good film concerning a wedding between two relatively wealthy families and the implications." 1978; 125m. *Class issues satirically presented through an ostentatious overdone wedding seen as high American cultural ritual. Might be used to compare to wedding scenes in* West Side Story, Our Town, Aaron meets Angela, *etc.*

AMERICA, AMERICA. ****Elia Kazan. 1963, 174 min. A classic version of the immigrant story, it is based on Kazan's own forebears and book. It's the tale of a young Greek's struggles to get to America. *A must to see and maybe use.*

AMERICAN GRAFFITI. ***1/2, PG. George Lucas. ". . . about the coming of age of a group of high-school students in Northern California. Superb rock 'n roll score." The movie led to the long-running TV series "Happy Days." 1973; 110m. *Portions useful to portray hegemonic 50s culture in an all-white California town whose adolescents are identified by the title as "American."*

AUTOBIOGRAPHY OF MISS JANE PITTMAN. ***** John Korty. "Superb TV movie traces black history in America from the Civil War years to the civil rights movement of the 1960s through the eyes of Jane Pittman, a 110-year old ex-slave." 1974; 110m. *May soon become a study in white views of black culture; elegiac in tone, elegant photography, obvious reconstructed Old South.*

BATTLE OF JOSIE, THE. [no ratings] *A hilarious "feminist" Western starring Doris Day, which is clearly anti-feminist in its interpretation & useful as such.*

BOUND FOR GLORY.* *** Hal Ashby. The story of Woody Guthrie, rich with songs. Like *Grapes of Wrath,* a story of Depression years. 1976, 147 min. *Issues of class, region, migration--the 1930s seen in terms of the 1970s.*

BOYS IN THE BAND. *** William Friedkin. "Award-winning film about a gay birthday party retains much of the qualities of pathos, bitchiness, loneliness, and jealousy that so enriched the play." 1970, 118 min. *A seminal work in 1970, still one of few works treating the emotional struggles of gay men.*

BOYZ N THE HOOD. **** John Singleton. 1992. A stunning account of young blacks growing up in modern Central L.A. neighborhoods. *No data in the movie books yet, but teachers are already using it widely. Family issues, role of fathers in black culture, rap music--a chilling anticipation of L.A.'s 1992 riots.*

CATTLE QUEEN OF MONTANA. ** "Barbara Stanwyck tries to protect her farm from land grabbers who have murdered her father, while the Indians are out to wipe out everybody." 1954; 88m. *Because a former president of the United States (Ronald Reagan) plays in it, teachers may find it has more impact than other Westerns as a demonstration of the way Hollyood constructed the history of the West in "B Westerns" of the era, how it portrayed Indians and women.*

CHARLIE CHAPLIN--THE EARLY YEARS, Vol. 1. Chaplin, Charles. ***** "A collection of early Chaplin shorts, including "The Immigrant," where Charlie, in love but broke on the boat to America manages to survive. B&W.1917; 62m.

CHINA GIRL. *** Abel Ferrara. "The Romeo-and-Juliet story in a contemporary gang format without becoming an ersatz *West Side Story*. In this case, the lovers hail from Little Italy and Chinatown in Lower Manhattan." 1987; 88min.

COLOR PURPLE, THE ***** PG-13. Steven Spielberg. "Spielberg's adaptation of Alice Walker's Pulitzer Prize-winning novel about growth to maturity and independence of a mistreated black woman. . . . Celebrates kindness, compassion, and love." 1985; 130m. *Although I did not like what it did to the book, most of my students by now have seen it--proving Alice Walker was right: the film opens doors for many who would not likely read her book.--BC*

CROSSING DELANCEY. *** Joan Silver. "Ethnic slice of life, romantic comedy with an upwardly mobile Jewish girl who is fixed up with a down to earth man who sells pickles for a living." 1988, 97 min.

DEATH OF A SALESMAN. Miller, Arthur **** Volker Schlandorff. "Thoughtful TV version of the aging, embittered Willy Loman (Dustin Hoffman), who realizes that he has wasted his life and that of his family." 1985; 135m. *Miller's classic could introduce themes of success and family relationships in "middle America" against which to compare those of other racial and regional groups.*

DO THE RIGHT THING **** Spike Lee. Tells the story of a hot day in Brooklyn's Bedford-Stuyvesant area where racial tension erupts into violence. Issues of police brutality, Korean-black tensions are dramatized. The roles Lee assigns to women have been challenged, but this is a fine film, with effective use of rap music. 1989; 120m. *A good film to teach with Ellison's* Invisible Man *for images of chaos related to race riots. Excellent for showing how emotions based on racial perceptions can escalate and explode.*

DOLLMAKER, THE **** Daniel Petrie. "Emmy Award for Jane Fonda's portrayal of a mother of five in Kentucky of the 1940s whose only personal happiness is sculpting dolls out of wood. Relocation when her husband is forced to leave to find work in Detroit causes hardship and setbacks." 1984; 140m. *South-to-north, rural-to-urban migration. Role of women, role of community.*

EL NORTE *** [n.d.] Brother and sister from Guatemala flee their homeland when parents are murdered and make the passage north to Los Angeles and "almost manage to realize their own version of the American Dream." 1984; 139min. *Excellent film; teaches well as a contrast to stories like "Ellis Island," below.*

ELLIS ISLAND. *** Jerry London. TV miniseries follows the lives of three immigrants to the U.S. at the turn of the century and their struggle for acceptance, happiness, and success in the promised land. 1984; 310m. *See my syllabus. It is so corny in its music and visual excess, it teaches quitewell.*

EMIGRANTS, THE. **** Jan Troel. With Liv Ullmann, Max von Sydow. "Touching story of the hardships of a Swedish peasant family who came to the American midwest in the 19th century. . . A stirring reaffirmation of the faith, bravery, and inner strength of human beings." 1971, 148 min. *A real classic!*

FOR LOVE OF IVY **** Daniel Mann. "Sidney Poitier delivers a terrific performance as a trucking company owner by day and gambling operator by night. Ivy (Abbey Lincoln), maid to a wealthy family, decides to leave their employ and the family's children, but they connive to get Parks to take her out and make her happy." 1968; 101m. *It's time to look again at this genre of films.*

GO TELL IT ON THE MOUNTAIN. ** Adaptation of James Baldwin's early novel about a Harlem family in the 1930s. 1985, 117min. *Worth using (with the book) if only for the singing at The Church of the Fire Baptized.*

GOD'S LITTLE ACRE *** Anthony Mann. Version of the Erskine Caldwell story that focuses on poor, itinerant farmers in Georgia. B&W; 1958; 110m. *Egad.*

GODFATHER EPIC, THE. Puzo, Mario ***** R. Francis Ford Coppola. "An expanded compilation of the two Godfather films for videotape; a masterwork that is is greater than the sum of its parts." 1977; 380m. *So they say.*

GONE WITH THE WIND. Mitchell, Margaret (adaptation) ***** Victor Fleming. "All-time classic of star-crossed lovers in the final days of the Old South in the Civil War." 1939; 222m. *Can be used for the same reason Willoughby teaches "Showboat"--to illuminate racist and sexist stereotypes in a 5-star blockbuster.*

GOOD EARTH, THE. Buck, Pearl. (adapt.)**** Sidney Franklin. "Richly detailed, Nobel Prize story and Oscar-winning film of a simple Chinese farm couple whose lives are ruined by greed. Outstanding photography." B&W; 1937; 138m. *It is interesting to have Asian American students evaluate this film.*

GUESS WHO'S COMING TO DINNER? *** Stanley Kramer. "One of the first films to deal with interracial marriage, daring in its day. 1967; 108m. *Useful.*

HESTER STREET **** PG. Joan Micklin Silver. "Beautifully filmed look at the 19th century New York City Jewish community with great period detail. Focuses on a young couple; he turns his back on old Jewish ways and she fights to hold on to them." *This is a favorite among college teachers.*

HISTORY OF WHITE PEOPLE IN AMERICA. ***1/2 Harry Shearer. "Martin Mull narrates a spoof on white heritage, hobbies, and food preferences that takes us to the Institute for White Studies and into the home of a very white family. Made for cable TV; unrated, contains obscenities and sexual topics."

1986; 48min.*[sic]*. *The very fact that a "two-volume" film (see Vol.II, below) with such a title has been made may be enough to drive home the point.*

HISTORY OF WHITE PEOPLE IN AMERICA (Vol. II). ***1/2. Harry Shearer. "Four episodes of the very white Harrison family: 'White Religion' has Mom and Dad (Fred Willard, Mary Kay Place) dealing with their daughter's teen pregnancy. 'White Stress' has Mom coming unglued, seeing a psychiatrist, and trying to relax. In 'White Politics' Dad runs for water commissioner because their water is polluted. Last, 'White Crime' finds Dad, son, and Martin Mull in court with Eileen Brennan as judge." Contains obscenities. 1986; 100m.

HOW THE WEST WAS WON. *** "Spectacle about the American pioneer spirit. A family of New England farmers heads west in the 1830s." 1963; 155min. *Shows values and exclusions typical of "old Western" (as distinct from "new Western") history--the construction of the West as antagonist to be "won."*

I KNOW WHY THE CAGED BIRD SINGS. Angelou, Maya (adaptation) ***1/2 Fleider Cook. "Maya Angelou's memoirs of her early life in the South during the Depression, detailing touching reactions to her parents' divorce and her grandparents' struggle to raise her and her brother." 1979; 100m. *Video version of a book that is a student favorite from reading lists for multicultural courses.*

INCIDENT AT OGLALA. Dir. Michael Apted, 1992, and THUNDERHEART, 1992. John Fusco. Dir. Michael Apted. "Nonfictional and fictional quests for the same truth--a thinking person's double feature. . . a directorial tour de force . . . a plea to social conscience that is difficult to ignore,"--*Time*, May 4, 1992. Both are about the G-men killed during a scuffle with AIM at the Pine Ridge Sioux reservation in 1975 and the framing of Leonard Peltier for the crime.

I REMEMBER MAMA. ***1/2 George Stevens. "Sentimental drama of a Norwegian family in San Francisco." B&W; 1948; 148m. TV series followed. *Sentimental? Does that mean women like it? Selected episodes are useful.*

I'M GONNA GIT YOU SUCKA! Wayans, Keenan Ivory. **** "Uproarious parody of the blaxpoitation flicks of the early Seventies. Wayans culled cast from the very films he brilliantly satirizes." 1989; 88m. *The uses of this film are suggested in that last sentence. Issues of race and gender.*

JESSE OWENS STORY, THE. *** Richard Irving. "Provocative insight into events behind the scenes that plague the not-always-admirable Olympic hero. . . A mirror of embarrassing racial attacks." 1984; 180m. *Consider pairing with the Jim Thorpe story (below) for analysis from modern perspectives.*

JEZEBEL **** William Wyler. "A spoiled Southern belle takes too long to choose between a banker and a dandy and loses it all." (Bette Davis received an Oscar in this role, given her as consolation for being turned down for the role of Scarlett O'Hara.) B&W; 1938; 103m. *Never mind the brouhaha over Davis--*

use it for the scene in which she sits on the porch in her farthingale surrounded by plantation darkies singing spirituals in perfect harmony, Hollywood style.

JIM THORPE, ALL AMERICAN *** Michael Curtis. "Burt Lancaster portrays the All-American Indian athlete who rose from obscure beginning to international fame. Sports fans will enjoy this." B&W. 1051 107m.. *See* Jesse Owens Story, *above, the essay by Shoots the Ghost, in Part II of this volume, and/or show after "Where the Spirit Lives" to inspire analysis and discussion.*

JOE *** R. John G. Avildsen. "A violent film about a bigot who ends up associating with the people he hates." 1970; 107m. *Class issues and clash between generations. I like this film for its comparison of two male American "types" and to compare to the generational gap in All in the Family.--BC*

LA BAMBA ** Written and directed by Luis Valdez, 1987. Based on the life of Ritchie Valens, the film has good illustrations of the musical interaction between Hispanic styles and 1950s rock. "Alive with the electricity of Valens' hits performed by Los Lobos as well as legendary sounds of Buddy Holly, Little Richard and Chuck Berry."--quoted from video package. 106 min.

LEARNING TREE, THE *** First film directed by Gordon Parks, famous black photographer. "Autobiography about growing up in Kansas in the mid-1920s provides a fresh perspective on being black in America." 1969; 107 min.

LIZZIE BORDEN. Louise Smith, Ellen McElduff. Compelling feminist docudrama of prostitution, the main character is Molly, a Yale graduate living with a female lover and working to become a professional photographer. Simulated sex, profanity, nudity, violence. 1987; 90m. *To some, an underground classic.*

MIGRANTS, THE *** "Worth seeing for Cloris Leachman's high-caliber portrait of an earth mother who breathes life into her clan even in the face of her own despair." 1974; 78 min.

MILAGRO BEANFIELD WAR, THE ***1/2. Dir. Robert Redford. "About a group of New Mexican villagers trying to recaim their water rights when a rapacious development company moves to turn the town into a golf course . . . engaging mixture of Capraesque populism and Latin mysticism . . ." 118m.

NEW LAND, THE **** Jan Troel. Stars Liv Ullmann, Max von Sydow. "The saga of the Oskar family documents their hardships in carving a new life in the growing U.S. in this remarkable filmed essay on foreign emigration to America." 1973, 161 min. *Sequel to The Emigrants, cited above.*

NINE TO FIVE. **** PG. Colin Higgins. "Comedic farce about three secretaries who decide to get revenge on their sexist, egomaniacal boss (Dabney Coleman)." 1980; 110m. *The critics panned it but many women loved it, and secretaries would go in groups to see it, howling and cheering together in darkened theaters over its episodes.*

PAWNBROKER, THE. ***** Sidney Lumet. "Somber, powerful portrayal of a Jew who survived the holocaust only to find his spirit still as bleak as the Harlem ghetto where he operates a pawn shop; dead emotions are shocked to life by confronting the realities of the modern city." B&W; 1965; 116m. *Yes!*

PURLIE VICTORIOUS. Davis, Ossie. ***1/2 "Alan Alda is a southern liberal. Davis and wife Ruby Dee are an evangelist couple who are trying to convert an old barn into an integrated church. Bigoted opposition from barn owner." Also known as *Gone Are the Days*. 1963; B&W; 93m. *Funny, funny, funny.*

PUTNEY SWOPE. **** R. Robert Downey. "Black man takes over a Madison Avenue advertising firm in a zany parody of American lifestyles". 1969; 88m.

RAISIN IN THE SUN, A. **** Daniel Petrie. "Limited opportunities open to blacks in the 1950s are portrayed in an enduring classic about a black family who tries to escape their crowded apartment life by moving to an all-white neighborhood." B&W; 1961; 128m. *A must! Today it's useful to show how opinions about Hansberry's classic have evolved, becoming more positive.*

RAP MASTER RONNIE--A REPORT CARD. *** Jay Dubin. "A look at the Reagan presidency through the eyes of writer Gary Trudeau." HBO special; unrated. 1988; 47m. *I saw a stage version in Washington, D. C. and thought it would be a fine teaching tool for American Studies. It is satire, of course, so biased throughout, but its use of smiling optimism as a club to impose hegemonic "American" values contrasts to angrier satires--it's subtler.--BC*

SOUNDER. ***** G. Martin Ritt. "Moving film of a black sharecropper family's struggle; when the father gets sent to jail, wife (Cecily Tyson) must raise the family, run the farm, and try to get the eldest son an education." 1972; 105m.

SOUTHERNER, THE. **** Jean Renoir. Stark life in the rural South before civil rights; dirt-poor tenant farmer struggles against insurmountable odds to maintain dignity and provide for the family. B&W. 1945; 91m. *An oldie.*

STREETCAR NAMED DESIRE, A. Williams, Tennessee. (adaptation) ***** Elia Kazan. Powerful drama of a sexually disturbed Southern belle no longer young who lives in a world of illusion that crumbles when she moves in with her sister and brutish brother-in-law. B&W; 1951; 122m. *North=male, South=female? Useful for considering together issues of region, gender, era and class.*

STREETWISE. ***** Martin Bell, et al. ". . . emotionally compelling and a highly recommended glimpse into the lives of homeless/displaced youths surviving as pimps, panhandlers, and small time drug dealers in Seattle. Explores a teenage wasteland with sensitivity. Violence and profanity." 1985; 92m.

TIME OF YOUR LIFE. Saroyan, William. ***1/2 H. C. Potter. Adaptation of a prize-winning play about the diverse regulars at Nick's Saloon and Entertainment Palace on San Francisco's Barbary Coast. B&W, 1948; 109m.

TO KILL A MOCKINGBIRD. Lee, Harper. ***** Robert Mulligan. Gregory Peck as a small-town southern lawyer defending a black man accused of rape; the children try to understand life in a small town. B&W; 1962; 129m. *A natural to pair and critique with episodes of the TV series, "I'll Fly Away."*

TORCH SONG TRILOGY. Fierstien, Harvey. (adaptation) *** R. Paul Bogart. Prize-winning comedy-drama about an insecure female impersonator looking for that one, all-encompassing relationship in a gay nightclub; Anne Bancroft is his unbending Jewish mama. 1988; 120m. *Many shocks of recognition!*

TREE GROWS IN BROOKLYN, A. **** Elia Kazan. Richly detailed, sentimental story of working class Brooklyn at the turn of the century; focuses on the happiness and tragedies of a poor Irish-American family ruled by an alcoholic father and strong-willed mother. B&W; 1945; 128m. *I loved it--BC.*

WISE BLOOD. **** PG. John Huston. Searing comedic satire on Southern do-it-yourself religion, about a slow-witted country boy who decides to become a man of the world. 1979; 108m. *An underground classic to Southerners.*

WOMAN OF DISTINCTION.* **1/2 Edward Buzzell. Rosalind Russell as a college dean who faces a tough decision concerning a professor. B&W; 1950; 85m. *Illustrates how women were once portrayed as strong in their careers.*

WOMAN OF THE YEAR. Ring Lardner and Michael Kanin ***** George Stevens. "Spencer Tracy is a sports reporter and Katharine Hepburn a famed political journalist who needs to be reminded of life's simple pleasures -- baseball; her attempts to learn the game are priceless." B&W; 1942; 112m. *Ditto, although I like "Adam's Rib" best of the nine Tracy-Hepburn films.*

==

AN AMERICAN MUSICOGRAPHY
A CHECKLIST OF FOUR CATEGORIES:
1) MUSIC ON VIDEO, 2) MUSICALS, 3) RECORDINGS, 4) BOOKS

compiled by Jan Petrie and Annette Hansen,
with occasional comment by Betty Ch'maj

CATEGORIES 1, 3, & 4: Unless otherwise indicated, the direct quotations are from the catalogs advertising the work. For more titles, write directly to the producers or consult your library's collection of media catalogs.--JP

I. MUSIC ON VIDEO

AFRO-AMERICAN MUSIC, ITS HERITAGE. 1972. (VSB) 16 min; VHS, EJ, 3/4U. 250 years of Black music, from the talking drums of West Africa to contemporary rhythm and blues, and gospel. Ancillary materials available. Prod/Dist: Communications Group West.

AMAZING GRACE. Bill Moyers (PBS) 60 min. A fine documentary tracing the history and variety of versions of a single song, examined in its contexts.

AMERICAN EXPERIENCE SERIES, THE. (The following titles from this excellent 29-program series are *primarily* about music):

BALLAD OF A MOUNTAIN MAN. Folklorist Bascom Lamar Lunsford's campaign in the 1920's to preserve the amalgamation of styles rooted in Scotch/English, African-American, Native American and other cultures which reflect America in music.

THAT RHYTHM, THOSE BLUES. In the small towns and cities of the South in the 1940's and 1950's, black rhythm-and-blues singers performed in warehouses, tobacco barns, movie theaters and halls. Endless one-night stands, makeshift housing and inadequate transportation were all a step toward the big time at the famed Apollo Theater in Harlem.

THE CALL OF JITTERBUG. 1989. (FL) 30 min; VHS. In the early 30's,the first art form to break through the color barrier swept the nation. At Harlem's Savoy Ballroom, blacks and whites danced together, probably for the first time in America. Interviews, lively vintage footage. The performers remember how dance was an antidote to the economic depression outside. Others recall bitter moments on the road where prejudice denied them a place to eat or spend the night.

THE COLORED MUSEUM, 1990. (PBS) 90min. Vibrant living theatre -- humorous sketches like "Celebrity Slaveship"; searing drama about black Vietnam soldiers, blues, gospel, dance, parodies of Arthur Miller, Shakespeare, and Hansberry's *Raisin in the Sun*. These 12 "exhibits" or skits are outstanding. Selected sketches, 5-8 min. each.

AMERICAN INDIANS OF THE PLATEAU REGION. JVC Anthology of World Music and Dance, Tape 27. Rounder Records, 61 Prospect St., Montpelier, VT 5602. (Video 2097, pt. 1-30)

AMERICAN MUSIC FROM FOLK TO JAZZ AND POP. Directed by Stephen Fleischman and Jonathon Donald. McGraw-Hill, 1967. B&W. 25 min.

AMERICAN MUSICAL THEATRE. 1986. 60 min.video in 4 parts. Presented by EAV, Pleasantville, NY. Four-part chronicle of the American musical stage from minstrel shows of the early 1800's to musical theatre of today. In Part III, Oscar Hammerstin's "Showboat" (1927) is used to mark a turning point, as the controversial subject of racial prejudice is introduced, which opened musical theatre to serious themes and social comment that followed in such shows as "Porgy and Bess." and "Pins and Needles" (an International Ladies Garment Union Revue featuring the song, "Sing Me a Song about Social Significance.") Part IV features "Oklahoma," "Pal Joey," "Lady in the Dark," Street Scene" and others based on serious themes, such as "West Side Story" and "Hair."--AH

ART BLAKEY AT THE SMITHSONIAN Director: Clark Santee, Della Gravelle Santee. "One of the great bebop drumming masters brings dynamic jazz to the Smithsonian." Blakey and the Jazz Messengers, joined by trumpeter Wynton Marsalis and saxophonist Branford Marsalis. 1982; 58 m.

BLACK MUSIC FROM THEN UNTIL NOW. ed. Roy Sandiford and George Bowers. Learning Corporation of America, Screen Gems Inc., 1971. 38 min. "Film begins with Nina Simone's feet. Enlarge to complete picture: A choir in robes sings gospel style behind her."

BLACK MUSIC IN AMERICA; FROM THEN TILL NOW. 1971. (LCA) 38 min; 16mm film. Introduces the contribution Black music has made to America in the forms of jazz, blues, spirituals, protest songs, swing, and rock and roll.

BLACK MUSIC IN AMERICA; THE SEVENTIES. 1981. Black Music Association. 32 min; 16mm. "A musical excursion through the world of Black music of the 1970's, from the Motown sound of Diana Ross to the disco beat of Donna Summer, narrated by Isaac Hayes & Dionne Warwick."

DISCOVERING AMERICAN FOLK MUSIC. Directed by Bernard Wilets. Biley Film Associates, 1969. 22 min. Color. Includes Louis Armstrong, Nina Simone, Mahalia Jackson, B. B. King, Leadbelly, King Oliver's Creole Jazz Band, Josephine Baker, Bessie Smith, Count Basie, Billie Holiday, Coleman Hawkins, Roy Eldridge, Duke Ellington.

DISCOVERING AMERICAN INDIAN MUSIC 1971 BFA Films and Video, Inc. 24 min; 16mm. "Introduces the rich and varied musical tradition of the American Indian in the songs and dances of tribes from various parts of the country, performed in authentic costumes."

DISCOVERING AMERICAN INDIAN MUSIC. Dir. by Bernard Wilets. Biley Film Associates, 1981. 24 min. Color. Music, dances and their meanings.

"GIVE MY POOR HEART EASE." Interviews and performances by B. B. King and James "Son" Thomas, Parchman Penitentiary work chants, and Wade Walton's barber shop boogie woogie. Color. 20 min. $50.00 from Center for the Study of Southern Culture.

GOOD MORNIN' BLUES. Mississippi Authority for Educational Television, 1978. Discusses roots of blues and its spread from South to North; includes Rob Johnson, Henry Spear, obscure blues singers, urban blues and jazz.

GRACELAND: PAUL SIMON IN CONCERT (PBS special).

HISTORY OF JAZZ WITH BILLY TAYLOR, A. 60 min. [source not cited] Covers background of jazz in Africa, riverboats, blues, swing, jazz in Europe, BeBop to the computer age.

HOPI: SONGS OF THE FOURTH WORLD. 1983. NY: New Day Films 58 min; 16mm. A compelling study of the Hopi that captures their deep spirituality and reveals their integration of art into daily life.

HUPA INDIAN WHITE DEERSKIN DANCE. 1958 Irwindale, CA: Barr Films. 11 min; 16mm. Shows how ancient cultural patterns are still followed by the Hupa Indians in their ceremonies.

INTERNATIONAL SWEETHEARTS OF RHYTHM, THE. 1986. (CG) 30 min. 16mm/video. "Award winning story of the multi-racial women's jazz band of the 1940's which featured some of the best female musicians of the day. Performed in major theatres and for American troops during WWII. In the South, the Sweethearts traveled, ate and slept in a bus because segregation laws prevented them from using restaurants and hotels. Examines the role of women and minorities in America in the late 30's to 40's. Interviews with surviving band members are interwoven with archival footage, musical performance, photographs and memorabilia." Rent/Purchase. *Contrast to the fictional all-white, all-girL band in the Marilyn Monroe comedy, "Some Like It Hot."*

JOPLIN: KING OF RAGTIME COMPOSERS. Narrated by Eartha Kitt. 15 min. Color. Discusses how ragtime combines European harmonies with African rhythms. Discusses life of Joplin.

ORNETTE--MADE IN AMERICA. "On Ornette Coleman, one of the most innovatIve forces in contemporary music. Performances in his home town, Fort Worth, with the local symphony orchestra. Interviews and rare early performances." With Charley Hayden, Don Cherry and Ornette's son Darnel.

ROCK 'N ROLL: THE EARLY DAYS. [no source] Featuring Chuck Berry, Fats Domino, Buddy Holly, Jerry Lee Lewis, Little Richard, Bo Diddley & more.

SONGS ARE FREE, THE. Bill Moyers interviews Bernice Johnson Reagon, founder of Sweet Honey and the Rock. (PBS) 1991. Order from Mystic Free Video, P.O. Box 1092, Cooper Station, NY, NY 10276. Tel. (800) 727-8433. *Illustrates well how to make connections between politics and poetics; good performances and commentary that is consistently interesting, about both music and culture; useful to initiate discussion on both race and gender issues--BC*

INTERNATIONAL SWEETHEARTS OF RHYTHM, THE. 1986 (CG) 30 min. 16mm/video. "Award winning story of the multi-racial women's jazz band of the 1940's which featured some of the best female musicians of the day. Performed in major theatres and for American troops during WWII. In the South, the Sweethearts traveled, ate and slept in a bus because segregation laws prevented them from using restaurants and hotels. Examines the role of women and minorities in America in the late 30's to 40's. Interviews with surviving band members are interwoven with archival footage, musical performance, photographs and memorabilia." Rent/Purchase. *Contrast to the fictional all-white all-gird band in the Marilyn Monroe comedy, "Some Like It Hot."*

TWO BLACK CHURCH SERVICES--at Rose Hill Baptist Church, Vicksburg, Miss., and St. James Church, New Haven, Conn. Produced by Yale University Films in association with the Center for Southern Folklore. Sermons, gospel choirs, faith healing, and spirit possession. 20 min. Color. $40.00 from Center for the Study of Southern Culture.

VISION SHARED--A TRIBUTE TO WOODY GUTHRIE AND LEADBELLY, A. 1988. Directed by Jim Brown. Bruce Springsteen, U2, John Cougar Mellencamp, Bob Dylan, Taj Mahal, Pete Seeger, Arlo Guthrie, Emmylou

Harris, Willie Nelson, and Little Richard pay tribute to folk pioneers, from backyard washboard bluegrass to Cougar's "Do Re Mi" and Springsteen's "I Ain't Got No Home" to Little Richard's "Rock Island Line," ending with a chilling collage of "This Land is Your Land." 1988. 72m.

WE SHALL OVERCOME. 1991. (CA) 58 min: VHS. "By tracing the sources of one song, this film uncovers the diverse strands of social history which flowed together to form the Civil Rights movement and set America marching towards racial equality. Rent/Purchase.

WILD WOMEN DON'T HAVE THE BLUES, 1989 (CA) 58 min; VHS. Through historic performances and recordings, captures the spirit of such pioneering blueswomen as Bessie Smith, Ma Rainey, and others. Affirms the role black women played in defining the independence of the New Woman of the 1920s.

WILLIAMSBURG, VIRGINIA: RECONSTRUCTED COLONIAL CITY: A MUSICAL DAY IN 1768. Colonial Williamsburg Foundation. "Shows some fine art and folk music popular during the 18th century. All buildings in Williamsburg have been restored to their original form, inside and outside. Williamsburg was the capitol of Virginia before it was moved to Richmond. The opening of the film shows some of the instruments from the Williamsburg museum collection of the 18th century." (Annotation by Professor Willoughby)

YOUNG, GIFTED AND BLACK. A historical overview that focuses on 12 singers. Some narrative serves to link performances by Louis Armstrong, Mahalia Jackson, Leadbelly, Josephine Baker, Bessie Smith, Billie Holiday, B. B. King, Edmund "Duke" Ellington, Julian "Cannonball" Adderly, Sly and the Family Stone, Irene Cara. (Annotation by Professor M. Rushkin)

II. AMERICAN MUSICALS: "BEYOND *WEST SIDE STORY*"

ED. NOTE TO CATEGORY II: The first thing to be said about the American musical is that it is a superb cultural resource for exploring multiculturalism, combining as it does music, dance, text, serious themes and "production values." The next thing to be said is that the American musical is very hard to define. As Larry Stempel has put it, despite a decade of unprecedented effort to produce "comprehensive, systematic reference works" on the subject, the definition has proved elusive. (Stempel, Book Reviews, American Music X,2 [Fall 1991]) Is King Vidor's "Hallelujah" a musical? "Girl of the Golden West"? "Shuffle Along"? "The Rise and Fall of the City of Mahagonny"? How shall we label the movie "Bird"? Where shall we list Virgil Thomson and Gertrude Stein's "Four Saints in Three Acts," Joplin's

*"Treemonisha," and Ross Lee Finney's "Weep Torn Land"? All are worth the
attention of multiculturalists, yet none appears on the checklist below.*

*Musicals being such important cultural documents, Jan, Annette and I
settled for a bibliography of general sources, followed by the "beginning of a
list." Sometimes we offer only a title, sometimes a comment--from me (in
italics) or a catalog.[1]. As in the videography, authors (when known) are named
first after the title, then (at times) directors; dates and running time (when
known) are added, but producers and actors are usually excluded.--BC*

A. MUSICALS: GENERAL SOURCES: *The video "American Musical Theater," cited above, provides a general overview. In addition:*

(1) "The single most important research tool" on the whole subject of American
    musicals, in Larry Stempel's opinion [ibid.], is Tommy Krasker and Robert
    Kimball's *Catalog of the American Musical: Musicals of Irving Berlin, George
    and Ira Gershwin, Cole Porter, Richard Rodgers and Lorenz Hart* (Washington
    D.C.: National Institute for Opera and Musical Theater, 1988) but Stempel also
    lists Cecil Smith and Glenn Litton, *Musical Comedy in America* (NY: Theatre
    Arts Books, 1981 [1950]), and Gerald Bordman, *American Musical Theatre: A
    Chronicle* (Oxford University Press, 1978; expanded, 1986) along with its
    three "spinoffs," *American Operetta* (1981), *American Musical Comedy* (1982),
    and *American Musical Revue* (1985).

(2) See also the three works edited by Stanley Green, *Encyclopedia of the Musical
    Theatre* (1980), *Encyclopedia of the Musical Film* (1981), and *Broadway
    Musicals Show by Show* (1985), and his own *The World of Musical Comedy*
    (rev. ed. 1968). A good source if you know the name of the musical is David
    Ewen's *The New Complete Book of American Musicals* (1970.) All these
    sources are cited by Jan under CATEGORY 4.

    In addition, try these titles: Gerald Boardman, *American Operetta, from HMS
    Pinafore to Sweeney Todd* (1981), Abe Laufe, *Broadway's Greatest Musicals*
    (1969), Julian Mates, *America's Musical Stage, Two Hundred Years of
    Musical Theatre* (1985), and Ethan Mordden, *Broadway Babies, the People
    Who Made the American Musical* (1983).

(3) For help in locating individual songs and tunes used in musicals, see the
    reference works by Allen L. Wolf, *Songs from Hollywood Musical Comedies,
    1927 to the Present: A Dictionary* (NY: Garland Publishing, Inc., 1976), Ken
    Bloom, *American Song: The Complete Musical Theatre Companion*, 2 vols.

---

[1]When ratings, from one to five stars, or direct quotations appear, they are taken from Mick
Martin and Marsh Porter, *Video Movie Guide 1990* (New York: Ballantine Books, 1990).

(NY: Facts on File, 1985), and Steven Suskin, *Show Tunes, 1905-1965* (NY: Dodd, Mead and Co, 1986) and the indexes by Nat Shapiro (to 1985) cited under CATEGORY 4. An interesting volume by B. Lee Cooper, *A Resource Guide to Themes in Contemporary American Song Lyrics, 1950-1985* (Greenwood Press, 1986) attempts to categorize all songs--not only songs in musicals--by theme: e.g., 21 songs are listed under "Discrimination and Prejudice" in a chapter on "Political Protest and Social Criticism," while a chapter on "Race Relations," covering some of the same works, subdivides and briefly describes works under the headings "Black Pride," "Brotherhood of Man," "Personal Concerns," and "Social and Economic Conditions."

(4) For discography, consult Jack Raymond, *Show Music on Record from the 1890s to the 1980s* (NY: Frederick Unger, 1982) and David Hummel, *The Collector's Guide to the American Musical Theatre*, 2 vols. (The Scarecrow Press, 1984).

B. MUSICALS: THE BEGINNING OF A LIST

AIN'T MISBEHAVIN.' A Musical Revue based on the music of the great black pianist and composer Fats Waller. 1978.

AL JOLSON STORY, THE. Dir. Alfred W. Green. Larry Parks lip synchs as Jolson sings in his life story of show business in vaudeville and on Broadway. His blackface innocence invites analysis from us today. B&W; 1946; 128m. *All you need of this is 10 minutes of Jolson singing "Mammie" to see the point.*

ANNIE GET YOUR GUN. Music and lyrics by Irving Berlin. Co-librettist Dorothy Fields. The Broadway hit starred Ethel Merman (Hollywood version starred Betty Hutton) in the title role. Based loosely on the life of Annie Oakley. 1950. *That this classic and beloved work is shot through with both sexist and racist content is a source of despair to those who love the musical--and Ethel Merman. The contrast between the life of real Annie Oakley and the one reconstructed for the musical, the use of egalitarian themes in "Anything You Can Do I Can Do Better," and the contrast of lyric versus music in Annie's song, "You Can't Get a Man with a Gun," as against the lyric and lullaby-like music of Frank's song, "The Girl That I Marry," are among the themes to explore when using the musical to raise issues relating to gender.--BC*

BABES IN ARMS. Rodgers, Richard and Lorenz Hart. Dir. Busby Berkeley. "The kids in town (Mickey Rooney, Judy Garland) put on a show!" Originally a Broadway musical. B&W; 1939; 96m. *Mickey + Judy putting on a show= hegemony personified, the route to stardom everybody expected to imitate.*

BIRTH OF THE BLUES. Jazz musical with Bing Crosby, Jack Teagarden, Mary Martin, "notable for its recognition of the role of black musicians in the number 'The Waiter and the Porter and the Upstairs Main.'"--Dan Kingman. 1941.

BLUES IN THE NIGHT. Music by Harold Arlan. A jazz musical. 1941.

CABIN IN THE SKY. "A folk tale fantasy about redemption; Ethel Waters was outstanding" in a cast that also included Lena Horne, Eddie Anderson, and Duke Ellington and his orchestra.--Dan Kingman. 1943. *A period piece.*

CRADLE WILL ROCK, THE. Music, lyrics, and book by Marc Blitzstein. 1938. Has been called "propaganda opera," a "New Deal opera," and a "leftist opera." *It is a favorite of mine for comparison to other arts of the 1930's. The songs are wonderful for introducing class issues and 1930s'protest and satire through distinctive musical styles. Strong, open advocacy of its views.--BC.*

EUBIE! Musical revue of ragtime pianist and songwriter Eubie Blake. 1978.

FLOWER DRUM SONG. Richard Rodgers and Oscar Hammerstein II. 1958. *An excursion into exoticism; the "Oriental" (not Asian) experience of America.*

GENTLEMEN PREFER BLONDES. Novel and play by Anita Loos (1920), music by Jule Styne, lyric by Leo Robin. Movie version 1953. *The version with Marilyn Monroe and Jane Russell provides a focus on sexism as intertwined with materialist culture in "golddigger" musicals and films. Compare, for example, Monroe's rendition of "Diamonds are a Girl's Best Friend" with Madonna's 1980s spoof of it in "Material Girl."*

GREASE. Music, lyrics, and book by Jim Jacobs and Warren Casey. About the subculture of high school kids in the rock and roll era.

HAIR. Music by Galt MacDermot, lyrics and book by Gerome Ragni and James Rado. The show opened in 1968; movie version 1979. A musical review that captures the youth culture of the 1960s, using mild rock and other new music.

JAZZ SINGER, THE. Dir. Alan Crossland. "The son of an orthodox cantor [Al Jolson] is touched by his father's wishes to continue in his footsteps but feels he must be a jazz singer." Considered the first talking picture. B&W; 1927; 89m. *Historically significant; might be used with THE AL JOLSON STORY.*

KING AND I, THE. Rodgers and Hammerstein version of Margaret Loudon's *Anna and the King of Siam.* 1956. Useful for the scene on "The Little House of Uncle Thomas" (Uncle Tom's Cabin). *Thanks to Marilyn Patton for showing how potent this scene is in speaking about sexism as well as racism.--BC*

LA CAGE AUX FOLLES. Music and lyrics by Jerry Herman. Book by Harvey Fierstein. 1983. Successfully introduced the theme of male homosexuality into the musical; deals with the social difficulties confronting gay culture.

LADY IN THE DARK. Music by Kurt Weill, lyrics by Ira Gershwin, book by Moss Hart. 1944. The Hollywood version starred Ginger Rogers in the lead. About a woman editor who is "in the dark" (having headaches) and must seek help from a psychoanalyst. He encourages her to give up her job and look for a man who can dominate her. Billed as "the first Freudian musical," the work has Rodgers dancing out the dream sequences in glorious technicolor with a huge cast of extras, which makes the musical useful to demonstrate how music works in tandem with visual production values to encode sexist ideas. *An excellent film to show how the "feminine mystique" emerged in popular culture at the end of World War II. The song "Jennie," however, pulls the rug out from under the heavy psychoanalytic content, its melody and comic bravura style empowering Jennie with an independence the lyrics belie.--BC*

LADY SINGS THE BLUES. 1972. Based on the life of Billie Holiday, starring Diana Ross. *Does this fit the definition of a musical?*

MADONNA, TRUTH OR DARE. B&W; 1991. For use with Madonna videos.

MEET ME IN ST. LOUIS. 1944. For hegemonic "middle-America" context.

MISS SAIGON. Music composed by Claude-Michel Schøenberg, lyrics by Alain Boubil. New York opening 1991. Vietnam mother raises her daughter to find her GI father; tragedy follows. *Deserves a whole essay of its own!*

MOTHER OF US ALL,THE. Book by Gertrude Stein in 1946, vocal score by Virgil Thomson in 1947. This is opera, not a musical, but wonderfully relevant to gender issues and feminism, centering around Susan B. Anthony and her colloquies with some very American characters (Daniel Webster, for instance). "Everything Americans feel about life and death, male and female, poverty and riches, war and peace, blacks and whites, activity and loitering is in it."--John Cage. "A memory book" of gospel hymns, "cocky marches, sentimental ballads, waltzes, darn-fool ditties and intoned sermons."--Virgil Thomson.

OKLAHOMA! The movie version of this Rodgers and Hammerstein classic was directed by Fred Zinnemann. "Laurie, a country girl, is courted by Curly, the cowboy, as the villainous Jud also pursues her." Important for its songs and its role in the history of musical theatre. 1955; 140m. *Check out the song, "The farmer and the cowman should be friends," as a study in cultural conflict.*

PORGY AND BESS. George Gershwin's music, Ira Gershwin's lyrics, libretto by Dubose Heyward. 1935. (Hollywood version, 1959) This opera is not a musical either but it certainly belongs to the study of black and white cultural interaction. How best to teach this important work? Perhaps begin with (a) manuscript studies--Wayne Shirley's in *Quarterly Journal of the Library of Congress*, 38, 1 (1981) and Charles Hamm's in the *Journal of the American Musicological Society*, 40, 3 (1987), or (b) with the stereotypes obvious to students, moving outward from these to the larger issues, or (c) with the story of how it was written, how popular it became, how influential it has been.

ROSIE THE RIVETER. 1944. *Apparently there was a musical with that title before the more recent documentary widely used in women's studies.*

SHOW BOAT, 3 versions in film, 1929, 1936 & 1951. Significant watershed in the history of musicals because it introduced serious themes; viewed today, parts of the script sound pretty embarrassing. *See Susan Willoughby's syllabus--she intends to use this work in future sections of her American Music course in order to focus intensively upon multicultural issues in music.*

SOPHISTICATED LADIES. Retrospective of Duke Ellington's works. 1981.

SOUTH PACIFIC. Music by Richard Rodgers and Oscar Hammerstein, book by James Michener. Major theme is prejudice. *The song "You've Got to Be Taught (to hate and fear)" is, of course, the most apt for courses on multiculturalism.*

STREET SCENE. Music by Kurt Weill, lyrics by Langston Hughes, book by Elmer Rice (based on his play). Gives a picture of New York tenement life, with diversity well represented in the diversity of "types" living close together. Subtitled "An American Opera," it is a hybrid form. *Perfect for our classes!*

TROUBLE IN TAHITI. A short opera in seven scenes, produced as a television show in 1952. Music and book by Leonard Bernstein. The story line focuses around the "hegemonic" American family of the fifties presumed to have found Nirvana in the suburbs. "An original and truly contemporary work"--Gilbert Chase. *Pertinent to the debate over "family values" in the 1990s.*

WEST SIDE STORY. Music by Leonard Bernstein, songs by Bernstein and Stephen Sondheim. Choreography by Jerome Robbins. Romeo & Juliet story set in New York. 1957. Film version, 1961, dir. by Robbins and Robert Wise. Sophisticated musical score; story told in movement, illustrating the importance of dance in multicultural analysis. Dissonance, lots of percussion. Excellent for a variety of multicultural themes. *See Hansen and Ch'maj, Essay #2.*

WIZ, THE. Music and lyrics by Charlie Smalls. Book by William F. Brown. New York opening 1978. Take-off on "The Wizard of Oz" in a hip black idiom.

WIZARD OF OZ, THE. Dir. Mervyn LeRoy. 1943. *I am told one teacher is using it as an innovative way to introduce the idea of heterogeneity (diversity) among friends united in a common quest, with a girl as their leader.--BC*

WOMAN OF THE YEAR. John Kander. Musical adaptation for Lauren Bacall and other 80s women of the 1942 Hepburn-Tracy movie. *(See Videography.)* 1981.

YANKEE DOODLE DANDY. 1942. A classic of its kind, with James Cagney as George M. Cohan. May be studied as a model of how an "American" identity was shaped under wartime pressures, and how the musical served to supply needed war songs to the nation for World War II. *Flag-waving galore!*

III. RECORD COLLECTIONS

ANTHOLOGY OF AMERICAN FOLK MUSIC. Folkways 2951-53. ed. Harry Smith. Eighty-four selections, on 6 LPs, of music from early recordings. Includes ballads, blues, gospel, and Cajun music as well as the old-time progenitors of country music.

ANTHOLOGY OF AMERICAN FOLK MUSIC. VOL 2:,Social Music. Folkways 2952. The basic anthology consists of commercial recordings of folk music made in the 1920s & 1930s. The notes contain a great deal of information, including discography and bibliography. This volume includes sermons and early gospel songs.

CHARLES IVES: THE 100TH ANNIVERSARY. Columbia M4-32504. This 4-LP set consists of a sampling of the music, but includes two sides of Ives playing his own music and a "bonus" record of excerpts from interviews for the oral history project *Charles Ives Remembered.* A lengthy, informative illustrated booklet is included.

HISTORY OF JAZZ, THE. Folkways. An 11 LP set (2801-11). An immense achievement for its time. See also the Smithsonian series.

GREAT BIG YAM POTATOES; ANGLO-AMERICAN FIDDLE MUSIC FROM MISSISSIPPI. 12 fiddlers, 42 tunes--recorded in 1939 for the WPA & Library of Congress. LP for $9.00 available from Center for the Study of Southern Culture, University of Mississippi, University, MS 38677.

JAILHOUSE BLUES. 24 selections from recordings made in the Women's Camp, Mississippi State Penitentiary at Parchman, Miss., in 1936 and 1939. LP $9.00, Center for the Study of Southern Culture, ibid.

MISSISSIPPI FOLK VOICES. "Sacred Harp, gospel, black fife and drum, work chants, blues, and country music by various artists." LP $7.00 from Center for Study of Southern Culture, ibid.

MOVING IN THE SPIRIT: WORSHIP THROUGH MUSIC IN CLEAR CREEK, MISSISSIPPI. "Varied styles of worship music plus a chanted sermon. LP $9.00." Available from Center for the Study of Southern Culture, ibid. (All descriptions quoted from Winter 1992 manual of the Center.)

MUSIC IN AMERICA No longer in print but available in many record libraries.

NEW WORLD RECORDED ANTHOLOGY OF AMERICAN MUSIC. This anthology (over 160 LPs to date) has many relevant recordings; the first 100 albums are indexed in Elizabeth A. Davis, *An Index to the New World*

Anthology of American Music (NY: W.W. Norton, 1981). Since New World's editorial policy is to avoid extensive treatment of groups and performers well represented elsewhere, this anthology is most useful as a well-annotated supplement, valuable for the added and different light it throws on certain areas.

SMITHSONIAN COLLECTION OF AMERICAN POPULAR SONG. A 7 LP anthology. Also on cassettes.

SMITHSONIAN COLLECTION OF BIG BAND JAZZ: FROM THE BEGINNINGS TO THE FIFTIES. Notes by Gunther Schuller and Martin Williams. A 6 LP anthology. Also on cassettes. Definitive collection.

SMITHSONIAN COLLECTION OF CLASSIC COUNTRY MUSIC. An 8 LP anthology. Also listed in Winter 1992 bulletin of Center for the Study of Southern Culture: "143 selections, more than 80 of which are not obtainable elsewhere. Accompanying booklet written by Bill Malone, Department of History, Tulane University. 8 cassettes. Originally $50.00. Now $40.00."

SMITHSONIAN COLLECTION OF CLASSIC JAZZ, original edition. A 6 LP anthology.

SMITHSONIAN COLLECTION OF CLASSIC JAZZ, revised edition. A 7 LP anthology. Also on cassettes. These two jazz collections are also excellent.

SONGS OF EARTH, WATER, FIRE AND SKY: MUSIC OF THE AMERICAN INDIAN. NW-246. First general album with excellent notes by Charlotte Heth.

TEXAS-MEXICAN CONJUNTO (Vol. 24). Border music featuring various groups with accordion, banjo sexto, tambora, vocals, playing polkas, rancheras, bolero, vols. 1935-66.

THE PROMISED LAND: AMERICAN INDIAN SONGS OF LAMENT AND PROTEST. 1981. Folkways FHJS-37254. Indian "message" music, an urban folksinging genre akin to work by Woody Guthrie.

THE STORY OF THE BLUES. Notes by Paul Oliver. A 2 LP set. Columbia CG 30008. *(See Oliver's book, The Meaning of the Blues, next section.)*

THE WORLD MUSIC INSTITUTE, "VOICES OF AMERICAS," 49 West 27th St., #810, NY, N.Y. 10001. Eight audio cassettes, each containing 60 to 85 minutes of music from North, South and Central America and the Caribbean. "The series features some of the most popular folk musicians in the United States, including a number of National Heritage Fellowship winners. Comes with a 64-page booklet that includes scholarly essays on the traditions as well as photographs and biographies on the musicians." (sales manual)

THE WORLD MUSIC INSTITUTE, "VOICES OF AMERICAS," 49 West 27th St., #810, New York, N.Y. 10001. Eight audio cassettes featuring music by recent immigrants from Afghanistan, the Arab countries, Cambodia, India, Iran, Laos, Morocco and Vietnam. 55 - 85 minutes of live music, most of which was recorded at WMI concerts from 1987 to 1990." (sales manual)

IV. BOOKS ABOUT MUSIC

Adler, John. *History of the U.S.: An Interpretation with Songs and Autobiographical Narration.* Iowa: Kindall/Hunt Publishing Co., 1990.

American Folksong. Compiled by Woody Guthrie, ed. Moses Asch. N.Y.: Oak Publications, 1961.

Anderson, Gillian, comp. and ed. *Freedom's Voice in Poetry and Song.* Wilmington, DE: Scholarly Resources, 1977. This compendious "inventory of political and patriotic lyrics in colonial American newspapers" concludes with a songbook with 92 songs and 8 poems.

Austin, William W. *"Susanna," "Jeanie," and "The Old Folks at Home": The Songs of Stephen C. Foster from His Time to Ours.* Music in American Life (series), 1989. A perceptive study of the complex array of meanings that Foster's songs have had in a variety of contexts.

Baraka, Amiri. *Blues People.* NY: Morrow, 1963. "A perceptive social study of African-American music by a prominent black writer (known as LeRoi Jones when the book was first published). The first six chapters are applicable to folk music." By now, it is a classic in its field, despite *seeming* opinionated.

Belz, Carl. *The Story of Rock.* NY: Oxford University Press, 1973.

Bierley, Paul E. *John Philip Sousa: American Phenomenon.* N.Y.: Appleton-Century-Crofts, 1973.

Bloom, Ken. *American Musicals: The Complete Musical Theater Companion.* NY: Facts on File, 1985. (2 vols.) Vol 1 has entries, by show, on over 3000 productions; Vol 2 has indexes by songs, people, & year of production.

Bob Dylan's Hard-Hitting Songs for Hard-Hit People. N. Y: Warner Bros., 1974. Compiled by Alan Lomax, notes by Woody Guthrie; music transcribed & edited by Pete Seeger. [Oak Publications, 1967] "May be the best collection concentrating on the period of the 1930s. Illustrated with fine photographs by Walker Evans &c. under auspices of the Farm Security Administration."

Bowers, Jane and Judith Tick, ed. *Women Making Music: The Western Art Tradition, 1150-1950.* Winner of the ASCAP-Deems Taylor Award and the Pauline Alderman Prize. Two good chapters on women in American music.

Broughton, Viv. *Black Gospel: An Illustrated History of the Gospel Sound.* Poole Dorset: Blandford Press, 1985.

Carman, Judith, et al. *Art-Song in the United States: Annotated Bibliography.* National Association of the Teacher of Singing, 1976.

Claghorn, Charles Eugene. *Biographical Dictionary of American Music.* 1973.

Courlander, Harold. *Negro Folk Music, U.S.A.* NY: Columbia University Press, 1963. Includes 43 complete songs. An excellent and far-ranging collection, edited by a noted authority.

deCesare, Ruth. *Myth, Music and Dance of the American Indian.* "An activity-oriented sourcebook of American Indian tradition, based upon the music and culture of 21 tribes. Includes brief information on each tribe represented, map, related classroom activities. Many songs in original language with pronunciation and singable English translation."

Denisoff, R. Serge. *Great Day Coming: Folk Music and the American Left.* Urbana: University of Illinois Press, 1971.

Dunaway, David King. *How Can I Keep From Singing: Pete Seeger.* NY: McGraw-Hill, 1981. "An ample and objective account of the career to date of the one outstanding survivor in the folk protest scene. Offers valuable firsthand insight into the entire procession of eras. A nearly complete discography."

Epstein, Dena J. *Sinful Tunes and Spirituals: Black Folk Music to the Civil War.* From the series Music in American Life. A valuable study, with extensive citations from contemporary sources."

Ewen, David. *The New Complete Book of American Musical Theater.* NY: Holt, Rinehart , 1970.

Ferris, Jean. *America's Musical Landscape.* [n.d.] "Survey of the elements of music and American music chronologically (Native American music omitted). Music examples cited in the text are generally available."

Floyd, Samuel A., Jr. ed. *Black Music of the Harlem Renaissance.* Greenwood Press, 1991. "Reasserts the centrality of music in what has been considered a literary movement."--Scott DeVeaux. Winner, 1991 Irving Lowens Award.

Forcucci, Samuel L. *A Folk Song History of America: America Through its Songs.* Englewood Cliffs, N.J.: Prentice Hall, 1984.

Fowke, Edith and Joe G. Lazer, eds. *Songs of Work and Protest*. NY: Dover, 1973.

Goldberg, Isaac. *Tin Pan Alley: A Chronicle of American Popular Music*. NY: Frederick Ungar, 1961. Includes introduction by George Gershwin, and supplement "From Sweet and Swing to Rock 'n Roll" by Edward Jablonski.

Gottschalk, L. M. *Notes of a Pianist*. Edition with notes by Jeanne Behrend. NY: Knopf, 1964. "One of the most perceptive and brilliant documents that we have of nineteenth-century American life and culture clashes as seen by a musician."

Green, Stanley, ed. *Encyclopedia of the Musical Theatre*. NY: Dodd, Mead, 1976. Reprint, Da Capo, 1980. Useful single-volume work, 492 pp. Entries by name, song, and show, with brief commentary on each show, and appendices on awards and prizes, and long runs.

Green, Stanley ed. *Encyclopedia of the Musical Film*. NY: Oxford University Press, 1981. Same organization and format as the preceding.

Green, Stanley,ed. *Broadway Musicals Show by Show*. Milwaukee, WI: Hal Leonard, 1985.

Greenway, John. *American Folksongs of Protest*. Philadelphia: University of Pennsylvania Press, 1960. A rather detailed account of protest songs, especially those used in the labor movement. Many examples, including music.

Hamm, Charles. *Yesterdays: Popular Music in America*. NY: W.W. Norton, 1979. This well-documented work has chapters relevant to nearly every aspect of popular secular music.

Harrison, Daphne Duvall. *Black Pearls: Blues Queens of the 1920's*. New Brunswick: Rutgers University Press, 1988.

Herskovitsz, Melville. *The Myth of the Negro Past*. NY: Harper Bros., 1951. "A landmark work, the result of studies begun in the 1930's. Traces Africanisms in New World black culture, daily life, and religion; one chapter deals with language and the arts."

Hicks, Michael. *Mormonism and Music: A History*. Music in American Life series 1989. Winner of 1989 Award in Criticism from the Association for Mormon Letters. "The history of Mormon music from the time of Joseph Smith to the present carefully and copiously documented. Chapters are devoted to charismatic singing, the popularity of brass bands, the famous Tabernacle Choir, and resistance to jazz and rock." --W.H. Baxter, *Choice*. 280 pp. Illus.

Hirshey, Gerri. *Nowhere to Run: The Story of Soul Music*. Penguin. "This definitive history of soul music wonderfully evokes the simultaneous interaction of personalities, music, and culture."--Stephen Holden, *The New York Times*. 1984, 384 pp.

Historical Records Survey, *Biographical Index of Musicians in the United States of America Since Colonial Times*. 1956.

Hitchcock, H. Wiley and Stanley Sadie, eds. *The New Grove Dictionary of American Music*. 4 vols. This is the best single source to investigate when seeking basic information on topics and artists related to American music.

Horn, David. *The Literature of American Music in Books and Folk Music Collections: A Fully Annotated Bibliography*. 1977.

Jablonski, Edward. *The Encyclopedia of American Music*. 1981.

Jackson, George Pullen. *White and Negro Spirituals: Their Life Span and Kinship*. NY: De Capo, 1975 (reprint of original 1944 ed.). "A well-documented study, but controversial in its conclusion that transmission of the material of spirituals was primarily from white to black. Dissenting views are presented by Epstein, Lovell, and Tallmadge under Garst, John F.

Jackson, Richard, ed. *Stephen Foster Song Book*. NY: Dover, 1974. Forty of Foster's songs in original published versions, with original sheet music covers and notes on the songs. All the important minstrel songs are included.

Jones, Bessie. *For the Ancestors: Autobiographical Memories*. 1983. A wealth of information is preserved here by a member of the Georgia Sea Island Singers.

Keck, George and Sherrill W. Martin. *Feel the Spirit: Studies in Nineteenth Century Afro-American Music*. NY: Greenwood Press, 1988.

Keil, Charles. *Urban Blues*. University of Chicago Press, 1966.

Levy, Lester S. *Give Me Yesterday: American History in Song, 1890-1920*. Norman: University of Oklahoma Press, 1975.

Lieberman, Robbie. *"My Song is My Weapon": People's Songs, American Communism, and the Politics of Culture. 1930-50*.

Lomax, Alan. *The Folk Songs of North America*. Garden City, NY: Doubleday & Co., 1960.

Mellers, Wilfred. *Music in a New Found Land: Themes and Developments in the History of American Music*. NY: Knopf, 1965. An English musicologist views American music; all the composers are given interesting and extensive treatment -- Ives as American hero, Ruggles as American mystic, etc.

Noebel, David A. *The Marxist Minstrels: A Handbook on Communist Subversion of Music.* Tulsa, OK: American Christian College Press, 1974. "An anti-Marxist perspective on the links between popular music and the political left."

Odum, Howard and Guy B. Johnson. *The Negro and His Songs.* Chapel Hill, NC: 1925. Reprint, 1964. A study of religious, social and work songs. A rather exhaustive treatment of the texts, with many complete examples. No music.

Oliver, Paul. *The Meaning of the Blues.* NY: Macmillan, 1960. Paperback Collier, 1963. "An exhaustive and perceptive study of blues subjects and milieu, in the form of an extensive commentary on 350 blues texts."

Rabin, Carol Price. *Music Festivals in America.* 1983.

Robb, John Donald. *Hispanic Folk Music of New Mexico and the Southwest: A Self-Portrait of a People.* University of Oklahoma Press, 1980. "The major summary in published form of many years of collecting by this scholar." The anthology (891 pages) includes many types of music--sacred, secular, and instrumental--with informative notes on each type. Songs include texts and English translations.

Roberts, John Storm. *The Latin Tinge: The Impact of Latin American Music in the United States.* NY: Oxford University Press, 1979. Deals with influences from all of Latin America; useful, even though the emphasis is on popular music.

Root, Deane L. *American Popular Stage Music, 1860-1880.* Ann Arbor: UMI Research Press, 1981.

Rosenthal, David H. *Hard Bop: Jazz and Black Music, 1955-1965.* Oxford University Press, 1990.

Scheurer, Timothy E. *Born in the USA: The Myth of America in Popular Music from Colonial Times to the Present.* University Press of Mississippi, 1990. The vision of America seen through the lyrics of its popular songs.

--------------. ed. *Readings from the Popular Press.* 2 vols. Bowling Green State University Popular Press, 1989. 36 short essays on American popular music aimed "to show popular music in an historic-cultural context."

Shapiro, Nat. *Popular Music: An Annotated Index of American Popular Songs.* NY: Adrian Press, 1964-73. Entries are arranged by year, and within each year alphabetically by title, with notes on the composers, lyricists, and publishers.

Shapiro, Nat. *Popular Music, 1920-1979: A Revised Cumulation.* Detroit: Gale, 1985. A three-volume rearrangement of the above, alphabetically with indexes.

Shaw, Arnold. *Black Popular Music i America.* NY: Schirmer Books, 1986. "Though dealing with a subject broader than jazz itself, this is invaluable in placing jazz in the context of black contributions to American popular music."

Southern, Eileen. *Readings in Black American Music,* 2nd ed. NY: W.W. Norton, 1983. A comprehensive, indispensable study of the entire field.

Stearns, Marshall. *The Story of Jazz.* NY: Oxford University Press, 1956. Early chapters deal with African influences and their transplantation here, both directly and via the West Indies. Also discussed are work songs, the blues, and the spiritual. Highly recommended, especially for its treatment of the beginnings of jazz, although by now later chapters seem outdated.

Stearns, Marshall and Jean. *Jazz Dance: The Story of American Vernacular Dance.* NY: Macmillan, 1968. Reprint, NY: Schirmer Books, 1979. This exemplary study fills a need, as an awareness of vernacular dance is indispensable to an adequate understanding of the popular music of the period.

Tinker, Edward Larocque. *Corridos and Calaveras.* Austin: University of Texas Press, 1961. Although this book deals specifically with the corrido and related forms as found in Old Mexico, it is excellent background reading on the corrido as a genre. Especially fascinating are the reproductions of old broadsides, with their drawings by the famous artist Jose Guadalupe Posada, a forerunner of Rivera and Orozco. A delightful book, in a very artistic format.

Titon, Jeff Todd, ed. *Downhome Blues Lyrics: An Anthology from the Post-World War II Era.* Music in American Life series. 128 blues lyrics convey the feeling of "down home," the African-American experience from which blues came. "Titon, a widely recognized blues authority discusses blues as a poetic form, blues music before and after World War II, and the meaning of the lyrics. Transcribed from recordings by black singers meant for black communities."

Tracy, Steven C. *Langston Hughes and the Blues.* 1988."Tracy's study leaves us with a far better understanding of the role of black music, and the blues in particular, as the central influence on the most original of black American poets." --Arnold Rampersad, author of *The Life of Langston Hughes.*

Travis, Dempsey J. *An Autobiography of Black Jazz* (intro by Studs Terkel). Chicago: Urban Research Institute, 1983. Jazz history, personal observations and photographs on the growth of jazz in Chicago and America. Insights into lives of Cab Calloway, Billy Eckstine, Franz Jackson, Eddie Johnson, others.

Vander, Judith. *Songprints: The Musical Experience of Five Shoshone Women.* Urbana: University of Illinois Press, 1988. Includes a 60 min. cassette.

A BIBLIOGRAPHY OF MULTICULTURAL FICTIONAL FAVORITES

by M. Kathleen Hanson

ED. NOTE: Borrowing from Lucy Lippard, Hanson calls this personalized list an "eccentric (and eclectic) bibliography" of works for classes on American multiculturalism. When she has no comment of her own, she has quoted from catalogs. For various reasons, a few works of autobiographical "non-fiction" are included.--BC

Abbott, Shirley. *Growing Up Down South.* Boston: Houghton Mifflin, 1991. A vibrant family memoir that is also a meditation on family myth and tradition. The author offers an honest look at the Southern Lady, country women and their families, servants, religion, and relationships.

Angelou, Maya. *I Know Why the Caged Bird Sings.* NY: Random House, 1969. Angelou uses her poet's gift for language and observation in this remarkable autobiography.

Antin, Mary. *The Promised Land.* Boston: Houghton-Mifflin, 1912. The work of a young woman (1868-1934) who emigrated as a child from Russia to Boston. A classic immigrant story. Compare with Cahan's *The Rise of David Levinsky.*

Arnold, June. *Sister Gin.* The Women's Press, 1979. "A very funny book. The characterizations, the wit of its dialogue and the flashing vigor of its southern colloquialisms see to that."--Alison Hennegan, *Gay News.*

Arnow, Harriette. *The Dollmaker.* NY: Macmillan 1954."Superb...a masterwork." --*The New York Times.* Also an ABC-TV movie. A story of personal triumph. The unique novel of a young woman's fight to keep her sense of dignity.

Barrio, Raymond. *The Plum Plum Pickers.* Sunnyvale, CA: Ventura Press, 1969. "Migrants are the scum of the earth. Anything they get over forty cents an hour is gravy." Against the backdrop of this management philosophy, Barrio recounts the year round drama of the lives of Manuel and Lupe Gutierrez, Mexican migrants, and their children.

Beam, Joseph. ed. *In the Life: A Black Gay Anthology.* Alyson Publications, Inc., 1986. "*In the Life* provides us with insight into lives we so commonly forget exist, and sends us on a journey to discover more about our culture than we ever imagined existed."--*Frontiers.*

Brant, Beth. *Mohawk Trail*. Ithaca, NY: Firebrand Books, 1985. A few lines of her poetry: "I close my eyes. Pictures unreeling on my eyelids. Portraits of beloved people flashing by quickly. Opening my eyes, I think of the seemingly ordinary things that women do. And how, with brush of an eyelash against a cheek, the movement of a pen on paper, power is born."

Bulosan, Carlos. *America Is In the Heart: A Personal History*. Seattle: University of Washington Press, 1973. The poet details his sensitive impression of Depression America in 1931, when his family immigrated from the Philippines.

Cahan, Abraham. *The Rise of David Levinsky*. Harper, 1960 edition. Cahan's character is not universal or wholly representative figure. He is a specific type. "Yet he combined a variety of traits characteristic of his ethnic heritage; he met the standard problems of cultural adjustment . . . and his life touched virtually every segment of New York Jewish society."--John Higham, the introduction.

Cather, Willa. *My Antonia*. Boston: Houghton Mifflin, 1918. Widely regarded as Willa Cather's finest novel, this famous portrait of a pioneer woman embodies all the strengths and passions of America's settlers.

Cather, Willa. *O Pioneers!* Boston: Houghton Mifflin, 1922. Cather introduces Alexandra Bergson, daughter of Swedish immigrant farmers, whose devotion to the land sustains her through the hardships and suffering of prairies life.

Chandler, Raymond. *The Little Sister*. Boston: Houghton Mifflin. "A California ocean. California, the department-store state. The most of everything and the best of nothing." This is the setting of Chandler's book, exposing the underside of the cultural experience known world-wide as the California Lifestyle.

Chesnutt, Charles. *The Conjure Woman*. Ann Arbor: University of Michigan Press, 1969. Lifts the spirits but also creates doubts in the shadows of the reader's heart and mind.

Chin, Frank et al., eds. *The Big Aiiieeeeee! The History of Chinese American and Japanese American Literature*. Garden City, NY: Doubleday Anchor, 1975. The forces which created and perpetuated the Asian American stereotype are exposed in this literary anthology.

Chung, C., A. Kim, A. K. Lemeshewsky. *Between the Lines: An Anthology of Pacific/Asian Lesbians*. Santa Cruz, CA: Dancing Bird Press, 1987. "Who are we? We are a small but growing group of Pacific/Asian lesbians. . . . we see this anthology as a seed, a beginning."--from the preface.

Clinton, Catherine. *The Plantation Mistress: Woman's World in the Old South*. NY: Pantheon Books, 1982. This pioneering study of the much mythologized

Southern Belle in the slave society before the Civil War is usually considered a work of social science, but reading the diary entries makes it a stunning collection of first person experiences.

Courlander, Harold. *The Mesa of Flowers.* NY: Popular Library, 1977. "A lovely novel . . . rooted in traditions & myths . . . perceptive . . . captures the pace of Indian life, the poetic quality of tales handed down, the deep commitment to natural harmony."--*Publisher's Weekly*

Cudjoe, Selwyn R.,ed. *Caribbean Women Writers: Essays from the First International Conference,* University of Massachusetts Press, 1990. "These voices, rich and varied in tone, transcend ethnicity and speak from a common heritage. This is a landmark work."--Barbara Paul-Emile, Bentley College.

Donnelly, Nisa. *The Bar Stories: A Novel After All.* NY: St. Martin Press, 1989. "The Bar Stories presents a panoramic view of the American lesbian nation, and celebrates lesbian scurvily in a world more often hostile than tolerant."--From the Publishers Notes.

Douglass, Frederick. *Narrative of the Life of Frederick Douglass.* NY: Dutton, 1968 Penguin edition. A must read for anyone interested in ethnic America.

Ellison, Ralph. *Invisible Man,* NY: Random House, 1989 [1957]. The adult black man in American society. Also a classic and a must!

Fedo, Michael. *Chronicles of Aunt Hilma.* St. Cloud, MN: North Star Press, 1982. Fedo captures the mood and spirit of Swedish-Americans of his boyhood years. Humorous reflections of life as it was in the 1940s and 50s in Middle America.

Frick, Aaron. *Reflections of a Rock Lobster, A Story of Growing Up Gay.* Boston: Alyson Publications, 1981. Story of the young man who made headlines several years ago by taking his boyfriend to this senior prom.

Gibson, Mary E. *New Stories by Southern Women.* Columbia, SC: University of South Carolina Press, 1989. This remarkable collection includes stories by Alice Adams, Toni Cade Bambara, Pam Durban, Bobbie Ann Mason, Jill McCorkle, Lee Smith and Alice Walker.

Gilman, Charlotte Perkins. *The Yellow Wallpaper.* Forward by Elaine Hedges. Old Westbury, NY: Feminist Press, 1973. This women's classic takes on new meaning today, especially with Hedges' interpretation.

Gonzales, Ray. *From the Restless Roots.* University of Houston, An Arte Publico Press Book, 1986. "The poetry of Ray Gonzales contain such unexpected light. Out of silent landscapes, the canyons, the 'faces of rock closing their eyes,' his images move continually toward transformation and redemption . . .

his language does more than speak and guide--it chants us into a powerful realm of clarity and potent vision."--Naomi Shihab Nye.

Griffin, John Howard. *Black Like Me.* Signet Press, 1959. This book is more than forty years old, but if you have young students who want to know why there was a Civil Rights Movement in the Sixties, they can still profit from a reading of Griffin's odyssey through the Deep South as a white man disguised as a black.

Gross, Theodore L. *The Literature of American Jews.* NY: The Free Press, A Division of Macmillan Publishing Co. Includes works of Abraham Cahan, Mary Antin, Emma Lazarus, and many others. An interesting commentary on the early Jewish experience in America.

Hurston, Zora Neale. *Their Eyes Were Watching God.* NY: Harper and Collins, 1990 [1937]. Hurston's most highly acclaimed novel, it was newly discovered a few years ago and has quickly become an enduring piece of American literature.

Houston, Jeanne Walatsuki and James D. Houston. *Farewell to Manzanar: A True Story of Japanese American Experience During and After the World War II Internment.* Boston: Houghton Mifflin, Boston, 1973. The title tells the story. Combine with Barrio's *The Plum Plum Pickers* and Bulosan's *America Is In the Heart* to tell the story of the ethnic experience from three viewpoints on the West Coast.

Jacobs, Harriet A. *Incidents in the Life of a Slave Girl: Written by Herself.* ed. Jean Fagan Yellin. Harvard University Press, 1987. The title of this book is self-explanatory, but it only begins to tell the story. Professor Yellin first read Jacob's autobiography in the early Sixties and dismissed it as a false slave narrative. But years later, schooled by the women's movement, she reexamined its radical feminist content.

Jen, Gish. *Typical American.* Boston: Houghton Mifflin, 1991. This is a wise and appealing story about Ralph and Helen Chang, young immigrants coming to terms with freedom.

Keyser, Jenny, ed. *Braided Lives: An Anthology of Multicultural American Writing.* University of Minnesota Humanities Press, 1991. "Includes writings by Naive American, African American, Asian American and Hispanic American authors. Its content shines.--*St. Paul Pioneer Press.*

Kingston, Maxine Hong. *The Woman Warrior.* Alfred A. Knopf, New York, New York, 1976. Prize-winning autobiographical novel by and about Chinese-American woman.

Koppelman, Susan, ed. *Between Mothers and Daughters: Stories Across Generations,* Old Westbury, NY: Feminist Press, 1978. A good collection.

Logan, Onnie Lee. *Motherwit, An Alabama Midwife's Story* (as told to Katherine Clark). NY: A Plume Book, Division of Penguin Books, 1991. "Oral history doesn't come much better than this."

Louie, David Wong. *Pangs of Love.* NY: Alfred A. Knopf, 1991. Louie has presented a sharp and quirky collection of short stories that capture the alienation he felt growing up as the son of a Chinese-laundry owner in a Long Island, New York, suburb.

Momaday, N. Scott. *The Way to Rainy Mountain.* University of New Mexico Press, 1976. A reflection on native art and literature of a particular historical migration. In the course of migration, a culture and psychological revolution occurred. The Kiowas began their journey as a divided and oppressed people; they ended it with honor and glory.

Moraga, Cherrie and Gloria Anzaldua, eds. *The Bridge Called My Back, Writings of Radical Women of Color,* foreword by Toni Cade Bambara. NY: Kitchen Table: Women of Color Press, 1981. This collection of prose, poetry and personal narratives intends to and does reflect an uncompromised definition of feminism. Chrystos, Andrea Canaan, Mitsuye Yamada, Neili Wong, Cheryl Clark, Merle Woo and Hattie Gossett are but a few of the authors represented.

Morris, Willie. *North Toward Home.* Boston: Houghton Mifflin, 1967. Morris attempts to explain his conscious struggle with his life in the context of a multicultural United States. This "mainstream" auto-biography illustrates ways in which an insider can feel like the outsider.

Morrison, Joan and Charlotte Fox Zabusky. *American Mosaid: The Immigrant Experience in the Words of Those Who Lived It.* 1992. "Powerful, dramatic, fascinating. . . . The voices and the testimony have the density and tenseness of fiction."--*Boston Globe.*

Mukherjee, Bharati. *Jasmine.* NY: Fawcett Crest Books, 1990. "Mukherje superbly delineates the tensions and contradictions encountered by these new Americans ...fine writing and unusual angle of vision on the immigrant dream make this a memorable and moving book."--*Boston Herald.*

Nguyen-Hong-Nhiem, Lucy and Joel M. Halpern. *The Far East Comes Near: Autobiographical Accounts of Southeast Asian Students in America,* Amherst, MA.: University of Massachusetts Press, 1989. "A forceful testimony of hardship and suffering, harrowing escape and the renewal of hope."--*Library Journal*

Neihardt, J. G. *Black Elk Speaks*. Lincoln: University of Nebraska Press, 1988. An old standard, with a new update--now that scholarship looks at the white man's retelling of the red man's tale.

Okada, John. *No No Boy*. Rutland, Vermont: Charles E. Tuttle Co. 1980. A novel of a Japanese-American, adrift in his own country, fighting his own private war of conflating loyalties. Set in the years after World War II, as Ichrio "Itchy" tries to pick up the threads of his life.

Petry, Ann. *The Street*. Boston: Houghton and Mifflin, 1991. Tells the story of an individual's fervent desire to maintain dignity, self-respect and a safe environment amidst the turmoil of a neighborhood in social and economic distress. Can be compared to *The Women of Brewster Place*.

Perlman, Robert. *Bridging Three Worlds: Hungarian-Jewish Americans, 1848 to 1914*. University of Massachusetts Press, 1991. A chronicle of an immigrant group's acculturation as citizens in a newly adopted land.

Pinero, Miguel. *Short Eyes*. University of Houston, Arte Publico Press Book, 1986. Native American viewpoint of Southwest culture.

Rivera, Edward. *Family Installments: Memories of Growing Up Hispanic*. NY: William Morrow Co., 1982. Intensely personal chronicle of a family's migration from a small Puerto Rican village to New York City captures the essences of the immigrant story. "An exceptional memoir . . . honest, simple, classical and true."--Phillip Lopate, *New York Times Book Review*.

Rivers, J. W. *When the Owl Cries, Indians Die: Poems of Mexico and the Southwest*. London & Toronto: Associated University Presses,Virginia Center for the Creative Arts, 1986. "J. W. Rivers's new book is chilling and beautiful. It so convincingly reinvents the lives of the poor, the dispossessed, the victimized . . . that immediately we believe in and care about them. A body of extraordinary, unforgettable poems." that add up to a novel.--Susan Ludvigson.

Rolvaag, O. E. *Giants in the Earth: A Saga of the Prairie*. NY: Harper and Row, 1991. This great American epic is one of the few books about the American westward movement that shows how much the land changed the people, instead of the popular American myth that says the people changed the land. *P. S. Douglas Moore has also written a moving opera based on the novel.--BC*

Rosen, Kenneth. *The Man to Send Rain Clouds, Contemporary Stories by American Indians*. NY: The Viking Press, 1975. "Nineteen stories convey the conflict between the Indian heritage and the Native American's problematic status in today's society."--Publisher's Notes.

Rosengarten, Theodore. *All God's Dangers: The Life of Nate Shaw*. NY: Random House, 1984. The author calls this book "the autobiography of an illiterate man." This work is rich in fact and perception as it chronicles the file of Nate Shaw (1885-193?) who displays a light level of intelligence and magnificent courage in his pursuit of the American Dream.

Silko, Leslie Marmon. *Ceremony*. NY: Penguin Books, a Division of Viking Press, 1977. Tayo, a young American Indian, returns to the Laguna Pueblo reservation after having been a prisoner of the Japanese during World War II. In an attempt to combat his growing sense of estrangement and alienation he turns back to his Indian past. The search into his own past becomes a ritual, a curative ceremony.

Steinbeck, John. *The Grapes of Wrath*. NY: Viking Press, [1939]. This old classic takes on new meaning as America sees more and more homeless people in shelters, as the number of unemployed grows, as the Western United States endures another year of drought--and as the book is set into the context of a course on multicultural America.

Stockel, H. Henrietta. *Women of the Apache Nation: Voices of Truth*. Reno: University of Nevada Press, 1991. Stockel talks to four women who describe their history, their lives and their hopes for the future.

Tan, Amy. *The Joy Luck Club*. NY: Ivy Books, 1989. Vignettes alternate back and forth between the lives of the four Chinese women in the pre-1949 China and the lives of their American born daughters.

Tan, Amy. *The Kitchen God's Wife*. NY: Putnam, 1991. Tan "is the weaver of a transcendent tale. The nagging mother we met in *The Joy Luck Club* bestows on the reader a story of her past life more glamorous than a fairytale and more sad. Tan has trumphed again."--*Time*, 1991.

Telemaque, Eleanor Wong. *It's Crazy to Stay Chinese in Minnesota*. NY: Thomas Nelson Inc., 1984. Who could resist such a wonderful title? The author relates a story both light-hearted and touching.

Toomer, Jean. *Cane*. NY: W. W. Norton, 1987. With an updated forward by Darwin Truner, the author's poetry lives again for a new generation.

Villarreal, Jose Antonio. *Pocho*. Garden City, NY: Doubleday & Co., 1959. About Richard Rubio, the youngest son of a Mexican migrant worker, a sensitive questioning boy whose coming of age in California was hastened by the poverty and primitive surrounding into which he was born.

Walker, Scott, ed. *The Graywolf Annual Seven: Stories from the American Mosaic*. St. Paul, MN: Graywolf Press, 1990. The Editor has provided the reader with a cultural 'salad bowl' in the form of stories and essays that demonstrate the richly diverse cultures that maintain their own characteristics while adding to the whole.

Welch, James. *The Death of Jim Loney*. Harper & Row, 1987. "A powerful novel about a modern American Indian, out of warpaint and costume, with no tribe, no real home."--*New York Times Book Review*.

Will, Roscoe, Coordinating Editor. *Living in Spirit, a Gay American Indian Anthology*. NY: St. Martin's Press, 1988. "one the most exciting books . . . since *Another Mother Tongue*. It reclaims for all the rich and diverse gay tradition of many tribes, the important roles reserved for gay women and men, and the gay contribution to traditional life."--*Feminist Bookstore, New York*.

Wasserstein, Wendy. *The Heidi Chronicles*, 1990. A play making the rounds of regional theatres. Wacky events in the life of a modern woman trying to balance career and personal life while engaging in severe self-scrutiny. With an array of colorful characters; "strikes nerves as well as the funny bone."--brochure copy.

Williams, John A. *The Man Who Cried I Am*. Boston: Little Brown, 1967. On a warm spring afternoon in 1964, Max Reddick begins to come to terms with not only his impending death but with his life. As an American Negro writer dying of cancer, he is forced to remember who he was and who he has become.

Wright, Richard. *Black Boy: A Record of a Childhood and Youth*. NY: Harper, 1989 [1945]. This classic, once thought sensational, tells with unforgettable fury what it felt like to be a "black boy" in the Jim Crow South.

===============================

POSTSCRIPT: *For other Fictional Favorites, check out resources that can be as hard to find as* Context *or as readily available as the* Heath Anthology:

Lewis, Judy, ed. *Context: Southeast Asian in California* (Folsom/Cordova Unified School District, Rancho Cordova, CA., 1991.) Lists of selected resources about the new immigration from Southeast Asia. For a collection of pamphlets, write directly to the district, Rancho Cordova, CA 95670. Tel. (916) 635-6815.

Paul Lauter, et al., ed. *Heath Anthology of American Literature*. 2 vols. (Lexington, Mass.: D. C. Heath & Co., 1990) This formerly controversial anthology is now widely used in literature classes, often displacing the Norton Anthology of American Literature because it is so multicultural. The selections are varied and, to my mind, quite wonderful!--KH

===================================

LIPPARD'S BIBLIOGRAPHY FOR
MIXED BLESSINGS[1]

ED. NOTE: In the field of visual arts today, no other volume is cited as often or respected as much as Lucy Lippard's Mixed Blessings: New Art in a Multicultural America. *Its bibliography of books and aticles is reproduced below. I have edited to shorten (NY for New York, etc.) but without eliminating unique information or omitting entries. I did, alas, have to omit her long list of exhibition catalogs, as well as reduce font size.--BC*

Books and Articles:

Allen, Paula Gunn. *The Sacred Hoop: Recovering The Feminine in American Traditions.* Boston: Beacon Press, 1986.

Anzaldúa, Gloria. *Borderlands/La Frontera: The New Mestiza.* San Francisco: Spinsters/Aunt Lute, 1987.

Araeen, Rasheed. "From Primitivism to Ethnic Arts." *Third Text* no. 1 (Autumn 1987), 6-24.

--------. *Making Myself Visible.* London: Kala Press, 1984.

Arrom, José Juan. *Mitología y artes prehispanicas de las Antillas.* Mexico City: Siglo veintiuno editores, 1975.

Aufderheide, Pat. "A Man Upside-down (Third World Artisits Explore Their Territory)." *The Progressive* (March 1987), 36-37.

Babcock, Barbara, ed. *The Reversible World: Essays in Symbolic Inversion.* Ithaca: Cornell University Press, 1978.

Basso, Keith. *Portraits of "The White Man": Linguistic Play and Cultural Symbols among the Western Apache.* NY: Cambridge University Press, 1979.

Beardsley, John and Livingston, Jane. *Black Folk Art in America: 1930-1980.* Jackson: University Press of Mississippi, 1982.

---

[1]*Mixed Blessings: New Art in a Multicultural America* (New York: Random House, Pantheon Books, 1990), pp. 260-70. In her introduction to the bibliography, Lippard--as earlier noted--states: "This is an eccentric (and eclectic) bibliography, reflecting the range of sources that informed this book . . . . Because there are no books specifically on this subject, my secondary sources were usually either articles and catalogs or outside the art field. (Primary sources were contact with or statements from the artists themselves.) . . . --LRL. Bibliography reproduced and reprinted by kind permission of the author.

Bernal, Martin. *Black Athena: The Afroasiatic Roots of Classical Civilization.* Vol. 1, The Fabrication of Ancient Greece 1785-1985. New Brunswick, N.J.: Rutgers University Press, 1987.

Bhabha, Homi. "Of Mimicry and Man: The Ambivalence of Colonial Discourse." *October* (Spring 1984), 125-33.

--------. "The Other Question--The Stereotype and Colonial Discourse." *Screen* (Nov./Dec. 1983), 18-86.

Bowling, Frank. "Formalist Art and the Black Experience." *Third Text* no. 5 (Winter 1988-89), 78-82.

Brett, David. "From the Local to the Global: The Place of Place in Art." *Circa* no. 29 (Summer 1986), 17-21.

Brett, Guy. *Through Our Own Eyes: Popular Art and Modern History.* Philadelphia: New Society, 1987.

Brookman, Philip. "California Assemblage: The Mixed Message." *In Forty Years of California Assemblage.* Los Angeles: Wright Art Gallery, UCLA, 1989.

-------- and Gómez-Peña, Guillermo, eds. *Made in Aztlán: Centro Cultural de la Raza, Fifteen Years.* San Diego: Centro Cultual de la Raza, 1986.

Buhle, Paul; Cortez, Jayne; Lamantia, Philip; Peters, Nancy Joyce; Rosemont, Franklin; and Rosemont, Penelope, eds. *Free Spirits: Annals of the Insurgent Imagination.* San Francisco: City Lights Books, 1982.

Cabral, Amilcar. "Identity and Dignity." *In Return to the Source.* NY: Monthly Review Press, 1973, pp. 57-69.

Camnitzer, Luis. "Access to the Mainstream." *New Art Examiner.* (June, 1987), 20-23.

--------. "La Segunda Bienal de la Habana." *Arte en Columbia* (May 1987), 79-85.

Candelaria, Cordelia, ed. *Multiethnic Literature of the United States: Critical Introductions and Classroom Resources.* Boulder: University of Colorado Press, 1989.

Cardinal-Shubert, Joane. "In the Red." *Fuse* (Fall 1989), 20-28.

Chernoff, John M. *African Rhythm and African Sensibility.* University of Chicago Press, 1979.

Chin, Daryl. "Some Remarks About Racism in the American Arts." *M/E/A/N/I/N/G* no. 3 (May 1988), 18-25.

--------. "Interculturalism, Postmodernism, Pluralism." *Performing Arts Journal* no. 11-12 (1989), 163-75.

Claerhout, G.A. "The Concept of Primitive Applied to Art." *Current Anthopology* vol. 6 (1965), 432-38.

Cliff, Michelle. *Claiming an Identity They Taught Me to Despise.* Watertown, Mass.: Persephone Press, 1980.

Clifford, James. *The Predicament of Culture: Twentieth-Century Ethnography, Literature, and Art.* Cambridge: Harvard University Press, 1988.

-------- and Marcus, George E., eds. *Writing Culture: The Poetics and Politics of Ethnography.* Berkeley: University of California Press, 1986.

Coe, Ralph T. *Lost and Found Traditions: Native American Art 1965-1985.* Seattle: University of Washington Press with American Federation of Arts, 1986.

Coutts-Smith, Kenneth. "The Myth of Artist as Rebel and Hero." *Black Phoenix* no. 3 (Spring 1979).

Crahan, Margaret E., and Wright, Franklin, eds. *Africa and the Caribbean: The Legacies of a Link.* Baltimore: Johns Hopkins University Press, 1979.

[Crawford, John.] "Editorial: Defining People's Culture." *People's Culture* vol. 1, no. 1 (Winter 1988), p. 3.

Creighton-Kelly, Chris. "Still Dreaming of a Multicultural Canada." *Border/Lines* no. 15 (Summer 1989), 4-5.

Davis, Angela. *Women, Race, and Class.* NY: Vintage Books, 1983.

Davis, Douglass. "What is Black Art?" *Newsweek* (June 22, 1970), 87-88.

Davis, Wade. *The Serpqnt and the Rainbow.* NY: Warner Books, 1985.

Deleuze, Gilles, and Guattari, Félix. "What is a Minor Literature?" in *Kafka: Towards a Minor Literature.* Minneapolis: University of Minnesota Press, 1986, pp. 16-27.

Deloria, Vive, Jr. *Custer Died for Your Sins: An Indian Manifesto.* NY: Avon Books, 1969.

Dockstader, Frederick J. *The Song of the Loom: New Traditions in Navaho Weaving.* NY: Hudson Hills Press/Montclair Art Museum, 1987.

Donelly, Margarita; Shirley Lim and Mayumi Tsutakawa, eds. *The Forbidden Stitch: An Asian American Women's Anthology.* Corvallis, OR: Calyx Books, 1989.

Dousihi, Anne. "Trickster: On Inhabiting the Space Between Discourse and Story." *Soundings: An Interdisciplinary Journal* (Fall 1984), 283-311.

Dower, John W. "Yellow, Red, and Black Men." In *War Without Mercy: Race and Power in the Pacific War.* NY: Pantheon Books, 1986, pp. 147-81.

Drinnon, Richard. *Facing West: The Metaphysics of Indian Hating and Empire-Building.* NY: Meridian Books, New American Library, 1980.

Durham, Jimmie. *American Indian Culture: Traditionalism and Spiritualism in a Revolutionary Struggle.* (Photocopied booklet, Chicago, n.d.; originally written in 1974.)

--------. "Here at the Centre of the World." *Third Text* no. 5 (Winter 1988-89), 21-32. (Includes an "interview" with the late Francisco Elso Padilla.)

-------- and Fisher, Jean. "The ground has been covered." *Artforum* (Summer 1989), 99-105.

Escobar, Elizam, "Havana Biennial and Art in Latin America." *Panic* (Aug. 1988), 25-38. (A reply to "Report from Havana, Cuba Conversation," *Art in America*, March 1987.)

Fabian, Johannes. *Time and the Other: How Anthropology Makes Its Object.* NY: Columbia University Press, 1983.

Failing, Patricia. "Black Artists Today: A Case of Exclusion." *ARTnews* (March 1989), 124-31.

Fanon, Frantz. *Black Skin, White Masks.* NY: Grove Press, 1964.

--------. *The Wretched of the Earth.* NY: Grove Press, 1968.

Fax, Elton C. *Black Artists of the New Generation.* NY: Dodd Mead, 1977.

Ferguson, Russell; Gever, Martha; Trinh T. Minh-ha; and West, Cornel, eds. *Out There: Marginalization and Contemporary Cultures.* NY: New Museum of Contemporary Art/Cambridge, Mass.: MIT Press, 1990.

Ferrero, Pat et al. *Hearts and Hands: The Influence of Women and Quilts on American Society.* San Francisco: Quilt Design Press, 1987.

Ferris, William, ed. *Afro-American Folk Art and Crafts.* Boston: G.K. Hall, 1983.

--------. *Local Color: A Sense of Place in Folk Art.* NY: McGraw-Hill, 1982.

Fine, Elsa Honig. *The Afro-American Artist: A Search for Identity.* NY: Hacker Art Books, 1982.

Fisher, Jean. "The Health of the People is the Highest Law." *Third Text* no. 2 (Winter 1987-88), 63-75. (On "ReVisions," an exhibition of Native American and Canadian art at the Banff Center, 1988.)

Foster, Hal, ed. *Discussions in Contemporary Culture Number One.* Seattle: Bay Press, 1987.

--------. *Recodings: Art, Spectacle, Cultural Politics.* Port Townsend, Wash.: Bay Press, 1985.

Freire, Paulo. *Pedagogy of the Oppressed.* NY: Seabury Press, 1973.

French, Laurence. "Multicultural Synthesis." In *Psycho-cultural Change and the American Indian: An Ethnohistorical Analysis.* NY: Garland, 1987.

Fusco, Coco. "Fantasies of Oppositionality." *Afterimage* (Dec. 1988), 6-9.

Gates, Henry Louis, Jr., ed. *"Race," Writing and Difference.* University of Chicago Press, 1986. (Essays originally published under the same title as a special issue of *Critical Inquiry,* vol. 12, no. 1, 1985.)

--------. *The Signifying Monkey: A Theory of Criticism.* NY: Oxford University Press, 1988.

Geertz, Clifford. *Local Knowledge: Further Essays in Interpretive Anthopology.* NY: Basic Books, 1983.

Gill, Sam. *Mother Earth: An American Story.* University of Chicago Press, 1987.

Goldbard, Arlene, and Adams, Don. *Crossroads: Reflections on the Politics of Culture.* Ukiah, Cal.: Institute for Cultural Democracy, 1990.

Goldberg, David. "Raking the Field of the Discourse of Racism." *Journal of Black Studies* (Sept. 1987), 58-71.

Goldman, Shifra. "Latin Visions and Revisions." *Art in America* (May 1988), 138-47.

-------- and Ybarra-Frausto, Tomás. *Arte Chicano: A Comprehensive Annotated Bibliography of Chicano Art 1965-1981.* Berkeley: Chicano Studies Library Publication Unit, University of California, 1985. Includes essays.

Goldwater, Robert. *Primitivism in Modern Art.* Cambridge, Mass.: Belknap Press of Harvard University, 1986.

Gómez-Peña, Guillermo. "The Multicultural Paradigm: An Open Letter to the National Arts Community." *High Performance* (Sept. 1989), 18-27.

-------- and Kelly, Jeff, eds. *The Border Art Workshop: A Documentation of Five Years of Interdisciplinary Art Projects Dealing with U.S.-Mexico Border*

Issues, 1984-1989. NY: Artists Space/La Jolla: Museum of Contemporary Art, 1989.

Goode-Bryant, Linda, and Phillips, Marcie S. *Contextures.* NY: Just Above Midtown, 1978.

Graburn, Nelson. *Ethnic and Tourist Arts.* Berkeley: University of California Press, 1976.

Gradente, Bill. "Art among the Low Riders." In *Folk Art in Texas,* ed. Francis E. Abernathy. Dallas: Southern Methodist University Press, 1985.

Green, Rayna, ed. *That's What She Said: Contemporary Poetry and Fiction by Native American Women.* Bloomington: Indiana University Press, 1984.

Harris, Marie, and Aguero, Kathleen, eds. *A Gift of Tongues: Critical Challenges in Contemporary American Poetry.* University of Georgia Press, 1987.

Highwater, Jamake. *The Primal Mind: Vision and Reality in Indian America.* NY: New American Library, 1981.

--------. *The Sweet Grass Lives On: Fifty Contemporary Native American Indian Artists.* NY: Lippincott & Crowell, 1980.

Hiller, Susan. "Anthropology into Art" (an interview) in *Women's Images of Men,* by Sarah Kent and Jacqueline Morreau. London: Writers & Readers, 1985.

Hooks, Bell. *Ain't I a Women? Black Women and Feminism.* Boston: South End Press, 1981.

--------. *Feminist Theory: From Margin to Center.* Boston: South End Press, 1984.

Hull, Gloria T.; Scott, Patricia Bell; and Smith, Barbara, eds. *All the Women Are White, All the Blacks Are Men, But Some of Us Are Brave.* NY: Feminist Press, 1982.

Igoe, Lynn Moody. *250 Years of Afro-American Art: An Annotated Bibliography.* NY: R. R. Bowker, 1981.

Jojola, Ted. "'Corn, or What We Indians Call Maize.'" *Village Voice* (Dec. 5, 1989), p. 110.

Joselit, David. "Living on the Border." *Art in America* (Dec. 1989), 120-29.

Joseph, Gloria L., and Lewis, Jill. *Common Differences: Conflicts in Black and White Feminist Perspectives.* Boston: South End Press, 1981.

Kahn, Douglas, and Neumaier, Diane, eds. *Cultures in Contention.* Seattle: Real Comet Press, 1985.

Korean-American Women Artists and Writers Association. *Symposium '89: Works by Korean American Women Artists.* Oakland: Mills College, 1989. (Text by Moira Roth.)

Kramer, Hilton. "Black Art and Expedient Politics." *NY Times* (June 7, 1970).

Kruger, Barbara, and Mariani, Phil, eds. *Remaking History: Discussions in Contemporary Culture No. 4.* Seattle: Bay Press, 1989.

Leon, Eli, ed. *Who'd a Thought It: Improvization in African-American Quiltmaking.* San Francisco Craft and Folk Art Museum, 1987. (Texts by Leon, J. Weldon Smith, and Robert Farris Thompson.)

Lewis, Samella. *Art: African American.* NY: Harcourt Brace Jovanovich, 1978.

--------. *Black Artists on Art,* 2 vols. Los Angeles: Contemporary Crafts, 1969-71.

Lippard, Lucy .R. "Captive Spirits." *Village Voice* (March 20, 1984).

--------. "Ethnic Images in the Comics." *Z* (April 1988), 70-71.

--------. "Ethnocentrifugalism: Latin Art in Exile." *Village Voice* (July 12, 1983).

--------. *Get the Message? A Decade for Social Change.* NY: E. P. Dutton, 1984.

--------. "Mestizaje." *Z* (March 1988), 58-59.

--------. "Native American Art Holding Up a Mirror to America." *The Guardian (New York)* (Dec. 16, 1987).

--------. "Native Intelligence." *Village Voice* (Dec. 27, 1983).

--------. "Not So Far from South Africa." *Village Voice* (Nov. 13, 1984).

--------. *Overlay: Contemporary Art and the Art of Prehistory.* NY: Pantheon Books, 1983.

--------. "Primitivism: Cultural Transfusions Enlivening Western Art." *In These Times* (March 12-18, 1986).

--------. "Re-Orienting Perspectives by Asian American Artists." *In These Times* (July 10-23, 1985).'

--------. "See Colorful Colorado." *In These Times* (April 23-29, 1986).

--------. "Showing the Right Thing for a Change." *Z* (Nov. 1989), 79-81.

Lipsitz, George. "Mardi-Gras Indians: Carnival and Counter-Narrative in Black New Orleans." *Cultural Critique* no. 10 (Fall 1988), 99-121.

Lugones, Maria C., and Spelman, Elizabeth V. "Have We Got a Theory for You! Feminist Theory, Cultural Imperialism and the Demand for 'The Woman's

Voice.'" *Women's Studies International Forum* vol. 6, no. 6 (1983), 573-81.

Machida, Margo. *Cultural Identity in Transition: Contemporary Asian American Visual Arts as a Vehicle for the Representation of Self and Community.* NY: Asian American Center at Queens College, forthcoming 1990-91.

Manhart, Marcia, and Manhart, Tom, eds. *The Eloquent Object: The Evolution of American Art in Craft Media Since 1945.* Tulsa: Philbrook Museum of Art, 1987.

Martí, José. *Our America.* NY: Monthly Review Press, 1977.

Mayer, Monica. *Translations: An International Dialogue of Women Artists.* Los Angeles: Monica Mayer, Jo Goodwin, and Denise Arfitz, 1980. (The account of an exchange between U.S. and Mexican women artists.)

Mesa-Bains, Amalia. "Meeting the Challenge of Cultural Transformation." *FYI* vol. 5, no. 3 (Fall 1989), p. 1.

--------. "Contemporary Chicano and Latino Art." *Visions* (Fall 1988), 14-19.

Metcalf, Eugene. "Black Art, Folk Art, and Social Control." *Winterthur Portfolio* (Winter 1983), 271-89.

Momaday, N. Scott. *The Names: A Memoir.* University of Arizona Press, 1976.

Moraga, Cherríe, and Anzaldúa, Gloria, eds. *This Bridge Called My Back: Writings by Radical Women of Color.* NY: Kitchen Table: Women of Color Press, 1981.

Mosquera, Gerardo. "Bad Taste in Good Form." *Social Text* no. 15 (Fall 1986), 54-63.

Muñoz, Braulio. *Sons of the Wind: The Search for Identity in Spanish American Indian Literature.* New Brunswick, N.J.: Rutgers University Press, 1982.

Murray, Pauli. *Song in a Weary Throat.* NY: Harper & Row, 1987.

Neumann, Marc. "Wandering Through the Museum: Experience and Identity in a Spectator Culture." *Border/Lines* no.12 (Summer 1988), 19-27.

Norwood, Vera, and Monk, Janice, eds. *The Desert Is No Lady: Southwestern Landscapes in Women's Writing and Art.* Yale University Press, 1987.

O'Brien, Mark, and Little, Craig. *Reimaging America: The Arts of Social Change.* Philadelphia: New Society, 1990.

P.A.D.D. (Political Art Documentation/Distribution). "Out of Sight Out of Mind I: Black and Native American Art." *Upfront* no. 6-7 (Summer 1983), 18-22.

--------. "Out of Sight Out of Mind II: Asian and Hispanic Art." *Upfrint* no. 9 (Fall 1984), 17-21.

Pau-Llosa, Ricardo. "Art in Exile." *Americas* (Aug. 1980), 3-8.

--------. "Landscape and Temporality in Central American and Caribbean Painting." *Art International* (Jan./March 1984), 28-33.

Pincus, Robert L. "The Spirit of Place: Border Art in San Diego." *Visions* (Summer 1989), 4-7.

Pindell, Howardena. "Art (World) & Racism: Testimony, Documentation, and Statistics," *Third Text* no. 3-4 (Spring/Summer 1988), 157-90.

Pinkel, Sheila. "Interview with Sheila Pinkel, Project Director of 'Multicultural Focus: A Photography Exhibition for the Los Angeles Bicentenial.'" *Obscura* vol 1., no. 4 (1981), 2-11.

Price, Sally. *Primitive Art in Civilized Places*. University of Chicago Press, 1989.

Qoyawayma, Polingaysi (Elizabeth Q. White). *No Turning Back*. Albuquerque: University of New Mexico Press, 1964.

Quirarte, Jacinto. *A History and Appreciation of Chicano Art*. San Antonio: Research Center for the Arts and Humanities, 1984.

--------, ed. *Chicano Art History: Selected Readings*. San Antonio: Research Center for the Arts and Humanities, 1984.

Raven, Arlene, ed. *Art in the Public Interest*. Ann Arbor: UMI Research Press, 1989.

--------. "Colored." *Village Voice* (May 31, 1988).

--------. "Feminist Rituals of Re-Membered History: Lisa Jones, Kaylynn Sullivan, Joyce Scott." *Women and Performance* no. 7 (1988-89), 23-41.

--------, Langer, Sandra; and Frueh, Joanna, eds. *Feminist Art Criticism: An Anthology*. Ann Arbor: UMI Research Press, 1988.

Richard, Nelly. "Postmodernism and Periphery." *Third Text* no. 2 (Winter 1987-88), 5-12.

Rivera, Tomás. *Into the Labyrinth: The Chicano in Literature*. Edinburg, Tex.: Pan Amercan University, 1971.

Roth, Moira, ed. *Connecting Conversations: Interviews with 28 Bay Area Women Artists*. Oakland: Eucalyptus Press, 1979.

Rothenberg, Jerome. *Shaking the Pumpkin*. Doubleday, 1972.

Rubin, Arnold. Accumulation: Power and Display in African Sculpture." *Artform* (May 1975), 35-47.

Rubin, William, ed. *"Primitivism" in 20th-Century Art: Affinity of the Tribal and the Modern*, 2 vols. NY: Museum of Modern Art, 1984. (See also *Artform* April and May 1985 for an exchange of letters between Rubin and Thomas McEvilley.)

Rushing, W. Jackson. "Another Look at Contemporary Native American Art." *New Art Examiner* (Feb. 1990), 35-37. (In reply to Clare Wolf Krantz's "Bridging Two Worlds," in Nov. 1989 issue, pp. 36-38; see also letters column, May 1990, p. 3).

Saakana, Amon Saba. "Mythology and History: An Afrocentric Perspective of the World." *Third Text* no. 3-4 (Spring/Summer 1988), 143-49.

Said, Edward W. *Orientalism*. NY: Vintage Books, 1979.

--------. *The World, the Text, and the Critic*. Harvard University Press, 1983.

Sanchez-Tranquilino, Marcos, ed. "Art and Histories Reconsidered." *Journal* (Winter 1987). (A special section including Harry Gamboa, Jr., "The Chicano/a Artist Inside and Outside the Mainstream [pp. 20-29] and Tranquilino's "Mano a Mano: An Essay on the Representation of the Zoot Suit and Its Misrepresentation by Octavio Paz" [pp. 34-42].)

Schechner, Richard. "Intercultural Themes." *Performing Arts Journal* no. 33-34 (1989) pp. 151-62.

Scully, Vincent. *Pueblo: Mountain, Village, Dance*. NY: Viking Press, 1975.

Simonson, Rick, and Walker, Scott, eds. *The Graywolf Annual Five: Multicultural Literacy*. Saint Paul, Graywolf Press, 1988.

Sims, Lowery Stokes. *"Heat* and Other Climatic Manifestations: Urban Bush Women, Thought Music, and Craig Harris with the Dirty Tones Band." *High Performance* no. 45 (Spring 1989), 22-27.

--------. "The Mirror/The Other: The Politics of Esthetics." *Artform* (March 1990), 111-115.

--------. "The New Exclusionism." *Art Papers* (July/Aug. 1988), 37-38.

Sollers, Werner, ed. *The Invention of Ethnicity*. Oxford University Press, 1989.

Soyinka, Wole. "The Fourth Dimension." *Semiotext(e)* vol. 4, no. 3 (1984), 69-72.

Spivak, Gayatri Chakravorty. *In Other Words: Essays in Cultural Politics.* NY: Routledge, 1988.

Stewart, Kathryn. *Portfolio II: Eleven American Indian Artists.* San Francisco: American Indian Contemporary Arts, 1988.

Sullivan, Michael. *The Meeting of Eastern and Western Art.* Berkeley: University of California Press, 1989.

Swann, Brian, and Krupat, Arnold, eds. *I Tell You Now: Autobiographical Essays by Native American Writers.* Lincoln: University of Nebraska Press, 1987.

Tate, Gregory. "Cult-Nats Meet Freaky-Deke." *Village Voice Literary Supplement* (Dec. 9, 1986), p. 5.

Thévoz, Michel. *Art Brut.* NY: Rizzoli, 1976.

Thompson, Robert Farris. *Flash of the Spirit: African and Afro-American Art and Philosophy.* NY: Vintage Books, 1984.

Traba, Marta. *Propuesta Polemica sobre Arte Puertoriqueño.* San Juan: Libreria Internacional, 1971.

Trinh T. Minh-ha. *Woman, Nature, Other: Writing Postcoloniality and Feminism.* Bloomington: Indiana University Press, 1989.

Tuan Yi-Fu. *Space and Place: The Perspective of Experience.* Minneapolis: University of Minnesota Press, 1977.

Tupahache, Asiba. *Taking Another Look.* Great Neck, NY: Spirit of January Publications, 1988.

Turner, Victor. *Dramas, Fields, and Metaphors: Symbolic Action in Human Society.* Ithaca: Cornell University Press, 1974.

--------. *Process, Performance, and Pilgrimage: A Study in Comparative Symbology.* New Delhi: Concept Publishing, 1979.

Villa, Carlos, ed. *Other Sources: An American Essay.* San Francisco: San Francisco Art Institute, 1976.

Vizenor, Gerold. *Earthdivers: Tribal Narratives on Mixed Descent.* Minneapolis: University of Minnesota Press, 1981.

Vlach, John Michael. *Afro-American Tradition in the Decorative Arts.* Cleveland: Cleveland Museum of Art, 1978.

Wade, Edwin, ed. *The Arts of the North American Indian: Native Traditions in Evolution.* NY: Hudson Hills Press/Tulsa: Philbrook Art Center, 1986.

-------- and Strickland, Rennard. *Magic Images: Contemporary Native American Art*. Norman: University of Oklahoma Press, 1981.

Walker, Sheila. "Candomblé: A Spiritual Microcosm of Africa." *Black Art: An International Quarterly* vol. 5, no. 4 (1984), 10-22.

Wallace, Michele. "'I Don't Know Nothin' 'bout Birthin' No Babies.'" *Village Voice* (Dec. 9, 1989), p. 112.

--------. "Michael Jackson, Black Modernisms, and 'The Ecstacy of Communication.'" *Third Text* no. 7 (Summer 1989), 11-22.

--------. "Multicultural Blues: An Interview with Michele Wallace" by Jim Drobnick. *Attitude* (Spring 1990), 2-6.

Wallis, Brian, ed. *Blasted Allegories*. NY: New Museum of Contemporary Art/ Cambridge, Mass.: MIT Press, 1987. (Anthology of artists' writings, including a number of artists of color.)

Weatherford, Jack. *Indian Givers: How the Indians of the Americas Transformed the World*. NY: Crown, 1988.

Weisman, Alan. "Born in East L.A." *Los Angeles Times Magazine* (March 27, 1988), 10-25.

--------. *La Frontera: The United States Border with Mexico*. NY: Harcourt Brace Jovanovich, 1986.

West, Cornel. "The Dilemma of the Black Intellectual." *Cultural Critique* no. 1 (Fall 1985), 109-24.

--------. [Interview by Anders Stephanson.] *Flash Art* (April 1987), 51-55.

--------. "Postmodernism and Black America." *Z* (June 1988), 27-29.

Williams, Raymond. *Culture and Society 1780-1950*. NY: Columbia University Press, 1983.

Williams, Reese, ed. *Fire Over Water*. NY: Tanam Press, 1986. (Anthology incl. texts by Theresa Hak Kyung Cha and Cecilia Vicuña.)

Wilson, Judith. "Art." In *Black Arts Annual 1987/88*, ed. Donald Bogle. NY: Garland Publishing, 1989.

Yau, John. "Official Policy." *Arts* (Sept. 1989), 50-54.

Ybarra-Frausta, Tomás. "The Chicano Movement and the Emergence of a Chicano Poetic Consciousness." *New Scholar: VI* (1977), 88-108.

Special Issues of Periodicals:

Art in America. "The Global Issue" (July 1989). (Articles around the issues raised by the "Magicians de la terre" exhibition at the Centre Pompidou in Paris.)

Art Papers. "The Black Aesthetic Issue" (Nov./Dec. 1985); [Multicultural issue] (July/Aug. 1990).

Artes Visuales. [Special issue on Chicano Art] (June 1981).

Bridge. "Asian American Women" (Winter 1978-79; Spring 1979).

Broken Line/La Linea Quebrada. Border Art Workshop/Taller de Arte Fronteriza, San Diego. (Each issue focuses on border issues and is "special" in format; no. 3 is a boxed exhibition; no. 4 is "The Latino Boom . . . BOOM!!")

Les Cahiers du musée national d'art moderne. "Magiciens de la terra" (Summer 1989). (Almost the entire issue was translated into English in the Spring 1989 issue of *Third Text.*)

Cultural Critique. "The Nature and Context of Minority Discourse." Nos. 6 & 7 (Spring and Fall 1987).

Cultural Democracy. "Campaign for a Post-Columbian World." No. 37 (Fall 1989).

Discourse. "She, The Inappropriate(d) Other." No. 8 (Winter 1986-87).

--------. [On ethnography and the politics of representation.] No. 11 (Spring 1988).

Feminist Review. "Difference: A Special Third World Women Issue." No. 25 (Spring 1987).

Flue. [Special issue as catalogue for the exhibition "Multiples by Latin American Artists" at the Franklin Furnace, New York.] Vol. 3, no. 2 (Spring 1983).

Frontiers. "Chicanas in the National Landscape" (Summer 1980).

Heresies. "Racism Is the Issue." No. 15 (1982).

--------. "Third World Women: The Politics of Being Other." No. 8 (1979).

Ikon. "Art Against Apartheid." Second Series, no. 5-6 (Winter/Summer 1986).

--------. "Without Ceremony." [Asian American Women.] Second series, no. 9 (1988).

International Review of African American Art. "Art in Public Places." Vol. 7, no. 2 (1987).

Sage: A Scholarly Journal on Black Women. "Artists and Artisans." Vol. 4, no. 1 (Spring 1987).

Screen. "The Last 'Special Issue' on Race." Vol. 29, no. 4 (Autumn 1988).

Visions. "Acculturation and Assimilation" (Fall 1989).

Periodicals:

Afro-American Art History Newsletter. Edited by Judith Wilson. New York.

Bridge: Asian American Perspectives. NY: Basement Workshop. (No longer publishing.)

Calladoo: A Black South Journal af Arts and Letters. Lexington: Department of English, University of Kentucky.

Community Murals. Ed. by Tim Drescher. San Francisco. (No longer publishing.)

Contact: A Poetry Review. Edited by Maurice Kenny. Bowling Green, N.Y.

Cultural Democracy. Minneapolis: Alliance for Cultural Democracy.

East Wind: Politics and Culture of Asians in the U.S. San Francisco: Getting Together Publications.

The International Review of African American Art. Jamaica, N.Y.

Journal of Ethnic Studies. Bellingham: Western Washington University.

The Spirit of January. Edited by Asiba Tupahache. Great Neck, N.Y.

Third Text (Third World Perspective on Contemporary Art and Culture). Edited by Rasheed Araeen. London: Kala Press.

Upfront. NY: P.A.D.D. (Political Art Documentation/Distribution). (No longer publishing.)

ABOUT THE AUTHOR/ EDITOR AND OTHERS

Betty Ch'maj pronounces her name SHMAY (rhymes with day). The apostrophe is optional and does not appear (nor does her middle initial M.) in publications prior to 1988. Her ethnic identity is Finnish-American, on both her mother's and father's sides. Ch'maj received her Ph.D. in American Studies from the University of Michigan in 1961. She has published and lectured in the United States and abroad on a wide range of topics in American Studies--among them, the American arts, American women, Emerson, Charles Ives, the radical right, and multiculturalism.

The concern with multicultural American studies evident in this volume extends from Washington, D.C., where the American Council of Education is addressing the issues, to the campuses of California universities where Ch'maj and her student assistants collected their findings.

RIGHT: Ch'maj with Reginald Wilson, ACE, consultant to the book, in Washington, D. C. BELOW (left to right): Ch'maj, Kathleen Hanson, Annette Hansen, and Jan Petrie in her office at California State University at Sacramento.